Forest Recreation

Third Edition

Forest Recreation

Robert W. Douglass

Chairman, Division of Parks and Recreation Administration,
The Ohio State University

Third Edition

WAVELAND PRESS, INC.
Prospect Heights, Illinois

For information about this book, write or call:
Waveland Press, Inc.
P.O. Box 400
Prospect Heights, Illinois 60070
(708) 634-0081

G U
1 9 1
.4
D 68
1 9 9 0

Contents

The present quest for recreation is associated with the recognition that recreation is an integral part of American life.
Source: Forest Service, USDA

About the Author

Robert W. Douglass (Ph.D., University of Minnesota) is the chairman of the Parks and Recreation Administration Division of The Ohio State University. His previous academic experience includes teaching and research at The Pennsylvania State University and The University of Houston. He has a diverse background in forestry, soils, recreation, and manufacturing. His professional fields of interest are resource-based recreation planning and remote sensing. The application of remote sensing to recreation planning has been the main concern of his research and led to the completion of his Ph.D. Dr. Douglass has published many works in recreation, applications of remote sensing in water-oriented recreation planning, and in uses of high-altitude photography.

Preface

Recreation presents America with a paradox. When times get difficult and the American economy has trouble, recreation continues to become more important to individual Americans. The organization and growth of publicly funded recreation programs that got started during the depression years are understood in the light of social welfare. The individual quest for recreational opportunities of the 1980s is disconnected from the concept of social welfare. It is more associated with the recognition that recreation is an integral part of American life.

The big rise in importance of forest types of recreation came coupled with the environmental awareness movement of the 1970s. The quest for environmental quality has always been led by those articulate and resourceful persons who have seen their unique recreational activities threatened by communal or corporate action. National policy decisions and national legislation had been influenced by the impact of the recreation-environmental coalition. The national forests were being restricted as to cutting practices during a period of lumber scarcity and anti-strip-mining legislation was pushed in the coal-producing states during an energy crisis. Today national parks are assessing ways to limit use when public pressure to use them appears overwhelming. Environmental impact statements are required whenever federal actions are taken on natural resources. All of this reflected a shift in the attitude of the American people toward the allocation of the nation's natural resources. Even in the 1980s, federal government's attempt to encourage American industry, the recreation-environmental interests have held the backing of the American people.

Recreation research is now getting onto firm footing and is now producing much information to aid in giving the land managers and technicians many of the answers that are needed to cope with the recreational needs of the American public. This book strives to consolidate into one publication the scattered findings of many researchers, the problems that confront forest recreation administrators, and the desires of the using public.

The research completed to date just scratches the surface of the problem that faces the land managers. Many recreation-management decisions still must be based on the seat-of-the-pants management or intuitive reasoning that comes with experience until more concepts of management can be developed by researchers.

This book has been written to provide the forest land manager with a broad background in the generalities of forest recreation needs and in forest recreation planning. Also, it provides the reader with specific recommendations on how to do the job at the technician level. Land managers, forest technicians, professional foresters, park technicians, and private landowners can use the information assembled here to aid in planning, developing, and administering forest recreation areas.

Recreation is serving as the catalyst to bring comprehensive land-use planning to the public. It is bringing diverse and often antagonistic groups together to plan statewide or regional allocation of resources. While recreation can claim some credit for comprehensive land-use planning advances, it must also accept much of the blame for making it necessary.

PART I

1

Introduction
to Part I

Forests were once thought of as areas to be cleared or to be used and their products put to use for the good of the nation. The production of timber was the dominant reason for forest management except in local areas where mining or grazing was strong enough to infringe on this domain. During the early 1900s, timber began to give up its role as king of the forests to a newcomer called water. Water became important because local areas slowly ran out of it or suddenly had too much of it. Water was found to be the key to economies throughout the United States as it had been the foundation of civilizations throughout history. Forested areas were set aside to protect headwaters of major waterways. Large areas of denuded land were planted to stop the erosion of the land and the silting in of reservoirs and watercourses.

As the economy of the United States developed after World War II, the force of recreation was felt upon the forests. The pressures of forest recreation, however, were slow to show themselves to land managers who misunderstood and mistrusted their impact. Forest recreation was discussed and given lip service, but the problems it posed were never faced. In 1960, recreation finally became recognized for its real value at all levels. Recreation was no longer a poor sister to other forest products, but was, rather, recognized as a major part of the forest resources. In some areas of heavy public use, recreation became the most valuable use of the forest. Certain influential foresters feel that the Forest Service should declare recreation as the most important resource of the national forests of the northeastern United States. Federal and state agencies are falling over one another in their bids to meet the needs of the recreation demand that has been so well outlined by the Outdoor Recreation Resource Review Commission in 1962. Private capital has begun to flow into developing all forms of recreation fields. The demand for forest recreation facilities that was being made by the American population in the 1960s continued to increase through the 1970s with no end in sight.

The economic confusion that began the 1980s caused some reflection upon the government's role in providing recreation and upon the individual's willingness to pay for it. Outdoor recreation, however, has become so well ingrained in the fabric of America that it is now an essential component of the general society's lifestyle and economic base. The economic situation has highlighted some changes in attitudes about recreation. Americans are continuing to spend much money for their own leisure activities but will not raise their support for public-funded recreation programs. One out of eight dollars spent by American consumers in 1980 was spent for some leisure activity.

Running counter to the facts highlighting consumer interest in recreation, some foresters seem to have hitched a ride on the mythical pendulum that some say is swinging back from having reached too far over to the amenities side. Even annual meetings of the Society of American Foresters have become saturated with timber production philosophies at all costs. Apparently some land managers have short memories or else they believe that the "supply side" of economics of the 1980s excludes the nation's largest industry—the leisure industry. Americans will spend more on recreation and leisure each year than they will on national defense. In its August 10, 1981 issue, *U.S. News and World Report* stated that leisure spending increased in inflation-adjusted dollars by 321 percent during the 16-year period from 1965 to 1981. Foreign visitors have begun to flood certain recreation facilities as their relative affluence coupled with mobility continue to rise.

The public has turned to the forested areas of the United States to satisfy much of its recreation need. The forests provide a natural and logical direction for the pressure to force itself. The forest areas are generally large enough to provide solitude of the varying degrees that different recreation interests desire. By definition, a forest is a collection of trees and associated vegetation that creates its own climate or environment. Space, solitude, inspiration, habitat for wildlife, and above all, an opportunity for a person to practice a slight degree of self-reliance can be found in the forests by those who seek it. Some campers and hikers come to the forest because they prefer to pursue their recreation interests in the atmosphere created by the forest. Many come for other reasons. Social status, group pressures, economics, and even the desire for companionship may bring visitors to the forests. Whether the attraction is being John Muir or David Douglas, Daniel Boone or Nathaniel Bumpo for a short period of time, or whether it is just to escape to the cool, quiet climate of the mountain woodlands, people usually enjoy being out in the woods. Perhaps people are not even sure why they participate in forest-oriented outdoor recreation. Actually, many campers admit to favoring closely packed neighbors. The fact that many people are willing to spend large sums of money in order to bring the conveniences of the modern home into the forest environment has created the multimillion-dollar recreation vehicle business. Often, the woods support a secondary feature that is the attraction that the public seeks. The rivers, streams, and lakes that provide millions with water-oriented activities have proved to be the major attraction to recreationists. The cover and habitat provided to wildlife attract additional people to the forests for hunting, nature study, and sight-seeing. The forest provides the backdrop for these activities, but it does not make them exclusively forest-recreation activities.

Outdoor recreation has become a major influence on our modern society. Areas that had not been able to develop a stable economy in recent decades suddenly have become centers for the new flood of outdoor recreationists. Land values have skyrocketed as a result of the demand for vacation homes coupled with state laws and interstate compacts that limit the amount of land available for home development. The sudden and overwhelming demand for outdoor recreation has caused many realignments in policies concerning land manage-ment. The wave of ecological awareness on the part of the voting public has pressured law makers into passing legislation that forces land managers to be concerned with the impacts of land-use decisions on the recreation resource. Even the federal emphasis on getting industry started up again in the early 1980s has not changed the public's interest and concern for the environment.

Professional forest-land managers have always considered recreation in their management planning; in the past, however, forests primarily have served the more pressing demands of timber, grazing, and water. Now that the recreation needs of the public must be satisfied, qualified personnel must be trained in the field of outdoor recreation. Professional foresters, forest technicians, conser-vationists, landscape architects, and others that are involved in forest land management require training to enable them to cope with the various facets of the recreation demand.

Part 1 of this book treats outdoor and, more specifically, forest recreation from the planning standpoint. It presents a general background of the prob-lems connected with forest recreation and the "whys" of the solutions. Outdoor recreation's history, its impact, and its future are important in planning and developing forest recreation. Part II is more concerned with the operation and management of forest recreation areas.

2
Outdoor Recreation

INTRODUCTION AND HISTORY

Outdoor recreation has a complexity of meanings and includes a variety of disciplines such as landscape architecture, forestry, ecology, physical education, conservation, and civil engineering. The problems concerning definitions and responsibilities are those problems associated with a new and dynamic discipline.[24] Outdoor recreation, as treated by this textbook, is the wholesome recreation that is done without the confines of a building. It covers a broad field of topics from a backyard barbecue to a Boy Scout Jamboree. It can mean recess on the paved playground of a downtown grade school or a two-week pack trip into the Bob Marshall Wilderness area in Montana. But whatever its form, it is part of an entity known as "recreation," and this word must be explained before such terms as "outdoor recreation," "forest recreation," and "water-oriented recreation" can be understood.

Any action that refreshes the mental attitude of an individual is recreation. Recreation is a wholesome activity that is engaged in for pleasure; therefore, it is play. The man who works long, hard days in a foundry or a coal mine may consider the working of crossword puzzles or the reading of short magazine articles the answer to his daily recreation needs. Mental activity in the evening balances, to an extent, the physical workload of the day. Since this worker pursues these activities for pleasure, he considers them a form of play and thereby recreation. The woman who spends her long day taking care of domestic chores, administering to the needs of three youngsters from sunrise to after their bedtime does not want to play horseshoes in her own backyard; she wants a change of environment. What she actually does is not necessarily important so long as it is different from her daily pattern and away from the ever-present surroundings of the home. A quick trip to the nearby lake might be a hectic evening's experience, but it makes the trip back into the house a pleasure.

Recreation may take various routes, but the results are the same. Recreation revitalizes the spirit. It restores a person's vitality, initiative, and perspective of life, thereby preparing the individual to return to his toil.

Today, people not only hope for recreation, they demand it as part of their

6

life. The interest in various types of recreation has varied as the population's way of living has varied. Conditions affecting leisure time and its use have changed quickly during the last 50 years. In 1910, the United States operated on a rural economy that had 90 percent of its population living in rural areas.[13] Transportation was slow and limited. The population had not achieved the mobility or the freedom from sustenance requirements that would give the time and the means for recreation.

A look at the lifestyle of Americans shows that recreation is a major driving force in their total decision-making package. Recreation influences where Americans desire to live, their career aspirations, and even their family composition. The massive population surge into the Sunbelt and Rocky Mountain states reflects a search for better climates and a higher level of recreational activities than are possible in the northland climates. The large growth in University natural resources and recreation programs that followed the ecology awareness boom highlight the young adults' interest in jobs related to what they perceive as recreation or quality of life awards even when salaries could be low. Pursuit of recreational opportunities early in life is often cited by young people who delay marriage. Indeed, this theme has been played up with great success by the population-control advocates who preach that young married couples could have fun together now if they postponed having children.

Most recreation researchers today speak of the surging recreation demands that have become a major factor in our present-day economy. Government publications tend to treat all recreation in their present-day terms and thereby ignore the recreation activities of 50 years ago. True, the conditions affecting leisure time and its use have changed; at that time, however, the people were active in outdoor recreation. It was during this period that the large railroad excursion picnics took place. People would use their limited leisure time to its best advantage by attending parks developed along railroad lines by private companies or by the railroads to promote business. They would use the community commons for picnics, for parties, or just for walking.

Rural living then, as today, provided closer contact with the natural environment. The people were not beset by the problems of social frictions that develop as people become crowded together. Outdoor living and contact with nature were part of everyday living. With this relatively immobile and largely rural population busy fulfilling its existence and subsistence requirements, the United States government had no policy on recreation. In the isolated areas where urbanization had taken place, a local need for recreation was recognized. New York's Central Park was designed in 1850 and Philadelphia, Chicago, and Boston established municipal parks within the next 50 years. These city parks were local attempts to provide open areas for outdoor recreation within the city. No popular pressure existed for parks or other forms of recreation areas at the national level. Even the establishment of the Yellowstone area as a 3,000-square-mile federal park by President Grant was brought about by the efforts of individuals who did not represent the thinking of the majority of Americans. Men such as John Muir, David Douglas, and Gifford Pinchot could see the value in holding in public trust areas of special beauty for future enjoyment.

Because Judge Cornelius Hedges held out for the public ownership of Yellowstone at the time the land was practically valueless and lost in distance from civilization, he was able to win his fight in 1872.[25] His victory and that of John Muir for a national park at Yosemite were the results of individual fights and conservation-minded presidents. They were harbingers of future demands, but not a reflection of national policy. The Yosemite Grant, The Kings Canyon Park, Yellowstone Park, and similar early parks were carved out of public domain lands of the western mountains.

Although government actions concerning recreation were scattered and dealt with specific situations, they became more common and more inclusive as time passed. The Antiquities Act of 1906 provided the authority for the federal government to establish historic, scientific, or cultural sites as national monuments. A need for a general policy was recognized in 1916 by the establishment of the National Park Service within the United States Department of the Interior. Today, the National Park Service is one of the five bureaus within the Department of the Interior that are concerned with outdoor recreation. The Departments of the Interior, Agriculture, Commerce, and Defense are all in today's outdoor recreation business. More than 30 federal agencies have recreation programs.[11] In 1962 the Bureau of Outdoor Recreation was created within the United States Department of the Interior to correlate the recreation efforts of all the other interested bureaus.

With the exception of New York and California, the state governments did not enter the outdoor recreation field until they received a big federal push in the 1930s. Many state parks in the eastern states are on lands that were turned over to state governments at the end of the Federal Submarginal Land Program.[18] Many of the structures and established conservation measures that serve as the foundation for many of today's parks were built by the Civilian Conservation Corps in the 1930s.

At the time that the National Park System was getting its slow start on western public domain lands, the state forestry-conservation movement began in the eastern states that had seen their forest lands ravished by logging, fire, charcoaling, erosion, and other related activities. Maine, Michigan, New York, and Pennsylvania organized state agencies to care for the forest lands of their states during the late 1800s.[15.8]

The industrialization of our agrarian society placed people out of touch with outdoor living. Hunting, fishing, and even picnicking were not convenient activities. At the turn of the century, a work week was 60 hours long and the people were being swept up by the new rush toward urbanization. Pay scales varied with forms of work and manual labor was looked upon as activity for the lower class. Manual activity therefore gradually fell into disrepute. As a result of its unfavorable view of manual activity, the United States placed little emphasis on physical fitness. Poor physical fitness became the vogue. This misguided attitude goes beyond driving cars or the use of labor-saving devices. In the 1950s, three out of seven American youths who were at the peak of their physical careers flunked the Army physical examination. But one does not need to turn to the U.S. Army for examples. Any man over 25 caught playing touch football was viewed with distrust in many neighborhoods. The problem reached such proportions that President Kennedy thought it necessary to establish a committee on physical fitness. This Council on Youth Fitness received wide publicity and made thousands of Americans conscious of their physical conditioning. As people turn to outdoor recreation in greater numbers, they are finding the opportunity to enjoy exercise as part of their recreation. In some cases, good conditioning is a prerequisite for outdoor recreation. Many skiers are injured each year because of the lack of the simple physical toughness that is required in preparation for taking to the slopes. The phenomenal increase in bicycling that swept the country in the 1960s provides some indication that a segment of the American population is combining exercise and recreation with transportation.

By the close of the 1970s, fitness activities had regained status throughout America. A study of the Washington D.C. area indicated that 69 percent of the population was involved in exercise during their leisure time.[19]

Jogging or running has become the most popular form of fitness activity. The fitness boom that began at the close of the 1970s has been unprecedented in this country. It is the first time in our history that Americans have had a peacetime fitness movement. In spite of the fitness movement, one out of six children aged 10 to 17 is still physically underdeveloped.

Outdoor recreation has become a major factor in modern living. Federal, state, and local governments have formed policies to guide outdoor recreation development. Private interests have entered into the rush to recreation by providing facilities for public use and by creating manufactured products for the recreationists' every dream. Even throughout every energy crisis new types of adult recreational toys are big selling items.

The Eighty-fifth Congress of the United States passed a law establishing a bipartisan Outdoor Recreation Resource Review Commission (ORRRC). This committee was charged with studying the present and future needs for outdoor recreation and with determining the available and future supply of outdoor recreation resources. In 1962, this commission made its report to the president and the Congress. The Outdoor Recreation Resource Review Commission Report covers 27 volumes of study reports on outdoor recreation. The findings are summarized in *Outdoor Recreation for America*, which is available from the Superintendent of Documents in Washington, D.C.[18] This ORRRC report stimulated much activity in the field of outdoor recreation at all levels of government and in private industry. The findings of this report were questioned by some researchers on the basis of the sampling techniques that were used; however, the federal government employees using the information included in the ORRRC report claimed that it held up under use. Regardless of the accuracy of the data contained in it, the report has done more for outdoor recreation in the United States than any other piece of research in that field.

Over 70 percent of our population now live in approximately 200 cities.[13] Every state except Vermont and Wyoming now has at least one major metropolitan area. The federal interstate highway system has made us the most mobile population in history. Travel from the cities to outdoor recreation sites is no longer the limiting factor that it was 20 years ago. Even with the rising cost of fuel, people can get into the family car and travel hundreds of miles for a short vacation. More than 25 percent of vacation trips are longer than 1,000 miles.[18] The high cost and possible scarcity of gasoline combined with the unfavorable economic situation in the early 1980s to cause some decrease in long automobile trips. Americans are flocking to recreation areas near home and foregoing trips to far away parks.[5]

As more and more research produces more involved and longer publications concerning the recreational use of leisure time, the difference between outdoor recreation and forest recreation becomes more indistinguishable. Forest recreation is any form of outdoor recreation that takes place in forested areas, whether or not the forest provides the primary purpose for the activity. This is an oversimplified definition because of many confounding issues, but it is generally true. Sightseeing can be outdoor recreation on Fisherman's Wharf in San Francisco, but it becomes forest recreation when done at Franconia Notch in the White Mountains of New Hampshire.

Whether the activity requires using the forest directly for consumption or indirectly as a background setting, that activity is included as forest recreation. If managing and altering of the forests would have an impact on the activity, that activity should be considered as forest-recreation management.

BASIC FACTORS INFLUENCING OUTDOOR RECREATION

Americans prefer the simple, more convenient, and less expensive forms of outdoor recreation that do not require great expenditures of money or time. Swimming, picnicking, outdoor games, attending sports events and concerts, and walking for pleasure were the most popular outdoor recreation activities in 1970.[8] Driving and sightseeing were replaced by picnicking and outdoor games in the top five activities as listed in 1960. Driving for pleasure had slipped from the number one position in 1960 to the number three position by 1965 because it is directly linked with population increase and is not exhibiting any increase in individual popularity.[7] Also, driving is less fashionable in times of energy shortages. The air pollution problem, the rising automobile operation costs, and the energy crisis probably will continue the slip of driving as a recreational activity.

The popularity of bicycling skyrocketed in the 1960s to the point where availability of quality bicycles appeared to be the limiting factor to continued growth. [7] Even in 1980, more bicycles than cars were sold in the United States. There are approximately 90 million bicycles in use by Americans. [2] A leveling off of bicycling popularity occurred in the late 1970s as racket sports and jogging became more popular. The boom in bicycling seems to have been the precursor of the personal conditioning and physical fitness activities that are popular as we move into the 1980s. A 1979 study by the A.C. Nielson Company determined that the top ten participant sports were swimming, bicycling, camping, fishing, bowling, jogging, running, tennis, pool, and softball in that order. [4]

Whether jogging, mass road races, cycling, and similar fitness activities are substitutes for the other recreational activities or just additional activities will not make much difference to the recreation-land manager. The new activities just mean different new demands on the resource base without alleviating any of the existing demands.

The most popular forms of outdoor recreation give some hints as to the factors involved in popularity. Money and time are factors since the most popular activities are also the least expensive and the most convenient forms of outdoor recreation. The supply of available facilities is also important in that people tend to use the facilities available to them. High transportation costs and fuel scarcity have caused a trend away from the big regional parks. Community and local parks are more attractive to the general public. Urban residents expect the public sector of recreation to provide more classes on crafts, physical fitness programs, and more organized sports. Table 2.1 lists the basic factors influencing participation in Outdoor Recreation. The influence of people, money, time, and communications on recreation is discussed in this chapter. Supply covers such extensive material that it is discussed singly in Chapter 3.

Table 2.1. Basic Factors Influencing Outdoor Recreation Participation.

People	Population size
	Living areas—urban, suburban, exurban, rural
	Age
	Education
Money	Disposable income
	Affluence
Time	Occupation
	Mobility
Communication	Mass media—social status, advertising, enlightenment
	Personal—convenience
Supply	Availability
	Accessibility

People

Population Size

People are the fundamental factor influencing recreation use. Since all recreation usage and values are based upon use by people, the number of people in existence or population becomes important. If the population increases while all other factors remain static, an increase in recreation area usage is likely to result. Any changes in the other factors influencing participation in outdoor recreation that are coupled with a population change will be accelerated and multiplied by the population change. The increase in family funds will change the standards of living and thereby change the participation pattern which will act along with many other factors to confound attempts to make accurate predictions about outdoor recreation. The assumption has been made that the future world political situation will continue along the same line that it has been following. Any great upheaval in politics or the economy would alter the outdoor recreation demand discussed here. The economic problems of 1978–1980 caused many cutbacks in the public sector leadership in outdoor recreation; it did not, however, decrease the overall public participation. The demand for recreation experience continued to rise during that period but it exhibited a shift in activities.

The population growth of the United States has brought a change in our entire social and economic structure. The population of the United States increased from 76 million in 1900 to 180 million in 1962 and to 216 million in 1977.[13] A predicted population of over 380 million people by 2000 A.D., which was expected on the basis of earlier trends, apparently will not materialize because of the sharp decline in birth rates from 3.80 per woman in 1958 to 2.45 in 1970 and 1.8 in 1978.[2] The latest population projection is for 281 million U.S. population in the year 2000.

It is apparent to today's user that the intensive-use outdoor recreation facilities are inadequate for the existing demand. Beaches are jammed or closed to the general public. Campers are advised to be on hand at dawn to get a spot in the developed campgrounds or to use computerized reservation systems.

The overwhelming use of recreation areas is not properly explained by the population increase, but, rather, by the amount and style that each citizen participates in recreational activities. The Third National Outdoor Recreation Plan (Table 2.2) indicates that reported participation is increasing in nearly every reported activity. This participation rate is continuing to grow both in percentages of the population participating and in the number of activities performed by each person. Camping participation moved from one in twelve persons in 1960 to one in four by 1970.[7,8] By 1977, there were more than 56 million campers in the United States.[3]

Although the demand for forest recreation opportunities will increase with

Table 2.2. Percentage of Respondents Reporting Participation in Selected Outdoor Recreation Activities as Reported in the Third National Outdoor Recreation Report.

	Year of Survey			
Activity	1960 %	1965 %	1972 %	1977 %
Swimming	45	48		
pool			18	63
other			34	46
Picnicking	53	57	47	72
Pleasure Driving	52	55	34	69
Sightseeing	42	49	37	62
Walking and Jogging	33	48	34	68
Playing Outdoor Games	30	38	22	56
Fishing	29	30	24	53
Boating	22	24	15	34
Camping	8	10		
Developed			11	30
Undeveloped			5	21
Hiking or Backpacking	6	7	5	28

the rising population, that demand has not paralleled the exact population rise. As crowding occurs, satisfaction might drop off for some users. When the satisfaction level drops to a certain point, people will begin to turn to other activities that offer better returns for their investments of time, money, and energy. Recreation researchers refer to this switch in activities as "substitutions." At what level of satisfaction does substitution occur for each activity? What are the primary influences that cause substitution? The answers to these questions will help the land managers plan to provide the increasing population with the best possible recreation opportunities. To the present, pure substitution has not been evident. A seemingly endless line of new activities and styles of participation has kept ahead of the need for substitution. Tent camping is rapidly disappearing from the developed campground as the number of recreational vehicles continues to increase at a rate of 25 percent each year.[6] Another shift to small-tent camping in wilderness situations is developing as an alternative to the use of recreational vehicles.

Living Area

As the population grew, it caused a concentration of industrial, political, and commercial activities to take place around the cities. This concentration of activities and services caused the flow into the cities to increase. Economic opportunities were better in the city where the better jobs were to be found. Also, the technological advances in agriculture had reduced the demand for farm labor.

By 1962, nearly three-quarters of our population lived in metropolitan areas where the people are subjected to social friction and denied daily contact with the relaxing powers of outdoor recreation. Many individual irritations and even mass riots are rooted in problems caused by congestion or the rapid pace and grating existence of big-city living. Although the lack of both indoor and outdoor recreation cannot be considered as the sole cause for the riots that have swept the large cities in recent summers, it has been considered as a major contributor to the upheavals. The National Advisory Commission on Civil Disorders ranked the need for recreation programs and facilities as the fourth most intense grievance behind the city riots of 1967. Recreation certainly has political as well as sociological and economic consequences.

The cities themselves have changed character since the early 1900s. Before individual automobiles were available, the cities were compacted into a high density of inhabitants per square mile. The lack of mobility and communications forced the compact situation even though the railroad provided access to corridors reaching out from the city. [13] Because travel to the core of the city or to the railroad was limited by the capabilities of horse-drawn means, there was a distinct edge to the city. The transition from urban to rural was abrupt and the people lived either in the city or in the rural areas. The suburbs did not exist beyond what was referred to as the "outskirts of town."

With the introduction of the automobile and its attendant highway system, a backwash of people occurred in the flood toward urbanization. The 1950s brought on the great expansion of the densely settled cities into the great suburban development. Suburbia, U.S.A., reached its romantic peak by 1960. The dispersal of people and their increased mobility around the metropolitan areas has encouraged industry to follow the pattern. The horizontal growth of the growing cities is no longer considered in terms of suburban developments; rather, it has become urban sprawl. This urban sprawl consumes thousands of acres per year and shows signs of continuing to spread. Aside from the area it occupies, urban sprawl removes much more land from use for certain outdoor recreational uses. Hunting, shooting, field trials, and other extensive outdoor recreational activities are especially vulnerable to the pressure of urban sprawl. As people who are unfamiliar with the sporting use of firearms move into a previously rural area, they intrude upon lands where the use of firearms has been a historic fact. Concern for home and family prompts the homeowners of urban sprawl to press for elimination of the danger. The noise of the hunter's firearms indicates a danger to the housewife. Even if the danger is imagined, the annoyance is real. Unfortunately, there are enough thoughtless hunters and shooters to justify regulations of the use of firearms in heavily populated areas.

Living patterns of people affect the choice of recreational pursuits. Sightseeing and swimming are common activities of the city dweller. The suburbanite is much more active in outdoor recreation in that he is involved in more forms of outdoor recreation. He participates mostly in sightseeing, camping, hiking, and swimming. We must realize that the adage, "Access promotes usage" generally holds true in this field. It is the urban-area dweller, however, who is causing much of the increase in outdoor recreation demand. He wants to get away from the confines and irritations of the city for a short period. He wants to participate in some outdoor recreation such as skiing, hunting, fishing, or just relaxing in the forest environment.

The phenomenal rise in the number of single adults since 1960 has begun to have an impact on the activities that fit into the singles' lifestyle. Skiing, cycling, games, and sun-worship types of activities appeal to this group whenever it is looking for outdoor nonurban-related recreation action. The sudden affluence and mobility of the single-adult group have become a significant factor in molding the recreation style as presented to the American public. Sheer numbers of these young adults are having an impact on the social fabric of the nation that is bound to be reflected in the recreation patterns of the population as a whole.

Many city dwellers are elated at witnessing or participating in what their rural cousins consider daily routine. The success of recreation farms in the mid-Atlantic states area indicates that urban dwellers are quite willing to pay for the privilege of participating in farm activities for a vacation. Much of the push for institutionalized wilderness areas has come from urbanites. Since the land manager has spent much of his professional life in a rural or forested area, he may have difficulty in understanding the high, but intangible, value that the urbanite places on a sightseeing visit to the forest. The farmer participates in outdoor recreation much less than the men engaged in city-oriented activity simply because he works out of doors. The major exception here is in hunting, where access again promotes use. Snowmobiling seems to be another activity where the rural family participates more than its urban counterpart.

Regional differences are evident to some extent in the preferences of people toward forms of outdoor recreation. The differing land forms, climate, water availability, and social status symbols that occur throughout the country have a bearing on the people's choice of activity. The recent booms in ski touring (cross-country skiing) and in snowmobiling are limited to the northern tier states where the snow cover is sufficient. Many of the regionally associated forms of recreation described by the Outdoor Recreation Resources Review Commission in 1962 have lost their local claim. People everywhere are getting into just about every major form of outdoor recreation.

The flow of people to the Sunbelt and Rocky Mountain states suggests the influence of recreation on living style. While the search for warmer climates is part of the reason why the Southern and Mountain states are showing such large rises in population, the warmer climate by itself is only part of the picture. Longer seasons for outdoor recreation provide the flavor for the sunbelt lifestyle.

A search for variety of recreational pursuits coupled with affluence causes Americans to appear in constant search for recreation. The year 1978 showed the biggest winter vacation boom in history. Higher gasoline prices and relatively lower air fares had stimulated the winter vacation boom that had sunbelt citizens jamming the Colorado and Utah ski resorts, while the snowbelt citizens flocked to Florida and points south. An ensuing rise in air travel cost has caused some realignment of travel for recreation; however, the pattern of long vacation trips by air travel still holds up but it is not enlarging.[14]

Age makes a difference in the form of recreation in which an individual will participate. It is to be expected that younger people will participate more in the strenuous sports such as horseback riding and skiing. The only activity that shows an exception to less participation as age increases is walking.[18] Walking is a very flexible term to express participation in outdoor recreation. Because it is very inclusive in its meaning, walking for pleasure is recorded under most circumstances by nearly everyone.[7] Walking is convenient, healthful, relaxing, and enjoyable. Time available seldom precludes going for a walk; it just controls the length of participation. Walking for pleasure can be done anyplace where walking is possible. Beaches, boardwalks, city streets, open fields, and forest trails all provide the settings for pleasure walks. Since walking can be done on a short time basis for a stroll around the block or a circuit through the local park, it is the ideal outdoor activity for people with only small pieces of leisure time. Also, the physical act of walking is not too strenuous for many older persons who have been forced to limit participation in more active fields. It therefore provides the older person with the opportunity for some outdoor recreation activity.

The vigor and affluence of the aging Americans has had a major impact upon the leisure industry that had been geared for producing teenagers' sporting equipment. As the population continues to age, the economic impact of the elderly will have enormous affects upon the leisure industry in areas where older citizens gather.[28] Yesterday's emphasis on teenagers has shifted as the population takes on a middle-age spread. The young middle-age group of 35–49 years has grown by 31 percent. It is that group that contributes most to all forms of outdoor recreation as they get married, raise families, and make capital investments in recreation.[2] The "greying" of America will continue to influence both the private and public sector to deemphasize their love affair with youth and to accept their obligations for an older population.

Camping, sightseeing, and picnicking are three major forest recreation activities. They maintain their popularity among adults as age increases. Because of their popularity among people of parental age, these three activities, along with hiking and swimming, are the core attractions in the forest recreation demand. Although outdoor recreation can be treated by gathering information on individuals, it is most often a result of group or family participation. Family units or organizations are responsible for most of the recreational camping and picnicking done in the United States. Participation in one activity often leads to participation in others. Swimming areas attract family picnickers who may also be classed as sightseers. Many private campground owners have learned that water for swimming or boating is necessary for a successful campground.

Education

Generally, those persons who have the higher salaries also tend to have had the greatest education. Their influence on the demand for outdoor recreation, however, seems to be based on their affluence and not on their intellectual background. Therefore, it is discussed under the basic influence of "Money."

Money

Many people dream of horseback trips into wilderness areas of the Rockies, of skiing down the slopes of the White Mountains, or of sightseeing through Yosemite and Crater Lake National Parks. Millions do these things every year and many millions more just dream about them. For most people, a trip to a nearby state park or lake is possible on a weekend, but any long trip or specialized recreation is limited because of its cost. Activities such as boating or skiing require high initial investments. Continued participation in these activities requires funds that are not needed for more essential uses. Even the uncomplicated sightseeing trip requires the costs of transportation (35 percent of total cost), meals (25 percent of costs), and sometimes lodging (16 percent of costs). The total cost can be prohibitive to any family working on a tight budget.

Available money is a factor that restricts or encourages outdoor recreation. Americans spend approximately 50 billion dollars a year on vacation and pleasure trips. That is more than 3 percent of their entire income. In addition, they spend almost as much on consumptive items associated with their vacation.[14]

The general pressure on forest-recreation resources comes in two forms. The people who flee the concrete and asphalt labyrinths of their work-a-day world for an afternoon in the forest are generally associated with certain types of activities. Sightseeing, picnicking, and swimming fit the needs and finances of this group. Funds available often determine that a family will go for a picnic at the nearby lake rather than go water skiing at the seashore. The second form of pressure on the recreation facilities comes from the group that has vacation time and is doing some family camping. The camping itself is an enjoyable activity, but is also a means of allowing many families to be mobilized sightseekers. Foresters and wilderness enthusiasts should not be too critical of the windshield hiker.

In spite of what many article writers and hiking enthusiasts might claim, leisure camping and back-country trips are expensive. Perhaps the costs are not evident at first, but they are there. Time itself is equal to money. Time away from the job or time when house and car payments are running due while camping and travel fees are mounting makes the average wage earner head for home. Many families with young children have realized the pleasures of family camping and hiking; the majority of young families, however, must be able to drive to an attraction if they are to visit it at all.

Most people can drive to a national park to enjoy the scenic attractions available, but only a relatively few people can take long periods of time from work, hire a guide and pack animals, and arrange a wilderness trip into the back country. Although wilderness and back-country areas fill an important position in the supply of recreation facilities, they may be more important for their historical or ecological value than for their recreational values so far as the majority of Americans are concerned today. Research has shown that most wilderness or back-country users are in the upper income brackets. [16]

As our population has gained in affluence, it has put more of its wealth into recreation. The Outdoor Recreation Resources Review Commission Report supports the theory that available money is a basic factor in outdoor-recreation participation. The people who hold the higher-salaried jobs form the groups that participate the most.

About 400,000 of household heads between 25 and 34 years of age earn more than $25,000. Coupling the large income with the active age bracket produces the potential for increased recreation participation. [15] Participation in outdoor recreation is directly proportional to income. [18] As the family income increases, its participation increases accordingly. The money Americans had left over after the bills were paid—in other words, the discretionary income—rose by $250 billion during the decade from 1960 to 1970. By 1977, recreation and leisure-time activities had become the nation's largest industry. The American people were spending 160 billion dollars on recreational leisure. [3] This great increase in the affluence of the population portends a huge increase in participation and might indicate a greater use in the more costly forms of recreation. The impact of energy costs of the eighties could change user patterns, however, total recreation activity seems to continue to rise under all conditions.

At the present, most forest recreation planning is based upon the assumption that the least expensive activities will remain the most popular. Camping is expected to retain its popularity since many families use camping as a means to an end. Camping becomes a way of minimizing the costs of food and lodging while traveling. Picnicking requires only planning and transportation in addition to regular food expenses. The combined costs usually are lower than a meal at a mediocre restaurant. We are seeing some changes related to fuel-cost rises. Camping is being done in home state parks instead of across the country. Boating is continuing to rise in popularity, but it is being done closer to home.

Presently, personal income strongly controls participation in outdoor recreation and influences the form and intensity that the participation will take. With the changes in values that are taking place in our society, it is possible that participation and income may not remain so well correlated. For example, heavy use is being made of state and national parks by low-level spending young people traveling and camping together either as a temporary lifestyle or as a vacation experience. Also, the overnight camping experience associated with some large outdoor rock festivals is changing the image of camping from a family activity to a community, subculture activity. The pairing of young unmarried adults for wilderness and backpacking has become a common if not totally accepted social group.

Time

Time is listed as a basic factor influencing participation in outdoor recreation. Available time or the lack of it has an obvious effect on what people will do. Time as it is considered here has two facets, of which the first is available or leisure time. The second facet of time is mobility, which is a person's relative ability to move easily from one point to another. Some of the travel can be con-

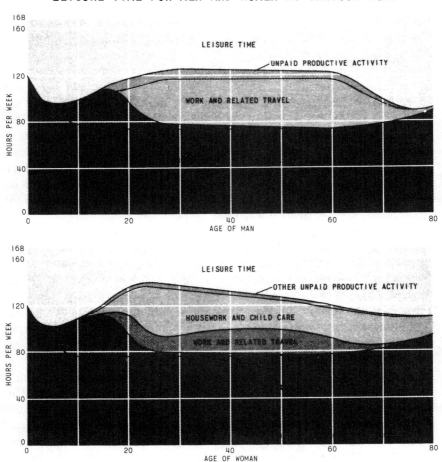

Fig. 2.1. Charts showing the hours spent per week by men and women performing tasks at various ages. (Courtesy of the Southern California Research Council.)

sidered as driving for pleasure or sightseeing. Up to a certain point, however, travel consumes leisure time.

Leisure time is the period in which a person is free to choose his own activity. Leisure time can be thought of as one of three blocks of time available to an individual.[9] Marion Clawson describes these three blocks as existence time, subsistence time, and leisure time. Any person must devote a certain amount of the day's time to existing. He must sleep, eat, and perform personal maintenance operations. After the basic existence requirements are met, the individual must take some time for meeting his subsistence needs. He must obtain food, clothing, housing, and transportation. Any time remaining after the existence and subsistence requirements have been fulfilled belongs to the individual as leisure time. Figure 2.1 shows the use of time by activity and age distribution of men and women as published by the Southern California Research Council.

It is the occurrence of this leisure time that has much to do with the types of recreation that people engage in. The increase of leisure time and the increasing means to do something with it are causing tremendous upsurges in recreation activity. Leisure time is available in daily, weekend, vacation, and retirement forms. It is how these pieces or forms of leisure time occur throughout the day or evening between or following the existence and subsistence needs of hygiene, working, household chores, and other daily regimen. These doses of daily leisure are often too short for engagement in forest recreation. These are the times spent at backyard barbecues, reading, or watching television. Physical relaxation is usually the rule when using daily leisure because this time is insufficient to prepare for, to equip, and to make an outing further than to the local bowling alley or movie theater.

Weekends provide a longer block of leisure time that has always been appreciated by school children. Weekends provide sufficient time to escape from the frictions of city dwelling for an outing or for an overnight campground visit. Shortening workweeks will continue to enlarge the blocks of time available for recreation in each day on weekends.

Vacation and retirement time provide the recreationist with leisure time that he requires to participate in outdoor recreation in depth. Vacations permit travel to distant points of interest. People with vacation or retirement time become users of recreational resources for the enjoyment of the activity. Vacationers camp and make investments in camping equipment because they enjoy camping as an end in itself or as a means to obtaining an end such as travel. This is quite different from the sightseer who is temporarily fleeing the steel and concrete cliffs for a quick, refreshing glimpse of the out-of-doors. Vacation leisure doubled in the 50 years from 1900 to 1950 and doubled again in the ten years from 1950 to 1960.[9] Predictions made in 1963 called for a fivefold increase during the last half of the 20th century. These predictions already appear to be too conservative in the light of changing philosophies of government and business toward national prosperity.

Union-management labor negotiations have begun to show an attempt to spread prosperity to all members of society by including longer vacations and a form of sabbatical leave in contracts. Coupled with the efforts of state and federal governments to keep the economy on the upswing, this increase in leisure time appears to be headed toward a great upswing within the next decade and it will be reflected in the increasing participation in outdoor recreation.

Occupation

With the advance in technology, there has been an increase in professional and skilled workers. These are the people who show interest and have the time and the financial means to participate in outdoor recreation. As their numbers multiply, so does the recreational demand. The length of the average workweek has gradually decreased to less than 39 hours. Today, it is approximately 36 hours. Unless a four-day workweek is adopted, any reduction in working hours will be dissipated into daily uses. Some companies started using a four-day workweek in 1972; however, no real trend in that direction has begun. It is the increasing length of paid vacations and annual salaries for skilled workers that have provided a major boost in the amount of time spent in outdoor recreation. Today, more than half the working population of the United States receives a paid vacation of three or more weeks. The extended vacation plan that was negotiated in 1963 between the United Steel Workers and the basic steel industry provides for 13-week vacations for 10 percent of the senior half of the workers each year. [1] This policy of prolonged vacations and the advent of semiretirements have enabled thousands of families to engage in recreation activities. In 1964, the first year of the contract, over 30,000 senior steel workers took advantage of the 13-week vacations. The adjustable work day, or flex–time schedules, being tried by some government and industry offices will serve to provide more time for local and short-trip recreation activities. Most of the adjustable workday schedules appear to be satisfactory in reducing traffic snarls among commuters; however, they lessen car-pool involvement and require more time for heating or cooling work spaces. The long-term impact on recreation impact is still to be determined.

Mobility

Time is used in traveling to and returning home from outdoor or forest recreation activities. This travel time becomes more critical as the distance increases or the mode of travel becomes more primitive. The railroad excursions of the early 1900s were all-day affairs that had to be planned well in advance and according to the railroad's schedule. A trip to the seashore by a Philadelphia resident took approximately two hours in 1950 if the traffic was not heavy. A total four-hour traveling time for the 140-mile round trip meant a long, hot effort to live for five or six hours on the beach. The individual's automobile, however, presented him with the choice of going or not going. It allowed him to set his own travel schedule to meet his particular needs or desires. The family car has provided mobility and is used for 90 percent of all vacation and recreation travel.[17]

Gasoline costs and shortages have had little effect on the private-commercial travel mix; they have, however, caused some adjustment away from long driving vacations. A sudden drop in vacation travel is expected by many recreation planners to occur when gasoline reaches $1.50 per gallon. Research by Warren in 1981 does not support the price elasticity theory. In her study of Ohio campers, Warren found that distance traveled for vacations has risen as the price of gasoline has risen over the 1978 to 1980 period.[27] Commercial transportation, on the other hand, has improved in some fields and deteriorated in others.

The most notable improvement in commercial travel has been the universal use of the jet airliner. Now, it is possible to fly from coast to coast in less than four and a half hours. The jetliner has increased mobility to the point where distance is now measured in time not in miles. This concept of distance equaling time more adequately fits into the overall recreation picture than does the mileage concept. Airlines are arranging package deals and pushing ads that extol the many reasons for visiting the American outdoors. Now, with airline deregulation occurring, many flights have been cancelled and the price of airline travel is skyrocketing. Domestic air travel fell off by 8 percent in 1980 after years of strong rises.[14] The airlines, however, are continuing a strong marketing campaign.

The 41,000-mile federal interstate highway system has had the most impact on the recreation style in the United States. The interstate highway system is nearing completion throughout the country, giving uninterrupted, controlled-access driving throughout the entire country. Pennsylvanians can camp in the Thousand Island camping areas in Canada and New York by following along Interstate Route 81 for approximately seven hours. The tedious and always dangerous trip across the Sierras on U.S. Route 40 has been made into a rapid and comfortable tour by the construction of a four-lane interstate highway through the beautiful Donner Pass. The smooth trip across this once forbidding wall of mountains is a far cry from the grisly adventure that faced the hapless Donner Party in 1847.

This relatively new mobility on a national scale brings the population into contact with the recreation attractions that exist in all parts of the country. The National Park Service policy that has been developed concerning accessibility and visitor-use limitations is directly related to the mobility afforded the American public through the interstate system. The interstate system is a self-continuing creation since it is funded by "earmarked" taxes on gasoline. As more miles are driven, there will be more gasoline consumed, especially with mileage-reducing pollution devices, and thereby more money to build more miles of highway.

Automobile sales had been averaging approximately eight million new cars per year. During the years from 1950 to 1980 the miles traveled by people in private cars and in airplanes increased by 100 percent. That increase in travel paralleled the increase in recreational visits during the same period. By 1970, Americans owned 100 million cars and were traveling a nearly completed interstate system that provided uninterrupted travel from coast to coast and into every part of the country. At the close of the 1970s, there were enough cars to seat every American in the front seat. Although the American automobile market collapsed in 1979, there will be plenty of cars around to transport recreationists. We know that the economy and availability of gasoline can have a sharp impact on the recreational patterns of Americans. When gasoline prices doubled, the visitation to distant national parks temporarily dropped by almost 20 percent and the recreational vehicle industry reported a 50 percent drop in sales.[14]

Because sightseeing is a prevalent outdoor recreation pursuit, scenic drives had been recommended for construction by the federal government.[20] This was a logical move for the government to take because such a costly undertaking is beyond the means of any other organization. The development of a system of scenic highways comparable to the Skyline Drive of Virginia would increase forest-recreation activities such as hiking, camping, picnicking, as well as providing general enjoyment of the forest vistas. Today more emphasis is being placed upon the development of accessible bike trails, jogging and fitness areas, and general hiking areas under such programs as "Rails to Trails."

Communication

Why do people want to participate in outdoor recreation? Relaxation, self-gratification, escape, and travel have already been mentioned as motives. Certainly, enjoyment is the immediate goal of recreation. But beyond the motivating forces lies the fact that people must know that outdoor recreation exists, that it is available to them, and that they could and would enjoy it. Communication provides the media to transmit these messages to the public. Mass and personal communication have continued to make technologic advancements to the point that now live television broadcasts can be transmitted around the world by an orbiting satellite system; overnight mail delivery is available in most metropolitan districts; and inexpensive long-distance telephone calls can be made by direct dialing. This case of long distance and mass communication creates an illusion of smallness for all of the United States.

People learn about outdoor recreation through communication. They can compare themselves with others engaged in outdoor or, more specifically, forest recreation. Although the comparison might be real or illustrative, it makes the people understand that they might also enjoy it. Mass communication media such as newspapers and television do more than expose the public to recreation ideas. They create an obligation to travel, picnic, camp, and to partake in other outdoor activities for social status as well as for personal gratification. Advertisements for products that are completely unrelated to forest recreation use mountain scenery or a forest-recreation activity for a backdrop. This motivation technique ties the product to the status or the enjoyment associated with wilderness trail riding, mountain stream fishing, or some other forest recreation activity. Most readers are familiar with cigarette or beer ads showing overwhelmingly delighted middle-aged men cavorting with very sexy 21-year-old girls in a bucolic setting. Besides the desired effect that it has concerning the product, the advertisement exposes the readers to the supposed or real pleasures associated with the forest and its environment.

Manufacturers of equipment associated with forest recreation are producing better and more elaborate gear to meet any demand. Besides making forest recreation easier for the devotee, new and better equipment stirs interests in nonparticipants. The advertising that is needed to present the equipment to the public eye also encourages the increase in the demand for the equipment and thereby an increase in forest-recreation participation. After the large financial expenditures are made, the new owner is placed in a position of use to continue justifying his purchase. Some economists have critized the author's reasoning that supply influences recreation demand. All one has to do, however, is look at the recreation-oriented items and ideas being huckstered across the land to see that the public could not have the demand for the toys they did not even know about before advertising spread the word.

Economic Aspects

Outdoor recreation is big business. It is no longer an adjunct to our economy. It has become a major influence in that it generated 3 percent of the gross national product in 1970. By 1977, total recreation had become the nation's largest industry in terms of dollars contributed to the gross national product. Visits to recreational facilities have tripled in the last 20 years and will probably increase tenfold before the year 2000. More than 160 billion dollars are contributed to the gross national product each year by recreation. [17,23,3] As outdoor recreation continues to grow, its contribution to the gross national product will become more and more significant. Some areas now hold recreation as one of the dominant factors influencing prosperity. The urban-industrial state of New Jersey considers recreation as its most important economic asset. [26] A new vacation industry has started with the recreation vehicle trade. A conservative estimate by the U.S. Department of the Interior states that there are more than five million motorized recreational vehicles in the United States. This includes snowmobiles, motorcycles, dune buggies, all-terrain vehicles, airboats, and hovercraft. [26]

Concern for energy consumption often brings recreation usage of fuels under question by those who are looking for some way to cut gasoline usage. In spite of the large economic contribution of motorized recreation to the nation's economy and to the enjoyment and well-being of its citizens, recreation vehicles consume less than 1 percent of the nation's total consumption. [3] Any government actions to conserve by cutting back on recreational fuel usage are symbolic, certainly not substantive. Even though it was withdrawn, the poorly worded proposal made by the U.S. Department of Energy to restrict the use of pleasure craft during severe gas shortages caused a 25 percent drop in boat sales in 1979. It was a naive and even foolish expectation that control of leisure activities could solve problems in this country. Fortunately, most of our elected leadership is responsive to the vital position of recreation in our nation.

All levels of government have become involved in recreation through efforts to satisfy the voting public. Millions are being allotted to recreation each year. The Land and Water Conservation Fund Act alone had contributed up to $800 million of federal funds per year to recreation. Many states have instigated their own multimillion-dollar recreation programs.

A National Recreation Advisory Council was established by President John F. Kennedy to study the needs of the country for recreation and to make recommendations to the president. Although this council was terminated by succeeding administrations, makeup of this council was a striking demonstration of the impact that recreation had on our society and its economy. Its members were the secretaries of the Interior, Agriculture, Defense, Commerce, and the secretary of Health, Education, and Welfare along with the administrator of Housing and Home Finance. Policy guidelines that were laid down by this group give recreation a leading place in our economy. They stated that "recreation is to be recognized on an equal basis with other beneficial water uses in management policies and programs." [21] This one statement opened the way for tremendous expansion of water-oriented recreation in the Tennessee Valley Authority and the Corps of Engineer impoundments where summer drawdown for low stream augmentation seriously hampered lake-shore development. Also, that statement placed recreation in competition with industrial and municipal users of water. It meant that pollution control was justified as part of a national recreation policy as well as part of a conservation and health program.

The government interest in water-oriented recreation is, in part, a reflection of the fact that freshwater boating is one of the largest generators of recreation dollars. Boating requires large initial investments and substantial sums for upkeep of the equipment. The boating industry generates more than $7.5 billion each year in retail sales of marine products and services. [23] A daily expenditure of $10 to $14 is associated with each recreational boating experience.

Supporting facilities such as docks, marinas, and restaurants are needed to meet the demand brought on by the increase in recreational boating. A study by Epp of the impact of recreational reservoirs in Pennsylvania showed that land values climbed more than enough to offset township tax losses related to the public action. [14] The factors most significantly related to housing development on these lakes were:

1. Presence of motor boating.
2. Presence of camping.
3. Age of reservoir.
4. Population between 51 and 85 miles from the lake.

Skiing is another sport that contributes to areas where outdoor recreation is an important business. The total effect of this one facet of forest recreation becomes apparent when the number of ski visits is known. There are more than 11 million skiers in the United States. An increase in participants of 42 percent occured between 1973 and 1976. [3] This compares with a 7 percent increase in the number of campers during the same period.

New activities requiring specialized equipment generate more economic activity as well as taking available money from some competing form of recreation. Ski touring is rapidly becoming a major winter sport in forested areas and with it has come the market for special equipment and supplies. Physical fitness awareness has encouraged many people to engage in jogging, skating, bicycling, and other exercise programs. Although much money is expended upon these pursuits in the outdoor setting, the generation of new recreation expenditures has not been documented.

Compatibility with Other Uses

Conservationists often align themselves with the recreation movement as called for in their version of multiple use of the forests. That concept of multiple use excludes timber values and calls for the forests to be used for hiking, sightseeing, camping, and other single-purpose uses. The overall forested areas produce too many products to be limited entirely to one of them such as recreation. Most informed people recognize the continuing need for forest products; therefore, they seek some sort of harmony among all of the uses.

Of course, specific, single-purpose sites are needed for recreation, timber, water, and wildlife management. These are intensive-use areas of small size and do not encompass an entire forest. However, wilderness areas and other large areas of unusual natural beauty have been established to preserve these areas in their natural state for the enjoyment of the public. The placement of large acreages into single-purpose management for recreation and scientific purposes is the cause of much friction among special interest groups concerned with forested land.

The removal of large tracts of forest lands from timber production is brought about by the formation of wilderness areas and national parks. The timber industry views this removal of land from production as a threat to its well-being. The timber industry argues that land presently producing tax money will be removed from the tax rolls when it becomes federal land. Timber land presently in federal ownership will no longer return a certain percentage of stumpage returns to the local counties, as is the case when timber is being sold from federal lands. With the removal of timber land from the market, job opportunities will be adversely affected. In general, the timber industry believes that the depressing effect of a large wilderness area or national park in certain areas will not be offset by the economic benefits derived from recreation. The contention here is that wilderness areas or large parks are usually established in locales where a large part of the economy is based on timber and not near the large centers of population where the expected users live.

The advocates of large park/wilderness areas devoted entirely to recreation and preservation contend that such areas are needed in order to preserve some vestige of the nation's heritage. Since these areas benefit the entire nation, they should not be justified on the basis of local economics. Also, the advocates of large parks do not agree with the timber industry's contention that the large-scale withdrawal of land from the production of timber will have a depressing effect on the local economy. Their belief is that the income generated from park maintenance, park administration, and tourism will more than offset the depressing affect on the timber-based economy caused by curtailing timber operations.

The conflicts between recreation and the timber industry on public lands is in the throes of a final solution. In theory, recreation has won. Recreation activities are given a high priority rating in public-forest activities in most cases. In other cases, it is too late, and the issue was decided by the bulldozer. Competitive recreational interest caused more eruptions over public-land policy in the 1970s than did multiple-use forest-management decision. Snowmobile and ski-touring, resorts and back country, summer home and undeveloped forest land, and motorcycle and archery hunting are the topics for discussion and court action on public land in this decade.

The requirements made by both sides of the preservation issue have come too fast in the lower forty-eight. The entire character of underdeveloped country has changed along with its designation as parkland or wilderness. Those areas have stopped producing revenue themselves; they have, however, become magnets attracting people, commercialism, nearby summer homes, and all of the clutter associated with any resort area.

Over the country as a whole, things might be different. The mood of the American population changed from being sympathetic to the need for development of private as well as public land to an attitude of caution about the total resource regardless of ownership. This concern has lead to some significant legislation involving statewide comprehensive land-use planning. New York passed a law in 1973 that strictly limits the development of the 3.7 million acres of private land within the Adirondack Park. It was the national concern over development that fueled the fight over preservation of the Alaska lands even though valuable oil and gas existed there for exploitation.

Growth-control efforts attempted by many local and state governments reflect concern over attractive areas being damaged by their own popularity. Justice William O. Douglas' opinion that "A quiet place where yards are wide, people few and motor vehicles restricted are legitimate guidelines" has been widely quoted in defense of growth limits.[10] In the total recreation picture, community growth controls parallel management decisions for recreational land use. During the relatively quiet economic era of a few years ago, the no-growth or preservation stance was possible. Some economists claim that the no-growth policy is doomed by the inflation economy present at the beginning of the 1980s.[10]

Some land developers have used the ploy of campground development to create what amounts to a rural slum by avoiding local laws covering sewage and water. Road construction is chewing up 200,000 acres of the United States each year, and another 500,000 acres fall to the developers' bulldozers. As these statistics continue to alarm law makers, more states will follow Vermont's lead in passing comprehensive land-use planning. On the other hand, the recreation segment of the recreation-preservation alliance may set the limits on the continued extention of preservation concepts. The wilderness visitor is recreating. In spite of other justification for wilderness and forest preservation, recreation activity is the overwhelming reason for visits to such places. As the eastern wilderness regulation impacts and the new national park costs become obvious to the recreating public, there is a shift occurring in the stance of the recreationists. The recreationists do not want to lose access to the land in order to preserve the existing or planned aesthetic conditions.

REFERENCES

1. Anonymous. 1965. Steel Firm Disenchanted on Vacation. *Chambersburg Public Opinion.* March 10, 1965, p. 25.
2. Anonymous. 1977. What Shifts in Population Will Mean for Industry. In *U.S. News and World Report*, May 30, 1977, pp. 60–62.
3. Anonymous. 1977. Americans Spend 160 Billion. In *U.S. News and World Report*, May 23, 1977, p. 63.
4. Anonymous. 1979. Racquetball is Fastest Growing Sport. In *Dateline NRPA*. National Recreation and Parks Association, December 1979, p. 8.
5. Anonymous. 1980. News You Can Use In Your Personal Planning. In *U.S. News and World Report*, June 2, 1980, p. 77.
6. Anonymous. 1973. Roughing It the Easy Way. In *Time* magazine, Time-Life., vol. 102, no. 1, pp. 60–61.
7. Bureau of Outdoor Recreation. 1965. *Outdoor Recreation Trends*. U.S. Department of the Interior. Washington, D.C. 30 pages.

8. ———. 1972. *The 1970 Survey of Outdoor Recreation*. Preliminary Report. U.S. Department of the Interior. Washington, D.C. 105 pages.

9. Clawson, Marion. 1964. In *Leisure in America: Blessing or a Curse?* Monograph 4, American Academy of Political and Social Science, Philadelphia, Pennsylvania.

10. Cohn, D'Vera. 1979. Bigger is No Longer Better. *Washington Post*, April 21, 1979, p. E-29.

11. Crafts, Edward C. 1964. Launched: The Bureau of Outdoor Recreation. In *Outdoor Recreation: Its Impact Today*. Soil Conservation Society of America. Ankeny, Iowa, pp. 12–14.

12. Epp, Donald J. 1970. *The Economic Impact of Recreational Water Reservoir Development on Land Use, Business Enterprises, and Land Values*. Bulletin 764, Agricultural Experiment Station, The Pennsylvania State University.

13. Erickson, Richard B. 1964. Urbanization and the Shooter. *The American Rifleman*, vol. 112, no. 12, p. 26. National Rifle Association.

14. McDowell, Edwin. 1980. Tourism in 1980: A Rocky Road to Summer. *The New York Times*, May 18, 1980, p. 1.

15. Marimow, William K. 1973. They're Making Money, Making it While They're Young. In *The Philadelphia Inquirer*, July 15, vol. 289, no. 15, p. 1.

16. Merriam, Ludwig, Ammons. 1965. *Glacier Park Chalet Visits: An Introduction to Wilderness*. Research Note No. 2, February 1965. School of Forestry, Montana State University, Missoula, Mont.

17. Newspaper Enterprise Association. 1969. *The World Almanac and Book of Facts*. Newspaper Enterprises Association, Inc., New York, N.Y. 1017 pages.

18. Outdoor Recreation Resources Review Commission. 1962. *Outdoor Recreation for America*. ORRRC Report to Congress. Government Printing Office, Washington, D.C. 246 pages.

19. Phillips, Angus. 1980. Watchout, Here Comes a Bunch Without Any Losers. In *Washington Post*, July 15, 1980.

20. Recreation Advisory Council. 1964. *A National Program of Scenic Roads and Parkways*. RAC Circular No. 4, Washington, D.C.

21. ———. 1964. *Policy Governing the Water Pollution and Public Health Aspects of Outdoor Recreation*. RAC Circular No. 3, Washington, D.C.

22. Robey, George. 1979. Boaters Buying in Face of Skimp. In *Columbus Dispatch*, section D, November 1979, p. 19.

23. Schroeder, George H. 1963. *Land Management Challenges for Industrial Foresters*. Special Publication No. 1, p. 43. Forestry and Conservation Station, Montana State University, Missoula, Mont.

24. Shanklin, John F. 1964. *Numbers and Types of Professionals Needed in Outdoor Recreation Leadership by Federal and State Agencies*. Proceedings of National Conference on Professional Education for Outdoor Recreation, July 9–11, 1964. BOR, Washington, D.C.

25. U.S. Department of the Interior. 1962. *Forest Conservation*. USDI Conservation Bulletin 42. Government Printing Office, Washington, D.C. 82 pages.

26. ———. 1971. *ORRV: Off Road Recreation Vehicles*, Task Force Study, U.S. Department of the Interior, Washington, D.C. 123 pages.

27. Warren, Loretta Ann. 1981. *Trend Analysis of Vacation Travel Patterns for Selected Ohio State Park Campers*. Unpublished thesis. School of Natural Resources, The Ohio State University. 58 pages.

28. Wooten, James R. 1978. Sunny Florida: Foreshadowing Our Future. In *U.S. News and World Report*, January 9, 1978, pp. 34–35.

3

Supply of Forest-Recreation Areas

INTRODUCTION

In a sense, the entire 2.3 billion acres of the United States make up the potential supply of recreation land.[15] Sightseeing is one of the leading outdoor and forest recreation activities, and it can take place anywhere. It is generally accepted, however, that other forms of forest recreation such as camping and picnicking do require areas that meet certain conditions. Because of the requirements of setting, attraction, space, and climate, the area that can be considered as available for outdoor recreation is limited to places that meet those requirements. The total area of land that is suitable for some sort of forest recreation activity constitutes the theoretical supply for forest recreation.

Today, there are approximately 775 million acres of forest land in the United States.[1] This seemingly large acreage of land must be many things to many people. Our population depends upon forest land for watershed protection, timber, wildlife habitat, recreation, and to a certain extent, forage. All of these demands upon the forest are growing larger each year. The legal battles over water that are wracking the Southwest highlight the desperate need for only one product of the forested lands. Many people rely upon forest products even while they are criticizing the forest management that made the products possible. Imposed upon this network of increasing pressures on the forests is the surge for various forms of forest recreation. Recreation is making heavier demands for a stronger voice in determining the use of forest resources.

Barring any catastrophic changes in our social system, recreation will continue to grow. Therefore, it must be given a voice in formulating land management policy. Forest land cannot, however, be turned over completely to recreation in spite of what some pressure groups may advocate.[24] Harmony must be reached among all forest land demands. Most of the demands are compatible with the others if there is a little compromising done by the land managers. Some forest uses seem to preclude other values; however, further inspection

30

may often show that the first impression is not correct. The forestry practice of even-aged management advocates clear-cutting in small blocks. That means that all the trees within the cutting area are either cut or killed. The loss of den trees horrifies the squirrel hunter and the apparent destruction of the beautiful woods causes the sightseer to write his congressman. The hunter and the sight-seer are partially in the right. A couple of compromises in the cutting tech-niques might have made everyone satisfied with the even-age management process. Den trees could have been left standing and strips of forest along the roads or in vista areas could have been left or cut under a less obtrusive system. Unfortunately, many forest land managers and landowners have abused the use of even-age management techniques by making huge and poorly planned cuts. As a result of not considering the public wishes, land managers have had some of their options removed by an aggrieved public with voting power.

Aside from the fact that compromises could have helped the forest manager overcome some ruffled feelings, the process of timber cutting is not completely destructive to all aspects of the forest community. Into the clear-cut area come deer to browse for much needed food. The ruffed grouse is absolutely depen-dent upon such openings in the forest canopy.[25] The cutting has simply changed the wildlife cover and habitat from that suitable for squirrel and turkey to that required by deer and grouse. Although the aesthetic values are sharply decreased at the time of cutting, they quickly return in the form of seedling and sprout reproduction. Sometimes the stand composition caused by planned cuttings is more pleasing to the sightseer than the previous, poorly formed second growth stand of timber that was removed. On the other hand, clear-cutting is not justified silviculturally in all cases, but becomes an expedi-ency for an overzealous timber marker. Clear-cuts are an aesthetic nightmare that can be brought back to haunt those responsible.

The Allagash River in Maine is an example of the part that management plays in maintaining scenic areas. Organizations and governments have pushed for a national scenic and canoe area to protect the shoreline from destruction by its private owners. Actually, the entire shoreline has been under forest manage-ment for years, and much of this so-called unspoiled area has been cut at least twice and has been open for public recreation for 100 years.[11] The Allagash Wilderness Waterway was the first state contribution to the Wild and Scenic Rivers System under Public Law 90-542. Obviously, all cutting does not im-prove the scenery or the wildlife, but with an effort the various demands on the forest can be harmonized and the growing demands for recreation, timber, and water all can be met.

The large forest areas are generally unused for recreation except for hunting. Even though each area cannot serve every purpose every moment, intelligent management will allow each activity to take place in a proper sequence. Camp-ing and hiking can go on in areas that are not scheduled for cutting. Hunting can follow the managed cutting. Recreation is a powerful force, but it should not become the dominant use of the forests. Putting too much emphasis upon estimated recreation dollar values would be attaching too much precision to too many variables. [24]

The actual supply of forest recreation land can include only those lands on which recreation is part of the present management plan or where it can be included with rational projections. Admittedly, any place might have recreational appeal to very narrow specialties such as snake hunters, rock collectors, or spelunkers. The more widely accepted endeavors such as camping, picnicking, hiking, hunting, fishing, and swimming generally require space, suitable climate, accessibility, appropriate setting, specific attractions, and water in the quantity needed for the area to be managed for recreation (Table 3.1).

Although the presence of land and water acreage is the limiting factor for forest recreation activities, other factors influence the actual supply of forest recreation land. Accessibility, major attractions, and public desires play an important role in whether or not an area is really part of the recreational inventory. Even the attractions of a wilderness area must be reached by modern transportation if they are to be enjoyed. Some of the most wild and beautiful country within the United States lies inaccessible and therefore unused in Alaska.

DISTRIBUTION OF FOREST RECREATION AREAS

Physical Distribution

The supply of developed forest recreation areas is inadequate, while the potential supply is much greater than could be required by any stretch of the imagination if the public wanted only highly developed sites. More than 360,000 square miles of the United States surface are in public ownership and are open for outdoor recreation. [27] Many millions of acres of private and public forest land could be included to swell the already adequate figure. Unfortunately, for the Easterner, most of the public land lies west of the Great Prairie. This means that most of the public land is in the West, while most of the people are in the East. The population density is 16 times greater in the Northeast than it is in the West, and the recreation pressure can be expected to be at least propor-

Table 3.1. The General and Specific Requirements
for Potential Recreation Areas

General	Specific
Space	Attraction
Suitable climate	Setting
Accessibility	Water
	Public desire

tionally greater.[27] Most of the acreage within the National Wilderness Preservation System (PL 88-577) lies west of the Great Lakes along with most of the Wild Rivers (PL 90-542).

In order to balance the discussion of forest recreation lands, one must realize that the ORRRC figures of 1962 tend to be somewhat biased in that the ORRRC Report equates federal land with recreation land. Actually, most forest land is in the eastern United States.[13] Some of the most heavily forested states are in the East. More than 80 percent of New England is covered by commercial forest land.[26] Energy crisis situations could have the effect of shortening road trips to the West for Easterners. Shifts in orientation of the Department of the Interior's National Park Service toward urban recreation responsibilities, the Eastern Wilderness Act, large increases in state park acquisition, and the National Recreation Recovery Act of 1978 indicate a national effort to present outdoor recreation opportunities closer to the population centers.

Increased mobility and longer periods of leisure time provides for some individual release from the overcrowding by permitting families to travel to the sections where recreation areas are more extensive. Of course, these same two factors tend to increase the pressure on the inadequate areas near the megalopolis or city complex as well as destroying the seclusion. The problem of getting people out of cities is now as acute as getting them into the cities was 15 years ago. This paradox of oversupply and shortage is found within the individual states as well as throughout the United States.

By the very nature of its urban society, the United States has its population grouped into megalopolises where the people overwhelm any outdoor or forest-type recreation that can be provided nearby. The detrimental effect of this heavy use lessens the effective area and makes the conditions worse. Many state parks that were designed in the 1930s have been placed in a high-density use situation that was not planned for. This heavy pressure has brought on deterioration of the facilities because the states, in an attempt to cope with the heavy use, have increased the numbers of campsites within their state parks beyond the limit that the areas can carry without adverse effects on the environmental conditions of the campground. An example of this situation occurred between 1955 and 1960 when the number of state-operated campsites rose by almost 50 percent.[22] During the same period, the number of campers has increased by approximately 100 percent and nullified any gains by the state park system.[16] Camping has continued a steady use in popularity right up to the present. There are approximately 60 million campers in this country.

Distribution by Ownership

The fact that the physical distribution of recreation areas is in an imbalance with the need has previously been discussed. Besides physical distribution, the supply is affected by the ownership and by the management of the land. Public forest recreation, as it is discussed in this book, takes place on land that is in either public or private ownership. The matter of payment for use does not preclude private land from the public recreation area unless it is a prohibitive cost or is accompanied by such standards as club membership or other precluding limitations. Usually, we should think of public-use recreation areas as those areas open to use by the general public regardless of ownership. This is opposed to land that is closed to public recreation use regardless of ownership. Approximately three-fifths of the country are in private ownership and are available for public recreation in widely varying degrees (Table 3.2). All forms of government from the town to the federal level operate forest recreation areas.

The four categories of ownership of recreation land are private, federal government, state government, and local government. Of these four categories of ownership of land, the federal land has been most actively developed for forest recreation while the private sector has lead the way in specialty and intense-use recreation. The federal government has usually taken the lead in recreation. The states have shown interest in recreation, but until recently, they have generally been too late to act. Local governments enter into the forest recreation field only on a very limited scale. The local governments are more concerned with the pressing problems of urban recreation on a daytime basis. Generally, municipal parks are relatively small. Even though they account for more than 80 percent of the parks in the United States, local parkland covers a total acreage of less than 1.5 million acres. [26] Playgrounds, ball fields, day camps, and supervised activities are needed to meet the needs of the community's youth. Some swimming and picnicking areas and urban organizations do provide local families with the opportunities for family-oriented recreation; however, recreation at the community level is a subject of its own and not covered in this text.

A slow but continuing shift of land ownership from private to public ownership has begun to cause some concern to Americans. A 1 percent shift in ownership has occurred between the ORRRC Study Report publication and 1978. In·

Table 3.2. Ownership of Land in the
United States by Percent.

Owner	Percent
Private	57
Public	41
Federal	34
State	6
County and Municipal	1
Indian	2
Total	100

the period from 1959 to 1974, approximately 17 million acres of land were transferred from private to public ownership. That is equivalent to the combined size of West Virginia, Delaware, and Rhode Island. Almost all of the land ownership shifted to local and state government. The federal land ownership has remained relatively constant.

Much of the land has been acquired by local and state governments for recreational purposes. Some has been used for highways, airports, and public buildings but most of it has gone into parks and wildlife refuges.[5]

Private Ownership

Of the 67 million acres of industrially owned commercial forest land, all but four million acres are open to some form of public recreation. This means that the public has access to 92 percent of the forest industry's land in the United States. Also, fishermen can pursue their sport on over 40,000 miles of streams on these same commercial forest lands.[1,2,13] The large forest landholding corporations keep their land open for public hiking, fishing, hunting, and camping and some go so far as to have campground areas established. Many of the larger landholders permit or encourage recreational use of their land more for good public relations than for profit. A blockade to the opening of some private land is the threat of liability for injuries to users. Often landowners are afraid to encourage or even to permit the public to use their land for recreational purposes. There is the possibility of a lawsuit against the landowner by persons injured while on his land. Being judged liable for injuries sustained by others can be disastrous to many landowners. Even being judged innocent of liability can be an expensive proposition. The defendant must pay legal fees and miss much gainful employment as well as having the anxiety of a lawsuit. Large companies feel that they are often the target of unjust or exaggerated liability claims. Such claims are considered to be nuisance claims where people hope to gain some compensation even though the matter of liability on the part of the defendant is doubtful.

Landowners are not alone in this fight against liability claims. Medical doctors and well-meaning volunteers are susceptible to charges of injuries caused during unsolicited care at accident sites. In order to protect interested citizens and physicians from damaging lawsuits, some states have passed laws to protect persons performing acts of mercy. These statutes are commonly referred to as "Good Samaritan Laws." Even though states where the public demands on private lands are heavy have attempted to lift this liability, they still recognize the owner's responsibility in willful negligence while attempting to protect the landowner from the growing fear of "nuisance lawsuits."

The increasing need for forest recreation is reflected in the overuse of campgrounds. As the number of publicly owned campsites is increased, the demand increases also and hence eliminates any actual gain on the need.[16] With an imbalance between the supply and the demand, the private investment system of capitalism comes into the picture. The use of private capital will permit areas to be developed on a risk-and-profit basis and thereby bring the supply into balance with the demand. Throughout the United States, private investors are developing forest recreation areas.

Some state park systems have helped to encourage this growth in private campgrounds by friendly cooperation with the owners, by not allowing pets into state park camping areas, and by catering to only one style of camping. The public sector is not in the position to keep ahead of the demand for any specific recreation activity. Only the private sector of the economy has the flexibility to adjust continuously to the desires of recreationists. Private campgrounds have grown in number to the point where they more than double the number of public campgrounds. With the exception of the Rocky Mountain and Pacific Coast states, the private sector provides most of the camping facilities within the United States.[28]

The 1960s was the era of small business enterprise entering the camping market. Private campgrounds developed in each state. Some private campgrounds have succeeded; many have not. The combination of good management, good work, good location, and good luck have made many small investors successful campground owners that still operate today.

A shift in the type of ownership and direction of private forest recreation took place in the 1970s. Large oil companies and motel chains recognized the potential of investment in campgrounds. By providing camping facilities near large resort attractions, companies could attract those people to the resort who would not be able or willing to pay the high cost of resort housing and dining. The permanent, or long-term, rental of campsites by trailer owners led to another step in the evolution of private enterprise in camping — the fee simple ownership of a campsite within a campground.

The 1980s are witnessing a general surge of people into vacation-home living. This is especially evident in the eastern United States where Southern Appalachia has become a dynamic second-home or vacation-home community. Camping has awakened an interest in mountain and forest environments. Now, people are moving all the amenities of home to the area that they find attractive.

Private land is open to public recreation use for three reasons. The first reason is a passive approach by the landowners. People are welcome on their land as long as they do little damage to it. Another facet of the passive approach is that of enforcement. Even if the public were not welcome there, its exclusion would be too difficult for the landowner to enforce and might even have other distasteful side effects.

Public relations is the second reason that much private land is open to the public. Large companies must produce a good image in the public eye and they must meet certain obligations to the social system that is responsible for their existence (Fig. 3.1) Attempts to avoid this responsibility cultivate ill will by the public toward the company. Good public relations are important to large companies for two major reasons. The first one is the obvious and the more direct reason of profit motivation. Rapid communication can spread a poor public image quickly and extensively to many potential consumers. A publicized company policy or action that causes widespread public disapproval can erase the benefits of a million-dollar advertising campaign. A more subtle reason for large landholders to cultivate good public relations is the threat of legislation that might influence the use of the forest land. Legislative attempts to alter or control land use are common at all levels of government. Owners of large forest holdings must gain the confidence of the voter and prove to him that the landowners' methods are best for the general good of the community.

The third and the fastest growing reason for opening private land to public recreation is the expectation of profit. With the advent of "Proposition 13" thinking and the subsequent tightening of the tax-money flow, park and recre-

Fig. 3.1. Public campsite near Effie, Minnesota, is one of thousands that are provided by commercial forest-owning industries for public goodwill purposes. (American Forest Products Industries photo.)

ation managers have turned to "privatization" of many facets of public recreation. The profit motive implies active participation by the landowner. He must develop facilities and manage the area wisely in order to turn a profit on his investment. The private ventures range from a small backyard campground to the elaborate developments featuring lodges, ski lifts, artificial lakes, and camping all rolled up into one large speculation. Hunting and fishing enterprises are developing in areas where people are willing to pay a fee for game or fish.

While LePage found that a definite fee elasticity existed in New Hampshire State Campgrounds—that is, that visits drop with fee rise—private campgrounds are finding a booming market for high-costing, highly-serviced campgrounds.[4,17] The apparent willingness of campers to pay up to $11.00 per night for the luxurious private sites while spurning state parks at $4.00 indicates a sorting of the users that might be used as a management tool.

Government officials realize that public agencies cannot meet all the demands for forest recreation. They believe that the privately owned lands and the private capital will become more important in meeting the future recreation requirements. There will be a continual proliferation of privately owned campgrounds of varying size and quality. Organizations of campground owners are being formed to help the investor and the user. Unfortunately, private campgrounds got off to a bad start because of poor planning, poor management, and hopes of high returns. Now that responsible managers have succeeded in recreation businesses and have organized, they are filling much of the need for recreational facilities. More people are realizing that $7 for each pheasant shot on a hunting preserve is a lower cost per bird than they would end up paying on open hunting areas if all the costs were tallied. Utility companies, paper companies, and other large landholders have increased the development of recreation facilities on their land to foster goodwill and to head off government control over the use of the land. Along with meeting their obligations to society in general, the large companies are expanding their lease arrangements with the Federal Bureau of Sport Fisheries and Wildlife and with state game-management agencies. These agreements allow government biologists to maintain and manipulate game habitat while the land is under private ownership.

Federal Ownership

The biggest forest recreation operator is the federal government, which owns one-third of the country. Approximately 761 million acres belong to federal agencies, departments, or commissions.[21,28] More than 30 agencies of the federal government operate approximately one million recreation areas throughout the United States, although 96 percent of the land is managed by the seven agencies providing outdoor recreation as part of their mandate (Table 3.3).[12,21,28] Forests, wildlife refuges, and grazing land constitute approximately 88 percent of the federal land, while dedicated parklands and historic

Table 3.3. Federal Agencies Providing the Most
Recreational Opportunities to the Public
in Order of Visitor Days.

Forest Service, USDA	(FS)
Corps of Engineers	(CE)
National Park Service	(NPS)
Bureau of Land Management	(BLM)
Bureau of Sport Fisheries and Wildlife	—
Tennessee Valley Authority	(TVA)

sites make up less than four percent.[5] The federal government's prominent position in recreation is justified by three assumptions. The first and most basic assumption is that the public has the right to use its own land. Since the people are the government, they are in a sense the real owners of all federal land. The second assumption states that the public has the right to obtain any values created by the use of public land. In a capitalist society, the investor is entitled to the profits; therefore, the public should receive any profit that results from the use of its land. The federal government's third assumption is that if the public is going to use its own land, it should use adequate and safe facilities. These adequate and safe facilities must be supplied by or under the auspices of federal agencies.[23]

Until the formation of the Bureau of Outdoor Recreation in 1962, no federal agency had ever been given the job of providing recreation for the American public; every one of the federal land-managing agencies, however, had been providing for the needs of recreationists for many years. The national forests and the national parks meet the general and specific requirements for potential recreation areas that are listed in Table 3.1 in that most of them are spacious, accessible, and have an attractive forest setting. The National Park Service and the Forest Service are the hosts to more than a billion recreationist visitors a year.

The huge water impoundments that have been constructed by the Tennessee Valley Authority and the Corps of Engineers have placed those two agencies squarely into the recreation business. Table 3.4 shows that recreation visits to Corps of Engineers' impoundments rose from 16 million in 1950 to more than 400 million in 1980.[7,23,28] The Corps manages more than 400 lakes with 47,000 miles of impoundment shoreline, more than 1,000 campgrounds, and 1,200 day use areas.

The Tennessee Valley Authority (TVA) has adopted the policy of local development. That means that the TVA has encouraged recreation development on its areas by the state and local governments and by the other federal agencies that are interested in recreation. Some lake frontage was sold to civic, service, or religious organizations; however, a reversionary clause was included in the sale contract to guarantee that the land was used for the purpose for which it was

Table 3.4. Recreation Visits to Selected Federal Lands Presented as Visitor Days.

Administrating Agency	Number of Visits (1,000s)			
	1950	1960	1970	1980
National Park Service	32,780	72,288	200,543	220,463[1]
Forest Service	27,368	92,595	178,109	820,000[2]
Corps of Engineers	16,000	106,000	300,000	420,000[2]

[1]National Park Statistical Abstract, 1980.
[2]Third Nationwide Outdoor Recreation Plan.

sold. The TVA undertook a large-scale effort to convert the 170,000 acres of second growth hardwood forest land between Lakes Kentucky and Barkley into a recreation area. The "Land-Between-the-Lakes," as it is named, was formally opened for recreation activities in 1964 after four years of planning.[31] That recreation area, managed as a recreation and environmental education demonstration area, draws approximately 2 million visitors annually.[28]

State Ownership

Approximately 6 percent of the United States is owned by the individual states for roads, parks, forests, and fish or game areas. State park systems have shown great increases in recent years. This growth from 5.7 million acres in 1962 to 9.8 million acres in 1975 amounted to a 72 percent increase in thirteen years.[5] The states had been given the pivotal role in outdoor recreation under the Land and Water Conservation Fund Act of 1965. How much public outdoor recreation is developed and what forms it will take largely depend upon the attitudes of the state governments. How much planning will the states do? How much money will they raise? How much flexibility will the state political systems allow? State recreation systems vary widely in facilities and services, although all the states claim to provide the same basic commodity of outdoor or forest recreation.[22]

States realize that it is their responsibility to provide balanced forest recreation opportunities for their citizens. State parks are active in land acquisition, preservation, and interpretation.[30] On one-third of the acreage of the National Park Service, state parks are accommodating twice as many visitors. State parks are faced with preserving a natural environment while responding to the needs of the recreationists by providing quality and quantity of experience opportunities. Table 3.5 indicates that simple proliferation of facilities does not appear to be the answer to overuse or to the overwhelming demand for forest recreation. Apparently, an adequate supply of satisfactory facilities attracts more people into the ranks of the participants or it encourages shifts from other areas or other interests to the satisfactory facilities. The shift of interest to state parks and local private recreation developments might continue to bear watch-

Table 3.5. Summary of State Park Systems.

	1950	1960	1970	1979
Areas	1,725	2,664	3,425	4,100
Acreage	4,657,000	5,602,000	8,555,000	9,000,000
Attendance	114,291,000	259,001,000	482,536,000	620,000,000

ing as the nation moves through its attempt to get control of its economy and energy demands.

Carrying Capacity of Land

The supply of forest recreation land cannot be measured in acres alone. The simple acreage figures do not provide the land manager with adequate information to plan for specific developments to meet a given demand. Most of the land tied up by recreation is not physically occupied by the user. The user does not intentionally consume the land that he occupies; however, he is doing that very thing. Deterioration of the occupied portions is the greatest threat to established recreation areas. The very presence of large numbers of people in one place changes the ecology of that area in many ways. The soil is compacted and eroded by millions of footsteps. Vegetation is killed directly by trampling or indirectly as a result of soil compaction when the infiltration and percolation regimes of the soil are altered and the pore spaces are eliminated. Normal wear and vandalism alter the site in an adverse manner. This deterioration of the occupied area is a real problem in the wilderness areas as well as in the Eastern state parks. [14,18,29]

Carrying capacity is a term used to quantify the relationship between an attraction's quality and the amount of use that the attraction receives. It is a management term that is dependent upon the management objectives for that area. Management objectives are a part of the carrying capacity concept because they establish the purpose for which the area is being managed. Management objectives reflect the intended quality level of the attraction and thereby set guidelines for the user's expectation. An accepted or a planned quality level is established by management decisions. An absolute carrying capacity does not exist for recreation areas.

Recreation managers use the term "optimum recreation carrying capacity." Optimum recreation carrying capacity denotes the amount of recreational use an area can withstand during a given period of time and provide the most appropriate protection to the resources and satisfaction to the users. [8] Both the physical carrying capacity and the social carrying capacity are considered along with management goals in determining the optimum carrying capacity. Table 3.6 lists general factors influencing the maintenance of the optimum carrying capacity of a recreation attraction.

Table 3.6. Factors influencing maintenance of the optimum
carrying capacity of a recreation attraction.

General Factors	Specific Example
Site Characteristics	• area and configuration of area • length of season • climate • elevation • surface drainage • soil • vegetation • topographic details • site amenities
Management	• control of antisocial behavior • water treatment • irrigation • visitor services • fertilization • insect control • litter control
Social / Psychological	• expectation • experience • activity compatibility • user population demographics

The amount of use that an area can support without any change in the recreational quality of the site is termed its physical carrying capacity. Wagar described recreation quality as the degree to which a recreation area normally contributes to the user's physical and psychic well-being.[29] Physical carrying capacity determines how durable the site is for recreation in the terms of user-days. It is the ability of the individual sites to hold up under user impact, or the physical capacity, that determines how large a supply of recreation land really does exist in the United States.

Social carrying capacity — the level of activity most acceptable to the user — is a very complicated concept. It involves the psychological items of mood, skill, experience, and expectations of the user along with the social considerations of group dynamics, weather, and events impacting on pleasure. A satisfaction model described by Chicchetti and Smith shows that the marginal satisfaction of each user decreases progressively with crowding even though the total satisfaction of the group is continuing to increase.[9] The theoretical social carrying capacity is reached when the aggregate satisfaction begins to decline with each increment of crowding.

Field studies have not supported the theoretical models of social carrying capacity. A study in 1980 by Manning and Cial did not establish dissatisfaction with incremental increase in use density.[19] The variables continue to change during field experience, thereby making any standard social carrying capacity designation very difficult. For instance, high densities of satisfied users occur at recreation sites when the weather is favorable. The users have a positive recreation experience in spite of the high use density when the conditions are favorable.

Space requirements per user-day have been roughly established to guide land managers in maintaining a given level of recreation quality. However, variables such as the level of recreation quality desired, soil characteristics, weather, season of the year, and the use of the area make such figures general "rules of thumb." Each site must be evaluated individually to determine its optimum carrying capacity. Site influences affecting this evaluation are discussed in detail in Chapter 6. Studies have shown that the independent variables that were significant at the 5 percent probability level were slope percent, aspect, and elevation. The vegetation is more hardy on steep northeast slopes at lower elevations.[10]

The management decision concerning the desired level of recreation quality must be made before the carrying capacity can be determined. Wagar gives the following example to explain the carrying capacity of forest recreation lands.[29]

1. Picnicking and its benefits would be at a certain level if the picnic area received 100 user-days of use each day.
2. If the daily use were increased to 200 user-days, character of the picnic area would change. It would adjust to the impact of the heavier use. Some wearing of the soil, a loss of grass, a higher noise level, and a loss of solitude would occur.
3. If the daily use were held at 200 user-days, the area would reach a new level of recreation quality and stabilize there. The area would now maintain that quality with a carrying capacity of 200 user-days use per day.

A Forest Service study of 38 independent variables revealed that six were significant in their effect on ground cover within camping units.[20] A multiple regression analysis worked out by this administrative study is being used to review the potential camping sites in the Southern Forest Service Region. Intelligent use of research findings precludes widespread adoption of this method without local checking. It is, however, an ongoing system that merits discussion.

The multiple regression resulted in the following equation:

$$\text{ground-cover index} = 81.28 + (-0.71A) + 0.21B + (-11.73C) + (-0.24D) + 0.82E.$$

Where ground-cover index, greater than 75 percent ground coverage by dead and living material is satisfactory; less than 75 percent cover is unsatisfactory.

A = potential pedestrian impact (PPI)
B = depth of B horizon in inches

C = percentage of surface rock
D = percentage of silt in C horizon
E = slope in percent
(percents are expressed as numbers: 33 percent is 33).

This equation has a standard error estimate of 4.7. In other words, the true percent of ground cover will be within 4.7 of the calculated percentage 68 percent of the time.

If 75 percent is the acceptable value for the dependent variable of ground-cover index, then a prediction formula can be developed to find an unknown potential pedestrian impact (PPI),* since all the independent variables can be determined at the site or from a detailed soil survey report. Determine the PPI rating for the design. If it is in excess of the PPI the site can tolerate, it must be reduced. Some reduction in PPI can be achieved by modification of the trail system. Major reduction of the PPI will require redesign of the campground or its relocation.

The system does not determine the number of visitor days that the site can tolerate. It determines the minimum PPI index that the design must accomplish to prevent deterioration. The Southeast Region (Region 8) of the U.S. Forest Service uses an acceptable minimum ground-cover index (GCI) of 75. If the GCI is below 75, deterioration would result at an accelerated rate when the area is used as planned. Therefore, modification of the fixed variable must be modified or compensated for in maintenance costs. The following example and detailed instructions are printed here by courtesy of Region 8 of the U.S. Forest Service.

Example

A. When solving for the ground-cover index (GCI) that will result when a given design is used on a known site (key to letters is given in text above):
$$GCI = 81.28 + (-0.71A) + 0.21B + (-11.73C) + (-0.24D) + 0.82E$$
B. When solving for allowable Potential Pedestrian Impact (PPI) with GCI measured on the Site:
$$A = 114.47 + 0.30B + (-16.52C) + (-.34D) + 1.15E - \frac{GCI}{0.71}$$
C. Instructions for determining PPI index:
   1. Select a map of a large enough scale to show the location of all facilities (1 inch = 50 feet or 1 inch = 100 feet).

---

*The *potential pedestrian impact* (PPI) is estimated by drawing straight lines on an accurate scale drawing to connect the center of each camping unit with each facility servicing that site — i.e., garbage can, water outlet, and toilet. The portions of lines that do not fall on facilities or on modified surfaces are measured to scale, totaled, multiplied by three (users per unit), and divided by the total area within the 50-foot radius of each unit.

2. Divide the development into individual camp loops or picnic grounds. The PPI of each will be determined separately.
3. Draw a 50-foot radius circle centered on each family unit activity area and determine the total area covered in the camp loop (shaded area in Fig. 3.2).
4. Draw a 15-foot radius around each family unit and service facility such as garbage cans, water hydrants, toilet building, and bulletin boards, and determine the total area enclosed.
5. Draw straight lines between the center of each family unit and each facility serving it. In picnic grounds, this will include the closest access point to the parking lot and other service facilities constructed to serve the picnic grounds such as bathhouses and craft shelters. Measure the total length of these lines falling outside of roads, surfaced trails, and

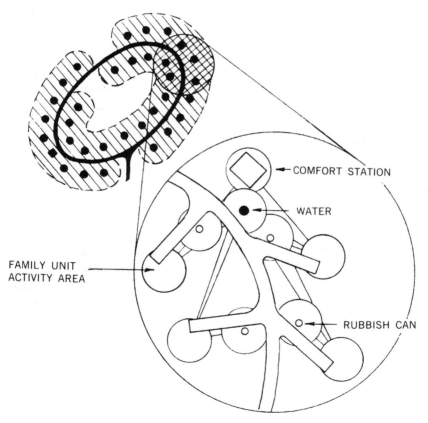

COMFORT STATION

WATER

FAMILY UNIT
ACTIVITY AREA

RUBBISH CAN

Fig. 3.2. In determining the potential pedestrian impact, the total area under 50-foot-radius circles at each unit is ascertained (shaded portion) along with total area within 15-foot-radius circles at each facility and family unit.

the circles drawn in Step 4 (15-foot radius around each unit and facility). Multiply this figure by 3 and add it to the total area of Step 4.

6. Divide Step 5 by Step 3 (total area within 50 feet of a unit center) to determine the percent of the total area potentially impacted by known pedestrian circulation. This percentage expressed without the percent sign is the PPI index to be used in the formula.

D. Instructions for determining Ground-Cover Index (GCI):

1. Draft site development area on map. This is the same as Steps 1, 2, and 3 in PPI instructions. (See Fig. 3.2.)

2. Establish transect lines across the developed area (determined in PPI Steps 1, 2, and 3) at 100-foot spacings. The first or base-line transect should be located without bias.

3. A sample is to be taken on the ground by following a compass bearing along the established transect line. Stop after four paces (two steps) keeping the left foot in place and on line.

4. Observe and record what is on the ground within an imaginary 3/4-inch circle immediately adjacent to the toe of the left shoe.

5. Repeat this procedure every four paces until the end of the transect line is reached. Hits on roads and surfaced trails are not recorded.

6. Calculate ground-cover index by dividing the number of hits on live ground vegetation, litter, moss, or rock by the total number of hits and multiply by 100.

The results of the study should imply management requirements. The formula states that for every unit increase in PPI, there is a corresponding decrease of 0.71 in GCI.

Ecological awareness and common sense dictate that studies be made for determining the environmental effects of various use levels. What happens then, when researchers find that the level of use is too high to maintain the present level of quality? The National Park Service has been taken to task and to federal court for trying to reduce the number of rafters using the Colorado River.[5] Site modification and permit limiting of users are being considered for the National Wilderness Preservation System. Each attempt to modify the use or limit the users, however, is construed by some group as an infringement upon the wilderness concept as institutionalized by Congress. The scientific studies related to carrying capacities must be made to provide sound basis for the political decisions as well as for design standards.

REFERENCES

1. American Forest Products Industries. 1962. *Forest Land Use—Everybody's Concern.* First Forest Land Use Conference, September 1961. AFPI, Washington, D.C.

2. ———. 1960. *Recreation on Forest Industries Land*. AFPI, Washington, D.C.

3. Anonymous. 1973. Life and Leisure: Troubled Waters. In *Newsweek* magazine, June 18, 1973, p. 62.

4. Anonymous. 1973. Roughing It the Easy Way. In *Time* magazine, vol. 102, no. 1, pp. 60–61.

5. Anonymous. 1978. The Shrinking Supply of Private Land. In *U.S. News and World Report*, February 20, 1978, pp. 64–65.

6. Bureau of Outdoor Recreation. 1971. *Outdoor Recreation Action*. Report No. 20. U.S. Department of the Interior, Washington, D.C. 30 pages.

7. ———. 1972. *Outdoor Recreation Action*. Report No. 24. U.S. Department of the Interior, Washington, D.C. 32 pages.

8. ———. 1977. *Guidelines for Understanding and Determining Optimum Recreation Carrying Capacity*. Prepared by the Urban Research and Development Corporation for the U.S. Department of the Interior. Washington, D.C.

9. Chicchetti, C.J. and Smith, V.K. 1973. Congestion Quality Deterioration and Optimal Use: Wilderness Recreation on the Spanish Peaks Primative Area. In *Social Science Research*, vol. 2, pp. 15–30.

10. Cieslinski, T.J., and Wagar, J.A. 1970. *Predicting the Durability of Forest Recreation Sites in Northern Utah – Preliminary Results*. U.S. Forest Service Research Note INT-117. Intermountain Forest Experiment Station, Ogden, Utah. 7 pages.

11. Clepper, Henry. 1962. The Allagash: Wilderness in Controversy. In *Journal of Forestry*, vol. 62, no. 11, pp. 777–781.

12. Crafts, Edward C. 1964. Launched: The Bureau of Outdoor Recreation. In *Focus on Resource Conservation*, vol. 1, pp. 12–14. Soil Conservation Service, Ankeny, Iowa.

13. Forest Service. 1973. *The Outlook for Timber in the United States*. Forest Resource Report No. 20. U.S. Department of Agriculture. Washington, D.C. 368 pages.

14. Hutchinson, S. Blair. 1962. *Recreation Opportunities and Problems in the National Forests of the Intermountain Region*. Intermountain Forest and Range Experiment Station, Ogden, Utah.

15. Johnson, H.A., and Tharp, M. 1963. Meeting the Demand for Outdoor Recreation. In *USDA Yearbook*, p. 309. Washington, D.C.

16. Kent, Joseph. 1965. Are Private Campgrounds the Answer? In *Better Camping Magazine*.

17. LaPage, Wilbur F. 1968. *The Role of Fees in Campers' Decisions*. Northeast Forest Experiment Station Paper NE-118. U.S. Forest Service, Upper Darby, Penn. 24 pages.

18. Lutz, H.J. 1945. Soil Condition on Picnic Grounds in Public Forest Parks. In *Journal of Forestry*, vol. 43, pp. 121–127.

19. Manning, R.E. and C.P. Cole. 1980. Recreation Density and User Satisfaction: A Further Exploration of the Satisfaction Model. In *Journal of Leisure Research*, vol. 12, no. 4, Forth Quarter 1980, pp. 329–343.

20. Orr, Howard R. 1971. Design and Layout of Recreation Facilities. In *Recreation Symposium Proceedings*, pp. 23–27. Northeastern Forest Experiment Station, U.S. Forest Service, Upper Darby, Penn.

21. Outdoor Recreation Resources Review Commission. 1962. *Public Outdoor Recreation Areas – Acreage, Use, Potential*. ORRRC Study Report No. 1. Government Printing Office, Washington, D.C. 200 pages.

22. ———. 1962. *Paying for Recreation Facilities*. ORRRC Study Report No. 12. Government Printing Office, Washington, D.C. 88 pages.

23. ———. 1962. *Federal Agencies and Outdoor Recreation*. ORRRC Study Report No. 13. Government Printing Office, Washington, D.C. 75 pages.

24. Rockefeller, Laurence S. 1962. The Future of Outdoor Recreation. In *Journal of Forestry*, vol. 60, no. 8, pp. 521–524.

25. Sharp, Ward M. 1957. *Management of Poletimber Forest for Wildlife Food and Cover*. Agricultural Experimental Station, University Park, Penn.

26. U.S. Department of Agriculture. 1977. *The Nation's Renewable Resources—An Assessment, 1975.* Forest Resource Report No. 21. Government Printing Office, Washington, D.C. 243 pages.
27. U.S. Department of Commerce. 1964. *Statistical Abstract of the United States—1963.* Government Printing Office, Washington, D.C.
28. U.S. Department of the Interior. 1979. *The Third Nationwide Outdoor Recreation Plan: the Assessment.* Government Printing Office, Washington, D.C. 264 pages.
29. Wagar, J.A. 1964. The Carrying Capacity of Wild Lands for Recreation. *Forest Science Monograph,* no. 7. Society of American Foresters, Washington, D.C.
30. Walters, William C. 1980. State Park Systems. In *Parks and Recreation,* August 1980, pp. 44–52.
31. Young, Gordon. 1973. Whatever Happened to TVA? *National Geographic,* vol. 143, no. 6, pp. 830–863. National Geographic Society, Washington, D.C.

4

Public Pressure and Legislative Response

INTRODUCTION

The years of and surrounding the "LBJ" era of President Johnson were the most significant dozen years in the recreation history of this country. From the groundwork of the Eisenhower administration to the middle of the Nixon presidency, the United States Congress passed legislation that significantly altered the government's policy toward the forest resources of the country. During this period of time, the federal government responded to the pressure of the citizens by assessing the recreation situation and moving to correct the deficiencies. Many of the decisions were made to a background of controversy that was far greater than the final votes indicated. Agencies, industries, and interests now act as though they always favored the recreation-oriented legislation against which some had fought bitterly.

These years saw the rise of a new pressure group of citizens interested in protecting what they held as valuable. This pressure group rose from a coalition of conservation/preservation-minded organizations such as the Sierra Club and the Issac Walton League to a powerful lobby for those persons wanting more positive action taken in protecting large areas of forest land from change. Membership in these organizations rose as they won court cases and pushed for more conservation-oriented legislation. It is interesting to note how the issues of conservation and recreation have been intertwined in legislation while they may be incompatible in application.

The eight federal acts selected for discussion in the chapter were chosen because: (1) they represented a significant response to the needs of the people, and (2) they had a major impact on recreation activities on forested lands. Certainly, other legislation was passed that could be covered here as well; it was not, however, because of the above criteria, limited space, and the intent of this text. Table 4.1 summarizes these selected laws. The Outdoor Recreation Review Act gave the American citizen the data that were necessary to outdate

Table 4.1. Selected Acts of Legislation Representing a Significant Response to Public Pressure for Recreation on Forested Lands.

Year	Act Number	Title	Purpose	Results
1958		Outdoor Recreation Resources Review Act	Created a high-level commission to: a. determine recreational needs in the United States; b. inventory present recreation resources and determine the need for 2000 A.D.; c. determine policies and progress required to meet those needs.	Report to Congress January 31, 1962, *Outdoor Recreation in America*; establish a national recreational policy.
1960	86-517	Multiple-use and Sustained Yield Act (Supported by the Forest and Rangeland Renewable Planning Act of 1974 and the National Forest Management Act of 1976.)	National forests are to be administered for recreation, range, timber, watershed, and wildlife.	Formalized the concept that the use of resources on national forest not be based on dollar returns.
1963	88-517	Outdoor Recreation Act	Charged the Secretary of the Interior with taking specific steps to assure adequate outdoor recreation opportunities for the American people.	Gave purpose to the Bureau of Outdoor Recreation which had been set up under Secretarial Order 497; the BOR organic act. BOR name changed to Heritage Conservation and Recreation, and new mission assigned by Order 3017 in 1978.
1964	88-577	Wilderness Act (amended by the Eastern Wilderness Act of 1974.)	Establishment of National Wilderness Preservation System for protecting the areas in their natural condition.	Originally aggregated 9.1 million acres into 54 wilderness areas and called for review of other primitive and roadless areas on national forests and parks; presently 80 million acres in 257 units.

1965	88-578	Land and Water Conservation Fund Act (as amended by Pl 90-401, Pl 91-485, and Pl 95-42)	This act is to assist in preserving, developing, and assuring access to such quality and quantity recreation that the nation's resources make possible.	Implemented a nationwide acquisition program; its large sums of matching funds encouraged comprehensive recreation planning and total involvement by all states and federal agencies.
1968	90-542	Wild and Scenic Rivers Act	Certain rivers and their corridors be protected in their present condition.	National River System contains 61 river sections and considering several more; several states have established state wild river systems.
1969	90-543	National Trails Act	Creation of trail system for public enjoyment of national and state forests and recreation areas.	693 trails are in the National Trails System; several states have established their own state trail systems.
1970	91-190	National Environmental Policy Act of 1969	Declaration of national policy encouraging harmony between man and his environment and to establish a Council on Environmental Quality.	Closed the "LBJ" era of single recreation acts; opened the legislative era recognizing the ecologic balance within the total environment.

old forest recreation concepts and to begin on the road to new policies that eventually culminated in the Environmental Policy Act of 1969. The Environmental Policy Act opened the door on a new era of environmental concern that has its roots deeply planted in the recreation-conservation movements of the past decades.

Some acts such as the Forest and Rangeland Renewable Resources Act of 1974 and the National Forest Management Act of 1976 are included within the "LBJ" era because they are extensions of the recreation-related concepts advanced by the eight federal acts selected for this chapter. The author believes that these acts are a reflection of the national concern reflected by the National Environmental Policy Act of 1969 and call for a reinforcement of the philosophy outlined in the Multiple-use and Sustained Yield Act of 1960.

One major shift in recreation that has occurred outside of the "LBJ" era has been the increased interest of the National Park System in the urban recreation system. Recreational needs of the urban populations were highlighted by the *National Urban Recreation Study* at the time local governments faced very tight financial situations. [29] Local taxpayer revolts and the passage of "Proposition 13" with its tax limits in California caused many cities to look for federal recreation assistance. The Urban Park and Recreation Recovery Act was passed as Title X of the National Parks and Recreation Act of 1978 (PL 95-625). [25]

Several actions have been taken by the federal government that, when considered collectively, indicate an attempted policy shift toward more federal involvement in urban recreation patterns. At the same time, the Secretary of the Interior, Cecil Andres, replaced the National Park Service director with a career man who did not espouse the "urban thrust" views of his predecessor. President Jimmy Carter froze all of the funding for the highly tauted Urban Park and Recreation Act at the first sign of economic stress in 1980. While the urban thrust of federal recreation is important to the overall recreation situation, it is not pursued at length in this book. The instability of the federal administration in supporting the post-NEPA legislation lends strength to the argument for the importance of the "LBJ era" legislation.

MAJOR RECREATION LEGISLATION

The Outdoor Recreation Resources Review Act of 1958

The growth of public interest in recreation demanded that a new approach be made to the federal government's role in outdoor recreation. President Dwight D. Eisenhower signed the Outdoor Recreation Resources Review Act on June 28, 1958, and started a blue ribbon committee on the way to studying, evaluating, and recommending recreation opportunities within the United

States. The law created the Outdoor Recreation Resources Review Commission that was to determine:

1. The outdoor recreation wants and needs of Americans for the present, in 1976, and the year 2000.
2. The inventory of recreation resources available regardless of ownership to meet those needs by 1976 and 2000.
3. The policies and programs that should be recommended to satisfy the recreation needs of the present and the future.

The Outdoor Recreation Resources Review Commission (ORRRC) was to deliver its report to the president and the Congress by January 31, 1962, and then to go out of existence.

The ORRRC made a study of all nonurban public recreation facilities and sampled approximately 16,000 persons to obtain data for its final report entitled *Outdoor Recreation for America*, which was submitted on schedule. *Outdoor Recreation for America*, commonly known as the ORRRC Report, was based upon 27 monograms treating various phases of outdoor recreation. The monogram titles are listed in Table 4.2. The major findings listed in the ORRRC report were:

1. The simplest activities are the most popular.
2. Outdoor opportunities are most needed near cities.
3. Although much land is available for recreation, it does not meet the recreation need because of location or management policies.
4. Not enough money was being spent on recreation.
5. Outdoor recreation is compatible with other resource uses.
6. Water is a focal point for outdoor recreation.
7. Outdoor recreation brings about economic benefits.
8. Outdoor recreation is a major leisure time activity that is growing in importance.
9. More needs to be known about the values of outdoor recreation.

The ORRRC Report recommended 52 steps to be taken in fulfilling the recreational needs of the American people. Primarily, the ORRRC Report recommended that a bureau (Bureau of Outdoor Recreation) be formed within the Department of the Interior to promote the cause of recreation. Other recommendations called for a national recreation policy, guidelines for management of the outdoor recreational resources, increasing existing recreation programs, and establishment of a grants-in-aid program to the states. The states were considered to be the key to the success of the recommendations.

Less than four months after the ORRRC report was given to the president and the Congress, Secretary of the Interior Stewart Udall signed Secretarial Order 497 to create the Bureau of Outdoor Recreation within the Department

Table 4.2. Numbers and Titles of the 27 Basic Studies
of the Outdoor Recreation Resources Review Commission.

Number	Title
1	*Public Outdoor Recreation Areas — Acreage, Use, Potential*
2	*List of Public Outdoor Recreation Areas — 1960*
3	*Wilderness and Recreation — A Report on Resources, Values, and Problems*
4	*Shoreline Recreation Resources of the United States*
5	*The Quality of Outdoor Recreation: As Evidenced by User Satisfaction*
6	*Hunting in the United States — Its Present and Future Role*
7	*Sport Fishing — Today and Tomorrow*
8	*Potential New Sites for Outdoor Recreation in the Northeast*
9	*Alaska Outdoor Recreation Potential*
10	*Water for Recreation — Values and Opportunities*
11	*Private Outdoor Recreation Facilities*
12	*Financing Public Recreation Facilities*
13	*Federal Agencies and Outdoor Recreation*
14	*Directory of State Outdoor Recreation Administration*
15	*Open Space Action*
16	*Land Acquisition for Outdoor Recreation — Analysis of Selected Legal Problems*
17	*Multiple Use of Land and Water Areas*
18	*A look Abroad: The Effect of Foreign Travel on Domestic Outdoor Recreation and a Brief Survey of Outdoor Recreation in Six Countries*
19	*National Recreation Survey*
20	*Participation in Outdoor Recreation: Factors Affecting Demand among American Adults*
21	*The Future of Outdoor Recreation in Metropolitan Regions of the United States*
22	*Trends in American Living and Outdoor Recreation*
23	*Projections to the Years 1976 and 2000: Economic Growth, Population, Labor Force and Leisure, and Transportation*
24	*Economic Studies of Outdoor Recreation*
25	*Public Expenditures for Outdoor Recreation*
26	*Prospective Demand for Outdoor Recreation*
27	*Outdoor Recreation Literature: A Survey*

of the Interior. By naming a professional forester, Edward Crafts, as director, President John F. Kennedy assured cooperation by the Department of Agriculture.[14]

The Multiple-Use and Sustained Yield Act of 1960

In 1960, the Eighty-sixth Congress of the United States passed an act that established a policy that the national forests were to be administered for outdoor recreation, range, timber, and wildlife and fish purposes. This act, which became Public Law 86-517, directed the Secretary of Agriculture to develop and to administer all the surface-renewable resources of the national forests under principles of multiple use and to produce a sustained yield of several services and products from them. Commonly known as the Multiple-Use Act, PL

86-517 is significant because it places recreation on the same level of importance as timber on Forest Service lands—an area that exceeds the combined land surface of France and Switzerland. [4] When wildlife is counted as a contributor to recreation, recreation assumes another dimension. In one state alone, Pennsylvania, there are more armed men (800,000) in the forests on the opening day of deer season than were in the field on both sides of the Vietnam War.

Multiple use was defined within the act as meaning the management of the forest resources so that they are used in the best combination to meet the needs of the American people. This has the familiar ring of Gifford Pinchot's doctrine that the national forests "should provide the greatest good to the greatest number in the long run." While the doctrine of multiple use does not dictate that every acre should be used for every purpose, it does mean that judicious use of all resources on large areas will provide latitude for adjustments to conform to all demands without hindering the production of the land. Single uses of some land were not excluded and wilderness was specified as a single use that was consistent with the purpose of the act.

The Multiple-Use Act states that the greatest dollar return is not the purpose of national forest management. This is the point that has been the most difficult for professional Forest Service employees and forest economists to adjust to. In this point lies the value of the entire act.

The concept of multiple use received further support with the enactment of the Forest and Rangeland Renewable Resources Act of 1974. [23] This act, now referred to as the Resources Planning Act (RPA), directs an assessment of all the nation's renewable natural resources on forest, range, and other associated lands. It also mandates that a comprehensive program be developed for all Forest Service activities in accordance with the principles set forth in the Multiple-Use and Sustained Yield Act and the National Environmental Policy Act. Essentially, the program is to be updated and submitted to the president every five years for the next forty years.

The framework for decision being used by the Forest Service in developing the program consists of seven resource systems. The seven resource systems are:

1. Outdoor Recreation
2. Wilderness
3. Wildlife and Fish Habitat
4. Range
5. Timber
6. Land and Water
7. Human and Community Development

These systems are analyzed with targets of output in goods and services against the funding level to meet the target levels. Alternate program directions are reviewed and the recommended program decision is made from that review. The basic factors used in influencing the final decision for the RPA program are economic effectiveness, environmental effects, public comment, and professional judgment.

The Outdoor Recreation Act of 1963

The Bureau of Outdoor Recreation had been created by secretarial decree on the recommendation of the ORRRC report and based on the legal support of an old reorganization act approved by Congress back in 1950.[16] Therefore, it was necessary to give statutory recognition to the Bureau of Outdoor Recreation (BOR). The Outdoor Recreation Act of 1963 (PL 88-29) became the organic act for the BOR on May 28, 1963.

Ironically, the very act that gave the BOR its mandate did not even mention the bureau. Rather, it gave the charge to the Secretary of the Interior. Some writers believe that this was a last-ditch effort to disarm the BOR by the National Park Service which might have hoped another secretary would delegate his authority in another direction.[16] In 1978, USDI Order 3017 did make some changes that reflected a weakening of the BOR's role as the nation's leading agency for recreation.

The purpose of the act was to declare the desirability of assuring adequate outdoor recreation resources and for all the levels of government and private interests to conserve, to develop, and to use those resources for the benefit and enjoyment of the American people. The Secretary of the Interior was authorized to perform the following list of activities and functions:

1. To prepare and to maintain a continuous inventory and evaluation of outdoor recreation needs and resources in the United States.
2. To prepare an outdoor recreation resources classification system for assisting in the management of those resources.
3. To formulate and to maintain a comprehensive nationwide outdoor recreation plan, to consider all federal agencies and levels of government recreation plans, to assess the present and the future needs and resources for recreation.
4. To provide technical assistance and advice to the states, political subdivisions, and private interests on the subject of outdoor recreation.
5. To encourage a regional concept in planning, acquisition, and development of outdoor recreation resources.
6. To engage in, to sponsor research, or to cooperate with educational institutions in establishing programs and encouraging public benefits from outdoor recreation.
7. To cooperate with, advise, and assist any federal agency in carrying out the purpose of this act.
8. To accept and use donations for the purpose of this act.

It was understood by Congress at the passage of Act 88-29 that Secretary Udall would delegate the charges to the BOR. This was done and the BOR played an active role in recreation until 1978.

Secretary of the Interior Cecil D. Andrus issued the USDI Order 3017 on January 25, 1978, establishing the Heritage Conservation and Recreation Service (HCRS) in the place of the BOR. Secretary Andrus acted under the authority given him by PL 88-29 and the Reorganization Plan of 1950. Recreation was added into the new bureau after some last-second manuevering by the recreation leaders who saw the possibility of Order 3017 killing a federal bureau interested in recreation. HCRS administer some of BOR's responsibilities as well as two additional areas. The National Natural Landmarks Program and the Office of Archaeology and Historic Preservation were moved from the National Park Service to HCRS. The new bureau lost major planning and study responsibilities for water, wild rivers, and trails to the National Park Service. [13]

On February 19, 1981, the opponents of BOR finally prevailed. Secretary of the Interior for the Reagan administration, James G. Watts abolished the HCRS to kill off the last vestiges of the BOR.

The Wilderness Acts

There has been a continuing saga concerning management of the nation's backcountry areas that has reached into all the biomes of the United States. A backcountry preservation system that was begun by the Forest Service with a half-million acres in 1924 has become institutionalized as the National Wilderness Preservation System, impacting on the management of more than 100 million acres of land.

On September 3, 1964, following its signing by President Lyndon B. Johnson, the Wilderness Act became law. It established a National Wilderness Preservation System that was to be composed of federally owned wilderness areas designated by Congress. The 54 areas that were designated by Congress were all in national forests and 87 percent of the 9.1 million wilderness acres were located in the western forests. [10,12] The department originally managing the designated areas—so far, the Forest Service—should continue to protect these areas, preserve their wilderness character, and disseminate information regarding their use.

The definition of wilderness as given in the act has limited any inclusion of eastern forests into the National Wilderness System by purist interpretation. Public Law 88-577 stated that a wilderness is:

an area where the earth and its community of life are untrammeled by man, where man himself is a visitor who does not remain . . . an area of undeveloped Federal land retaining primeval character and influence, without permanent improvements of human habitation, which is protected and managed so as to preserve its natural conditions and which

1. generally appears to have been affected primarily by the forces of nature, with the imprint of man's work substantially unnoticeable;

2. has outstanding opportunities for solitude or a primitive and unconfined type of recreation;
3. has at least five thousand acres of land or is of sufficient size as to make practicable its preservation and use in an unimpaired condition; and
4. may also contain ecological, geological, or other features of scientific, educational, scenic, or historical value.

The act did not name all the specific areas to become wilderness, but declared all areas previously named as "wild," "wilderness," or "canoe" areas to be designated as wilderness areas. The Secretaries of Agriculture and the Interior were directed to evaluate lands under their jurisdiction that could be considered for future inclusion within the National Wilderness System. In the years following the act's passage, the total area in statutory wilderness rose from 9,139,721 acres to more than 19,000,000 acres within the lower 48 states by 1979. [2] Fifteen million acres of that wilderness area are in 110 units within the National Forest System. Even when the Department of the Interior's recommendations are added to those of the Forest Service, most of the wilderness will be west of the Mississippi. Only 80,000 acres of wilderness were on the eastern side of the river in 1973. By February 1973, the National Park Service had studied 63 areas and had four of those areas, totalling approximately 201,000 acres, designated to wilderness status. All four areas are in the western part of the United States. Additionally, 56 million acres of Alaska were placed into the National Wilderness Preservation System through the Alaskan Lands Act of 1979.

The "purist" acceptance of the Wilderness Act argues against any wilderness existing in the East even though Point 1 of the act recognizes that man's activity can be blotted out, allowing the area to return to its natural state. To overcome the purists' objections, which were construed by wilderness enthusiasts as a stall, congressional leaders initiated legislative action specifying eastern wilderness.

An Eastern Wilderness Bill (PL 93-622) was passed by Congress in 1975, establishing 16 Wilderness Areas in the East and naming 17 more areas for study. When the Carter administration arrived in Washington, the Wilderness System got a boost from Assistant Secretary of Agriculture, Rupert A. Cutler. Pressure for a more comprehensive review of potential wilderness areas and Cutler's interest in the wilderness concept lead to a reordering of the Forest Service land area review procedures of its 62 million acres of roadless areas. The Roadless Area Review and Evaluation procedure being followed was revamped and the process repeated as the Roadless Area Review and Evaluation, II (RARE II). RARE II was completed in 1978 and serves as an environmental impact statement on the subject. [14]

President Carter responded to RARE II by recommending that Congress set aside 15.4 million more acres as part of the National Wilderness Preservation System, continue study on 10.6 million more acres, and open up the remaining 36 million acres to regular forest management. [15]

National Wilderness Preservation System, September 1, 1979

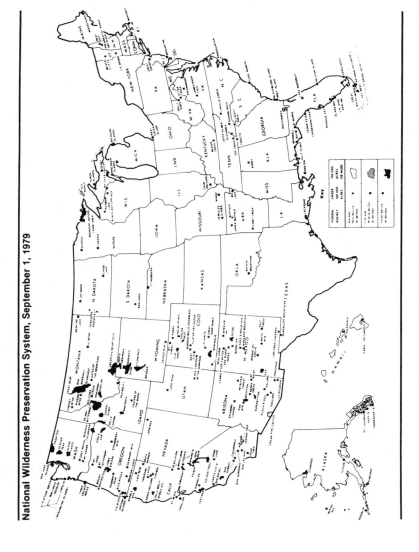

Fig. 4.1. Status map of the National Wilderness Preservation System.

Compromise permitted the passage of the Wilderness Act after severe attacks had stopped similar legislation in earlier years.[3] Aircraft and motorboats can be used where their previous use had been established even though the prohibition of roads, motorized vehicles, aircraft, or any form of mechanized transport is specified in the Wilderness Act. A special provisions section states also that prospecting and mining can be carried out as agreed to prior to this act. Until January 1, 1984, the old mining laws and mineral-leasing laws extend into the Wilderness System. This provision not only permits digging, drilling, and mining, it also states that the forests can be cut to support such activity.

Interested individuals have already joined the Forest Service in individual lawsuits to stop incursions into wilderness areas. It is plain that the pressure groups that brought on the wilderness areas stand ready to challenge the special provision compromises that do appear to be inconsistent with the intent of this act.

Grazing of livestock is to be permitted where it was established prior to the act. The use of wilderness areas for transmission lines, reservoirs, and similar public works projects including roads is permitted when deemed necessary by the president. It appears that the nation has a Wilderness System only if it can keep it. So far, the public pressure is to keep it, to enlarge it, and to make it more defensible.

The Land and Water Conservation Fund Act of 1965

No other single piece of legislation has done more to get all the federal agencies and states moving in outdoor recreation than has the Land and Water Conservation Fund Act of 1965 (LWCF).[11] The act provides funds to state and local governments and to federal agencies for the development of outdoor recreation on a planned, nationwide scale. The expressed purpose of the Land and Water Conservation Fund Act is to bring the supply of the nation's recreation facilities up to its needs.

Its tremendous success came partly because of the active role of the recreationists in pushing to achieve the benefits under the act. Huge sums of money were made available from the LWCF to those federal agencies and states that cooperated and complied with certain standards. The original act authorized annual appropriations of up to $60 million each year for eight years. The figure was moved up to $200 million in 1968 (PL 90-401), up to $300 million per yer in 1970 (PL 91-485), and up to $900 million per year in 1976.[4,7,11,12,18]

Land and Water Conservation Fund money is allotted to the states or spent by federal agencies for land acquisition. Sixty percent of the LWCF money is designated to go the state governments on a 50-50 matching basis. That means that for every dollar the state contributes to its planned outdoor recreation program under this act, the federal government will contribute one dollar until the state limit of federal assistance is reached. The technique of using matching funds will double the total money used by the states under the Land and Water Conservation Fund Act. The multimillion-dollar incentive of this act has caused all states to complete an acceptable comprehensive recreation plan as required for eligibility under LWCF. Forty percent of the money is available to federal agencies for land acquisition. The different level of funding between states and federal agencies served the intended purpose of giving a greater push to move the states up to the recreation level of the National Park Service, the U.S. Forest Service, and the Bureau of Sport Fisheries and Wildlife. [16]

No tax money was intended for direct use in funding appropriation under the LWCF. Income derived from admission fees, sale of surplus land, and the existing tax on motorboat fuels was to provide the revenue for this law. [5] Pressures for more allocations and objections to the fee principle brought about changes in financing LWCF activities. The admission fee schedule was dropped and offshore oil-leasing receipts and general treasury funds were added to the money available. Currently 85 percent of the fund comes from offshore oil receipts.

This act survived attacks by opponents who viewed it as a land-grabbing attempt by federal government agencies. Compromises were, of course, necessary, because of our form of government, to get the bill into law. The timber industry worked in provisions to block this act from being used to expand the national forests. Only private lands within the proclamation boundaries or up to 500 acres adjacent to the national forest can be purchased with LWCF money. Furthermore, 85 percent of the land added to the national forests must be east of the 100th meridian. To prevent any active advertisement campaign in favor of the recreation land acquisition, an inclusion to prevent such use of LWCF funds was placed in the bill.

The LWCF Act has all of the states cooperating with the federal government to create state, regional, and national comprehensive recreation plans. An investment in outdoor recreation resources of more than $2.5 billion has resulted from this act. More than 1,000,000 acres have been added to federal parks and recreation areas and almost 27,000 state and local projects were assisted on a matching basis. The success of the LWCF Act has lead to its modification. States became dependent on LWCF monies to purchase parkland faster than the states and local governments could provide management and operation funds. The Reagan administration has questioned that continuing use of LWCF and has suggested a shift in use of LWCF money to operation and management.

The Wild and Scenic Rivers Act of 1968

The United States Congress declared that as federal policy, certain selected rivers with their immediate environments shall be preserved and protected for the benefit and enjoyment of the public. [21] The Wild and Scenic Rivers Act of

1968 (PL 90-542) implements this policy by establishing a National Wild and Scenic Rivers System and by prescribing the methods to be used in adding to that system. Three levels of classifications of rivers are included in the act. They are described by the act as:

1. *wild rivers areas*—those rivers or sections that are free of impoundments and generally inaccessible except by trail, with watersheds or shorelines essentially primitive and unpolluted;
2. *scenic rivers areas*—those rivers or sections of rivers that are free of impoundments, with shorelines or watersheds still largely primitive and shorelines largely undeveloped, but accessible in places by roads;
3. *recreational rivers areas*—those rivers or sections of rivers that are readily accessible by road or railroad, that may have some development along their shorelines, and that may have undergone some impoundment or diversion in the past.

The act that named eight rivers to wild river status and named 27 more to be studied as potential additions was essentially an extension of the Wilderness Act of 1964. It grew out of the thinking, pressures, and deliberations that led to the establishment of the National Wilderness System. Final passage of the Wild and Scenic Rivers Act was the result of pressure from some members of Congress, conservationists, states, the Forest Service, Bureau of Sport Fisheries and Wildlife, Bureau of Outdoor Recreation, and similar agencies. Opposition came, not surprisingly, from the Corps of Engineers, Bureau of Reclamation, Soil Conservation Service, and other water-developing agencies.[6]

The eight rivers given wild rivers status by the bill were noncontroversial and mostly in public ownership. Figure 4.2 shows the status of the National Wild and Scenic River System as of September 1, 1979. Several states have complementary Wild Rivers Systems where they describe, establish, and maintain the rivers with technical help from the Department of the Interior.

The act states that the federal agency or the state government determine the boundaries to be in the Wild Rivers System. The land area included, however, cannot exceed 320 acres per mile on each side of the river. Also, no more than an average of 100 acres per mile can be purchased for development by the managing agency.

Unfortunately for the conservationists, the usual compromises were made with the mining interests to get this bill passed and signed into law. Existing mining claims cannot be stopped; however, areas within one-quarter of a mile of the stream banks are withdrawn from any new claims.

The National Trails System Act of 1968

Congress enacted Public Law 90-543, the National Trails System Act, in 1968, to establish trails near urban areas and within more remotely established scenic areas.[22] The act designated two major existing scenic trails, the Appalachian

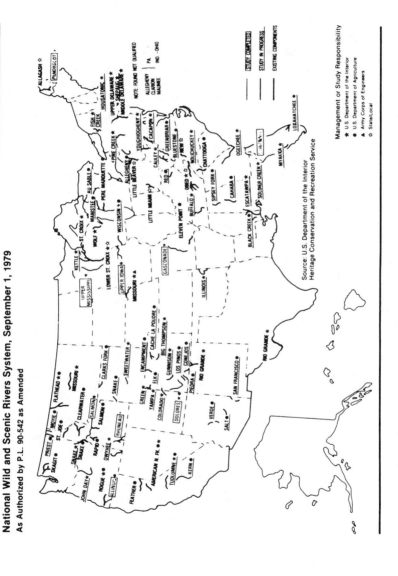

National Wild and Scenic Rivers System, September 1, 1979
As Authorized by P.L. 90-542 as Amended

Source: U.S. Department of the Interior
Heritage Conservation and Recreation Service

Management or Study Responsibility
★ U.S. Department of the Interior
● U.S. Department of Agriculture
▲ Army Corps of Engineers
☆ State/Local

STUDY COMPLETED

STUDY IN PROGRESS

EXISTING COMPONENTS

Fig. 4.2. Status Map of the National Wild and Scenic Rivers System.

63

and the Pacific Crest Trails, as part of the new system and presented the methods for adding new components to the system (Fig. 4.3). Fourteen additional trails were named for study as potential components. Eleven years after the act was passed, the federal government finally committed itself to protect vulnerable parts of the Appalachian Trail.

National scenic trails should have historic, natural, or scenic qualities that give the trail recreation-use potential of national significance and can be established only by the U.S. Congress; national recreation trails may, however, be designated by the Secretary of the Interior. A third category of federal trails is that of connecting or side trails. Another emphasis of the National Trails Act is on the establishment of state, local, and private trails. The Bureau of Outdoor Recreation grants-in-aid under the Land and Water Conservation Fund Act are available to state and local projects. [7]

This act has its roots in a study made by the Department of the Interior entitled *Trails for America*. [6] Senator Jackson submitted a bill that was backed by the Secretaries of Agriculture and the Interior to a receptive Congress. In spite of solid backing by conservation groups and apparently strong support everywhere, the bill ran into trouble because of its application of the right of eminent domain. [30] Several valid questions, which were raised by the local congressmen, arose on the location of the suggested trails. Eventually, compromise settled the issues with condemnation being prohibited without the landowner's consent when more than 60 percent of the entire trail was in public ownership.

In 1972, the corridor for the 3000-mile-long North Country National Scenic Trail was announced. It runs from Vermont to North Dakota. The North Country Trail will be the fourth national scenic trail.

Twelve years after this act was passed, the original two national scenic trails, the Continental Divide Scenic Trail and the North Country Trail were the only ones in their class. Two more are being considered in the late stages of review and several trail corridors have been identified. However, the process of establishing a national scenic trail is long and involved, requiring U.S. congressional approval. Also, national scenic trails are being routed to avoid cultural developments and to offer a primitive experience.

On the other hand, national recreation trails are to be located so as to serve the greatest number of people. The Secretary of the Interior or the Secretary of Agriculture can designate a trail to this category without approval from Congress. This is done with the consent of the agency or political subdivisions that have jurisdiction over the property. There are more than 600 national recreation trails throughout the 50 states. They vary in length from less than a quarter of a mile to 67 miles.

The National Trail Systems Act has lead 33 states to pass state trail system legislation. Also, it gave comprehensive direction to the Secretary of the Interior to consider trails as state outdoor recreation plans were made. That word-

National Trails System, National Scenic and National Historic Trails, September 1, 1979

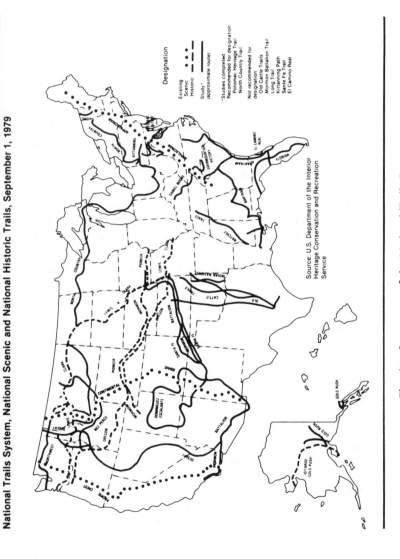

Fig. 4.3. Status map of the National Trails System.

65

ing brings the financial power of the Land and Water Conservation Fund Act into play.

The National Environmental Policy Act of 1969

A national policy toward the environment was established by the Ninety-first Congress and President Nixon. The National Environment Policy Act (PL 91-190) formalized an already established awareness of environmental relationships between man's activities and the earth's biosphere.[23] It replaced the specific reactions to scattered attacks on the aesthetic, cultural, and natural components of the environment with a comprehensive look at encouraging production and enjoyable harmony between man and his surroundings. This act spells out a national policy that culminates and closes the LBJ era of recreational-environmental legislation.

Title I of the National Environmental Policy Act (NEPA) declared a national environmental policy while Title II established the Council on Environmental Quality. Title I established six goals as necessary in establishing a national environmental policy. They state that the federal government should strive to:

1. fulfill the responsibilities of each generation as trustees of the environment for succeeding generations;
2. assure safe, healthful, productive, and aesthetically and culturally pleasing surroundings for all Americans;
3. attain the widest range of beneficial uses of the environment without degradation, risk of health or safety, or other undesirable and unintended consequences;
4. preserve important historic, cultural, and natural aspects of our national heritage, and maintain whenever possible, an environment which supports diversity and variety of individual choice;
5. achieve a balance between population and resource use which will permit high standards of living and a wide sharing of life's amenities;
6. enhance the quality of renewable resources and approach the maximum attainable recycling of depletable resources.

As a result of Title I, each federal agency will be required to make a detailed report relating to any proposed action that could significantly affect the environment. This "environmental impact statement" must discuss the impact that the action will have on the environment, alternatives to the proposed action, the relationship involved between local uses and long-term productivity, and any irretrievable resources that would be committed.

The Council on Environmental Quality was established by Title II of the act to ensure that unquantified environmental amenities and values are given appropriate consideration in decision making along with economical and technical considerations. This council is to be made up of three well-qualified individuals appointed by the president with senatorial consent. This council has been instrumental in shaping many of the president's decisions related to conservation on environmental protection.

The public involvement aspect of NEPA is a result of Executive Order 11574 setting up guidelines for the Council on Environmental Quality. That executive order directs agency heads to ensure that the public be fully and promptly informed so that interested parties can provide their views.

The environmental impact statement has become an end unto itself. It has become so well established in government activities as to generate its own creation industry. Arguments for and against the NEPA process point out the good or the harm that that process is creating. There is no doubt that the NEPA process has cost money in the short run as well as many long delays for projects. The public must judge if the long-term public good brought about by NEPA outweighs the inconvenience, frustration, and short-term inefficiencies asssociated with NEPA.

Title II also calls for the president of the United States to make an annual environmental quality report to the Congress. This report sets forth the condition of the environment, the trends in its quality, the adequacy of natural resources, and a review of programs affecting the environment.

CONFLICTS ARISING FROM NATIONAL POLICY

The federal land resources policy is firmly directed toward full utilization of those resources with the least possible damage to man's natural, cultural, and aesthetic environment. This means pressure for a land-use-planning system to follow on behind the nationwide comprehensive recreation plan. In its present mood, the American public has come to the conclusion that resource management decisions cannot be made solely on economic basis or even on professional judgment.[17] The public wants to have access to the decision making done related to the nation's resources.

Cost-benefit ratios were used by the Corps of Engineers to justify reservoir construction with great success until the 1960s. Local opposition was generally outwaited or swept away by favorable benefit ratios. Intensely developed recreation became a major factor in selling the dams to the public. Citizen opposition jelled to the point where the Corps of Engineers' dams are no longer quickly accepted by the public because of favorable cost-benefit ratios.

The National Park Service worked hard through the years from 1950 to 1966 to make the National Park Systems available for use by a maximum number of users. The impact of this policy, coupled with greatly increased mobility and recreation participation rates, crushed many of the parks under heavy use. A movement to reverse the trend to overuse our National Park System has caused a change in personnel at the top ranks of the National Park Service.

The Forest Service personnel administering the vast national forest system find themselves caught in the vice of public demand for recreation and public outrage over timber shortages. New and expanded timber markets have run the value of timber up to record high values. This is especially true of the hardwood forests of the Northeast where public-use pressure is greatest on the forest. Forest land values are skyrocketing because of the vacation home demand. As the vacation homes become numerous in one area, they bring together the urban ills that most developing communities have already faced. In addition to occupying forest land, these recreational dwellings, along with their accompanying sewage and refuse problems, expose more Americans to the forest environment which is in turn threatened by the recreation home market.

The role of the private sector in recreation is considered to be pivotal in our nation's effort to meet the growing needs of the recreating public. At a time that a market situation was getting well established in the camping field, the U.S. Congress removed all charges for recreation on federal land. Although further actions by the Congress probably will restore a fee schedule for federal areas, much damage has been done to private operators in a market that has been shown to be highly cost elastic.

During the 1960s, the coalition of recreation, conservation, and environmental groups was successful in the establishment of recreational areas and the passage of significant recreation-related legislation. However, the conflicts between saving and using quickly arose within this coalition. Generally, the conflicts are one-way problems. Those people wishing wilderness, solitude, or unmechanized forms of recreation are annoyed at the masses desiring other legitimate recreation uses of the land. Now, the federal land-managing agencies must zone their land selectively to permit or exclude various recreational vehicles.

In many situations involving natural resources, attempts to preserve areas have led to exploitation. Many purist groups were joined by recreation-user organizations to get preservation legislation passed only to find that the newly acquired status had caused widespread interest in the area to be preserved. Degradation and commercial exploitation of rivers named to be studied for inclusion in the National Wild Rivers System can be directly attributed to publicity related to the study.

As the clamor for vacation homes increased, there was a push to purchase land in isolated forest areas. In 1977, approximately 5 percent of the American households owned 3.5 million vacation homes. The states that attract vacation homes are also attracting residents. These are the Sunbelt and Rocky Mountain states that are showing the gain in the present population shift from the snow belt to the sun belt.

Recreation and Land-Use Planning

Each year 700,000 acres of land are paved for housing or roads. Thousands of additional acres are aesthetically destroyed or irreparably damaged by some form of economically justified activity. Approximately 250,000 square miles of the semiarid West are facing destruction under the drag-lines and shovels of the strip-mining operations.[7] Against such a backdrop, many Americans are acting to legislate an overall plan to protect the nation's resources by establishing forms of comprehensive land-use planning.

Land-use planning is attacked as "Un-American" by some developers and some large landowners because it prohibits freedom of choice to the owner. Most people agree, however, that a form of comprehensive land use is needed. Recreation can serve as the catalyst to bring together the interests of land speculators, agriculture, energy producers, and the urban residents.[28] The nation must consider land capabilities, national goals, and the available management techniques.

Much of the environmental interest aroused in the early 1970s occurred over issues calling for comprehensive land-use planning at the state or regional level. Diverse interests of housing developers, mining, agriculture, and energy productions must be coordinated if these environment problems are going to be worked out favorably for the nation in the long run. Combining planning skills and approaches to problems have been the foremost success of statewide comprehensive recreation plans developed in accordance with the Land and Water Conservation Fund Act. A people-oriented, natural-resource-coordinating agency is needed to tie together the marketplace interest of the economists, the profit-minded land developer, and the environmentally enlightened public to integrate the demands on the nation's physical resources. At this time, recreation has proved to be the only field capable of getting the competitive interests together.

REFERENCES

1. Anonymous. 1973. Saving the Land. In *Time* magazine, Time-Life, Inc., May 28, 1973, p. 96.
2. Anonymous. 1978. The Shrinking Supply of Private Land. In *U.S. News and World Report*, February 20, pp. 64–65.
3. Bockman, C.F. and Merriam, Jr., L.C. 1973. *Recreational Use of Wildlands*. McGraw-Hill, New York, N.Y. 329 pages.
4. Bureau of the Census. 1972. *American Almanac*. Grosset and Dunlap, New York, N.Y. 1017 pages.
5. Bureau of Outdoor Recreation. 1965. *Fact Sheet on the Land and Water Conservation Fund Program*. U.S. Department of the Interior. Washington, D.C. 6 pages.
6. ————. 1966. *Trails for America: Report on the Nationwide Trails Study*. U.S. Department of the Interior. Washington, D.C. 153 pages.

7. ————. 1971. *Outdoor Recreation Action*. Report No. 20. U.S. Department of the Interior. 30 pages.

8. ————. 1971. *Outdoor Recreation Action*. Report No. 18. U.S. Department of the Interior. Washington, D.C. 30 pages.

9. Campbell, J.P. 1971. Luncheon Talk. In *Proceedings: National Symposium on Trails*. Washington, D.C., June 2–6, 1971, pp. 6–10.

10. 88th Congress of the United States. 1964. Wilderness Act of 1964. PL 88-577.

11. ————. 1964. The Land and Water Conservation Fund Act of 1965. PL 80-578.

12. 89th Congress of the United States. 1965. National Wilderness Preservation System. House of Representatives, Document Number 79.

13. Fairfax, Sally. 1978. A Disaster in the Environmental Movement. In *Science*, vol. 199, February 1978, pp. 743–748.

14. Forest Service 1978. *RARE II*. Draft Environmental Statement. Roadless Area Review and Evaluation. United States Department of Agriculture.

15. Hornblower, Margot. 1979. Carter Will Open 36 Million Acres of U.S. Forests. In *Washington Post*, April 16, 1979.

16. Fitch, F.M. and Shanklin, J.F. 1970. *The Bureau of Outdoor Recreation*. Praeger, New York. 228 pages.

17. Hatfield, Mark. 1973. Speech to the General Session of the Congress for Recreation and Parks, Washington, D.C.

18. Josephy, Alvin J. 1973. Plundered West: Coal is the Prize. In *Washington Post*, August 26, p. C1.

19. Larson, Ray. 1973. Ripping Off Maine: A Peace Disturbed. In *Washington Post*, October 6, 1973, p. E1.

20. 90th Congress of the United States. 1968. Amendment of Title I of the Land and Water Conservation Fund Act and for Other Purposes. PL 90-401.

21. ————. 1968. Wild and Scenic Rivers Act. PL 90-542.

22. ————. 1968. The National Trails System Act. PL 90-543.

23. 91st Congress of the United States. 1970. National Environmental Policy Act of 1969. PL 91-190.

24. 93rd Congress of the United States. 1974. Forest and Rangeland Renewable Resources Planning Act. PL 93-378.

25. 95th Congress of the United States. 1978. Urban Park and Recovery Act of 1978. PL 95-625 Title X.

26. Outdoor Recreation Resource Review Commission. 1962. Recreation for America. ORRRC Report to Congress. Government Printing Office, Washington, D.C. 246 pages.

27. Underhill, A.H. 1970. The Wild and Scenic Rivers Act. In *Proceedings: National Symposium on Wild, Scenic and Recreational Waterways*, St. Paul, Minnesota, September 10–12, pp. 10–20.

28. Underhill, A. Heaton. 1973. *The Place of Recreation in Land Use Planning. Outdoor Recreation Action*. Report No. 27. Bureau of Outdoor Recreation. Washington, D.C. 33 pages.

29. U.S. Department of the Interior. 1978. *National Urban Recreation Study, Executive Report*. Superintendent of Documents. Government Printing Office. Washington, D.C. 185 p.

30. Verkler, Jerry T. 1971. The National Trails System Act — Discussion of Background and Provisions of the Act. In *Proceedings: National Symposium on Trails*, June 2–6, Washington, D.C., pp. 12–13.

5

Forest Recreation Planning

INTRODUCTION

Forest recreation planning is the intelligent use of the recreation resources in providing satisfactory recreation facilities and areas to meet present and future needs of the population. Good planning helps to determine types, quantity, location, and timing of recreation development. In order to make intelligent use of the recreation resources, the planner must understand the need for recreation in his area. He must know how much development is needed for each type of recreation and when it should be ready for public use. Also, he must know what sites can be developed for each type of recreation that is needed and what impact their development will have upon other forest uses.

Planning will prevent a hit-and-miss system of recreation that could put too much of the wrong thing in one place and not enough of anything in another. Haphazard developments based on available funds, sudden interests, or reaction to overcrowding will be partially avoided by a well-developed recreation plan. Anticipation of public needs is possible when investigations are properly performed and competently analyzed. By knowing what, where, when, and how much to develop, the private landowner and the public administrators will be in a better position to undertake successful recreation development ventures.

The recreation plan aids in the creation of related complexes of recreation opportunity instead of individual, unrelated, and competing facilities. These complexes should be grouped in such a way as to complement one another. Hiking trails should be accessible to campers, but the trail should not penetrate the campground. Fishing-stream improvement could be coupled with small campsites and day-use areas developed near population centers, around boat-launching areas, and adjacent to beaches. By grouping recreation complexes together in a rational manner, the planner can do much to fill the recreation need, increase dispersal of use, and reduce operation costs.

The principles used as criteria by the Tri-State Transportation Commission present a clear and concise outline for recreation planning.[12] They are:

71

1. *Coincide outdoor recreation space with land-use planning* (system). Systematically preserve the hillsides and headwaters in low-density use to provide space for regional parks and extensive recreation.
2. *Arrange recreation lands according to purpose* (service). Determine the tradeoff between land and travel that will optimize recreation service to the population. Small parks and ball fields should be scattered in highly developed areas with forest recreation areas elsewhere.
3. *Give priority to sites that can serve more than one purpose* (multiple use). Recreation can be combined with some other form of public use such as right-of-way usage or watershed management to give such sites priority over single-use ones.
4. *Save rare lands and historic sites* (distinctive locations). Preservation of unique features of a region gives recreation land a greater dimension.

These principles, as advanced by New York, Connecticut, and New Jersey, provide the proper prospective in which to consider the planning of forest recreation.

The forest is many things to many people, but it is also only one thing to each of many others. To these, it is a place for growing and harvesting timber, a place to scrape away in order to get at valuable minerals, a place to keep sacred and undisturbed, or a place to collect and store water. Now that recreation has moved into the forest environment, it has collided with the established uses of forest land and caused serious conflicts. Established and necessary uses of forest land are being attacked by recreationists who need more area. Also, some different types of recreation are incompatible when attempted on the same area. The demand for downhill ski resorts worries wilderness enthusiasts. Even at the local level, fishermen and water skiers are continuously battling. Recreation planning will help to make these collisions less inflammatory by pointing out potential conflicts in the use of the land and water before they happen and by suggesting ways of mitigating the impacts.

Timing of recreation development is very important for providing the optimal mix of facilities with the minimum investment. [4] Much of the total cost depends upon the advanced planning and the direct purchase of land. By looking ahead at the predicted need, the planner can make decisions on land purchases that could save substantial sums of money spent for land acquisition. Advanced planning is very important when long "lead-time" periods required for action could permit a high rise in the land value or allow commercial exploitation of the area before the recreation development could be started.

Timing is important even when the land is already administered by the government agency or private owner who is doing the planning because future recreation developments must be worked into the area's management plan. Management of forested areas requires long-term plans that give the forest manager an outline of the operations to be undertaken on the forest. If recreation planning information were available to the forester far enough in advance, possible recreation sites could be saved, specially cut, or cut far in advance of the time when they will be needed for recreation. This advance notice of land use for special purposes is commonly referred to as "earmarking." Sufficient lead time will permit lower costs for acquisition and earmarking of presently owned lands for future recreation uses.[4]

RESPONSIBILITY

Responsibility for recreation planning lies with the private landowners as well as with every level of government. The farmer who is considering converting part of his farm into a campground must make plans that are parallel to those made by the Forest Service. True, the farmer's plans are not as large in scope or magnitude as are those of the Forest Service, but they are similar in intent. That is, they give a comprehensive report on the needs of the potential users and the resources available or required to meet those needs.

At the national level, the Secretary of the Interior is responsible for preparing a nationwide outdoor recreation plan and submitting it to the president. The federal role in recreation planning is primarily one of encouraging action by other levels of government and by private landowners. With the passage of the Land and Water Conservation Fund Act of 1965 (PL 88-578), the federal government obtained a very useful tool for encouraging recreation action at all levels of government. States are required to complete a Statewide Comprehensive Outdoor Recreation Plan (SCORP) in order to be eligible for federal matching funds from the Land and Water Conservation Fund.

The largest landowner in the country, the federal government, finds itself deeply involved in forest recreation. There are some cases where the original purpose of the land management conflicts with recreation and therefore takes precedence over it. Military depots such as the sprawling Letterkenny Army Depot in Pennsylvania are often opened to public hunting; however, developments in Vietnam had caused munitions movements that interfered with public access and shooting on these depots. Another problem has been the use of some of these depots as private hunting preserves for the people in charge under the guise of costs or some other contrived excuse to deny public access. Fragile watersheds that could not withstand the trampling of millions of feet are not developed for intensive-use recreation because of the danger of permanently damaging the original value of the area.

In addition to developing a nationwide recreation plan and coordinating the actions of its own agencies, the federal government coordinates and encourages the recreation programs of other parties. Concessions systems on federal land encourage the use of private capital in fields where the federal government does not operate. Most of the nation's downhill ski resorts are on national forest land as a result of concession agreements. Technical assistance and planning aid is available to rural landowners who are interested in outdoor recreation enterprises. Unfortunately, technical assistance is the least important ingredient in a successful outdoor recreation enterprise. Management skills, foresight, and capital resources are the things most required for success; these very conditions, however, are usually lacking in the submarginal agricultural communities where the federal government is so active in pushing its technical assistance.

The state role in outdoor recreation is considered to be "pivotal" by the federal government. States should take on the responsibility of recognizing, developing, and managing public recreation resources that fall between national and local government control. [10] All states have completed their comprehensive statewide, long-range plans for outdoor recreation which is one necessary step in eligibility requirements for receiving federal matching funds under the Land and Water Conservation Act. Besides compiling the statewide plan, the state should coordinate all outdoor recreation within the state and assist the local governments in their recreation programs. In state programs, the concession method of encouraging private investment is used but to a more limited extent than at the federal level.

The local governments are the closest to the needs of the local population and should be able to transfer these needs into action. Actually, this does not appear to be true for the planning and development of forest recreation facilities. All too often, small towns and counties consider nearby state parks as their own community recreation area and do little or nothing beyond the political wrangling required to get the state to take care of local needs. Some local governments at the city and county level are planning and developing such intensive recreation areas as picnic grounds and campgrounds. In most cases, these have been a direct benefit to local users. But, since outdoor recreationists are often travelers, the local governments are often catering to tourists' money rather than to recreation needs of local citizens when they establish overnight facilities.

STATEWIDE COMPREHENSIVE OUTDOOR RECREATION PLAN

The Statewide Comprehensive Outdoor Recreation Plan (SCORP) is an analysis of the outdoor recreation and open-space needs within the state. SCORP outlines the policies that guide the development and improvement of outdoor recreation activities in both the public and private sectors of recreation. SCORP identifies outdoor recreation problems and issues with the state. It is supposed to outline the actions needed to solve the problems and to resolve the issues.

The states are supposed to produce a comprehensive recreation plan every five years. The SCORPs produced, however, have been inconsistent in quality among the states. Up to 1980, much of the material within the various SCORPs was not used locally because of poor quality or the inability of the states to supply information according to an individual's needs. There are still problems with using the SCORP for anything but a statewide view of outdoor recreation.

In 1980, the former Heritage Conservation and Recreation Service revised its guidelines for the SCORP. The new guidelines required an annual action plan (AAP) as an integral part of the SCORP and a five-year policy plan.

The policy plan presents a state's five-year plan for resolving recreation issues and problems. The annual action plan is the part of the recreation planning process that provides the yearly actions to be taken in addressing the priority items in the SCORP.

Uncertainties of changing national direction, regional autonomy within the former Bureau of Outdoor Recreation, and state initiative variations combined to make the SCORP process one of constant evolution instead of statement. Process development, not recreation planning, has been the result of SCORP across the country. Qualification to receive the state's share of the Land and Water Conservation Fund money has been achieved by each state. That appears to be the real local measure of success for the Statewide Comprehensive Outdoor Recreation Planning process.

Although the SCORP reports have not served the individual planning project or the resource manager very well, the reports do contain great quantities of inventory data that can be put to good use. Because the SCORP process was never completed and because the SCORP reports do not serve individual projects, this chapter will present methodology that can be used in conjunction with SCORP for recreation planning.

INVENTORY

How much of what types of recreation are needed and when will the areas be required? In order to answer this question, a recreation planner must analyze the need for recreation with the area to be served by the plan. Also, he must compile the facts on available recreation opportunities and compare the sum of available facilities with the sum of the demand. By subtracting the available opportunities from the need, the planner can ascertain the net amount of facilities required.

Recreation demand is the amount of outdoor recreation opportunities that the public wants. The former Bureau of Outdoor Recreation used the term recreation demand as "an expression of total participation in general outdoor recreation activities that could be expected if adequate facilities were available."[2] Therefore, demand really is composed of the actual use of existing facilities plus a latent demand that is not being reflected because of the lack of sufficient facilities. The general variables affecting participation in outdoor recreation are discussed in Chapter 2. For use in regional recreational planning, the demand analysis is divided into four parts.[2] The four steps or parts of demand analysis are:

1. Determination of effective population
2. Adjustment of participation rates
3. Determining existing demand
4. Estimating future demands.

Figure 5.1 gives a block diagram outlining the regional recreational planning process. The demand translated to acres minus the supply within the region gives the net recreational demand.

Effective Population

The size and distribution of the study area's population determine the "effective population." While the actual number of people within the zone of influence has a direct bearing on the effective population, the distribution of those people within the zone will govern the pattern of need. The majority of people live in metropolitan areas, but they seek outdoor recreation opportunities in rural and forested areas. Research shows that 90 percent of all outdoor recreation takes place within 125 miles of the participant's home.[3] Any metropolitan area that is within 125 miles of the study area should therefore be considered as being within the zone of influence (see Fig. 5.2).

Approximately 60 percent of outdoor recreation participation takes place within the day-use zone that has a radius of 40 miles. The weekend-use area has a radius of 40 to 125 miles and accounts for 30 percent of the recreation visits. The remaining 10 percent of the visits are made up of extended trips. Perhaps these zone radii will change with increased interstate travel; however, they are presently proving to be satisfactory figures with which to make estimates of demand.

In order that the effective population within the study area can be determined, each metropolitan area is centered in a circle with a 40-mile radius representing the day-use zone of its population. Also, a 125-mile radius circle is used to depict the weekend-use area for that metropolitan area. The area of the portion of the day-use circle falling within the study area is measured with a planimeter and expressed as a percentage of the entire circle area. Study areas are used in the regional planning sense in that they could be river basins, counties, or the like. Since 60 percent of the recreation use occurs within a day-use circle, 60 percent of the metropolitan area's population should be multiplied by the percentage of the circle within the study area to obtain the effective population within the day-use zone.[2] The participation rate per individual is included later.

By using the same reasoning, the effective population for weekend use can be determined by using 30 percent of the metropolitan area population as dis-

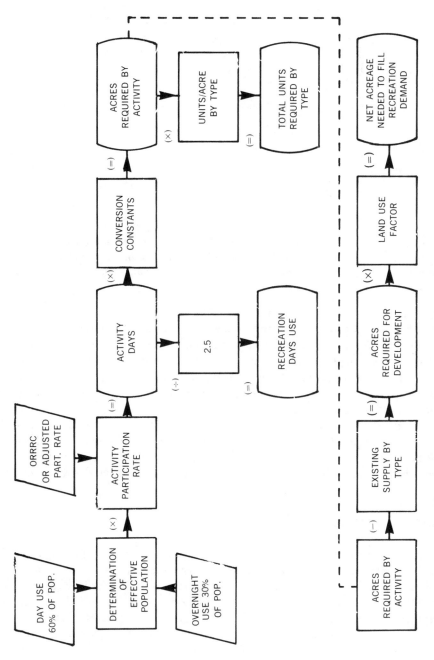

Fig. 5.1. Schematic of flow in regional planning to determine total acreage required in meeting recreational demand.

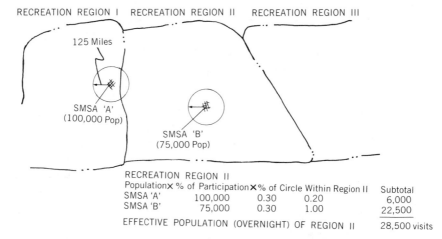

Fig. 5.2. Sketch showing standard metropolitan statistical area (SMSA) 'A' contributing 20 percent of its population (20,000) to the effective population for overnight use of Recreation Region II, while all of SMSA 'B' (50,000) lies within Region II.

cussed above. The same procedure is followed for each metropolitan area and the total is added to the nonurban population inhabiting the study area to obtain an estimate of the total effective population within the zone of influence.

This methodology assumes that the nonmetropolitan population living within the study area will have its recreational demands satisfied there. The amount of loss of nonmetropolitan population outflow would be offset by inflow from contiguous areas.

Demand is more than a reflection of population. It is a product of population and rate of participation in outdoor recreation. The determination of effective population for the zone of influence can be determined by the method given above. This means that the next step in ascertaining demand is the analysis of the participation rate for the effective population.

Adjusted Participation Rates

In order to estimate demand, the effective population's rate of participation must be determined. Chapter 2 discusses the variables that affect user participation. Research does show that participation rates remain relatively constant for each socioeconomic segment of the population.[2] The Outdoor Recreation Resources Review Committee Study Report 19 gives regional rates of participation for selected activities. The figures in that study report are based on interviews conducted by the United States Bureau of Census.[7] The regional participation rates as given in the ORRRC Study Report are shown in Table 5.1.

An adjustment of the regional participation figures can be made to make the

Table 5.1. Annual Participation Rates for Selected Activities by Region.*

Activity	United States Average	Northeast	Northcentral	South	West
	Days per Person in Effective Population				
Swimming	6.47	7.97	5.34	5.54	7.63
Sightseeing	5.91	5.11	6.64	5.09	7.46
Picnicking	3.53	3.77	3.64	2.77	4.30
Boating (all forms)	2.59	2.39	2.68	2.54	2.65
Nature walks	2.70	2.79	2.42	2.67	2.88
Camping	0.86	0.55	0.65	0.79	2.00
Hiking	0.42	0.41	0.35	0.35	0.72

*ORRRC Study Report 19.

data more suitable for state or area use. This adjustment to reflect more localized conditions can be based upon an index that considers all of the factors influencing participation in outdoor recreation; such an index might, however, be confounded by the interactions among variables or be too difficult and too expensive to determine. A citizen-user survey is generally used to adjust participation rates. Telephone sampling of family units has been used in SCORP preparations with apparently satisfactory results. Many planners have used the BOR published participation rates as they appear in Table 5.1 and are apparently satisfied with the results. The ORRRC data, however, are far outdated and should be updated by some method such as a citizen-user survey. Most SCORP reports give the participation rates by regions within the state; however, those rates are so general that they should be adjusted for individual planning problems.

Determining Existing Demand

The current recreation demand by activity is the product of the existing effective population and the adjusted participation rates. An example of current recreation demand tabulation is given in Table 5.2.

The standard unit for determining primary outdoor recreation benefits is the recreation day and not the recreation occasion that has been determined in Table 5.2. Since research has shown that a participant engages in an average of two and a half activity occasions for each visit to an area, the activity occasion figure should be divided by 2.5 to get the proper estimate of recreation day use.[2] The Forest Service uses a 12-hour day as a recreation-use day so that two 6-hour visits total up to one recreation day. While this definition of a recreation day makes for neat and realistic bookkeeping, it is unwieldy for regional planning. In planning, a turnover factor is employed for each facility to compensate for more than one user in a day. The turnover factor varies for

Table 5.2. Present Demand for Forest-Oriented Outdoor Recreation as Estimated by Multiplying the Effective Population by the Adjusted Participation Rate.

Activity	Effective Population (thousands)	Adjusted Annual Participation Rate	Annual Activity Occasions (thousands)
Sightseeing	2555	7.07	18,064
Swimming	2555	5.96	15,228
Picknicking	2555	3.88	9913
Boating*	2555	2.85	7281
Camping		0.69	1763
Nature walks		2.58	6592
Hiking	2555	0.37	945
		Total	59,786

*Including water skiing, canoeing, and sailing.

each activity. Campers occupy the campsite once during a day, thereby establishing a turnover factor of one. Tennis courts might be used by approximately seven groups during a day; therefore, tennis could have a turnover factor of seven.

Those people who travel over 125 miles for extended trips are not considered directly in demand estimation because there is no valid way to determine their contribution to the recreation demand within the study area. It is believed by most planners that this 10 percent of recreationists, the extended vacationists, do contribute a significant portion of the demand. For this reason, recreation-use figures that are compiled for recreation plans are conservative in spite of what some critics might suggest.

Estimating Future Demand

The simplest method of obtaining an approximation of future recreation demands is by multiplying the predicted population by the predicted participation rate. By using the years 1976 and 2000 as target years, the planner can use the projection given in the Outdoor Recreation Resources Review Commission Study Reports 19 and 26.[7,8] The estimated future demand is based upon assumed availability of sufficient resources to satisfy the demand completely.

An acceptable prediction of the percentage increase in participation rates based upon the ORRRC Study Report 26 is given in Table 5.3. The planner can apply the predicted percentage increases shown in Table 5.3 to the base figures given in Table 5.1 to arrive at the participation rates for the years 1976 and 2000. The estimated future demand is the product of the increased participation rates and the predicted population for each target year.

An increase in both quality and quantity of recreation facilities on a per

Table 5.3. Percentage Increase in Participation Rates over 1960 Base for Selected Activities by 1976 and 2000.[a]

Activity	Percent Increase (1960–1976)[b]	Percent Increase (1960–2000)
Swimming	90	300
Sightseeing	108	374
Picknicking	67	209
Boating	96	317
Nature walk	[c]	[c]
Camping	149	545
Hiking	148	511

[a]ORRRC Study Report 19.
[b]With full opportunity.
[c]Lack of sufficient data.

capita basis is assumed for the data in Table 5.2. Because of this, the predicted demand is not restricted as a result of insufficient satisfactory facilities. At first appearances, this assumption leads to liberal prediction; however, in light of the overcrowding and the drawing powers of newly developed recreation areas, the "full-opportunity" predictions may prove to be conservative ones.

SUPPLY

The planner must compare the available and planned supply of recreation facilities to the present and future demands in order to estimate the area's needs. This requires an inventory that accounts for all the recreation areas that are open for public use regardless of ownership. Also, it should analyze the land-use patterns of the study area to determine what acreage of land will be available for future development. Generally, the three-stage time sequence used in tabulating the data is: (1) the areas that exist at the time of the inventory must be tabulated; (2) all areas that are programmed for completion by 2000 should be included; and (3) the inventory should include all those areas that have been identified as potential recreation sites by the administering agency or landowner.

Existing Recreation Areas

Areas that are small can be inventoried personally by the planner; large areas, however, present too great a problem for first-hand inventorying. Also, the work has already been done by some public agency that will cooperate in supplying the needed information. The Department of the Interior has inventoried the publicly owned areas as part of its work on a nationwide recreation

plan and through the SCORP process. This inventory includes all lands
dedicated to public, outdoor recreation. The Public Sector Inventory lists each
area by name and gives its government administration level, size, use, location,
and major classification of development as appear in Table 5.4.

For planning purposes, the six BOR inventory classes are often grouped into
three groups. Because of similar use and facilities, the six classes are combined
as follows:[2]

1. Intensively developed—Classes I and VI
2. Extensively developed—Classes II and IV
3. Undeveloped—Classes III and V

State recreation plans, the Soil Conservation Service, the National Association of Soil Conservation Districts, and various state campground associations
can supply the planner with information concerning private and public recreation facilities within the study area.

The land areas available to recreation are affected in a large measure by the
land-use patterns within the study area. A review of the land within the study
area is therefore necessary to determine what percentage of the land is available
for outdoor recreation activities. Urbanized areas, cropland, and pastureland
usually are not available or desirable for outdoor recreation. The U.S. Department of the Interior lists forest lands, water, and miscellaneous land as having
the highest recreation resource potential.[2]

The use capacity of the existing land can be estimated by using the use figure
given in column C of Table 5.4 for each of the three development-intensity
groups. This is probably the simplest method of determining the resource
capacity. It is necessary to convert supply from area to recreation-days use for
comparison to recreation demand by multiplying the man-days use recommended in column C by the number of acres available.

Table 5.4. Recreation Area Classification System.[a]

Class (Column A)	Description (Column B)	Man-days Use/acre/year[b] (Column C)
I	Intensively developed and managed for mass use	2000
II	Extensively developed for general outdoor recreation	75
III	Natural environment; little or no development available	2
IV	Outstanding natural area	—
V	Primitive	—
VI	Historic and cultural area	—

[a]BOR Public Sector Inventory.
[b]Based upon Clawson, *Land for the Future*.

The Forest Service has used a classification system for developed recreation areas that is based upon experience levels.[14] This is a five-point scale with near wilderness experience as Experience Level 1 and grading to regional parks and commercial trailer camps as Experience Level 5. Table 5.5 lists the criteria for each experience level used in the Forest Service recreation planning.

The distribution of the recreation supply must be analyzed to see if it adequately serves the study area. Although sufficient land area might exist within the study area, it might be distributed in such a way as to be inaccessible to most of the population. It is at this point where the planner must make or ask for a policy decision governing the user group. Should the recreation developments be user-oriented, resource-oriented, or mixed?

The philosophy of recreation planning is occasionally attacked on the grounds that it mistakes the spending of time and of money for actual enjoyment. In defense of this philosophy, it must be said that tax money, at any level, must be spent to the greatest advantage of the taxpayers. Private operators can look toward other philosophies, but not public agencies. A certain percentage of the sites should be developed in inaccessible areas where the land is inexpensive; these areas, however, should be considered a small segment of the planned recreation "mix."

DETERMINATION OF AREA NEEDS BY USE TYPE

By comparing recreation-day demands with recreation-day supply, the total surplus or total deficit of supply can be determined. The planner must then decide how to turn a total deficit of recreation days into meaningful terms that would be applicable to the development of a forest recreation area.

Some regional offices of the former Bureau of Outdoor Recreation had derived the methodology to obtain the total acreage required for each type of use planned for the study area.[3] The methods given here can be used to determine area requirements by use types for the development plan that is discussed in the next chapter.

The first step to take is to determine the developed area or the area that is actually occupied by the facilities. The second consists of converting developed area into total area. Since the predictions of use are based upon maximum use of the facilities, the use days are determined by totaling the number of weekdays, weekend days, and holidays, and equating them to weekend days.

A summer season usually extends from Memorial Day through Labor Day and includes 14 weeks. The 14 weeks have 98 days of which 30 are weekend days or holidays. By assuming that three weekdays of use equals the use on one weekend day or holiday, the planner can equate the weekday's use to holiday use by dividing the 68 weekdays in the period by 3. This result is added to the 30 weekend days occurring in the summer period. This means that the facilities

Table 5.5. Summary of Experience Level System Used by the Forest Service in Planning Recreation Areas.*

Experience Level	Description	Normal Site Capacity (persons)	Normal Site Density (persons/acre)
1	No public mechanized access; a bare minimum nonwilderness development with basic site protection facilities principally, but minimum facilities for visitor comfort and convenience; requires well-developed camping skills by user.	Campground: 15–50	4–8
2	Usually a primitive road access; minimum development with limited controls; hunter camps and boat landings are typical.	Campground: 50–100	9–12
3	Good roads; typical medium-density forest campground or picnic area; flush toilets and water supply.	Campground: 100–375 Picnic area: 55–125	13–16
4	Very good accessibility; not rustic, having contemporary facilities and convenience features. Flush toilets and water supply.	Campground: 375–1000 Picnic area: 130–250	17–25
5	Excellent accessibility; designed for convenience of users, heavy site modification and contemporary design; associated with trailer parks and regional parks; showers, and flush toilets used.	Campground: 600–1500 Picnic area: 255–500	26–75

*Region 8 Forest Service, USDA.

are based upon 53 capacity days per year. Swimming is an exception to this assumption. Because of its susceptibility to being curtailed by inclement weather, swimming is computed at 80 percent of its capacity. Therefore, 42 days of swimming are assumed for each summer season.

All of the land required for one person to engage in the selected activity is included in the figures given in Table 5.5. This includes all the development that is necessary for that person.[3]

The information in Table 5.6 can be inserted in the formula given here to determine the area required to meet the predicted demand.

$$\text{Acreage required (AR)} = \frac{\text{demand for activity} \times \text{area/person in sq. ft.}}{\text{capacity days} \times \text{turnover factor} \times 43{,}560}$$

$$= \frac{D \times a}{CD \times TF \times 43{,}560}$$

Example:

$$\text{area required for picnicking at a 15 table/acre density} = \frac{9{,}913{,}000 \times 726}{53 \times 1.5 \times 43{,}560} = 2078 \text{ acres}$$

Sightseeing and walking require relatively little additional developed land and do not figure into the process of estimating required acreage. Therefore, the summation of the four listed activities will present an approximation of the developed area required to meet the recreational needs of the study area.

Extensively developed land has approximately 15 percent of its area developed. This means that for every acre of developed land, an extensive recreation area would have 6.7 acres of undeveloped land. Class 1 or intensively developed land has approximately 70 percent of its area developed. Therefore,

Table 5.6. Assumptions and Standards Used in Developing Conversion Factors for Translation of Demand into Acreage Needs.[a]

Activity	Number of People per Car	Area Required per Person Including Parking (ft²)	Turnover Factor (TF)
Swimming	4	302[b]	1.5
Boating	3	544[c]	2.0
Picnicking	4	2725 to 726[d]	1.5
Camping	4	3640 to 907[e]	1.0

[a]Based upon Report on Water-Oriented Outdoor Recreation — Lake Erie Basin.
[b]Includes beach area.
[c]Includes ramp, car, and trailer.
[d]4 to 15 tables per acre: 4 persons to a party.
[e]3 to 12 camping units per acre.

for every acre of developed land that it has, an intensively developed recreation area has 1.4 of undeveloped land.

The extensive-use factor of 6.7 and the intensive-use factor of 1.4 can be averaged together to get a working index factor of 4 to apply to the demand acreages. By multiplying the index factor of 4 by the number of required developed acres, the planner can estimate the total acreage needs of recreation in the study area.

THE RECREATION PLAN

The recreation plan is a report that presents decisions concerning the recreational development of the study area. It is an outline of what is to be done in order to establish the recreation areas needed to meet the present and future demand deficits that have been estimated by the demand-and-supply inventories. A three-part recreation plan is used to present the proposed program for recreation development.

Part 1 of the recreation plan deals with philosophies, policy decisions concerning the type, quantity, placement, timing, and the cost of the recreation facilities within the study area. This part should include statements to aid in the interpretation of the graphic section that follows.

Part 2 deals with the conflicts with other uses. It should recognize any conflicts that will result from the implementation of Part 1 of the recreation plan. Specific steps should be laid out in this part of the plan to coordinate with all interested parties to alleviate any conflicts that will be caused by the development of recreation facilities within the study area.

Statements explaining policy on water-pollution prevention, fire protection, hunting and fishing, and timber production should be included in this part of the report. Another topic that fits in here is the discussion on economic considerations resulting from the planned recreation facilities. Explain this effect on the local tax base; the new service-type facilities such as gasoline stations, motels, and restaurants that will follow the development phases; and the expected effect on regional employment that will be the result of increased recreational use of the study area.

Part 3 of the recreation plan is the graphic or visual aids section. It includes the maps, overlays, and photographs that are combined with the acreage and facility requirements to give an overall picture of the study area. The graphic section should be arranged very carefully so as to facilitate its use because it is the section of the plan that will be of interest to most people. Maps and graphs should be included to show the distribution of the effective population, of the recreation supply, and of the planned development areas.

The recreation plan should contain all the information and make all of the policy decisions that are needed to begin the development plans for each planned area. The recreation plan is neither a discussion of on-the-ground resource development nor is it a management plan for the study area.

TYPES OF USERS

Whatever facilities are built should depend upon their users. The types of facilities and the amount of site modification should depend upon what the user wants. User wants are difficult to sample because use or even satisfaction does not mean preference. Enjoyment, enthusiasm, and satisfaction are relative with the individual and the situation. Campers may be satisfied to stay in a worn-out, underserviced, and ill-equipped campground because they have never been to better facilities or because it is the only campground near their destination. Recent studies have shown that people were recreating in given areas by choice and therefore favored the conditions that existed at that recreation area.[5,11] Another problem in gaining information concerning the recreationist deals with the samples taken. Concern about the types of people who do or who do not answer questionnaires or submit to interviews is showing up in the writings of researchers.

This text employs the facilities-oriented categories outlined in Table 5.7 because a major portion of planning is concerned with facility location and type. Forest recreation opportunities are quite broad; therefore, the facility orientation permits some sorting of demand to assist in the planning process.

FINANCING RECREATION DEVELOPMENT

The planner must realize what forms of financing recreation facilities are available to private investors and to government agencies. It is one thing to sit at the drawing board and plan recreation developments; it is another problem to find the money for financing them. With the emphasis on user-oriented recreation areas where large effective populations exist, more costly facilities are needed to satisfy the ballooning demands. As more people become outdoor recreation oriented, they want more variety in the selection of activities available. Beaches and marinas of the summer are being supplemented by ski tows and toboggan runs during the winter months. Lodges, rental cabins, and elaborate camping areas probably will continue to be in demand. These are all very expensive facilities that may be out of reach of many landowners and government agencies. There is the possibility that a shortage of capital for these facilities could prevent their being available to help meet the growing recreation demands by the public.

A comprehensive discussion of recreation financing from a public agency viewpoint is presented in the ORRRC Study Report 12.[6] This report explains

Table 5.7. Categories of Facility-Oriented Users.*

Categories	Brief Description
1. Wilderness enthusiasts	Want no commercial development; perhaps no site modification that would interfere with their sense of isolation; relatively small group.
2. Sportsmen	Desire minimum of facilities; adhere to parts of wilderness approach, but conflict sharply on others; accept the need for capital investments for improvements better than any other group.
3. Day-use participants	Picnickers and swimmers generally accept and even require much site modification; willingness to pay; produce the most number of private successful ventures in some regions.
4. Campers	Generally families; fastest growing segment of forest recreation; widely varying opinions on site modifications; willingness to pay for elaborate facilities.
5. Winter sports enthusiasts	Rapidly growing in number; require the largest capital outlays; obtain biggest returns.
6. Boating enthusiasts	Great impact in recent years; cruising, water-skiing, and fishing have developed with reservoir construction in areas where recreation opportunities were previously scarce; adequate facilities of marinas, lodging, and service are very expensive.
7. Resort users	Goes to resort, not to an activity; uses urban facilities in outdoor or forest setting; various activities enhance stay at resort.
8. Sightseers	Extensive recreation users; use vistas, roadside rests, curio shops, marked trails, restaurants, and similar service facilities.

*ORRRC Study Report 12.

some of the financing methods available to recreation planners as well as outlining problems involved in financing this form of investment.

Many problems beset the planner who must be concerned with where the money comes from. Planners must count on construction work to progress on a seasonal basis and in locations where costs probably will be high because of inaccessibility. As mentioned earlier in this chapter, the facility may be under construction at the very time the public is losing interest in that form of activity. To help lessen the danger of obsolescence, the planner should include as much flexibility as possible. While flexibility helps to protect the capital investment, flexibility also raises the costs.

Four of the five broad classes of financing outdoor recreation facilities that are listed in Table 5.8 are based upon those described by the Outdoor Recreation Resources Review Commission. One additional category has been added in this text to give credit to private enterprise for being in forest recreation without government prodding.[6] Each category is described briefly in the following paragraphs.

Table 5.8. Broad Classes of Forest Recreation Financing.

No.	Class	Capital	Land Ownership	Management	Comments
1	All private	Private	Private	Private	Own attractions
2	Satellite	Private	Private	Private	Dependent upon nearby heavy use public facilities
3	Concession	Private	Public	Private	Large, government-administered attraction
4	Combination	Public and private	Public	Private	—
5	All public	Public	Public	Public	—

All Private

Over 70 percent of the rural land in the United States is in private owner-ship.[15] The use patterns of private lands will therefore have a great influence on the development of forest recreation in one form or another. Although the Bureau of Outdoor Recreation attempted to remedy the problem, the unfortunate fact remains that most of the publicly administered forest, parks, and water frontage lie far from the population centers.[13] The United States Department of Agriculture claims that "it is inevitable that a very high propor-tion of future outdoor recreation in this country will take place on or in associa-tion with privately owned facilities."[13] This certainly has been the case in spite of the publicity given to the creation of state and federal recreation acquisition and development. Nationally, private campgrounds outnumber public ones by a 2-to-1 ratio; record crowds mob resorts—both natural and man-made attrac-tions; one large resort completely changed the recreation pattern of the eastern seaboard when Disney World opened in central Florida.

Privately enterprise can stand on its own two feet in forest recreation at any size level. Smaller private endeavors included in this class must have some at-traction to bring visitors, must be situated to gather in the enroute transients, or must fill a local need for that particular type of recreation. Large resort devel-opments can create their own attractions such as lakes, golf courses, ski tows, lodges, and cabins. The need for these forest resort cities is acute in the eastern megalopolis as has been demonstrated by the instant success of the large ven-tures that have opened there during the last couple of years.

Private enterprise has the advantage over public development because pri-vate investment does not have to justify itself directly to the masses of taxpayers that must be served by publicly financed recreation. Private capital can there-fore be placed into specialized projects that meet a more limited desire than can public capital.

In recognizing that private land and private capital must play a widespread role in supplying the needed recreation facilities, the federal government took steps to encourage private enterprise to enter this field by supplying technical assistance and even financial help in the form of loans. The main emphasis of this effort has been aimed at the rural landowner who could diversify his activities and get into outdoor recreation for a profit.

Unfortunately, many people at all levels of government view recreation as an "out" or the "missing industry" of poverty areas. As a result of this thinking, much of the federal assistance has been slanted toward marginal farmers. The assistance has been limited mostly to design details, planning assistance, and low-cost credit while ignoring the more important problems of business management.

Managerial skill probably is the most important factor in making the business venture a success.[1] Also, foresight and available capital are two other leading reasons given for success or failure of a recreation enterprise. Managerial skills, foresight, and available capital are not generally possessed by the marginal farmer that the government invited into the recreation business.[4] The situation is now changing. Large companies have moved into recreation, bringing with them the managerial skills and financing that produce the flexibility needed to succeed. Instead of reacting to old data and standard recreation concepts, some of these corporations lead the way in new trends. The vacation home industry, country club campground resorts, turnpike camping sites, and the condominium approach to camping have all developed on a big scale as a result of large-corporation entry into the outdoor recreation field.

Satellite System

The second method of obtaining capital for recreation facilities is the reliance upon the satellite class of development. The satellite class, or gateway system, is made up of private capital on privately owned and operated areas near and dependent upon a large public recreation area. This system is officially recognized by the proponents of large public recreation areas as a way to preserve areas in a more natural state. Because of the mobility of today's visitors, public parks can be serviced by facilities located off the public land, thereby encouraging private investments that are dependent upon the park to draw the users.

The typical example of the satellite system in operation can be observed around Gettysburg, Pennsylvania. Here, the Gettysburg National Monument attracts tourists and Civil War buffs by the hundreds of thousands without providing them with any facilities or services other than information and minimal toilet facilities. Visitors to the national monument must rely entirely upon private capital ventures for all services and facilities.

A secondary satellite system has developed around a well-known state park that receives much camper use from Gettysburg tourists. Since dogs are excluded from Pennsylvania state parks, would-be campers with dogs are turned away to seek facilities elsewhere. Three private campgrounds have been established around this state park to cater to the needs of the dog owners and overflow crowds. So the camper that has been attracted to the Gettysburg National Monument is excluded from the state park and ends up staying in a private campground.

The satellite system has received much criticism from those who believe that it creates a "honky-tonk" or "tourist-trap" atmosphere. True, the public agency's lack of control over the private development could prove to be a serious disadvantage. Poor-quality accommodations and low-caliber services can spring up under these situations. Visitors to the Great Smoky Mountains National Park can attest to the low quality of development that sometimes develops under the satellite system. In spite of the low aesthetic quality of the commercialism surrounding some large national parks, the National Park Service is being forced to rely on this system much more heavily in the future as it limits camping and automobiles within the parks.

Proponents of private enterprise can answer the criticisms on the lack of controls by reviewing the theory of supply and demand. If these tourist-trap conditions exist, as they often do, it is a result of the user-public's need. As this need for goods and services becomes large enough, competition becomes keen and the overall quality of the private developments increases. The pleasant environment and high standards of development surrounding the Gettysburg National Monument are credits to both an interested local population and private enterprise.

Whatever the arguments, the satellite system is working and it will continue to expand. It is to be hoped that the tourist-trap atmosphere will not gain the upper hand and spoil the entrances to all the heavily used park areas.

Concession System

The use of private capital and private management on public land makes the concession system of financing recreation.[6] This permits private capital to come into large public areas where there is heavy use and to operate a business without competition. The price paid for this privilege is regulation. The public agencies set standards for structures, services, and profit. A compromise between restrictions and profit is necessary in order to make this system work.

This compromise must be based upon some common-sense assumptions in order to establish an equitable solution. The concession system is needed to obtain facilities and services to meet the growing recreation demand. Its success depends upon the fairness of this compromise between the public agency, which is obligated to protect the public interests, and the private investor, who wants to make a profit. Table 5.9 lists some of the problems that a concessionaire must consider when entering into a concession agreement with a governmental agency.

Federal agencies have been the biggest exponent of the concession system al-

Table 5.9. Summary of Advantages and Disadvantages
of the Concession System for the Investor.*

Advantages	Disadvantages
1. Attractive location maintained by government	1. Shifting government policy
2. Lack of competition	2. Harsh and uncertain wording of the
3. Captive clientele	contracts appears to favor the
4. Free publicity	government
5. Successful concession is in public interest	3. Political interference

*ORRRC Study Report 12.

though the states have participated to a limited extent. The Departments of Agriculture, the Interior, and Defense are the major agencies involved in supervising concessions within their jurisdiction. Of the individual bureaus, the U.S. Forest Service is the most deeply committed with over 1,500 concessions involved.[6]

Combination Class

The combination of private management of publicly owned facilities on public lands is the fourth basic method of financing recreation facilities. This method has been widely used by the states and to a limited extent by the federal government.

This method of financing recreation facilities has worked with varying degrees of success; it has, however, produced facilities when they would otherwise have been lacking. By charging rent for the facilities, a government agency relieves the operator from the long-term investment of funds. This is often the situation at state-owned day-use areas where the public wants to buy prepared food, curios, and miscellaneous necessities.

The other advantages of this system to the operator are captive clientele, lack of competition, and attractive surroundings which are similar to the advantages of the concession system. The disadvantages to the operator of political interference, fluctuating policy, and unequal appearing contracts are also similar. In this system, however, the operator may be less of a businessman than those involved in the large concession ventures. He may view the operation as a part-time undertaking to provide his family with a summer's vacation. True, efficient businessmen do perform well in this system; however, the poorer managers have a good chance of becoming involved in these activities even though they do not have to have large sums for investment to qualify for the concession-system class. True, the agency having the responsibility for the public interest in the area does have the final control over quality of operation in that it can refuse to renew the lease agreement.

All-Public Class

Public ownership and management of facilities on public land is the fifth basic method of financing recreation developments. This method is very popular with state organizations which often view it as a way of avoiding concession-caused problems, of maintaining absolute control, and of producing a profit for the state. Private businessmen might question the efficiency of the state employee who does not have a true profit incentive.

One obvious problem here is that this situation favors political interference. All too often these facilities simply become another source of patronage jobs to be handed around by the politicians in power.[6] When this happens, the quality of employee drops.

REFERENCES

1. Agnew, R. 1965. *Profitable Private Campground Construction and Operation.* Rajo Publications, New York, NY. 50 pages.
2. Bureau of Outdoor Recreation. 1966. *Outdoor Recreation Requirements for the Upper Mississippi River Basin.* Unpublished. Lake Central Region, BOR, Ann Arbor, Mich.
3. ———. 1966. *Water Oriented Outdoor Recreation, Lake Erie Basin.* Unpublished. Lake Central Region, BOR, Ann Arbor, Mich.
4. Gould, E.M. 1964. Forest Managers and Recreation Research. In *Proceedings of Society of American Foresters, Allegheny Section,* Baltimore, Maryland.
5. LaPage, Wilbur F. 1968. *The Role of Fees in Campers' Decisions.* Northeast Forest Experiment Station. U.S. Forest Service. Research Paper NE-118. Upper Darby, Penn. 24 pages.
6. Outdoor Recreation Resources Review Commission. 1962. *Paying for Recreation Facilities.* Study Report 12. Government Printing Office, Washington, D.C. 93 pages.
7. ———. 1962. *National Recreation Survey.* Study Report 19. 394 pages.
8. ———. 1962. *Prospective Demand for Outdoor Recreation.* Study Report 26. 61 pages.
9. Peterson, R. Max. 1980. *Looking at Recreation Through Forest Service Eyes.* Parks and Recreation, March 1980, pp. 42–48.
10. Recreation Advisory Council. 1964. *General Policy Guidelines for Outdoor Recreation.* Circular no. 2, Washington, D.C.
11. Shafer, Jr., Elwood L. 1969. *The Average Camper Who Doesn't Exist.* Northeast Forest Experiment Station, Upper Darby, Penn.
12. Tri-State Transportation Commission. 1969. *Outdoor Recreation in a Crowded Region.* 100 Church Street, New York. 19 pages.
13. U.S. Department of Agriculture. 1962. *Rural Recreation—A New Farm Business.* Washington, D.C.
14. U.S. Forest Service. 1973. *References for Recreation Development,* Section Number 1. Regional Office, Atlanta, Georgia. 21 pages.
15. Wooten, H., and Anderson, J. 1954. Major Uses of Land in the United States. U.S. Department of Agriculture. *Agricultural Information Bulletin,* no. 168. 31 pages.

6

Site Selection

INTRODUCTION

In selecting the place, or site, of any recreation development, the planner is limited or guided by a set of principles and a number of basic site-influencing factors. These principles and factors as discussed in this chapter are applicable to any form of forest-oriented recreation. Generally, the higher investment and more identifiable intensive-use areas receive most of the planner's attention. Camping, picnicking, skiing, and boating are typical examples of activities that require a relatively high degree of development. Other activities such as hunting and sightseeing are less identifiable as activities requiring development of sites except in the large picture of highways, restaurants, and gas stations.

The configuration and variability of forest land present a host of problems to the planner who is attempting to locate the most desirable site for an intensive-use recreation development. Everything will not be perfect. It is most likely that every site investigated will have some characteristic that will adversely influence the quality of the site's recreation potential. In each situation, the planner must weigh the advantages of the site against the price of overcoming its disadvantages. It must be looked at in this manner rather than from the point of view of advantages versus weakness because many site-selection criteria become limiting factors if they are unfavorable. A swampy area would not serve well for a golf course, but under unusual circumstances site modification could be done to permit such an establishment. The relative demand for such a development must be coupled with the available sites within the general location of the recreation development.

Three general principles of site selection should be observed in choosing sites that are to serve as recreation areas. One of the primary purposes of a recreation development is to satisfy the user. The user must be satisfied with the development, or eventually it will fail. This principle applies as readily to private enterprise undertakings where one might readily consider the making of money as the primary purpose. Profit is certainly the motive for going into business, but the profit realized will usually depend upon the extent to which the users' requirements are satisfied. If a public agency establishes recreation areas without

94

serious regard to user needs, that agency is self-seeking or negligent in its duty to the tax-paying public.

Second, user convenience must be the prime reason for the selection of a site. Forest recreation is becoming people oriented rather than resource oriented. Development areas must therefore be selected with regard to their convenience to the public rather than to the convenience of the resource manager. This principle has been part of the private investor's thinking right along. Public agencies and large landowners not seeking a profit from recreation have long considered recreation as a by-product to be fitted in at the convenience of resource management. If the site cannot be chosen for user convenience, that convenience must be built in. If sufficient lake frontage is unavailable to supply a lodge with a marina, then lagoons can be dug or lake frontage created to bring the user and the attraction together for the users' convenience.

Easy access to the area is a must. Back-pack hikers must first get to the wilderness area before they begin their hike into the back country. In this case, convenience to the user refers to high-quality access roads and secure trail heads. Other forms of convenience might include such things as running water, sanitation facilities, charcoal burners, or even fully furnished cabins.

The third principle is concerned with the relationship between resource and user satisfaction. The resource must be adequate to provide sufficient enjoyment to the users. Tennessee Valley Authority lakes, Yellowstone National Park, and Vermont's Battenkill River are proven attractions that provide the users with almost unlimited opportunity for enjoyment.

There are attractions to bring the visitors to the area. Also, each has a sufficient amount of land around the area or as part of it to provide for sufficient developed sites, proper setting, and additional side attractions. Some private recreation areas have invested thousands of dollars to bring the resource level up to that required to attract users. Additional attractions can stretch the resources of an area. A golf course at a ski area is an accepted way of keeping the public satisfied all year around. Also, the lake that serves as a hazard on the fifth or sixth hole can supply the water for the snow-making machines in the winter.

SITE-INFLUENCING FACTORS

Certain factors influence the quality of recreation that can be developed on an area. These factors limit the type of development possible on a given site. The higher-quality site will have a favorable summation of these influencing factors. Although individual factors can be ignored if the planner has unlimited capital, they are important enough to be limiting without the expenditure of funds to change them. Each site-influencing factor constitutes a scientific field of its own and cannot be covered completely here. This chapter briefly relates the role of each factor to its influence on an intensive recreation area. Table 6.1 lists the five major site factors that influence the quality of an intensive forest recreation area.

Climate

Climate is defined by Webster as "the average condition of the weather at a place over a period of years." The climatic data that are compiled over many years are composed of the many elements of weather such as temperature, humidity, precipitation, and prevailing wind direction. Climate is generally considered to mean a summary of weather variations on a regional basis.[2] Therefore, the argument can be raised that this chapter is dealing with microclimate, that is, the local weather conditions that exist at one small area and are influenced by the conditions at that area. The major weather elements that form the climate of an area are temperature, major air movements, and precipitation. Microclimate on any given site is influenced by the factors of temperature, aspect, air drainage, exposure, wind, rainfall, and position on the slope.

Microclimate

Temperature

Data concerning temperature give the planner a great deal of insight into the expected quality of a site. Daily or monthly mean temperatures can be compared with the regional means to determine if the site is adversely or favorably affected by microclimatic influences. Mean summer temperature will influence the vegetation that can be grown on an area and therefore has a direct relationship with forest recreation.[2] Temperature ranges are important in site selection. A large spread between the mean daily high temperature and the mean daily low temperature is undesirable for recreation areas. Sites with more uniform temperatures should be sought. The mean daily high (or low) temperature can be determined by recording the highest (or lowest) temperature reached each day of a month and averaging those figures.

Although pressure systems and frontal changes influence the weather regionally, they have slightly varying impacts on each different site. These varying im-

Table 6.1. Site Factors Influencing Quality of Forest Recreation Areas.

Climate
Topography
Soils
Water
General environment

pacts are brought about by the factors affecting the microclimate of a site. Aspect, exposure, elevation, and air drainage influence the temperature at a given site and cause some sites to be more favorable than others for recreation.

Aspect

The compass direction in which a slope faces dictates its aspect. Foresters have long recognized that certain aspects were better than others for timber growth. Timber growth is only of parallel interest to recreation; the things that cause better or poorer timber growth, however, could have some effect on forest recreation quality. The east slope receives morning sunshine and afternoon shade and may be the best aspect for campgrounds. The morning sun can warm the rising campers and dry out the campsite. Since most camping is done in the summer, afternoon heat is a problem. By placing the campground on the east slope, the planner can take advantage of the afternoon shade to cool the campground. In far northern states, any aspect might be satisfactory for winter sports. Perhaps the southerly slopes will help to warm skiers or skaters. In most locales, however, the north slopes are most favorable because of the protection they offer to the snow. West or southerly aspects are best for swimming beaches. People tend to swim during the afternoon and generally prefer the sun to the shade. Vistas and scenic overlooks must be placed where they are most effective; however, a northerly aspect is best wherever a choice exists. The northerly aspect places the sun at the observer's back and not in his eyes. Also, the sunlight gives better accent and lighting on the scene when viewed from that aspect. Studies in West Virginia and in Utah found that aspect is a significant independent variable influencing vegetation. [1] Higher-quality forest cover occurs on the northeast aspect and the poorest growth is on the southwest aspect in the Appalachians. Also, the Utah study indicates that the northeast aspect had the best vegetation survival at the end of a season of recreation trampling and the southwest aspect had the poorest survival rate.

Air drainage

Air drainage plays an important role in microclimate in that it affects temperature, humidity, and fog. Colder air sinks to the lower levels. Cold air and humidity collect in low areas where they remain during periods of quiet air. During clear, calm evenings, heat is lost by radiation, causing a further reduction in temperature. If the air temperature is below saturation point, radiation fog is formed. [2] Although smog is usually associated with cities, it is common in campgrounds and picnic areas where poor air drainage exists. A blue-gray blanket of smoke and cooking gases hangs over many crowded campgrounds. This problem is not serious if there is a wind strong enough to form turbulence and thereby improve the air drainage. Smog is a local phenomenon that occurs when air temperatures rise with increasing altitude instead of falling with altitude, thereby prohibiting the fouled air from escaping by normal convection currents.

Poor air-drainage areas can be avoided by keeping the recreation area out of the low places and off stream bottoms. Air drainage can be improved within picnic and campground areas by creating "chimney effects" in the overhead cover to permit better ventilation.

Exposure

The exposure of an area to sunlight plays an important role in determining microclimate. Exposure differs from aspect in that exposure refers to the ability of sunlight to fall on an area. The southern aspect would be expected to have the greatest exposure; however, the lower portion of the slope may lie within the shadows of another mountain and thereby have a low exposure time. Sites with high exposure times tend to become hot and not desirable except as swimming areas or for use in late fall, winter, or early spring when the heating effects of long exposure time are welcomed.

Wind

The prevailing wind should be considered when positioning cabins, tents, and camping unit interiors. The door of a cabin or tent should not face directly into the prevailing winds nor should the tent pad be located just downwind from the fireplace. Wind blowing over a long water surface can cause relatively large waves on lakes; boat landings therefore, should not be placed at the end of the long axis of a lake when other sites are available.

Winter sports are severely affected by wind. Ski slopes and sledding hills can be scoured clean of snow by winds. On the other hand, constant drifting at an inconvenient location will require snow removal funds to be expended. Ice skaters prefer to skate where there is little or no wind; therefore, an artificial barrier might be required if the site does not lie in the lee of a natural windbreak. Climatic data obtainable from the local weather station will provide the overall picture concerning the winter weather over the area; however, an on-site investigation should be made to determine the prevailing wind directions during the snow season. On the ground, observations will give an indication of what to expect. Also, the valuable knowledge of local citizens probably will provide the investigator with the most specific information.

Rainfall

The amount of rain that falls is generally uniform over a large region so that alone it does not influence the individual site selection to a great extent.

Fig. 6.1. Shelter to protect picnickers from New Mexico sun.

However, when combined with other site-influencing factors, rainfall becomes very important in influencing the quality of a recreation site. Satisfactory outdoor recreation areas have been developed on the wet Olympic Peninsula of Washington as well as on the Big Bend National Park in Texas. However, the amount of rain that falls does affect greatly the impact that other factors have on the quality of the site.

Dampness, dreary weather, mud, and damage to the ground are problems that occur more readily in areas that are wet during the heavy-use period. More daylighting or removal of overstory vegetation is required to dry out areas. Also, more shelters are needed to provide people with wet weather activity space. In the hot, dry Southwest, shelters are constructed to provide shade for the users.

Dust, limited vegetation growth, and recreation area damage are problems to be faced on dry-site recreation areas. Irrigation may be necessary to provide enough water for the vegetation to recover from trampling and to grow. Plantings of all kinds may be necessary to provide an adequate ground cover and shade in areas of dry-season use.

Position on slopes

The placement of the recreation area on the terrain is important to the user because this decision has a great bearing on user comfort throughout the life of the development. The hillside should be divided into the lower, the middle, the upper third of the slope and each third considered as to its effects on recreation. The position on slope has some effect upon the exposure of the site to sunshine, air-drainage patterns, and temperature extremes. Although exposure is related to aspect, it is not identical. Lower slopes are exposed to sunshine for a much shorter period than the upper slopes of the same aspects; the lower slopes therefore tend to be cooler and damper with poorer air drainage. As a result of poor air drainage, the smoke-filled and moisture-laden air lingers on the lower slopes. Convection currents move the cool air downslope at night so that the cold air collects in the bottom of valleys.[2]

The upper slopes have the greatest extremes in temperature. They get very hot during the day when they are exposed to the sun. In the eastern mountains, the overstory vegetation is of poor quality on the upper slopes as a result of exposure and dryness of site. The poorer-quality overstory that is found on the upper slope permits more sunlight to strike the forest floor. In the evening, the sparser vegetation permits relatively more heat loss by radiation than do the closed canopies on the lower slopes. The upper slopes are more exposed to wind than the other slope positions and are considerably drier as a result. Fire, which is the third major problem in recreation, is a relatively more serious threat on the dry, windswept upper slopes than it is on the lower slopes.[6]

The middle slopes offer the best microclimatic conditions for recreation area development. Morning updrafts and evening downdrafts produce good ventilation and provide a moderating effect on the temperature. Middle slopes may lack sufficient benches or other gently sloping terrain to establish recreation areas without a great amount of earth moving. Middle-slope sites, however, are superior to upper- and lower-slope sites and should be considered for development whenever possible.

Topography

The relative configuration of the land, or topography, plays a major role in determining the recreational quality of a site. The influence of land relief exhibits itself as the steepness of slope, the position on slope, the aspect of the slope, and the relative position of attractions to possible hazards or detractants.

A site's steepness, or its degree of slope, plays a basic role in determining its use for recreational development. Obviously, moderately steep slopes make better ski runs than softball fields. Since campgrounds should be developed on slopes that are less than 10 percent, the location of such gentle-sloping areas strongly guides the placement of campgrounds and picnic areas. [5] While the rugged mountains provide a picturesque setting, the more level spots provide the sites for recreation site development. If level places do not exist for parking, tenting, and playing, they must be made. Steeper slopes mean greater costs for building level sites.

Steeper slopes require longer trails, more steps, or steeper grades. Road and trail layout is restricted by steep slopes which also limit accessibility. Also, the dangers of erosion and slides are greater than they are on more gently rolling land. Level land, however, is not without hazards. Level areas might be poorly drained and therefore unsuitable for dispersal fields, heavy traffic, or structures. Although most intensively developed sites should be built on slopes of less than 10 percent, the survival rate of ground cover was higher on the steeper portions of the units. [3,4]

In some parts of the West and Southwest where forest and bush fires are hazards to human life, certain features of topography become important. Box canyons with only one easy exit should be avoided in site selection. The dangers of flooding or washouts should influence the choice of sites along rivers and streams.

The relative position of the selected sites to the attraction, ease of movement between them, and access to the sites are reflections of the general configuration of land. Cliffs, rock outcrops, and swamps can be attractions or hazards to recreation development depending upon their nature and location.

Soils

The problems associated with soils are many and difficult to overcome. Generally, an understanding of the physical properties of the soils in an area is needed in order to avoid problem soils and to choose the ones favorable to the selected use. Erosion, compaction, trafficability, drainage, and slope are five of the physical properties of soil that must be considered in site selection. These five properties are considered as hazards to any kind of management that takes place on the ground. Unfortunately, use restrictions owing to soil conditions are even less practical in forest recreation management than they are in any other kind of forest resources management.

Recreation areas should be located on gently sloping areas that have deep, well-drained soils that are of medium textures. The heavier soils of silt and clay are more susceptible to puddling (loss of soil structure because of use when too wet or too dry), surface runoff, and erosion. Very coarse soils such as sands are not as desirable as the loams of the medium-textured soils because the coarse-textured soils tend to be droughty. As a result, they will not support the grasses and understory that are so desirable in recreation areas. One advantage to the very coarse soil materials is the lack of dust and mud. A study by Orr showed that the six significant independent variables affecting ground cover survival on a recreation site included four that were related to the soil profile.[3] They were:

1. Thickness of B horizon in inches (positive).
2. Percentage of surface rock (negative).
3. Percent of slip in C horizon (negative).
4. Depth of water table in inches (negative).

A more complete discussion of these variables has been presented in Chapter 3 under "carrying capacity."

Adverse soil conditions do not always preclude the use of an area, but they do demand special attention if the area is to prove satisfactory. Experienced, trained soil scientists should be consulted to gain information about the soils in specific spots.

Water

Water is an essential ingredient of most recreation areas. It is required for the existence needs of cooking, washing, and drinking and for the recreational needs of swimming, boating, or fishing. Chapter 15 deals extensively with the supply of water needed to meet existence needs. The problems of water quality, quantity, source, treatment, and distribution must be considered by the planner to develop a safe and adequate water system.

Recreation water is required for successful operation of most forest recreation

Table 6.2. Sources of Water for Existence and Recreation Needs.

Recreation	{	Wells Springs Streams Ponds Lakes Rivers Oceans	}	Existence

areas. It is an attraction; therefore, sites should be located with a view of the water whenever possible. Care must be taken to avoid locating the development along the edge of the water where the development could spoil the attraction. Although recreational water quality need not be as high as existence water, minimum standards do exist. Some states permit public bathing in water with a coliform organism count of 2,400 per 100 milliliters of water. Most areas consider the safe limit for bathing water to be 1,000 coliform organisms per 100 milliliters of water.[6] Hazards such as dangerous undertow, swift current, or rocky bottoms should be considered in choosing a site with water as an attraction.

General Environment

A junkyard and the county dump would not make good neighbors for a forest recreation area. In general, the quality of an area is affected by the aesthetic level of its surroundings. The problem of the character of the surroundings falls into the category of general environment. Is the area large or small? Is it accessible? What is the cover type on the area? What building materials are natural to the area? These are some of the questions concerning the general environment. In general, a planner should search for accessible areas within a setting that would not be adversely influenced by adjacent developments. Occasionally, the area to be developed is the local eyesore such as was the case with Kickapoo State Park in Illinois, which is an abandoned stripmine turned into a state park complete with camping, picnicking, and fishing. As the size of a recreation area increases, the impact of the surrounding developments decrease. When the recreation areas cover thousands of square miles, the internal facilities can remain somewhat immune to the conditions outside.

The nature of the vegetation cover is of some concern to the planner because it tells him how much modification will be required to raise the site quality to the prescribed level. The percentage of wooded or cleared land can help him determine the costs of cutting or of planting. The presence of noxious weeds such as poison ivy or poison oak will mean an eradication program.

The presence of local building material may prove to be a cost-reduction factor as well as a good way to provide a more natural flavor to the construction projects.

No matter how many site-influencing factors are considered in site selection, the most important thing to strive for is the primary purpose of a recreation area. The primary purpose of a recreation area is to produce user satisfaction.

REFERENCES

1. Cieslinski, T.J., and Wagar, J.A. 1970. *Predicting the Durability of Forest Recreation Sites in Northwestern Utah—Preliminary Results.* USDA Forest Research Note, INT-117, Ogden, Utah. 7 pages.

2. Neuberger, H., and Stevens, F. 1948. *Weather and Man*. Prentice-Hall, New York. 272 pages.
3. Orr, Howard R. 1971. Design and Layout of Recreation Facilities. In *Recreation Symposium Proceedings*. Syracuse, N.Y., October 12–14, pp. 23–27.
4. Pennsylvania Department of Forests and Waters. 1969. *State Park Planning and Guidelines*. Bureau of State Parks, Harrisburg, Pa. 90 pages.
5. U.S. Forest Service. 1963. *Recreation Management*. Title 2300 of *Handbook and Manual*. U.S. Department of Agriculture, Washington, D.C.
6. U.S. Public Health Service. 1965. Environmental Health Practice in Recreation Areas. U.S. Department of Health, Education, and Welfare. *Public Health Service Bull*. No. 1195. Washington, D.C.

7

Recreation Area Development

INTRODUCTION

The next step after recreation planning is the development of specific recreation areas. How many campsites? How many picnic tables? Where will they be located? Can day-use and overnight areas be developed on the available spaces? Where will the roads be located? How will the drinking water be supplied? These questions and others are answered in the development plan. The purpose of the development plan is to get the on-the-ground layout plans completed.

As considered here, a developed area is a relatively small area of contiguous land that will be administered and managed by one supervisor and whatever staff is required to assist him. Development plans are confined to specific locations that are joined together by the same attraction. As such, development plans are resource oriented in that they are based upon the recreation resources of the designated area that can be used to satisfy the recreation demand. The recreation plan as discussed in Chapter 5 is generally population oriented and provides the general information needed to arrive at the number of various types of facilities required. This chapter on recreation area development is concerned with the on-the-ground problems associated with the creation of intensive-use recreation sites. The actual selection of individual sites, the design and layout of recreation areas, and construction specifications for the facilities are part of recreation development.

Certain assumptions are made at the beginning of the development program.[9,12] These assumptions are based upon data compiled in the recreation plan. For small areas or private land where no overall recreation plan exists, these assumptions are based upon the landowner's desire and upon information gathered during the early stages of development planning. Examples of the basic assumption needed for the creation of a specific development plan are:

1. The recreation development is wanted, authorized, or needed.
2. The predicted use is given or is obtainable.

Generally, the development plan is based upon the predicted use and the land available. These factors are brought together in the investigation phase, which is the first half of the development plan. By working with the resources and demands, the developer can create the working report which is the second half of the development plan.

For its purpose in area planning, the Forest Service usually limits development areas to approximately 100 acres.[19] This size, however, constitutes the area of substantial modification and does not include the general environment or setting requirements. For the purpose of this book, the development area will be dictated by resources available and the quantity of land that can be managed and administered under one superintendent and his staff.

INVESTIGATION OF THE PROBLEM

The purpose of the problem investigation is the location selection and the layout of the recreation facilities. This is accomplished by determining what facilities are required to meet the demand and then by placing them on the most desirable sites whenever possible.

Types of Activities

The type of recreational activity developed will be dictated by the decisions made in the planning stages. These decisions will be influenced by the expected demands of the perspective users and by the resources available. A scarcity of land will limit both the type and the quantity of recreation development. On the other hand, large tracts of available land with a varied landscape offer many opportunities for diversity in development. A small area near a large population center will be able to serve the greatest number of people if it is developed for day-use activities such as picnicking where there can be a high turnover rate among users and where a high density of use can be achieved. If the day-use demand is not overwhelming, a small tract of land in a scenic setting and near an attraction could be developed into a campground. Since the larger tracts of land permit more versatility of design and variety of type of activities, they are more desirable to work with. The presence or absence of recreational water certainly will alter decisions concerning the type of recreation. Water for swimming is practically a must for successful private recreation areas and very desirable for all day-use areas.[11].

Available funds might limit the actual development in spite of what the plan might call for. Private developers might operate on a fractional level to test public response or to gain income. Also, costs of campgrounds might force their postponement in favor of the more profitable picnic areas when funds are limited. Even though these approaches to the problem might prove to be detrimental to the success of private recreation areas, they are resorted to as a result of insufficient capital.[10]

Predicted Use

The predicted use of the different types of facilities can be obtained from the recreation plan, from estimates based on location and attractions, or by checking on use at nearby developments that offer similar facilities. This method, the comparable demand method, can be rather reliable in specific areas of obvious heavy use. The expected use is estimated by analogy with the similar facilities in the area. Evidently, the success of this method is predicted on the comparability of the two areas and on the unsatisfied demand for facility.[13]

In some instances, use will be intentionally limited by the developer who is interested in maintaining a prearranged quality level. The ability of the attraction to withstand use without deteriorating beyond a certain point determines the carrying capacity (see Chapter 3).

Required Facilities

Turning the predicted use figures into required facilities is a trick that often appears to be sleight of hand. The most reliable technique for this operation is that of using constants to convert predicted use into required acres of land for each type of use. A complete discussion of converting demand figures into required facilities is included in Chapter 5 of this text. Also, the use of the constants technique is included in Example B of the development plan given later in this chapter.

Many central camps exceed a density of 12 camping units per acre and some states are attempting to achieve a picnic table density of 15 tables per acre. Observation has shown that density on privately operated areas probably varies with nearness to major attractions.[1,12] In areas where land values are high and the demand is heavy, the units are crowded more closely together for the purpose of gaining more use per acre of land. By using the same logic, one can reason that the private operator must offer something more attractive when his land is not overrun by people desperately clamoring to camp or picnic at a very popular resort.

As mentioned earlier in this chapter, the size of the development might be limited to the available resources and by the desire of the landowner. After the basic assumption that the recreation area is needed has been made, the resources available might dictate the types and quantity of recreation facilities even more than the predicted use. If recreational water is available, it should be developed for swimming and boating.[10] The site selection factors that are discussed in Chapter 6 should be reviewed so that the developer is familiar with the physical factors that influence the recreational quality of the site. The amount of land that has high potential for recreation will help determine size, location, and amount of recreation facilities.

Another resource to consider here is that of operation personnel. Some types of developments need more watching or administration than others. If operating personnel will be a problem, the size or type of developments will be limited. Family-operated picnic grounds may be based upon the amount of work each member of the family can contribute. The hiring or reliable outside help might be too expensive or even impossible.

Inventory

The heart of the investigation is the inventory of the area. What possibilities exist? Where are the most desirable locations? What limitations must be placed on their use? Are they accessible? These are just some of the many questions that the inventory will answer for the developer. Before he can act wisely, the developer should have a thorough working knowledge of the area. He must know:

1. The legal boundaries of the area and have them clearly marked.
2. The configuration of the landscape as it includes drainages, ridges, slopes, springs, cliffs, and other topographical features.
3. The geology of the underlying rock.
4. The soils that comprise the area.
5. The vegetation types and associations that cover the soil mantle.
6. All cultural improvements that lie on or that directly influence the area to be developed.
7. Past management history.
8. Any zoning or planning ordinances that might restrict his decisions.

Graphic reconnaissance

There are many tools available to the developer who is willing to gather them together. The most basic step in the graphic reconnaissance is that of obtaining a copy of the legal plat or map of the property. The plat and legal description of the property are on record at the county Recorder of Deed's office and are usually obtainable through the county surveyor's office. If there is any doubt concerning the property boundaries, the county surveyor should be contacted. In the event that the property boundaries require relocation, the landowner's capital investment will not have been placed in jeopardy by the developer's lack of investigation and poor professional competence.

The title should be checked for encumbrances that could cause legal problems in the future. Property record books are public records and as such are available at the county courthouse and can be searched by the developer himself. In many cases, a relatively small investment in legal assistance at this point in the investigation will save much heartache and cost later on. The legal fees and even the resurveying costs are small prices to pay for the security and benefits they offer.

Some of the tools available in making the graphic reconnaissance are topographic maps, aerial photographs, geology maps, county highway maps, and soil maps. Skillful interpretation of the information displayed on these publications will enable the developer to compile much pertinent data concerning the site. These maps were compiled by experts in each of the fields and thereby present more information than any developer could collect by himself. The topographic map, soils map, geology map, and aerial photograph usage in graphic reconnaissance are discussed in the following paragraphs.

Topographic maps. The most familiar tool in the graphic investigation is the United States Geologic Survey (USGS) quadrangle sheet. The quadrangle sheet or "contour map" is produced by the Army Map Service and published for civilian use by the United States Geologic Survey. It graphically displays such topographic features as land configuration and streams, cultural features such as roads and buildings, and optionally such vegetative cover as forests and orchards. The original USGS sheets included 15 minutes of longitude and 15 minutes of latitude and usually were printed at the scale best suited for general use in that portion of the country. In areas where problems of national significance occur, the scales of 1:31,680 or 1:24,000 were used. Areas of average national importance were surveyed for publication at a scale of 1:62,500.

After World War II, the 15-minute quadrangle was generally abandoned in favor of the 7½-minute quadrangle sheet which shows greater detail. Most of the nation is now scheduled for resurvey into 7½-minute quadrangles. The new quadrangle sheets give a very good presentation of the natural and cultural features of the land. Unfortunately, four 7½-minute quadrangle sheets now replace one 15-minute sheet. This means more shuffling of papers in the office or field to get the proper coverage. The use of scissors and rubber cement will pay great dividends before the project is complete. It is strongly recommended that one map showing the entire tract and its immediate surroundings be constructed from whatever number of 7½-minute sheets required.

Free status maps showing the completed survey work for each state are available from the Geological Survey Distribution Section, Washington, D.C., for areas east of the Mississippi River and from the Geological Survey Distribution Section, Denver, Colorado, for states west of the Mississippi River. Also, a free folder explaining the topographic maps and symbols can be obtained from the same places.

The quadrangle sheets can be obtained at local distribution points within each state as explained on the back of the state's status map. However, highly satisfactory service is rendered to those who choose to deal directly with the regional distribution sections in Washington and in Denver. Order forms and the

Table 7.1. Scales Commonly Used on USGS Standard Topographic Maps.

Reference Fraction	Engineer's Scale	Contour Interval
1:24,000	1 inch = 2000 feet	1 to 100 feet
1:31,680	1 inch = ½ mile	1 to 100 feet
1:62,500	1 inch = 1 mile (approx)	10 to 100 feet
1:63,360	1 inch = 1 mile	(Alaska only)
1:125,000	1 inch = 2 miles (approx)	20 to 250 feet
1:250,000	1 inch = 4 miles (approx)	20 to 250 feet

price list accompany the status maps and should be used in ordering maps whenever possible.[21]

Geology maps. Geology maps are available for each county from the state office of U.S. Geological Survey. These are generally high-quality maps that are accompanied by an excellent description of each geologic stratum and its effect upon the landscape. Knowledge of the underlying rocks is helpful in interpreting the topography, evaluating possible sites, locating roads, and searching for water supplies.

Soil maps. The United States Soil Conservation Service has the responsibility for soil correlation and mapping in the United States. Copies of soil association maps are usually available from the county work unit conservationist or from the state office of the Soil Conservation Service. This department is readily available and quite willing to help on all soil and related problems. The soil association map should be accompanied by brief descriptions of the soils found in each association stating their capabilities and limitations. A knowledge of the soils in the area is of the utmost importance if future problems are to be minimized. In limited areas, the Forest Service soil scientists have produced outstanding maps of soils occurring in and around national forests. Information can be obtained from these maps by contacting the appropriate forest supervisor.

Aerial photographs. The use of aerial photographs for graphic reconnaissance is rapidly becoming very popular. A wealth of information concerning topography, vegetation, geology, and existing roads and structures can be obtained from aerial photographs. Much information can be gained from simple imagery interpretation if the observer has some knowledge of aerial photographs. More specific facts can be obtained by basic photogrametric techniques of height and distance measurements.

Aerial photographs are intended to be taken with the camera perpendicular to the earth's surface or at a planned angle from the perpendicular. The former, or vertical photography, is the most commonly used and the easiest to obtain.

The latter, or oblique photography, shows a good perspective scene, but is not suited for accurate interpretation by anyone except highly trained and well-equipped specialists. The oblique photograph does have a display value for the recreation developer. The relative landscape is more discernible to the public when viewed on the familiar high oblique that shows the horizon than it is on the vertical photographs. These high-oblique photographs are more difficult to obtain; however, they do help in advertising or in public relations when they can be obtained.

The vertical photograph can be easily obtained at various scales from the regional office of Agricultural Stabilization and Conservation Service (ASCS). The ASCS distributes the photographs taken for other agencies as well as those flown for ASCS purposes. If the owning agency is unknown, the order should be handled by the coordinator of Aerial Photograph Work at the Washington office of the ASCS. The regional laboratory offices of ASCS are:[2]

Eastern Laboratory
Aerial Photography Division
ASCS—USDA
45 South French Broad Avenue
Ashville, North Carolina 28801

Western Laboratory
Aerial Photography Division
ASCS—USDA
2505 Parley's Way
Salt Lake City, Utah 84109

The Aerial Photography Status Map of the United States is produced each year by the ASCS and is free upon request to that agency. A booklet listing the status of aerial photography held by the United States Department of Agriculture can be obtained from that department without cost. This regularly updated publication graphically depicts the coverage by states.

The first step in purchasing the required photographs for the job is to obtain a photo index sheet of the county concerned. The photo index sheet is a picture taken of all the aerial photographs that have been matched together on a flat surface so as to give the appearance of a county map. More than one photo index sheet may be required to give entire county coverage. These index sheets can be viewed at the local ASCS office, the U.S. Soil Conservation Service office, or by contacting the county agent of the state university extension service. The photo index sheets can be requested from the regional ASCS office. Order blanks can be obtained from the county ASCS office or by writing directly to the regional ASCS office.

In most cases, existing photographs are adequate for the purpose of recreation development. They are taken on black and white panchromatic film with high-precision equipment and are printed on single or double-weight semi-matte paper. If the ASCS-supplied photographs are not adequate for the developer's needs, he can contract with any of several competent private businesses to fly the required photographs. One note of caution should be sounded here. Reliable firms with long records of success should be contacted. If color film is to be used, the cost of the delivered prints may run twice as much as for panchromatic film; one should therefore avoid contractors who have not had a great amount of experience in color photography.[7]

Although the single vertical aerial photograph is not a map in the photogrametric sense, it does serve as a very good guide to the landscape. An experienced interpreter can evaluate several factors that aid in identifying images shown on aerial photographs. Avery lists shape, size, tone, pattern, shadow, topographic location, and texture as the seven most important factors.[3]

Single photographs, usually at a scale of 1:15,840, make excellent field sheets and are often carried by soil scientists and foresters who make notes directly on the photograph surface with soft pencil. This mapping or sketching technique permits spots to be pinpointed on the photograph by the person looking at that location. The location of specific landmarks both on the photographs and on the ground eliminates any need for mistake-producing measurements.

By use of conjugal pairs, or overlapping photographs, a third-dimension model of the overlapped area can be viewed. This third dimension or stereoscopic model is similar to the view that an airplane passenger would have when looking vertically downward upon the photographed area.

The use of conjugal pairs and a few simple photogrametric techniques will enable the trained interpreter to select possible sites for the developed facilities, to lay out roads, to analyze the vegetative cover, and to make other tentative development decisions.

By judicious use of USGS quadrangle sheets and aerial photographs, the developer will be able to preselect several possible sites for the developed areas without making the expensive field trips that would otherwise be necessary. When the possible sites have been marked on the topographic map or on one aerial photograph, the developer can make his way directly to each one for an on-the-ground reconnaissance. This will greatly reduce the time required in investigating the area and help to prevent the developer from wandering around in the woods hoping to stumble onto a suitable site.

Working map. A final working map will be needed to develop the second portion of the development plan. It is a good idea to begin the first draft of the working map while involved in the graphic reconnaissance. As data concerning possible sites are compiled, they can be recorded directly upon the working map. Also, as the graphic reconnaissance progresses, the picture of possible sites will become clear on the working map, whereas it would be a jumble of facts and figures in a notebook.

Scales of 1 inch equals 400 feet or 1 inch equals 500 feet have proved to be satisfactory for development planning. The former scale is probably more favorable on areas of less than 1,000 acres. An advantage of making the working map at a scale of 1 inch = 400 feet is the similarity to the scale of the 40 inch × 40 inch aerial photograph enlargements available from the ASCS. Al-

Table 7.2. Partial Data Concerning Aerial Photographs Available from the Agricultural Stabilization and Conservation Service.

Scale (approx.)	Engineers' Scale (approx.)	Print Dimensions (inches)	Cost per Print*
1:20,000	1 inch = 1667 feet	10 × 10 (contact)	$ 2.00
1:15,840	1 inch = 1320 feet	10 × 10 (contact)	2.00
1:15,840	1 inch = 1320 feet	12 × 12 (enlargement)	6.00
1:7920	1 inch = 660 feet	24 × 24 (enlargement)	8.00
1:4800	1 inch = 400 feet	38 × 38 (enlargement)	25.00

*Costs are given for double-weight semimatte paper for 1981.

though the scale is neither uniform nor exact at all points on the photograph, it is approximate enough to use in locating cultural improvements and vegetative covers that are not shown on the quadrangle sheet.

Most quadrangle sheets are sufficiently accurate to serve as the working map. The purpose of the working map is to diagrammatically show the proposed recreation sites and the road network required to serve them. All the developer has to do is to reproduce the desired portions of the quadrangle sheet at the proper scale for his working map. Changing scales is a relatively simple problem that can be easily overcome. The steps for redrawing the topographic map at the larger scale when a projection table is not available are given below:[16]

Step 1. Block off the development area on the quadrangle sheet so that it forms a rectangle with the left sideline running north-south.

Step 2. Grid the rectangle. Construct parallel north-south lines with one-quarter-inch spacing. Then construct parallel lines that are perpendicular to the north-south line with quarter-inch spacing. This divides the area into blocks that are one quarter of an inch square.

Step 3. Letter each north-south line and number each east-west line for identification. This gives each line intersection an identity.

Step 4. Divide the desired scale by the quadrangle scale to get the conversion factor (CF).

Example:

$$\frac{\text{desired scale}}{\text{quadrangle scale}} = CF$$

$$\frac{\frac{1}{400}}{\frac{1}{2000}} = 5$$

Step 5. Grid the sheet of drawing paper with the lines placed so that they are spaced according to the product of the original spacing and the conversion factor. In the case of the example, the interline spacing should be 5 inches.

Step 6. Letter and number the grid lines as in Step 3.

Step 7. Transfer data from the topographic quadrangle to the working map by using the point where the contours, natural feature, and cultural improvements intersect the grid lines.

Ground reconnaissance. Nothing will substitute for an on-the-ground inspection of prospective sites and water sources. The developer and whatever technical assistants that he requires must get out to take a look at the land. Aerial photographs and maps are only tools to assist the developer and to make his job easier. They do not replace the need for him to see the area with his own eyes, to walk over the ground, and to check out his graphic interpretations of slope, vegetative cover, soil, drainage, rock cover, and water sources. When he is on the ground at each site, the developer can use a check list of the recreation-site-influencing factors listed in Chapter 6.

Ground reconnaissance can be expensive if one simply strolls through the woods observing things as one goes. A developer's time is better spent in doing what he is being paid to do, which is to develop a recreation area. Therefore, he must rely upon his graphic interpretation for guidance unless the area is very small and easily traversed. Anyway, the stereoscopic view of the aerial photographs generally gives the observer a better perspective of the landscape than he can get by standing on the site. This is especially true in heavily forested areas.

While making the ground reconnaissance, the developer must make up his mind which sites will be best suited for each planned activity. He must locate the needed acres for picnicking, for camping, for bathing, and for whatever other activities are required by the master plan.

Site maps. After the sites are chosen, each site should be mapped to a scale of 1 inch equals 60 feet to make the working drawing of that area's layout. Each campground, picnic ground, beach, and other type area is shown on the master working map as a diagrammatic outline along with its road network. The individual sites become the focus of attention while their internal layouts are planned. The detailed map of each area should be made in the field using either plane table or transit methods. The telescopic alidade and stadia rod will produce a very satisfactory plane table map showing five-foot contours. If a smaller contour interval is required, the transit and grid technique should be used. However, this technique is not too satisfactory on wooded land or where expenses are limited. Some Forest Service developers demand that a one-foot contour map be made. This is an expensive and even doubtful venture on wooded land; however, it may be necessary where the land is nearly flat, where extensive paving is to be done, or where doubt exists about the placement of septic tank drain fields and water lines.

Using the layout techniques discussed in Chapters 8 through 13, the different facilities should be drawn on the 1 inch equals 60 feet working map so as to take advantage of the topography. The layout should show all roads, trails, structures, units, water lines, absorption fields, and power lines where applicable.

THE DEVELOPMENT REPORT

The development report describes the planned recreation sites, the proposed facilities, the proposed timetable of development, and the estimated costs involved. The facts gathered and the decisions made during the investigative phase of the development plan are presented and explained within this report. A suggested outline for this report is presented below. This outline is presented as a guideline and is open for modification to fit the circumstances. [1,9,20]

Suggested Outline for Development Report

I. Introduction
   A. Objective of development plan
   B. Description of the area
      1. Size and ownership
      2. Location and setting
      3. General topography
      4. Accessibility
   C. Statement of recreation needs in area
      1. Present and predicted use of nearby facilities
      2. Estimated use through year 2020 (Table 1)
II. Required Areas and Facilities
   A. Conversion of predicted use into facilities and costs (Table 2 and 3)
   B. Proposed sites and their development timetable (Table 4)
III. Detailed Descriptions of Each Proposed Site
   A. Data Sheet
      1. Name
      2. Type of recreation activity
      3. Location
      4. Size
      5. Area description
         (a) Vegetative cover
         (b) Topographic features
         (c) Advantages
         (d) Disadvantages
      6. Proposed facilities and costs
IV. Appendix A
   A. Working map
      1. Scale at 1 inch equals 400 feet

    2. Showing
      (a) Diagrammatic outlines of each selected area
      (b) Contours
      (c) Roads and trails
        (1) Proposed
        (2) Existing
      (d) Other topographic features
        (1) Natural
        (2) Cultural
  B. Detailed map of each proposed area
    1. Scale at 1 inch equals 60 feet
    2. Showing
      (a) Countour lines (5-foot to 1-foot intervals)
      (b) Detailed layout within area
  C. Detailed drawing of standard unit designs for applicable activities
    1. Picnic units
    2. Camping units
    3. Amphitheater
V. Appendix B
  A. Engineering specifications and drawings
    1. Roads and trails
      (a) Size
      (b) Surface
      (c) Grade
    2. Water treatment and distribution
      (a) Equipment needed
      (b) Specifications
    3. Sanitation
      (a) Sewage
      (b) Refuse
    4. Structures and site modification

The suggested outline for the development report has four parts. In addition to the appendices, the report covers (1) the general introductory material in Part I, (2) the required areas and facilities in Part II, and (3) a detailed description from specific data gathered in the investigative portion of the development plan. Much of the latter two parts of the report is dependent upon that information as it is reflected in the working map of the area. It is the working map that graphically exhibits the selected sites for each facility.

Part I. Introduction

Part I of the report is concerned with a general description of the area and of the

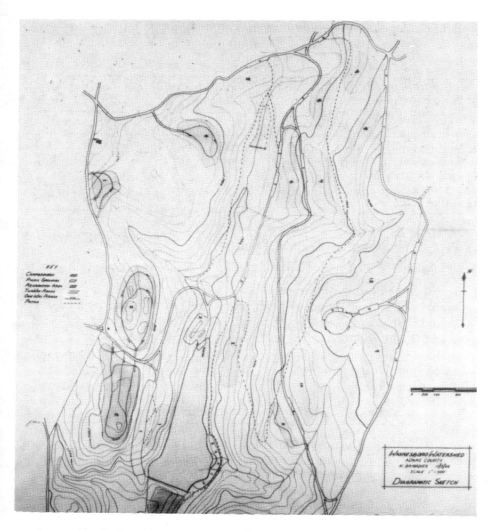

Fig. 7.1. The final working map gives the diagrammatic outline of the proposed recreation sites.

anticipated demand on that area for recreation facilities. In the recreation planning stage, this demand should have been projected through the next 35 or 40 years so as to permit the construction of adequate facilities from the beginning. Although these are considered to be planning figures, the estimated-use figures should be shown in Table A of the introductory part of the report so as to give a basis for making succeeding assumptions or estimates. The example in Table A is presented to show predicted-use figures that could be compiled for a proposed reservoir-based recreation development.

Example A

Table A. Predicted Recreation — Days Use With and Without Project.

Use of Area by Purpose of Visit Class	Estimated 1980 Days Use	Predicted Days Use Without Project		Predicted Days Use With Project	
		1990	2020	1990	2020
	(1000)	(1000)	(1000)	(1000)	(1000)
Campgrounds	2.0	10	15	35	60
Picnic sites	12.0	20	40	50	75
Swimming	3.0	12	18	35	55
Boating	0.5	3	5	50	90

Part II. Required Areas and Facilities

Part II of the development report is concerned with determining the types and numbers of facilities needed and their costs. If conversion factors are used, they should be shown in Table B of the report. Example B gives the format of Tables B and C as they should appear in Part II of the development report.

Example B

Table B. Usable Recreation Acres Needed in Year 2020.

Area Class	Estimated Visitor-Day Use	Converting[a] Factors	Acres Needed[c]	Number of Units
Campgrounds	60,000	0.0016[b]	96	298
Picnic sites	75,000	0.0008[b]	59	236
Swimming	53,000	0.0001	6	5[d]
Boating	90,000	0.0002	18	5[d]

[a]Based upon formula for determining acreage requirements in Chapter 5.
[b]Three units per acre.
[c]Rounded upward to nearest acre.
[d]Swimming and boating units are based upon usable locations required to satisfy the demand.

The method of using the converting factors is employed to save arithmetic on projects where visitor-day use is the only variable. When the space requirements of the user, length of season, and turnover factor remain constant for an activity, they can be worked up as a converting factor to be multiplied by the number of visitor-day use to estimate the required acres of development. The formula for estimating the area required is discussed in Chapter 5. An example of computing the converting factor is given below:

(a) Compute converting factor for campgrounds that will have three units per developed acre (formula in Chapter 5).

$$\frac{\text{area required}}{\text{for picnicking}} = \frac{(\text{demand}) \times (\text{area}/\text{person})}{(\text{capacity}/\text{day}) \times (\text{turnover factor}) \times 43,560 \text{ ft}^2/\text{acre}}$$

Example:

$$\frac{75,000 \times 2725}{53 \times 1.5 \times 43,560}$$

(b) Make a converting factor y by:

Let

$$y = \frac{a}{cd \times TF \times 43,560}$$

$$y = \frac{2725}{53 \times 1.5 \times 43,560} = 0.008$$

(c) Therefore:

area required $= D(y) = 75,000(0.0008) = 59$ acres

(d) Units required $=$ acres $\times$ (units per acre) $= 59 \times 4 = 236$ units

The completion of Table B in Part II of the development report provides the developer with the number of units required by activity type. The next step to take is the cost determination for the project by completing Table C. Table C is a cost summary of the recreation development. It uses the data from Table B to determine the number of each type of facility that is required and the estimated cost for it. Example C shows Table C as it should appear in the development report. Although the tables shown in the examples are very large developments, they are still set up and used in the same manner for small developments.

Example C

Table C.

Area Class	Number of Units	Unit Cost[a]	Total Cost per Class
Campsites	298	$ 3500	$1,043,000
Picnic sites	240	3000	720,000
Swimming	5	40,000	200,000
Boating	5	60,000	300,000
Total costs			$2,263,000[b]

[a]Cost estimates including pro-rata share of roads, sanitary system; however, costs used here are examples and do not reflect the full impact of today's inflationary spiral.
[b]Not including contingency, planning, and overhead fees.

The Table D that is suggested in the outline for the development plan is a summary of planned areas and a timetable for their construction. It serves as the heart of the development report when used in conjunction with the working map. It gives a complete summary of the planned recreation development by the areas that are identified on the working map. The area names and numbers that appear in Table D must be the same as those shown on the working map, which is part of the report's appendix. Example D shows Table D as it should appear in Part II of the development report.

Example D

Table D. Summary of Planned Areas and Their Construction Timetable.

No. Location	Net Usable Area (acres)	Units Camp site	Units Picnic site	Units Swimming	Units Boat- ing	Completion Schedule* Percent completed by 1990	Completion Schedule* 2000	Completion Schedule* 2020
1. Spring Run	30	24	40	1	1	100	100	100
2. Bear Trail	45	24	25	1	1	—	—	100
3. Big Bend	240	60	85	1	1	50	100	100
4. Deer Flat	500	169	50	1	1	50	100	100
5. Indian Creek	180	21	40	1	1	50	100	100
		298	240	5	5			

*Completion schedule dependent upon predicted-use figures and available capital.

The sample outline and the examples listed above will help guide the developer in producing the development report. The development report and the investigation phase should be presented in such a way as to make them as usable as possible. Emphasis should be placed on complete and clearly understood tables and summaries that can be correlated easily with the maps contained in the appendix.

If the developer is working for someone other than himself, he must, of course, render the best possible service to his client and perform in a professional manner. Beyond this, however, he should strive to make his report as interesting and as understandable as possible. Neat, colored maps or photographs with overlays are more than just "merchandizing"; they are important in aiding the client to understand the development plan quickly. If the developer has done a professional job of preparing the plan, he would not feel guilty in using a little "eyewash" to sell his product to someone who might not have the time, interest, or technical understanding to read beyond the first couple of pages.

Part III. Detailed Descriptions of Each Proposed Site

The third part of the development report gives a detailed description of each proposed site. Each proposed site should be named by this point in the report so that easy correlations can be made between the detailed descriptions and the areas drawn on the working map. The detailed description of each site should contain information on the site's location, size, vegetative cover, and topographic features. Succinct statements concerning the site's apparent advantages and disadvantages should be included as part of the detailed description. Also, a list of the proposed facilities and their costs should be included.

The description for each site should be presented in tabular form so as to make the information readily available to interested readers. The tabulation format should be kept uniform whenever possible in order to lessen the time needed to locate details about the site.

The maps made of each site should be drawn at a scale of 1 inch equals 60 feet and included in Appendix A of the development report.

Part IV. Appendices

Appendix A

Appendix A is the proper location for all pertinent maps that will be included in the development report. The working map of the development area should be drawn at a scale of 1 inch equals 400 feet (1 inch equals 500 feet if the area is greater than 1,000 acres) and should be included in Appendix A. Each of the site maps should be placed in the same order as the sites are numbered in Table D of Part II.

Appendix B

The engineering specifications and working drawings should be included in

Appendix B so that they will not clutter up the body of the development report. Care must be taken to present the appendix material in an orderly and uncomplicated fashion so as not to frustrate the user who is looking for the details that have been filed in the appendix.

The average developer would like to believe that his work is completed without worrying about engineering specifications and drawings. Unfortunately, things do not work out that way. The purpose of the development plan was stated at the beginning of the chapter. Its purpose is to get the on-the-ground layout plans completed. The person who is responsible for getting the job done must have the specifications and designs in order to determine costs, to prepare for purchases, and to obtain the necessary approvals by regulating agencies.

Much information concerning water supply, sanitation, and layout can be obtained from various chapters in this book. Working drawings of standard structures and facilities are easily obtainable. The Forest Service has assembled a set of working drawings into one publication entitled "Working Drawings of Basic Facilities for Campground Development" which can be purchased from the Superintendent of Documents.[17] The use of the word campground in the title is somewhat misleading in that the working drawings included in that publication are for structures usable in almost any popular forest recreation activity.

Costs on individual items vary greatly according to circumstances; therefore, local bids should be solicited for materials and labor. This section should be used only to achieve broad estimates for budgeting purposes. Construction costs have been so greatly affected by inflation that any cost figures given in this textbook would be subject to considerable error.

Some cost lists in publications espousing outdoor recreation as an enterprise appear to be slanted to encourage landowners to get into the camping or picnicking business. As a result of conflicting published cost estimates, the developer would do a more professional job by obtaining bids and determining the actual costs for the given project as part of his own work rather than relying upon published estimates for more than guidelines. These data should come through as part of the development plan by using the specifications in Appendix B and the site layouts in Appendix A to get the cost bidding completed.

REFERENCES

1. Agnew, R. 1965. *Profitable Private Campground Construction and Operation.* Rojo Publication, New York. 50 pages.
2. Agriculture Stabilization and Conservation Service. 1966. Order for Aerial Photography. Form ASCS—441. January 1966.
3. Avery, T.E. 1964. *Interpretations of Aerial Photographs.* Burgess, Minneapolis, Minn. 193 pages.
4. Cooper, C., and Smith F. 1966. Color Aerial Photography: Toy or Tool? In *Journal of Forestry*, Vol. 66, pp. 373–378.

5. Cordell, N.K., and James G.A. 1972. *Visitor Preferences for Certain Physical Characteristics of Developed Campsites*. Southeast Forest Experiment Station. Forest Service Research Paper SE-100. 21 pages.
6. Doell, C.E. 1963. *Elements of Park and Recreation Administration*. Burgess, Minneapolis, Minn. 340 pages.
7. Holcomb, Conklin, and Winch. 1964. *Opportunities for Private Campgrounds as an Alternative Use of Land*. Agriculture Extension Service Circular No. 792. Virginia Polytechnic Institute, Blacksburg, Va.
8. Lane, R.D. 1964. Private Recreation Enterprises—Pie in the Sky? *Proceedings of 19th Annual Meeting of Soil Conservation Society of America*. Jackson, Miss.
9. Mackie, D.J. 1965. Site Planning to Reduce Deterioration. In *Proceedings of Society of American Foresters Meeting—1965*. Detroit, Mich.
10. Pennsylvania Department of Forests and Waters. 1969. *State Park Planning and Guidelines*. Bureau of State Parks, Harrisburg, Pa. 90 pages.
11. Reidesel, Wilson. 1969. *Developing Campgrounds for Recreational Vehicles*. State of Wisconsin, Bureau of Commercial Recreation. Madison Publishing Division, Appleton, Wisc. 23 pages.
12. Soil Conservation Service, USDA. 1977. Recreation Ready Reference. Northeast Technical Service Center Technical Note Number 1.
13. Tracy, J.C. 1934. *Plane Surveying. A Textbook and a Pocket Manual*. John Wiley, New York. 162 pages.
14. U.S.D.A. Forest Service. 1962. Working Drawings of Basic Facilities for Campground Development. In *Agricultural Information Bulletin*, no. 264. U.S. Department of Agriculture.
15. ————. 1962. Forest Recreation for Profit. *Agricultural Information Bulletin*, no. 265. U.S. Department of Agriculture.
16. ————. 1963. *Recreation Management*. Title 2300 *Handbook and Manual*. U.S. Department of Agriculture, Washington, D.C.
17. ————. 1963. Supplemental Report of the Impact of the Proposed Rowlesburg Reservoir on the Monongahela National Forest. Unpublished Regional Office. Upper Darby, Pa.
18. U.S. Geologic Survey. 1972. *Topographic Map Symbol Sheet*. USGS, Department of the Interior, Washington, D.C.

PART II

8

Introduction to Part II

There is a point at which planning must be turned into action. Someone must turn recreation plans and development reports into facilities that the public can use. Bridging the gap between paperwork planning and on-the-ground development is a difficult step. It requires an understanding of the planning reports and a knowledge of the specific improvements to be undertaken. Also, initiative is required on the part of the land manager if he is to maintain actual control over the development of the recreation areas.

Many facilities come about by management decisions or expansion improvements and not as a result of a large-scale recreation plan. When the time arrives for the manager to concern himself with the specifics of getting the facility onto the ground, the manager must have an adequate source of detailed information concerning recreation developments and their operation and management. The planning stages of recreation areas are horizons apart from the successful construction, maintenance, and operation of a forest recreation facility.

Part II of this book provides a technical approach for getting the job done. It is the "how-to" approach to recreation facilities, management, and operation. In Part II, the land manager can find the specifications and recommendations for sanitation, water supply, and various forms of developments. Also, he can obtain the suggestions, methods, and techniques for operating and managing recreation areas under varying circumstances.

Although Part II gives many details concerning the design, management, and operation of forest recreation areas, it cannot give the three qualities that are most important to a recreation area manager. A good recreation area manager must have initiative, interest, and imagination. He must find the opportunities to improve his areas wherever possible. A certain aggressiveness will be needed to obtain a positive approach to management.

9

Campgrounds

CLASSIFICATION OF CAMPGROUNDS

Camping is one of the major forms of forest recreation and it is still growing in popularity.[2] Although it does not compile the large day-use statistics as do swimming and picnicking, camping does provide the image of forest recreation for most Americans. There are more than 1.1 million campsites in the United States. That number had been increasing by 5 percent per year until 1982. The mention of forest recreation conjures up visions of tents standing among the high-reaching trees in some secluded forest glen, of wood smoke, and of a cool dip in a mountain stream. The camper knows, however, that the typical scene includes trailers, buslike recreational vehicles, or pickup mounted units lined up—each to its own cubby hole of gravel or asphalt. Some campgrounds do not provide facilities for open fires. Wood fire is rarely used for cooking in developed campgrounds. Swimming is as likely to be done in a pool as in a stream.

Camping popularity has led to modification of style. Values associated with camping are changing rapidly and those who want to adhere to certain values are moving into specialized forms of camping. Trailer and recreation vehicle camping is still growing in popularity. However, a sharp rise in tent camping has accompanied the boom in backpacking. The camping opportunity spectrum offers opportunities for participation at many levels of sophistication.

A generalization claims that people camp at or near major tourist attractions to avoid the high cost of motels and restaurants but that they camp in the secluded areas for outdoor environment enjoyment.[33] Studies of camper motivation show that people are doing the style of camping that they are satisfied doing.[17,18,23] In this observation lies a shortcoming of most studies that attempt to create demand curves and to evaluate visitor preferences. Also, the population of nonrespondents might be different from the population willing to give answers. Very little literature is based upon unmarried couples using public campgrounds or upon the preferences of the thousands of young people in vagabondage around the nation during the warmer months of each year. Also, there is the uninhibited participation in backpacking activities by young adults sharing recreational experiences regardless of their marital status.

Table 9.1. The Number of Campers in the United States for Selected Years.

	1955	1964	1970	1976
Campers	(1000) 6,200	(1000) 13,000	(1000) 35,200	(1000) 58,102

Campers expect many different things of the campgrounds where they stay. Their tastes run from expensive mobile campers to backpacks; however, they all demand the three major features of sanitation, safety, and attractive sites. The *Forest Service Handbook* describes campgrounds as sites primarily developed for overnight use by campers. [27] Campgrounds are improved areas that provide visitors with attractive sites, sanitary facilities, and safe fire areas along with such general safety as can be accomplished through proper administration. The primary management objectives of having campsites are to provide a service to the user, to protect the user, and to protect the resource. Often, these objectives are lost because of indifferent bureaucracy within public parks, overzealous administrators, or overrestricting regulations. Most campers, hunters, and fishermen realize the need for certain limitations; however, they show justified resentment toward being treated as delinquent book borrowers by bossy park superintendents or worrisome campground owners.

Generally, campers are a loyal group and prefer to return to favorable sites year after year. Many campers even become possessive and refer to a particular campsite as their camping spot. In his study of high participation campers, LaPage found that the 25 percent of the campers who accounted for 80 percent of all reported camping prefer to return to the same privately owned campground. [25] These people are important to the camping movement in forest recreation. In many cases, they have been camping in an area longer than the park administrator has been on the job. These "regulars" can contribute much to the planning and managing of a campground; however, they are very sensitive to changes that are not compatible with their feelings.

Camping is the essential element of forest recreation for some people, while it is just a means to an end for others. Many people spend their vacation camping in order to go places because of simple economics. The savings caused by camping will quickly amortize the investment in camping equipment. Indeed, studies in Minnesota indicate that campers use campgrounds as a substitute for resorts or vacation homes. [18] Even the high cost of quality backpacking equipment can be rationalized as inexpensive when compared to today's resort costs.

There is a wide variation among campers as to their needs. Some want to be isolated back in a wilderness area, while others enjoy the social amenities of citylike camping. A general effort at transposing urban lifestyles to parks and forests appears to be a common practice with most campers. [18] The campers seeking isolation, solace, and relief from the frictions brought on by social contacts are still found in highly developed campgrounds. Enjoyable times occur for many camping families as they get together with the campers crowded around them. There are other conflicting interests among campers. Some want conveniences to varying degrees while others prefer pure wilderness. There are those who demand easy accessibility and those who look forward to packing-in by foot or horse. Others want as much wilderness as they can drive to. West found that respondents at the extremes, between primitive and highly developed campgrounds, tended to have highly intense feelings about their respective preferences. Campers in the middle had less intense feelings about what they preferred. Research findings have supported the contention that people camp where they are satisfied camping. People camping in central campgrounds stated that they were satisfied with small camping units while campers in a Forest Service forest-type camp felt that camping units should be well spaced, screened, and reasonably private.[12,15] Careful planning can make land available to meet most of the varying demands for camping areas.

This chapter treats the development of campgrounds that are to be used by the campers who are traveling or vacationing as families, as small groups, or as individuals. Camps used by organizations such as the Boy Scouts, YMCA, or church groups have different problems of design and administration. The organization camps are discussed in a later chapter.

A system of campground classification is necessary to order to allow the land manager to choose the type of campground that is suitable for the needs in his area. This book has adopted the Wagar system of classification because of its flexibility and its overlapping types that permit freedom of use without over-classification.[30] Any new field needs definitions; however, it must fight off hair splitting and overclassification. Wagar's system of campground classification should serve as a guide and not as a set of rules for campground development.

CENTRAL CAMPS

Whenever the conditions occur that consistently attract large numbers of people to a relatively small spot, the best class of campground to provide is the central camp. Central camps are just a few steps away from city living in that the camping units are crowded together in designated locations and each unit is oriented next to its neighbors in a geometric pattern. This placement of units allows maximum use of the land area and permits easy maintenance and administration. State parks and private campgrounds use the terms "modern" or "highly developed" to describe their central camps that have the complete set of facilities and closely set units less than 100 feet between centers.

The formal layout and closeness of the campsites permit intensive use of the area. The intensive use in turn justifies the investment of capital to provide services for the camper. Because of this intensity of use, flush toilets are necessary to maintain satisfactory sanitary conditions. Hot showers, electrical and water hookups, a general store, and laundry facilities are part of life in a complete central camp. More than 85 percent of privately owned campgrounds have water, electrical, or sewage hookups. Less than 25 percent of public agency campgrounds have any hookups.[25] Many camping purists and some non-campers find the central campground, as it is described here, distasteful, while others completely disdain any pretense at searching for nature and seek the luxuriant campground resorts that provide a transient country-club atmosphere. Certainly, the person who camps for the purpose of obtaining seclusion and an expression of self-reliance would not be content to stay in a central camp. Central camps, however, have many advantages over the more primitive forms of campgrounds. Central camps provide security, comfort, social life, and convenience.

Security is a need that must be recognized in camping as well as in hometown living. Few campers will admit in public that they consider their physical security when they select a campground; however, every serious family head is concerned with the safety of his family. Many camping families have driven into and then out of an isolated and deserted campground after dark. Everyday living brings people into constant contact with many other people in familiar surroundings where legal governments provide communities with police protection. Therefore, the individual is not equipped to provide for his own security. As most experienced campers know, any physical danger is very small; however, camping puts people into unfamiliar situations in places where formal law enforcement is not evident. The large number of people in a central camp provides a feeling of security, as well as justifying the salaries of the attendants and managers who are responsible for the campers' safety.

Comfort in camping is a relative term, dependent upon the campers and their desires. Central camps provide the maximum comfort obtainable in normal camping situations. The comfort level of a central camp is one rung lower than it is for cabin living. Research has shown that the comfort level of a campground is one of the four major conditions affecting user satisfaction.[4] The many conveniences available in central camps raise the comfort level, while

Table 9.2. Classification of Campgrounds and their Purpose.*

Classification	Purpose
Central camps	Provide maximum conveniences and headquarters for large numbers of campers.
Forest camps	Mix naturalness with conveniences.
Back-country camps	Unrestricted camping and no conveniences.
Peakload camps	Handle large numbers of campers for short period of time.
Long-term camps	For campers staying one month or more.
Traveler's camps	Provide for needs of en route campers.

*J.A. Wagar.

overcrowding lowers it. Recreational vehicles provide many of the urban comforts of home to the camper as well as providing insulation against crowding.

Major site modification is required to overcome the effects of high-density use. Nature must be assisted by planting, fertilization, irrigation, and construction. Native vegetation is often replaced with more durable ornamental plants. Paving protects the roads, parking areas, and heavily used portions of the campsite from the deterioration effects of heavy traffic. The pretense of rustic construction is abandoned in favor of more suitable and less expensive materials to provide administration buildings, storage sheds, wash houses, and other required structures. Barriers of wood, masonry, or plants control the flow of traffic.

The social instinct of people remains active while they are camping. Even those who venture into the back country remember the chance meetings with other hikers as highlights of the camping trip. Central camps bring people together from widely separated sections of the country. Although the campers are from different parts of the country and have diverse backgrounds, they all have camping as a common interest. Some experienced campers prefer to spend part of their camping vacation in large central camps in order to exchange fireside chatter with other campers. Many people who prefer central camps because of available facilities and services are also those people who want to follow a daily living pattern that is not greatly different from their normal pattern. Etykorn concluded from his research in California that people do not choose camping as a way of escaping and that they tend to follow their home activities when camping.[7] Those campers who do the bulk of camping tend to have more of a social attitude toward camping than do the less active campers.[14] Their evenings are taken up by entertainment or a social engagement. The activities and the setting are different, but the evening's format remains unchanged. Group singing or slide talks by park personnel replace television and the fireside chat with neighboring campers takes the place of an evening of bridge or pinochle.

The convenience of the central camp is an important factor to the traveling vacationer. A central camp is near the attraction that the camper will come to see and it will serve as a base of operations for him. From this base of operations, the camper can make day trips to nearby points of interest. Often, neighboring scenic attractions can be protected from destruction by trampling or by the encroachment of campsites if the campers can be congregated into a central camp.

A central camp must meet three minimum requirements to be successful. First, it must be near to a major attraction that will bring the crowds of campers needed to justify the high-density development and the many facilities and services available at a central camp. This should be a durable attraction that will hold its value over an indefinite length of time and under heavy use. An extensive area of unusual beauty would satisfy this requirement, but a small fishing stream would not. The heavy fishing pressure brought on by the users of the central camp would destroy the attraction by overuse. Private central campgrounds can, in themselves, be destination points with sociability and facilities being the attraction.

Second, the central camp must be accessible from a major highway, not necessarily an interstate highway, although the camp itself can be several miles off the major highway to discourage the curious motorists from taking a casual side trip through the camping area.

Third, it must be flexible if it is to continue to provide returns on the initial investment. Methods of camping are changing and the campground should be flexible enough to accommodate the new methods as they become popular. With the majority of campers using recreation vehicles, the electric, water, and the sewage hookups are popular at private campgrounds. Campers who do the most camping tend to have large investments in camping equipment, prefer private campgrounds with utility hookups, and are repetitive in their choice of campgrounds.[14] Dumping stations for sewage disposal are now a necessity to handle the self-contained camper units. Changes in tent designs are requiring different pad arrangements. Economy of size is a factor in the success of private campgrounds so that expansion has been the norm in successful operations.

Central camps such as the ones at Yellowstone, Yosemite, and Crater Lake National Parks are large enough to include several hundred units and to accommodate large numbers of campers. The smallest central camp should exceed 50 units in order for it to accomplish its purpose of supplying the maximum conveniences to the campers. The overhead required for 50 units can usually accommodate 100 units, so expansion should be planned. It is the large numbers of campers grouped together that enable the central camp to support the cost of construction and maintenance of flush toilets, showers, laundry facilities, a general store, and other conveniences associated with a central camp. Smaller central camps can act as a base for surrounding campgrounds that maintain a more rustic atmosphere. In this case, the central camp can supply facilities and services that are not found or desired in the other classes of campgrounds that are nearby.

Caravan campgrounds for large groups of recreation vehicles are modifications of the central camp. Figure 9.1 shows a design of a caravan camp suggested by the Pennsylvania Bureau of Parks for large destination parks.[21] Such a specialized area or group camp requires a large, level site of approximately 160 feet in diameter that is in grass cover and separated from other campgrounds or picnicking areas. At least one set of flush-type toilets and shower facilities should be built for each 200 units. Trash receptacles should be placed every 200 feet apart at the maximum. A large playground area and a campfire ring are desirable within the circle.

FOREST CAMP

The forest camp utilizes individual camping units that are designed to handle a family or a small camping group. The units are scattered to provide a degree of

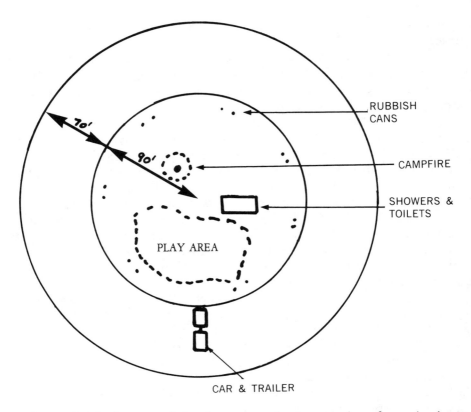

RUBBISH CANS

CAMPFIRE

SHOWERS & TOILETS

PLAY AREA

CAR & TRAILER

Fig. 9.1. Sketch of a caravan designed to accommodate large numbers of recreational vehicles traveling in convoy or rendezvousing at a destination.

privacy, but they are grouped close enough to permit construction of limited facilities. The forest camp is the typical campground that is associated with forest recreation. The camping units are located along a looping road that winds through a wooded area where the natural environment has been maintained as much as possible. The forest camp is a blending of the formal campground layout with the naturalness of the forest, with units spaced more than 100 feet apart for a density of four to six units per acre.

Forest camps have the four strong points of family living, convenience, solitude to a degree, and site protection (see Fig. 9.2). Families have the campsites to themselves without much disturbance from passersby or neighbors. This situation allows the family or camping group to perform as a unit within its own campsite. Families form the largest group of campers and forest camps are a popular type of campground. The feeling of solitude that encourages family living is a feature of forest camps that comes from spacing the units at intervals of at least 100 feet. Many campgrounds are developed without regard to this

Fig. 9.2. A forest camp is a blending of a formal campground layout with the naturalness of the forest. Forest camps provide family living, convenience, a degree of solitude, and site protection.

minimum distance between camping units. The attempts to conserve space or money by crowding the units together are an unfortunate choice of conservation. Many state parks contain new campgrounds with a 50-foot spacing between the centers of the units. These subminimum spaced units do not produce a forest camp, but, rather, they make a modified central camp. They do not fill the needs of a central camp nor do they meet the minimum requirements for satisfactory forest camps.

Convenience is a strong point favoring forest camps. The user is able to drive right into the campsite that is laid out for his needs. The family can be set up for overnight living in a minimum of time. Water, sanitary facilities, and refuse collection stations are within a couple of hundred feet. The user has easy access to and from the campsite and to nearby attractions. Ease of access and limited facilities favor the visitor who does not plan a long stay, although many forest camps now have flush toilets, utility hookups, and hot showers. Many successful private campgrounds have a density of three to four units per developed acre, which could have those campgrounds included in the forest camp category if the units are not all crowded into a central camp layout. Many publicly owned forest camps have a two-week limit on occupancy to permit as many people as possible to use the camps. On the other hand, private campgrounds can cater to the long-term camper. The same features are desirable for the campers who use the campsite as a base of operations while visiting surrounding attractions. The users should find the forest camp convenient to them while they are participating in certain forest recreation activities such as fishing, sight-seeing, and hiking. It does not qualify as an outdoor motel in that it is not right on the major highway. The forest camps should serve a particular area or attraction and should be far enough away from the major throughway to discourage their use for picnicking or en route camping.

Solitude, as it is found in the forest camp, is not based upon isolation from other humans, but, rather, it is developed by clever design of a relatively high-density use area. As mentioned above, the spacing of the units helps to produce the feeling of solitude; however, the distance between units can be stretched so far before they become single, scattered campsites, and this does not appear to serve any purpose.

Site modification is the amount of change in an area during its improvement to campground status. The site modification for forest camps is done in such a way as to maintain as much of the area's rustic flavor as possible. Improvements are made with natural material whenever possible. Buildings are constructed of logs or wood slabs, and barriers are made from rocks, logs, or other native material. The layout of the campground is such that campers are not required to cut through other campsites when following the shortest route to the facilities such as toilets, water supply, wash house, or to the swimming area.

The dispersal of the campsites acts to protect the site from destruction by overuse. Judicious location of forest camps can help to justify a central camp nearby. Forest camps are sometimes located as satellites to a central camp that supplies their users with the more elaborate services and facilities that do not fit in with the spirit of the forest camp.

People who regularly camp in forest camps prefer the campground that is relatively small. Lime's study of campers on the Superior National Forest indicated that a forest campground should have less than 25 camping units.[15] Small scattered campgrounds present management problems. The forest manager must provide service, maintain the site quality, and keep a safe place. Trying to meet management objectives on scattered campgrounds will cost too much money. Therefore, a designer or planner will be smart to combine what has been learned by studying user preferences and by recognizing the impacts those preferences will have on the management budget. Loop roads can be used to tie several small campgrounds together into one management area. Each loop road can have approximately fifteen units and can be tied in with other loops to form a larger campground where the smallest aspect apparently has been maintained.

BACK-COUNTRY CAMP

The back-country camp is designed to provide limited facilities for camping in wilderness areas that are far removed from civilization. They are in the wilderness or back country where they can be reached by walking, horseback riding, or boating. Back-country camps vary widely in the kinds of services and facilities that they supply; however, they maintain the wilderness flavor of the area as much as possible. A fireplace and a clearing are usually provided for each campsite. Other improvements might include such things as corrals, tables, safe drinking water, lean-tos, and toilets according to the specific needs of each area. Site modification is limited to the facilities and clearing and is not applied to the general area. However, the increasing use of favorable camping spots is causing site deterioration. Site modification and rehabilitation are techniques of restoring a campsite to a condition approximating the original; however, wilderness campers do not want any site modification that would spoil the original purpose of the wilderness area. As user pressure justifies the need, more facilities should be used in laying out primitive units to concentrate use on the modified site.

Many people go camping in wilderness areas to escape from crowds and regulations. These wilderness campers like being free to wander and to camp where they want to without interference. In general, they do not want any cultural improvements to mar the solitude of the wilderness. Unfortunately, the campers' presence is enough to change the environment.[13] Even slightly used areas show considerable wear and tear. Also, wilderness campers have a tendency to follow familiar trails and to camp near the old camps of others. Site deterioration has been accelerated in wilderness areas by a sharp increase in their use. Pack animals and riding horses eat more vegetation in a week than they can carry. With an average of 2.5 horses per person in the wilderness, the forage is quickly consumed.

Wilderness, back country, or primitive areas have slightly different connotations when used by different federal or state agencies; however, they are basically large tracts of land that have no public roads or other cultural developments. Campers gain their enjoyment in these areas by communing with nature without interference from crowds or regulations. The back-country campers make up a relatively small, but outspoken, segment of the camping public.[10,27] Backpacking, however, has become a rapidly growing sport in the last couple of years. The lightweight pack frame was introduced in the early 1950s and the rip-stop nylon equipment in the late 1960s.[24] Since then, backpacking equipment sales have nearly doubled every year.

In local areas, formal back-country camps tend to concentrate use during overnight camping and thereby protect the surrounding site. When used in conjunction with an established trail system, the back-country camps can be used to spread use over the entire wilderness preserve. Therefore, back-country camps serve to protect the wilderness character by concentrating camping use in widely scattered campsites. These camps will increase in number and in public acceptance as the user pressures on the wilderness areas continue to rise along with all other forest recreation pressures. The lean-to campsites maintained along the 2,000-mile Appalachian Trail by volunteer labor have been a very successful form of back-country camps. The National Trails System and the Wild and Scenic River Acts of 1968 have created extensive recreation areas strung out over long distance without vehicle access. These recreational undertakings will require an extensive system of back-country camps to accommodate the boaters and hikers using them.

Forest Service guidelines for back-country facility design suggest that a linear layout of facilities should be used to minimize trampling of the site by visitors.[8] Since the best route between any two facilities is along the single, nearly straight path, the need for shortcutting is eliminated. The linear layout of the back-country camp should be off the main hiking trail and available over a well-marked access trail. Figure 9.3 presents the linear layout of a back-country camp.

The boat-in campground is an adaptation of the wilderness camp that is designed to accommodate those campers traveling by boat. Usually, these campgrounds are relatively small with only a few units. Although they are not accessible by car, boat-in areas generally do have maintenance access roads for servicing and refuse removal. Units consisting of tent site, table, and fire ring or stove should be spread out more than 100 feet apart to maintain the wilderness setting. Hand pumps are generally used to supply the water. For sanitation, pit toilets are the rule except when situations dictate chemical toilets. Two single-pit toilets are needed to service eight units with 600 feet being the maximum distance from any unit.[21] Some boat-docking development might be required; however, gentle shorelines usually serve the purpose.

PEAKLOAD CAMP

The peakload camp, or overflow, is designed to handle large numbers of campers for short periods of time with the minimum of services and facilities. This form of campground serves those people who arrive too late to occupy a regular campsite. A designed and well-marked peakload campground keeps the overflow crowds in a designated location where sanitation and regulations can be enforced. Without the overflow area, many campers would not stay in the area, or they would set up their own campsites throughout the surrounding woods. Both of these alternatives are unsatisfactory.

Records show that campground use comes in spurts during short periods of seasonal attractions such as opening day of fishing season, hunting season, or the Fourth of July weekend.[5] A 1970 sample of private campgrounds in New York reported an average occupancy of 70 percent on weekends and 29 percent

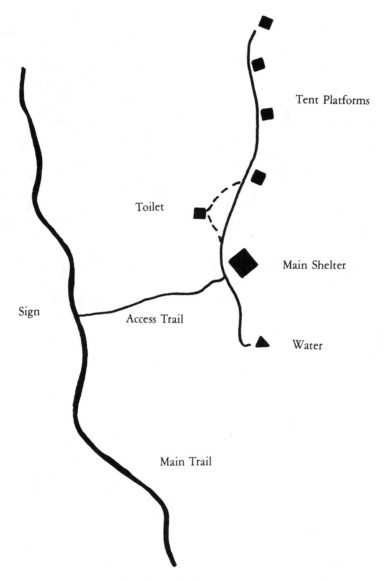

Fig. 9.3. Forest Service, USDA, suggested linear layout of a back-country camping area.

on weekdays.[3] It would be economic folly to attempt to construct camping facilities to meet the peak demands that occur a few times a year. This would produce large, rambling, and empty campgrounds for the normal season. The costs of this pursuit would be ruinous; another solution to the peakload problem has therefore been adopted. The peakload, or overflow, campground is

Fig. 9.4. Peakload camps serve to satisfy the user who cannot find space in a regular campground.

provided to handle the crowds that cannot find a campsite in the forest or central campgrounds (see Fig. 9.4).

These overflow areas usually have portable facilities and a minimum of sanitary developments. Water is generally supplied by a tank trailer if at all, and the fireplaces are usually portable iron grilles. Pit toilets are provided, but are centrally located to minimize the number required. Occasionally, picnic grounds are planned so that they can be turned into peakload campgrounds when the need arises. This planning allows for better facilities and a more permanent development. Of course, this approach assumes that the peak demand for camping does not coincide with the demand for picnicking; therefore, the doubling up of the picnic and the peakload sites can be done successfully only in limited locations.

The degree of site modification for peakload camps varies widely and does not parallel the use. Generally, peakload camps are set up in an old field or clearing that is near the regular campgrounds. Sometimes, much site modification is done on a small area to provide for intense use. Native vegetation is planned to provide shade and barriers. Occasionally, open areas are mowed during periods of light use in order to maintain the grass cover and to keep out volunteer trees. In specific locations where very heavy use occurs sporadically, log barriers are constructed to limit motor vehicles to designated areas.

The advantages of peakload camps are site protection and user satisfaction during periods of extraordinary use. If the landowner allowed the indiscriminate locating of campsites, he would be violating the definition of a campground. Facilities for fire and sanitation must be provided in a campground. These things would be unavailable or inconvenient in unrestricted camping. The area would be subject to serious deterioration and the visitors would be dissatisfied with the available facilities and the location of their camping neighbors. New trails would be formed indiscriminately and damage to the vegetation would occur over a widespread area. Although the peakload camps often do not provide a pleasant view, they still satisfy the user under the circumstances for which they were designed. Campers, fishermen, and hunters generally understand why they have been directed to a peakload camp and make the best of it.

Occasionally, some campers prefer to use the peakload camp instead of the forest or central camp because of their unusual equipment, such as buses and trucks, and their dislike for the more formal campsites. Many recreational vehicle owners prefer to park in the middle of a mowed field. This is particularly evident in areas of high humidity, large insect population, and where electrical hookups permit air conditioning. The peakload camp should be held for over-flow crowds if it is to serve its purpose. The other campgrounds should be flexible enough to handle special camping equipment and to provide for various camping tastes.

Peakload camps are usually located near the campgrounds they serve; however, they should not be placed closer to the attraction than are the regular camps.

LONG-TERM CAMPS

Long-term camps are designed to provide accommodations for campers who wish to stay in an area for more than two weeks. People who stay in one location can be centered in one area that is specially equipped to meet their requirements. By grouping the long-term campers in one place, the administrator keeps them from tying up the short-term camping facilities.

Cabins, tent cabins, truck campers, and camping trailers are often used for long-term camping.[13] The standard canvas tent is being replaced by these other facilities. The demand for more conveniences increases as the camper's stay lengthens and thereby raises development costs. Hot showers and laundry facilities are needed for maintenance of personal health standards and ready access to stores is needed to keep the group supplied during the prolonged stay.

Public agencies usually attempt to serve the greatest number of people that they can; therefore, they tend to avoid establishing long-term camps. Campers who intend to stay in a camping area for a long period of time give a predictable income to a private campground. Because of this, private capital is interested in providing long-term camps to users on a profit-motive basis.[20,30] Generally, rate schedules established for private campgrounds decrease in proportion to length of stay.[3,22] The long-term discount rate that is commonly followed sets the weekly rate at six-day charges and the monthly rate at three-week charges. Research suggests that while seasonal discounts raise the occupancy level, they can reduce seasonal income.

Some eastern states have removed rental cabins from their parks and placed a time limit on the camping areas in an attempt to cut down on long-term camping on tax-supported land. States can no longer justify expenditures for long-term campers while many more short-term campers cannot find adequate facilities. Federal recreation managers are encouraging private capital to meet the need of the long-term camper by the use of the lease and concession agreements. The Forest Service is now attempting to stop undercutting the private campground by raising camping fees up as high as eight dollars per day. Also, the Forest Service is expanding its permit program to encourage private capital in the development of resorts, campgrounds, marinas, and other recreational uses of the national forest system.

Site modification is usually heavy around long-term camps because of the need for paving roads, trails, and living areas. Traffic control and artificial materials are obvious to the user.[4] Occasionally, long-term camps are established under more natural conditions; however, the general rule calls for many services and facilities. Flush toilets, utility hookups, and running water are necessary for this class of campground. Garbage collection, laundry facilities, hot water, and hot showers are provided. Campgrounds appealing to long-term campers have higher investments in recreation and convenience facilities.[3]

A major attraction is usually near a long-term camp. Although the users want to relax and live out of doors, they generally need something to maintain their interest in an area. Extensive scenic attractions, good fishing, or boating are some things that will help to make a long-term camp a success. Long-term campgrounds near major attractions such as the Atlantic seaboard attract large numbers of high-participation campers with a large investment in equipment. Some situations permit the owner to leave the camping vehicle stored on the campground property and to have it moved into place on a campsite during the owner's visits.

Long-term campgrounds do raise some questions. Is the campground just a way to circumvent zoning restrictions? Will the population density be too high when all planned units are occupied? Are the water and sewage facilities complete and the roads dedicated? Will the entire area become a transient, rural slum polluting the environment while the purchasers are left to face the problems?

TRAVELER'S CAMPS

Campers en route between their destination and home often stop overnight at camps that have been designed to serve the traveler. A large percentage of campers stay at traveler's camps at some time during their trip because these camps provide cheap and convenient accommodations.

Money saving and convenience are the major advantages afforded the users of these camps. Land managers recognize the values of having the traveling campers located together for safety, sanitation, and regulation. However, there is a question concerning federal and state development of traveler's camps. Should the public agencies get into an outdoor motel business? Many western states and the federal government do provide this service to en route campers. Traveler's camps have proved to be a successful venture for private capital if they have good locations along a major highway and in an area where campers are traveling past.

Traveler's camps should provide the minimum facilities that the traveler needs to spend a night and to prepare his meals. Toilets, water, fireplaces, and tables are the usual facilities found at these camps, although some of the more popular franchised areas have swimming pools and recreation buildings. Maintenance of these areas is a larger problem than it is for other classes of campgrounds because of the rapid change of occupants. Although they permit tenting in most cases, en route campgrounds have developed in favor of the recreational vehicle. Site modification is usually very heavy because of the heavy use and smaller space requirements. No attempt should be made to maintain the natural setting. The units can be crowded together to 30-foot centers. Paving should cover much of the area that is to carry vehicular or foot traffic. Screening vegetation and barriers should be used to compensate for the lack of space in giving privacy and in protecting the site from excessive wear. [20] In general, the traveler's camp does not offer a scenic or recreation appeal. It provides overnight accommodations and should be located so that it does not become a peakload camp handling the overflow crowds from nearby campgrounds.

Traveler's camps should be located adjacent to a major throughway in as pleasant surroundings as possible. Many small-town chambers of commerce in New England and elsewhere have constructed traveler's camps to encourage en route campers to spend a day in their town. States are incorporating traveler's camps into their statewide recreation plans to encourage tourists to visit the state's attractions.

APPLICATION OF CLASSIFICATION SYSTEM

As mentioned earlier in the chapter, this classification system of campgrounds should serve only as a guide in campground development. It has already had wide distribution through Forest Service publications and is generally accepted as a guide in many areas. Any attempt to force every campground entirely into one or another category would defeat the flexibility inherent in this system. A system of campground classification designed to accommodate every different interpretation of needs would be so cumbersome as to be completely useless except in classrooms.

Each situation requires its own solution in campground development. Quite often, the manager inherits an existing campground that is completely inadequate to meet the demands of the campers. He must scrape together enough money to patch up facilities that will serve the number of users without much concern for their desires. When the time comes that the manager can begin to follow a development plan that refers to forest camps, central camps, and overflow camps, he is too saddled with the "Topsey-style" monster that just grew.

Many of the eastern states have attempted to combine the forest camp with the central camp. That is, they have attempted to preserve the natural beauty of the forest surrounding the family camping unit while placing the units on 50-foot centers. Presently, this method is proving to be popular in the eastern states where extremely heavy use dictates crowded conditions. Many of these areas are relatively new and have not shown how well they will maintain the forest atmosphere under such heavy use. As dust, mud, and dying vegetation force the managers to turn to artificial measures such as paving and barrier plantings, these campgrounds probably will move into the central campground category. Necessity has fathered some very interesting innovations in campground layout. The loops and turns of the interior campground roads provided many wasted sites because they did not provide vehicular access to each isolated spot. Also, steep hills along an interior road had previously prevented the establishment of camping units there. Now these areas have become "walk-in" camping units. The cars are parked in a designated spot and campers walk approximately 100 yards to their unit. This walk-in unit enables the manager to make use of these corners that are unaccessible by automobile. Also, it allows the camper to get a little way off from his neighbors so that he can have some isolation.

Many campers wish to hike a couple of miles into an isolated camp that has many of the facilities associated with an improved camping unit. They want to make an attempt at roughing it only in the fact that they must hike in to the area. Once there, they want the comforts afforded by the forest-type campground. Attempts to meet this demand are most notable on the West Coast. Certain campgrounds are operated in such a way that the campers leave their equipment and supplies at the manager's office. The equipment and supplies are trucked over maintenance roads to the camping unit while the campers are hiking in. This system completely ignores the wandering college-age adventurer who is certainly camping under primitive conditions while tied to the modern modes of transportation. Indiscriminate camping done with recreational vehicles does not fit into any of the listed categories even though it is done in large numbers. Readers should keep in mind that this text is classifying campgrounds and not camping lifestyles.

Although each campground must be designed to meet the demands of its users, it must be based upon the sound principles of safety, comfort, convenience, economics, and conservation. It is the primary responsibility of the campground designer to provide camping units that are as safe as possible from hazards.

CAMPGROUND DEVELOPMENT

Camping Units

A camping unit is an area that has been developed to accommodate a party of campers. Usually a group of eight campers is the maximum design load for a camping unit. The three major purposes for a camping unit are:

1. To provide for the comfort, living, and activity requirements of the campers.
2. To provide the camper with a planned area for fires and sanitation.
3. To provide definite use and traffic patterns within the campgrounds.

Although there is some variation among formal camping units, there is an overall similarity in their composition and arrangement. The usual camping unit is 25 feet wide and 30 feet long with a buffer zone surrounding it. The buffer zones are strips of woodland that have been left to provide privacy and to help protect the soil and vegetation from destruction. The width of the buffer zones between camping units varies from 25 feet in central camps to over 100 feet in forest camps.

In order for a camping unit to provide adequate accommodations, it must contain a stove or fireplace, a table with benches, a tent or trailer space, and a parking space.[29] Water and sanitation are major facilities that affect the location of camping units within a campground. Water and sanitation, however, generally are not provided within each camping unit except when trailer hookups are provided.

The interior of the camping unit should be planned to provide ease of movement from table to tent, car, or fireplace (see Fig. 9.5). The table is the center of camping activity and should be placed between the parking area and the tent space. Campsites with the facilities grouped together around a central point are preferred to those that have the table, fireplace, tent pad, and spur spread over a large area or in a line.[6]

Tables and fireplaces have changed little since their design evolved in the pre–World War II period.[31] The tables should be made of pressure-treated wood, fiberglass and galvanized steel tubes, or concrete, and bolted into place

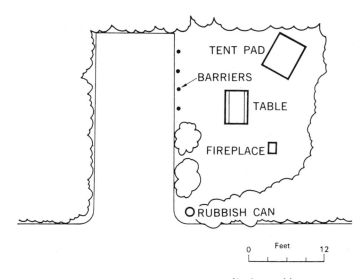

Fig. 9.5. Camping unit layout perpendicular parking spur.

to prevent movement. Concrete piers should be used under each leg to assure that the bench remains level if the table is not chained to a pad. Fireplaces generally should be of the small, low design. They do not need to be the elaborate stone structures that were built by the Civilian Conservation Corps prior to 1940. The fireplace should be placed so that it is downwind from the tent and table during periods of the prevailing winds. Fireplaces have become secondary cooking places for the many campers who use gasoline pressure stoves or other cooking devices such as charcoal grills.

The need for the disposal of burning charcoal in camping and picnic areas has led to the use of concrete rings for containing the discarded charcoal. These concrete rings are two to three feet in diameter and twelve to eighteen inches high. They are placed in contact with mineral soil so as to provide a safe receptacle for burning material. Campers have accepted the use of the charcoal ring. In many cases, they prefer to build their fires in the safe confines of the ring instead of the fireplaces. Some park administrators state that they are replacing fireplaces with the concrete "firerings" in new sites to save on development costs.

A camping unit should be oriented so as to take advantage of any scenic view and of the land conformation. Besides increasing the attractiveness of the unit, judicious orientation minimizes the need for major site modification by heavy, earth-moving equipment. Site modification is usually necessary to provide the required comfort levels. The forest canopy should be opened to allow for the admission of sunlight and to provide for air movement. The deep shady forest generally does not provide man with a good living atmosphere for camping.

Tents, clothes, and other materials are wet in the morning and will require sunlight to dry out. Smoke, gasoline fumes, cooking odors, and other smells will linger under a closed canopy that does not allow for the proper air drainage. Sunlight will dry the campsites and cause convection currents in the air that will carry off the collected fumes and replace them with fresh air. Care should be taken not to overdo the daylighting since studies show a positive relationship between canopy closure and desirability. Those sites with more shade are more desirable than those with less shade. This was one of the most important factors in camping-unit selection by campers participating in a study of microsite effects on campers preferences.[6] The effect of shade, however, on camping-unit desirability becomes insignificant when water views are involved. Campers desire to camp within sight of water when possible.[15] Enough trees should be left to provide adequate shade and to maintain the natural setting of the camping unit. About 60 to 80 percent canopy closure is needed to produce the optimum shade on camping units that have surfaces reinforced with gravel, paving, mulching, or similar materials. Campgrounds with natural surfaces should have more area in sunlight to encourage minor vegetation growth and soil drying. The remaining or "leave" trees should be chosen for their apparent health, size, location, and species, in that order of importance. On unreinforced sites where screening vegetation and ground cover is being encouraged, the large canopy trees should be considered for removal so as to permit more sunlight to strike the forest floor.

The area within the camping unit should undergo a periodic clean-up to remove dangerous snags or diseased trees that threaten the safety of the camper. In some cases, organic litter and vegetation should be removed to reduce the possibility of fire spread. The litter, however, protects the soil from compaction and helps to prevent site deterioration.[16] In most cases of heavy use, the ground litter should be augmented instead of reduced. Sawdust, wood chips, or shredded bark is frequently spread over the camping unit to protect the soil from wear and to help keep down the dust.

Although camping units should be on slopes of less than 10 percent, they are seldom level enough for proper tent or table pads; some mechanical grading must therefore, be done.[27] Level camping units are more desirable than sloping ones if they are well drained.[7] In some of the more formal camping units, the tent site is designated and the spot modified to provide tie downs and a level pad. The specified tent location centralizes wear in one spot that can receive special treatment. Many state parks and private campgrounds do not have designated tent sites within the camping units and permit the tent to be set up anywhere within a loosely defined area. This practice leads to damage of all the trees and vegetation within the unit.

Each camping unit should include a parking area for at least one car and, in most cases, for a trailer. Since camping units generally are designed to accommodate one family, it is usually assumed that one parking space is adequate.

However, approximately one-fourth of single-family camping units is occupied by two or more families even when empty units are available.[11] Occasional units should be designed as multifamily camping units; the majority of camping units, however, should be operated as single-family units with one parking space.

The car should be parked within the camping unit on a gravel or paved parking spur that is at least 12 feet wide and at least 30 feet long. The spur should be located so that it will provide the campers with easy movement between the car and the table. Log or stone barriers should be placed so as to restrict the car to the parking spurs.

Proper placement and construction of the parking spurs are very important considerations in the establishment of safe and efficient camping units. Generally, the parking spurs are located perpendicular to a two-lane road and at a 45-degree angle to a one-lane road. The perpendicular spurs are designed as head-in parking areas, while the 45-degree spurs are either head-in or back-in parking places (see Fig. 9.6).

Evolution of safer and more efficient camping-unit design is continuing to take place to meet the needs of the campers. Back-in parking spurs are becoming the most popular design in newly constructed camping units. The large increase of trailer campers has created a need for larger parking spurs. The minimum size standard for a trailer parking spur is a width of 14 feet and a length of 55 feet.[26,27] They should be of the back-in or of the newer drive-through design. The drive-through parking area is a small loop just off the campground road. It allows a car and trailer to enter at one end, park parallel to the campground road, and exit at the other end of the loop. The exit end of the parking loop serves as a back-in parking spur for the car while the trailer remains set up for camping. A pull-off site is a modified drive-through site that is used where space is limited but trailer camping is expected. It is designed for the right-hand side of the road so that the trailer and vehicle serve as a screen between the campground road and the camping unit.

The users of recreational vehicles do not need a tent site but they do want to back their pickup trucks and trailers further from the road to obtain more privacy so that 55-foot spurs should be included to accommodate the larger vehicles if they are to be permitted in the campground. Trailer doors open on the right-hand side of the trailer; therefore, camping units should be designed so that the door faces away from the road and into the camping unit.[27] Tree limbs should be trimmed to allow clearance for the trailers.[26]

Camping Layout

The campground should be designed, or laid out, to provide for the comfort and enjoyment of the user, for efficiency of maintenance, and for the preservation of natural beauty. The campground layout is concerned with the place-

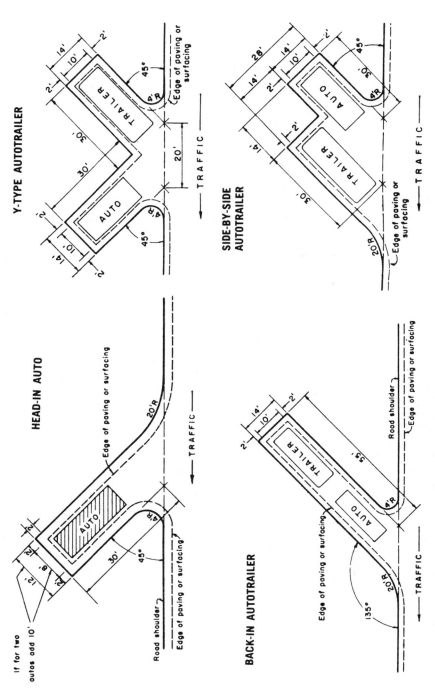

Fig. 9.6. Details of parking spurs (U.S. Forest Service).

149

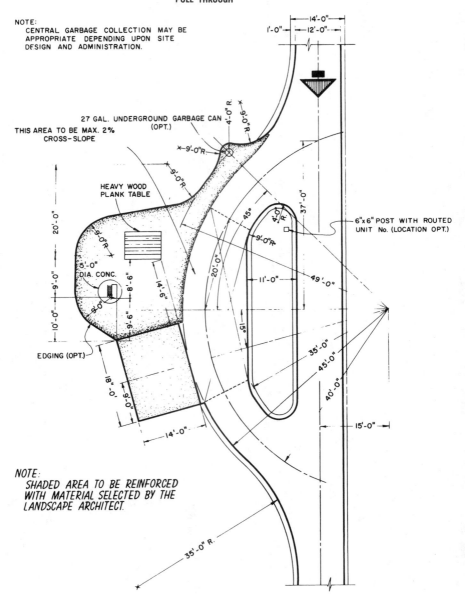

PULL THROUGH

NOTE:
CENTRAL GARBAGE COLLECTION MAY BE
APPROPRIATE DEPENDING UPON SITE
DESIGN AND ADMINISTRATION.

27 GAL. UNDERGROUND GARBAGE CAN
(OPT.)

THIS AREA TO BE MAX. 2%
CROSS-SLOPE

HEAVY WOOD
PLANK TABLE

5'-0"
DIA. CONC.

EDGING (OPT.)

6"x 6" POST WITH ROUTED
UNIT No. (LOCATION OPT.)

NOTE:
SHADED AREA TO BE REINFORCED
WITH MATERIAL SELECTED BY THE
LANDSCAPE ARCHITECT.

Fig. 9.6. (Cont.)

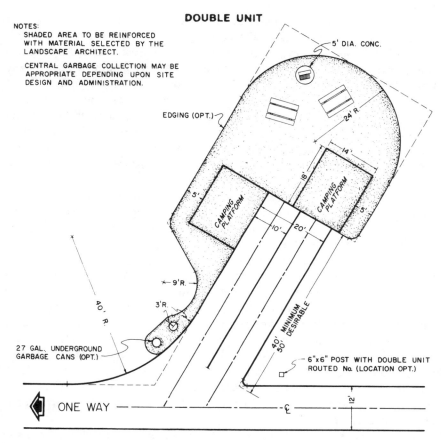

Fig. 9.6. (Cont.)

ment of camping units, roads and trails, sanitation facilities, and water supply. There are many kinds of campers; therefore, the campground layout should be designed for the campers who will use it.[26] Site selection and predicted user groups should be considered carefully in the planning stages that are discussed in Part I of this book.

The proper location of individual camping units in forming a campground is necessary in central, forest, and long-term camps. Most of the requirements are the same for the central and the forest camps except for spacing. Long-term camps are basically either central or forest camps depending on their location and design.[4] At least 100 feet should separate the camping units except in central camps where they are set together with 50 feet between center points.[27] The American Camping Association recommends that the number of camping units be limited to three per acre.[1] However, the placement of four to seven camping units per acre is more common throughout the country.

The centers of the units should be placed at least 50 feet from the edge of campground roads and at least 100 feet from streams or lake shores. People following their desire to camp as close to water as possible are causing serious damage to many shoreline areas; therefore, camping units should be placed away from the water as much as possible within the designated campground. This is not contrary to the doctrine of user satisfaction even though campers indicate a desire to be next to the water because keeping the camping away from the water helps to protect the waterfront quality for everyone's enjoyment. A view of water is a major condition in camping unit selection by visitors. Every effort should therefore be made to arrange the units so that water vistas are maximized. Extra vegetation thinning can be used to increase vistas of the water. The units should be oriented in such a way that the campers in one unit do not travel through other units to reach the major attractions. In most cases, the actual location of the individual units should take place after the internal campground roads have been located.

Campground roads are classified as either entrance or internal roads. Entrance roads are designed to allow movement between the major highways and the campground. The entrance roads are an important part of the campground setting because they present the first and last impressions of the campground they serve. These roads must be designed so as to allow reasonably rapid travel at the same time that they provide the proper setting expected for a campground. They should be well identified by signs, should be two lanes in width, and should be surfaced with crushed stone or paved. The sharpest curve permitted in an entrance road should have a 50-foot radius of curve. the turnoff from the main road onto the entrance road should have a radius of curve that is greater than 100 feet.

Entrance roads should be marked with a sign that is clearly visible from 300 feet on a main highway or from 150 feet on a forest road. Deceleration lanes should be constructed along the main highway for 150 feet in both directions from the intersection.[1]

The internal roads of a campground should be one-way loops whenever possible. Traffic flow and topography will require some two-directional roads; these two-lane roads, however, should be kept to a minimum for safety to the camper and for lower costs to the builder. The roads should be laid out in gentle loops that have 200-feet minimum diameters to allow for the placement of units and facilities within the loop. One-way loops permit better utilization of existing grades, and allow flexibility in placing units and central facilities. Occasionally, an internal road will end in a turn-around area. In this case, the road should be at least one and a half lanes wide with intervisible turnouts to allow for passing. Internal roads should be hard surfaces or covered with crushed stone to make them usable in wet weather and to prevent blowing dust in dry weather.

Speeding automobiles have become a problem in some campgrounds. Managers have reported success at controlling speeders by making the loop roads two-way and by planting trees right at the road edge. These actions tend to slow down automobiles by introducing a hazard factor to the driver. However, any relation between the net gain in hazard reduction in the campground obtained by two-way loop roads and edge planting is questionable.

Internal campground roads should be kept at least 200 feet from the water's edge. Access to the water should be provided by a boat-landing road if necessary and also by well-marked trails. Formal trails are an important part of the campground layout because they channel the people's movement within the area. A well-marked trail system will assist the camper to find his way around; it will help to keep the campers on given routes and out of other people's camping units; and it will aid in preventing the widespread destruction of the campground setting by keeping the trampling feet in the designated routes of travel. Admittedly, some campers will take short cuts or wander all over the other camping units, but the majority of campers will be eager to use a well-designed trail system within the campground. In areas of unusually heavy use such as around wash houses or toilets, the trails will require surfacing to prevent soil wear and to eliminate muddy spots. Chapter 12 has a more complete discussion of trails.

The location of the water supply and the sanitary facilities is a critical decision in campground layout. The high costs of installation and maintenance must be balanced against user satisfaction and safety. Sanitary facilities are more often criticized than any other part of a campground.[9] The Forest Service considers one outlet to be the minimum water supply for every four camping units.[27] A nonthreaded, self-closing faucet should be placed within 150 feet of each camping unit if water under pressure is provided. Also, some threaded faucets should be available at intervals for fire protection. Small or remote campgrounds can be served adequately by hand pumps or springs. Some peakload camps have water supplied at pickup stations by tank trucks. However, this is unsatisfactory except as an emergency step in the overflow camping areas where people should stay for only one night.

Water under pressure encourages excessive use.[29] Standing water around faucets will quickly turn the area into an unsightly and unhealthy mess. Water should be drained away from faucets by underground drains or surface paving. Sanitary water disposal becomes a problem wherever water is available to a large number of campers. Too often, no facilities are supplied for the disposal of wash water or dishwater so the water is thrown into the brush around the camping unit. The soil in the camping area becomes saturated with chemicals and grease contained in discarded dishwater. Aeration and normal infiltration of water in the soil are blocked, causing damage to the protective vegetation. Under severe conditions, waste water causes sanitation problems as well as aesthetic devaluation. To cope with the problem of waste-water disposal, slop sinks should be conveniently placed throughout campgrounds that receive heavy use.

Liquid-waste drains or slop sinks should discharge into the general sewer system if one exists. Where sewer lines are not available, the slop sink should drain directly into a seepage pit that has been constructed exclusively for liquid waste from washing and cooking. This type of disposal needs the approval of the local health authority.[29]

Another major consideration in campground layout is that of refuse disposal. Some ranger districts are already operating municipal-type garbage trucks.[13] Each camper produces approximately 1½ pounds of refuse per day.[29] This refuse must be collected and disposed of as part of a daily maintenance operation.

The four reasons for refuse removal that are listed in the forest Service manual on recreation management are:[32]

1. To eliminate conditions favorable to disease-spreading insects and rodents.
2. To minimize obnoxious odors.
3. To prevent the pollution of the water supply.
4. To prevent the defilement of natural beauty.

The campground layout generally includes a refuse can for each camping unit. The use of one can could be stretched to serve two camping units, but this practice is not recommended for areas of heavy use. The refuse container should be located at the front edge of the camping unit or adjacent to the road so that it will be accessible for pickup as well as convenient for the users. The conventional 20- or 30-gallon galvanized cans with tight-fitting lids are usually satisfactory refuse containers. These can are watertight, nonabsorbent, and easily washed. Disposable plastic liners are available at an approximate cost of 10 cents each and have become popular for home use. The plastic liners aid in maintaining cleanliness and reducing the need for frequent washing of the containers.[34] In campgrounds where bears or dogs are a nuisance, some modifications must be made to prevent the animals from scattering the refuse. The containers should be made of a heavier gauge metal and they should be securely anchored to the ground. Specially constructed swinging lids help to block entrance of the animals into the cans. In recent years, the use of centrally located dumpsters has been tried in place of individual unit trash cans. Dumpster use appears to be successful in areas accommodating experienced campers or nature-oriented campers. Most people seem to be willing to carry their refuse to the dumpster if the trip is not out of the way. One dumpster can serve one loop of up to 25 units if it is placed properly. The best place for the dumpster appears to be on the trail near the toilet building.

A campground should be laid out so that there is a toilet within a 300-foot radius of every camp and one toilet for each sex for every ten units. Although some state health codes require the distance between a camping unit and a toilet to be less than 200 feet, private investors prefer to stretch the minimum distance to 500 feet in order to provide more elaborate and therefore more expensive facilities.[10,19] The location of toilets was an important factor in camping-unit selection. Campers prefer to be away from the toilet house but still accessible to it. A study by Cordell and James discovered that the optimum distance between toilets and camping units appeared to be 200 feet with a definite decline in desirability with decreasing distance.[6] This study agreed with others that the area within 50 feet of the toilet building is considered to be undesirable to almost everyone. Six types of sewage disposal systems that are used in campgrounds are:

1. Simple sanitary pits.
2. Watertight, pump-out pits.
3. Chemical tanks.
4. Composting system.
5. Septic tanks.
6. Sewage treatment plants.

The sanitary pit, pump-out pit, and compostor are satisfactory where use is light or running water is not available.[32] The privies are acceptable if they are kept orderly, clean, and relatively odorless. Although the privies are cheaper to construct than flush toilets, they are more expensive to maintain. Chemical tank toilets should be used in places where pit toilets cannot be used because of possible high-water conditions. Composting toilets can be used where water is scarce and use is relatively light.

Flush-type toilets require an adequate water supply, soil conditions that are favorable for dispersal afield, and heavy enough use to justify their costs. Specific details on sanitation facilities are given in the next chapter. Toilets should be well marked and easily located. Barrier plantings are desirable to screen the toilet structures; however, the screening should not hide the buildings from view.

REFERENCES

1. Anonymous. 1962. *Tent and Trailer Sites.* American Camping Association, Bradford Woods, Indiana.
2. Anonymous. 1977. Americans Spend $160 Billion on Recreation. In *U.S. News and World Report*, May 23, 1977, pp. 63–64.
3. Brown, T., and Wilkins, B. 1972. *A Study of Campground Businesses in New York State.* Department of Natural Resources, Cornell University. 22 pages.

4. Burch, William R. Jr. 1964. Two Concepts for Guiding Recreation Management Decisions. In *Journal of Forestry*, vol. 62, no. 10, pp. 707–711.

5. Burke, H.D., and Rushmore, F.H. 1963. *A Planning Guide for Outdoor Recreation in Washington County, Maine*. Department of Public Information and Central Services, University of Maine, Orono, Maine.

6. Cordell, H.K. and James, G.A. 1972. *Visitor Preferences for Certain Physical Characteristics of Developed Campsites*. Southeast Forest Experimental Station. Forest Service Research Paper Se-100, Atlanta, Georgia. 21 pages.

7. Etykorn, P. 1964. Leisure and Camping: The Social Meaning of a Form of Public Recreation. In *Sociology and Social Research*, vol. 49, no. 1, pp. 76–89.

8. Fay, S.C., S.K. Rice, and S.P. Berg. 1977. *Guidelines for Design and Location of Overnight Backcountry Facilities*. Northeastern Forest Experiment Station, Durham, New Hampshire. 22 pages.

9. Fine, I.V., and Werner, E.E. 1960. *Camping in State Parks and Forests in Wisconsin*, vol. 1, no. 3. University of Wisconsin, Madison. 18 pages.

10. Halcomb, Carl J., Howard E. Conklin, and Fred E. Winch Jr. 1963. *Opportunities for Private Campgrounds as an Alternate Use of Land*. Agriculture Extension Service V.P.I. Circular No. 792. Blacksburg, Va. 16 pages.

11. Hopkins, Walter S. 1965. Outdoor Recreation on Small Woodlots. In *Proceedings of the 62nd Annual Meeting of Association of Southern Agricultural Workers*. Dallas, Tex. February 1.

12. Hultsman, J. and R.L. Cottrell. 1978. *Camp Unit Design Guidelines*. Tennessee Valley Authority. Golden Pond, Ky. 21 pages.

13. Hutchinson, S. Blair. 1962. *Recreation Opportunities and Problems in the National Forests of the Intermountain Region*. Intermountain Forest and Range Experimental Station. Paper 66. Ogden, Utah. 33 pages.

14. LaPage, W.F. and D.P. Ragain. 1971. *A Second Look at the Heavy Half of the Camping Market*. Northeast Forest Experiment Station, Upper Darby, Penn. USDA Forest Service Research Paper NE-196. 9 pages.

15. Lime, D.W. 1971. *Factors Influencing Campground Use in the Superior National Forest of Minnesota*. North Central Forest Experiment Station, St. Paul, Minn. USDA Forest Service Research Paper NC-60. 18 pages.

16. Lutz, H.J. 1945. Soil Conditions on Picnic Grounds on Public Forest Parks. In *Journal of Forestry*, vol. 43, pp. 121–127.

17. Marquardt, R., A. McGann, J. Ratlift, and J. Routson. 1972. The Cognitive Dissonance Model as a Predictor of Customer Satisfaction Among Camper Owners. In *Journal of Leisure Research*, no. 4, pp. 275–283.

18. Merriam, L., A. Mills, C. Ramsey, P. West, T. Brown, and K. Wald. 1972. The Campers in Minnesota State Parks and Forests. In *Agriculture Experiment Station Bulletin*, vol. 510. University of Minnesota. 19 pages.

19. Ohio Department of Health. 1964. *Camp Sanitation Laws, Regulations, and Recommendations*. 22 pages.

20. Outdoor Recreation Resources Review Commission. 1962. *Paying for Recreation facilities*. ORRRC Study Report 12. Government Printing Office, Washington, D.C. 88 pages.

21. Pennsylvania Department of Forests and Waters. 1969. *State Park Planning and Guidelines*. Bureau of State Parks, Harrisburg, Penn. 90 pages.

22. Riedsel, Wilson. 1969. *Developing Campgrounds for Recreational Vehicles*. State of Wisconsin. Bureau of Commercial Recreation. Madison Publishing Division, Appleton, Wis. 23 pages.

23. Shafer, Elwood L. Jr. 1969. *The Average Camper Who Doesn't Exist*. Northeast Forest Experiment Station. Forest Service Research Paper NE-142. Upper Darby, Penn. 27 pages.

24. Silka, Stephen. 1973. Being a Modern Backpacker Means Owning the Earth. In *Philadelphia Inquirer*, July, 15, p. 7E.

25. U.S. Department of the Interior. 1979. *The Third Nationwide Outdoor Recreation Plan: The Assessment.* Washington, D.C. 264 pages.
26. U.S. Forest Service. 1962. Forest Recreation for Profit. *USDA Agriculture Information Bulletin*, no. 265. Government Printing Office, Washington, D.C. 26 pages.
27. ————. 1963. *Recreation Management.* Title 2300. *Forest Service Handbook.* Government Printing Office, Washington, D.C. 26 pages.
28. ————. 1973. *References for Recreation Development.* Region 8, Atlanta, Ga.
29. U.S. Public Health Service. 1965. *Environmental Health Practice in Recreational Areas.* P.H.S. Publication No. 1195. Government Printing Office, Washington, D.C. 134 pages.
30. Wagar, J. Allan. 1963. *Campgrounds for Many Tastes.* Intermountain Forest and Range Experiment Station Research Paper Int.—6, Ogden, Utah. 10 pages.
31. Wagar, J.V.K. 1946. Services and Facilities for Forest Recreation. In *Journal of Forestry*, vol. 44, pp. 883–887.

10

Picnic Areas

INTRODUCTION

The word picnic is so much a part of the everyday language that it rarely needs definition. As just about every American knows, a picnic is an outdoor meal where the members of the party consume the food they brought along with them. Commonly, a picnic infers a trip away from home and not dinner on the patio. Advertisements still picture a picnic as a basket and blanket set on the ground near a sports car by a young, cigarette-smoking couple. Although picnickers may or may not smoke cigarettes, they are not epitomized by the young couple. Rather, picnickers tend to be family or organized groups that use tables and other facilities in a developed recreation area.

Although picnicking does take place endemically throughout the forests and along the roads, it is generally considered to be an activity requiring developed facilities. Developed facilities not only add to the convenience, safety, and enjoyment of the users, they also serve to keep the people grouped together in places designed to accommodate them. This centralizes wear, reduces soil and water pollution, consolidates the rubbish, and facilitates cleanup and maintenance.

If researchers do not count the sport of "just relaxing," they should name picnicking as the number-one forest recreation activity. The Third Nationwide Outdoor Recreation Plan states that 72 percent of the respondents to its 1977 survey have participated in picnicking.[11] Table 10.1 shows that picnicking has been the most popular activity in most of the Department of the Interior outdoor recreation surveys. The forest setting is ideal for picnicking in that it is shady, pleasant, and in some cases quiet. Most certainly, it is different from the dining room. Picnicking is classed as a day-use type of activity. That is, the users participate during a portion of the day or evening and do not require overnight accommodations. Actually, many publicly administered picnic areas have established closing times. In areas where recreation water for swimming or boating is not plentiful, picnicking is the dominant day-use activity. When water for recreation is available, picnicking becomes co-dominant with such activities as swimming, boating, fishing, and water skiing.[9]

Table 10.1. Comparison of Rank Order Popularity of Outdoor Recreation Activities from Four National Recreation Surveys.*

	1960	1965	1972	1977
First	picnicking	picnicking	picnicking	picnicking
Second	swimming	swimming	fishing	swimming
Third	fishing	fishing	swimming	fishing
Fourth	biking	biking	camping	camping

*The Third Nationwide Outdoor Recreation Plan.

Most successful picnic areas are within 30 miles of a population center so that people can make the one-way trip in less than 45 minutes. [4,5] Many states are keeping this travel distance in mind when planning new day-use recreation facilities by striving to build a park within 25 miles of every citizen.

THE PICNIC UNIT

The picnic unit is approximately 400 square feet in size and is oriented around the table. In addition to the table, a picnic unit usually contains a fireplace of some sort and a refuse container. Water supply, sanitation facilities, and a parking spot are located nearby to the picnic unit. When many units are placed together to form a large picnic ground, fireplaces are not included with every unit because most people prefer to bring prepared foods or to do their cooking on gas stoves or charcoal grills.

The table should have the seats attached and should be made from durable materials. Although pressure-treated lumber costs more than untreated lumber, it lasts so much longer that it is worth the extra cost. One argument for using nonpressure-treated wood is that costs are low enough to permit disposal of rotted tables. This sounds reasonable but does not work out in practice. Regardless of economics, the tables are not thrown away until they have passed through several seasons in poor condition, while the rot was getting extensive enough to justify disposal. Some managers do store and refinish picnic tables each winter to preserve them, but this is a costly and difficult way to protect wood.

Combination wood or fiberglass and metal tubing table-bench combinations are becoming popular in many larger picnic grounds. These are made of wood plank or fiberglass table tops and benches connected with metal tubing. They are being accepted by the user-public in many large recreation areas where they are commonly used in spite of the fact that metal tubing does not fit into the preconceived idea of naturalness that a picnicker might expect.

It is becoming more evident with heavy use of picnic areas that tables should be tied down so that they cannot be moved. That is because there is an area of concentrated wear that occurs around a picnic table. This wearing and compaction of the soil kill the overstory vegetation and open up the area to direct sunlight. In order to gain the benefit of shade, the users move the table out of the sunny spot and into the shade, thereby moving the circle of wear. By tying down the tables, the manager can stop the circle of wear from creeping outward and destroying the shade-producing vegetation in widening areas.

The idea of fastening down picnic tables has been advocated for more than 25 years; however, it has been resisted by some park managers for various reasons.[6] "Why shouldn't the users have the privilege of placing the tables where they want them?" is one argument against permanent table locations. Another one claims that it would cost money to build tie-down points and therefore the park could not afford to do it.

The latter argument can be summarily dismissed by stating that the park management cannot afford not tying down tables if it wishes to protect the quality of the area. The former point of public privilege requires more tact. After all, the users are either paying customers or taxpayers. Either way, they have a right to demand that their needs be fulfilled. The site must be protected from destruction as a service to all taxpayers including the immediate users or as a capital investment by the private owners. If the public wants the tables moved about, it is obvious that their needs have not been met in the layout design. All too often, the movement of tables is permitted as a cover-up for poor layout design or managerial laziness.

Fireplaces are not as important in picnic unit designs as they once were, but they cannot be eliminated. People still want the experience of the campfire. Some even prefer to cook in fireplaces, and other people need a place to dump burning charcoal. The waist-high, cast-iron charcoal grill is an ideal departure from the ground-level-oriented concept of picnic cooking. These grills are set at approximately waist height by a heavy metal post. In areas where use is limited to daytime, these grills are very satisfactory. However, if the area is to be available for evening use, it should have some fireplace structure at ground level. Visitors will tend to ignore the waist-high grills and build their campfires on the ground.[7]

The concrete fire rings (described in Chapter 9), that are made from sections of sewer pipe, have proved to be an inexpensive and easily installed container for fire. Each ring is more than 30 inches in diameter and weighs approximately 300 pounds. The walls are three inches thick and ten inches high. The size and weight of the concrete rings deter most picnickers from moving them.

The refuse container should be located near each table but in a position that facilitates its being emptied by the maintenance crews. These containers should meet the standards outlined for refuse containers in the chapter on sanitation (Chapter 14).

PICNIC GROUND LAYOUT

Picnic grounds must serve a variety of users under differing circumstances. Although picnicking is classed as a day-use activity, all participation is not limited to daylight hours. Certain users prefer picnics as a summer's evening activity even though most picnicking is done in the daytime in conjunction with other day-use activities. Picnicking is usually thought of as a destination type of use; with the increase in mobility, however, there has come an increase in en route picnicking that is reminiscent of the railroad tour stops of past decades.

The picnic ground should be situated in such a position as to afford the best view possible; however, it should be kept back at least 150 feet from the water's edge. This 150-foot buffer strip is recommended for two reasons. First, the presence of the picnic ground near the water will concentrate the use where it will do the greatest damage to the area's natural environment. Second, the picnic ground is kept back from the water's edge to discourage swimming in unauthorized areas. Gentle slopes of less than 20 percent are the most favorable sites for picnic areas.[10]

Well-marked trails are necessary to tie a recreation area together. Trails and stairs should be constructed when necessary to guide the user to such nearby attractions as the beach or the boat landing. In order to satisfy the differing needs of picnickers, this text recommends four general classifications of designed picnic grounds. They are (1) the general-use picnic grounds, (2) the reserved group area, (3) the forest cluster, and (4) the enroute picnic ground.

General-Use Picnic Ground

The general-use picnic ground probably is the most commonly designed picnic ground. It incorporates flexibility by catering to most forms of picnicking tastes. The unit density varies from 10 to 50 per acre; however, 15 tables per acre is the most favorable density in the general-use areas.[8] This is the maximum level that, under normal use, will permit growth of durable grasses.

The entrance road should divide into one-way loops that provide access to the parking lots. This keeps traffic flowing into and out of the lots in one direction only, thereby lessening the traffic danger to pedestrians. Service roads needed to maintain the area should be eight feet wide and should be closed to the public's vehicles so that they can serve as trails within the picnic grounds.

General-use picnic grounds should contain at least 100 units to make them efficient to operate and to provide enough flexibility.[13] Approximately half of the tables should be placed in groupings of twos or threes to serve small user groups that require more than one table. When units are coalesced into a grouping of tables, one fireplace or barbecue pit can serve the multiunit grouping.

Fig. 10.1. Picnic tables that were dragged into a semicircle around a bonfire indicate that the picnic ground layout did not satisfy the demand for evening campfire use.

Those users who desire to participate in evening picnicking around a bonfire will need to be considered in the layout design. People like to sit next to the fire in the evening. Since the ground around picnic fireplaces usually is dusty or muddy, people sit on the tables and attached benches. If the tables are not properly oriented to the fire, they will need to be turned before they are satisfactory for use as seats. Figure 10.1 shows a group of tables moved into a circle around a fireplace by evening users. True, tables that are permanently fastened down would be difficult to move, but the real purpose of designing a picnic area is not to frustrate the users but to anticipate their needs. The purpose of design layout is to give the user satisfactory and safe facilities while protecting the quality of the natural environment at the highest level compatible with use. Therefore, allowances should be made to satisfy the evening picnicker by arranging small groups of tables around fireplaces at a couple of points within the area.

The trails leading to the evening picnic sites should be clearly marked and well maintained. Since these units will be used after dark, they should be readily accessible from the parking lot. This makes night travel between the units and the parking lot less hazardous and also permits easy checking at closing time.

Drinking water is less essential to picnicking than it is to camping because

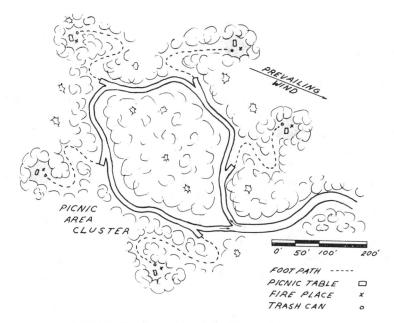

Fig. 10.2. Sketch of cluster picnic ground layout.

many picnickers come ready equipped for the meal and have a limited need for additional water.[12] They need little or no water for cooking or dishwashing. Therefore, the water outlets need not be very close to each unit. They should be placed so that every picnic unit is within 50 to 70 yards of drinking water. This method of placing water outlets differs from the method used in campground layouts in that it is based upon approximate radii and not directly upon the number of units.

The U.S. Public Health Service recommends that water be available within 150 feet of each picnic unit.[13] This is a specification that should be adhered to in a high-density, heavy-use area; however, the distance can be stretched to approximately 200 feet in less heavily used areas. All faucets should be self-closing and nonthreaded to conserve water. Exceptions to this faucet design should be made where strategically place outlets are designated for fire suppression purposes.

Since the turnover factor for picnic areas is estimated to be 1.5, more than one family or group will use each table on a given day.[1] Also, some administrators believe that the shorter-staying picnickers are not as careful to maintain the cleanliness of toilets and washhouses as are campers. The toilets can be as much as 500 feet away from picnic units and still meet the U.S. Public Health Service's suggested standards concerning distance.[13] Flush toilets should be used in all general-use areas whenever possible because of the heavier use from each unit and the larger number of units within the effective radius of each toilet facility.

The parking of the automobiles poses an interesting problem in layout design because of the importance placed upon nearness of the automobile to the picnic unit. Research by Burke shows that people want to picnic within 250 feet of their automobiles and that they will not use a table that requires a walk of more than 400 feet to reach it.[3] Investigations made in New York State indicate that the public desires nearness to the parking area above all other considerations.[6]

Observations of the recent phenomenon involving van and pickup-truck use in park areas substantiate the premise that nearness to the vehicle is of primary importance to many picnickers. Vans, cars, and pickup trucks of young and not so young adults often line the road edges and beach areas of recreation sites from Galveston Island to Lansing, Michigan and from the California beaches to the Jersey shore. Only legal restrictions or fee charges seem to limit the wave of young people picnicking on the hood of their vehicle to a cacaphony of loud music emanating from musical sound systems.

Parking facilities can provide a good control over usage of a picnic ground if parking can be restricted to the designated areas. The theory here is that one table in use means one car in the lot.[8] Unfortunately, there is the problem of parking on the grass, in the woods, and in other unauthorized places. Posts, high beams, ditches, curbs, and other barrier materials can be incorporated in the layout to help restrict vehicles to the roads and parking places. The barriers used to restrict vehicles should be as subtle and unobtrusive as possible.

Parking lots should be hard surfaced or graveled according to intensity of use. The costs for asphalt-surfaced lots are approximately one-third higher than for gravel-covered lots.[2] Asphalt-surfaced lots are preferable to graveled lots because the maintenance costs are lower and the user-satisfaction level is higher. Three hundred square feet of paving is recommended for each parking space within the lot. This permits room for parking, for backing up, and for maneuvering.

Two or three central parking lots, rather than several small ones, are recommended for general-use picnic areas. Narrow forested strips should be used to break up the central lot and prevent the larger lots from looking as though they belong to the suburban shopping center. If the wooded strips are oriented in an east-to-west direction, they will provide shade for much of the paved areas of the lot.

General-use picnic grounds must be planned to incorporate the collection of units into the natural beauty of the area. Cox points out that this incorporation requires a well thought out blending of man-made angles and lines with nature's curves and colors.[6] The designer must not confuse informality with haphazardness. The placement of each unit must be considered on the basis of individual site problems as well as on its part in the overall aesthetics and operation of the picnic ground.

The recreational use of parklands by mechanized young people is a legitimate form of picnicking even though it is somewhat different than the conventional style that has been accepted by park planners, managers, and others. Exclusion of that segment of users can usually be obtained by charging an admission fee or by overenthusiastic enforcement of petty rules. However, the exclusion of the mechanized youth from recreation areas raises the question of even-handedness. There is a shift taking place in the picnicking activity. The young people are more openly attached to the vehicle than are the classical picnickers who will walk a couple yards away from the car.

Design, planning, and management of recreation areas near population centers should consider the picnic trend of the mechanized youth. Eating and drinking at the immediate vehicle site while engaging in frisbee playing, lounging, or girl/boy watching is the style of picnicking that is gaining popularity. Parking-area control can accommodate that style by judicious changes in traffic flow, parking locations, and form of enforcement. One-way flow of traffic causes more even movement than two-way traffic. One-way traffic can reduce hazards and confusion. Also, one-way traffic better serves the pass-in-review aspect of mechanized picnicking. Peripheral parking provides better observation for the picnickers interested in seeing and being seen. Peripheral parking permits the manager to save some central open area for strolling, congregating, and playing. Contrary to what some managers think, the presence of law enforcement officers is welcomed by this group of recreationist. However, the confrontation atmosphere occurs so often that mutual distrust quickly builds up between these users and the management persons. Much of the confrontation occurs because of the lack of communication and recognition of other's rights.

Group Picnic Grounds

Group picnicking is a common activity throughout the United States and should be recognized as a need during recreation planning. These groups should be catered to by providing a separate area. The separate area for large groups has many advantages that should help the manager as well as the user group. First, the group has a place that was designed to accommodate a large group. Because of administrative policy, the area can be reserved during certain days for large organized groups or open to the general public during heavy-use days. Second, the group obtains privacy in separation from the general-use areas. By having their own area, the group does not overrun sections of the general-use picnic area and place an overload on the facilities there. Bus loads of people invading a general-use area conflict with the families and small groups of users that feel preempted from the facilities or annoyed by the overcrowding.

The group picnic ground should be separated from the general-use area by enough distance to prevent casual invasion by nongroup members. This means that parking, water, and sanitation facilities must be supplied for exclusive use of the groups. Entrance roads should pass the other picnic areas prior to reaching the group picnic ground so as to minimize the need for restricting signs and gates to keep out nongroup users.

Play areas and special cooking areas for barbecues or clambakes are favored by large groups because these users tend to engage in planned play activities and commonly prepared meals. By placing the tables into formal arrangements, the designer places the group together for meals and business meetings. The formal grouping of the tables provides more unoccupied space for play areas and general environment. Also, it concentrates wear and rubbish into one location. This reduces the destruction of the surrounding forest and makes cleanup easier.

Shelters are of particular importance to the success of group picnic areas. By providing protection from inclement weather, they permit planned group outings to continue when they would otherwise be canceled because of rain.

Cluster Picnic Grounds

The cluster picnic ground is a low-density picnic facility designed for use by families and small groups that desire privacy. These areas have a density of four units per acre and incorporate the least site modification of all types of picnic grounds. The units are grouped in clusters of three to five units for lower construction costs and easier maintenance. Spacings of approximately 100 feet are left between each unit within the cluster.

A longer walk from the road to the unit is more justified at the cluster units than in the general-use areas. The longer walk may be necessary to achieve privacy while keeping the road-construction cost down. Unpaved, one-lane service roads can serve as trails throughout the cluster areas and thereby reduce the development costs.

The cluster units cause a dispersal of users over a large area; therefore, they should be limited to lighter-use locations or in conjunction with large general-use picnic grounds. Pump-out pit toilets might be satisfactory in these areas because the lighter use will not justify the cost of flush toilets.

The units and layout of the cluster picnic ground are somewhat similar to the units in the forest type of campground except that the parking spurs can be 400 feet from the unit and there are no tent pads. The variable distance from the parking spur accounts for the need to consider clusters of units instead of the uniform spacing that is found in forest campgrounds described in Chapter 9.

Although maintenance of cluster areas is somewhat more difficult because of the traveling distance, the flexibility of layout is a great aid to the park manager. Cluster picnic units can be fit into rough terrain or into small areas of particular scenic interest without destruction of the attraction. A certain spreading of the wear circle will occur even though the table is anchored in one place;

however, wear circles should remain confined to the location of each unit and not coalesce into one big bare spot. The recreation area manager must remain prepared to limit use and rehabilitate the sites when wear becomes excessive.

En Route Picnic Grounds

One of the most heavily used recreation facilities is the roadside picnic table on a major highway. Roadside tables and rest areas have long catered to the traveler who wishes to prepare a meal rather than to visit a restaurant. With the increased number of people taking longer and more frequent trips, the demand for these facilities is rising rapidly. The proliferation of single tables simply complicates the problem because it makes cleanup costly and involves the motorist in a miserable game of "luncheon roulette" while trying for the next table down the highway.

Roadside rest areas that contain many tables appear to be the answer for en route travelers on the major highways. With the interstate road system devoid of restaurants, many motorists combine picnicking with long-distance traveling. By having the tables grouped in evenly spaced rest areas, the planner facilitates operation and maintenance and he enables the traveler to plan on the rest stop ahead of time.

Roadside rests should include picnic tables, sanitary facilities, and drinking water as well as a safe place to pull off the highway. Grills and fireplaces are not necessary in the layout because the rest area is designed for rapid turnover. Flush toilets should be installed whenever an adequate water supply is available and sewage treatment can be accomplished (Chapter 14).

REFERENCES

1. Bureau of Outdoor Recreation. 1966. *Water Oriented Outdoor Recreation*. BOR, Lake Central Region. U.S. Department of the Interior, Ann Arbor, Mich.
2. ———. 1966. *Wabash River Basin Comprehensive Study—Louisville Reservoir, Helm Reservoir*. BOR, Lake Central Region. U.S. Department of the Interior, Ann Arbor, Mich.
3. Burke, H.D. 1964. Picnic-Table Use Depends Upon Distance from Parking Area. In *Journal of Forestry*, vol. 62, no. 10, p. 753.
4. Crites, R.S. 1966. *Handbook of Outdoor Recreation Enterprises in Rural Areas*. Farmers Home Administration, Government Printing Office, Washington, D.C. 122 pages.
5. Cohee, Melville H. 1972. *Recreation Areas and Their Use*. Technical Bulletin No. 55. Department of Natural Resources, Madison, Wisc.
6. Cox, L.D. 1940. The Design and Development of Picnic Grounds. In *Bulletin New York State College of Forestry*, vol. 13, no. 3-c. Syracuse, N.Y.
7. Hultsman, J.T. and R.L. Cottrell. 1978. *Camp Unit Design Guidelines*. Tennessee Valley Authority. Golden Pond, Ky. 21 pages.
8. Mackie, D.J. 1965. Site Planning to Reduce Deterioration. *Proceedings of the Society of American Foresters*. Annual Meeting, Detroit, Mich.
9. Outdoor Recreation Resources Review Commission, 1962. *The Quality of Outdoor Recreation*

as Evidenced by User Satisfaction. ORRRC Study Report 5. Superintendent of Documents, Government Printing Office, Washington, D.C. 65 pages.

10. Pennsylvania Department of Forests and Waters. 1969. *State Park Planning and Guidelines.* Bureau of State Parks, Harrisburg, Penn. 90 pages.

11. U.S. Department of Interior. 1979. *The Third Nationwide Outdoor Recreation Plan: The Assessment.* Washington, D.C. 264 pages.

12. U.S. Public Health Service. 1962. *Manual of Individual Water Supply Systems.* Public Health Service Publication No. 24. U.S. Department of Health, Education, and Welfare, Washington, D.C. 121 pages.

13. ———. 1965. *Environmental Health Practice in Recreational Areas.* PHS Publication, No. 1195. U.S. Department of Health, Education, and Welfare, Washington, D.C.

11

Organization Camps

Organization campsites are areas that are developed to serve an organized group of people who have similar interests. The organization camp provides supervised activities, social and educational opportunities, meals, and lodging incidental to the forest recreation experience. Organization camps are designed and operated to provide for the existence needs of the user as well as to provide him with a full schedule of supervised activities. This type of camp generally caters to the young people from the ages of 8 to 16; however, this is not always the situation in that some organized camps provide for the wants of adult users or family groups. Communities, church organizations, large associations, and youth groups often sponsor organized camping on a nonprofit basis.

Historically, the organization camp traces its roots to the idea of private summer camps for children that still thrives throughout the country. Frederick Gunn started the movement in 1900 when he took the students of his Gunnery School for Boys camping in Connecticut.[1] Summer camps are serving a definite need for the children of urban areas whose parents can afford to pay the costs of room and board at the camps. The educational and character-building organizations such as the YMCA and Boy Scouts of America were the next group of organizations to get into the camp business following the success of privately owned camps. As the organized camp idea caught on and spread to political units, lodges, and government-sponsored groups, the character of the camp itself began to change.

Generally, the early organization camps were based on fun, enjoyment, and relaxation. Unfortunately, this casual air did not last after the professional educators and frustrated military officer–type of individual took charge of the organized camp movement. Camplife evolved into a nightmarish mixture of "Boot Camp" and reform school with bugle calls, company streets, and a packed schedule of formal activities. This misguided approach to physical activities and recreation lead to rebellion and over fatigue.[2] It was this era in organization camp history that soured many children and parents on this form of forest recreation, thereby leading to jokes about packing the screaming kids off for the summer.

Today, the organized camps have matured in their outlook and purpose. The educators now realize that their 1930 approach is not in keeping with modern theories on child behavior and training. Military leadership principles remain the same, but the techniques of leadership have changed markedly even within the Army. Experience has taught the military that seven or eight persons is all that one man can effectively control. As a result of these changes, the organized camp has undergone a modification that influences its physical layout and is of importance to the recreation developer. Formal, pseudomilitary camp arrangements are losing popularity and the informal camps made up of scattered units are now recommended to provide the best atmosphere for education, self-expression, and relaxed recreation.

Activity-theme camps have gained in popularity during recent years. Adults and entire families, as well as children, are attending camps that provide programs for attaining higher skill levels in specific recreation or athletic competence. Tennis camps, wrestling camps, and other athletic specialty camps became popular during the 1960s as a way for young athletes to improve in their chosen sports. Those camps generally were conducted on college or school campuses and employed physical education staff for the summer months.

The success of those campus programs has lead to the development of outdoor recreation–based activity-theme camps located in forest and mountain settings that can serve the entire family. Private sector efforts combine activity training with a complete forest recreation resort area. The activity-theme camps can accommodate various themes too as popular movements change. However, the attraction of a pleasant forest resort will remain to provide the vacation appeal.

The organization camp has a place in forest recreation.[7] From the user's standpoint, these camps fill a need that cannot be satisfied by any other type of development. To the land manager, organization camps provide a way of relieving some of the pressure on the regular camping and day-use facilities. By providing special areas for organization camping, the manager will be able to keep the organized groups from overrunning facilities that were designed for family camping groups. Approximately eight million youngsters go to organized camps each summer at the cost of $500 to $1,500 each.[1]

Approximately two billion dollars are spent on organized camps each year. Ninety-five percent of the two million acres of organized camp land is in private ownership. Therefore, organized camping has a significant impact on local economics and on the recreation land base.

The American Camping Association has an accrediting system; however, only 3,500 of the estimated 10,500 organization camps in the country have qualified for accreditation. Accreditation includes health and safety standards for camps. Several attempts have been made to pass state and federal legislation to regulate health and safety conditions at organized camps. Those attempts at regulation have failed on the national level because the overall camp industry death and injury rates are in line with home and school rates. Hiding within the relatively unalarming averages are some substandard safety situations.

The Forest Service makes every effort possible to provide opportunities for this type of recreation. Although its federally supplied funds are not used to build, to operate, or to maintain the highly developed organization camps, the Forest Service does list the organization camp fourth on its priority list for available sites. Public campgrounds, picnicking areas, and water-sport sites take precedence over organization camps for available sites on the national forests.

SITE SELECTION

The principles of recreation site selection that are outlined in Chapter 5 are applicable for locating organization camps as well as any other popular type of forest recreation area. On the other hand, requirements for the general location of the site are different from those for any other type of recreation because of the nature of the user group. Privacy, size, accessibility, and topography all present problems unique to organized camps.

Privacy

Privacy is an important ingredient of site selection for an organization camp. The activities performed in many camps require the feeling of complete isolation from civilization for enthusiastic involvement by the participants. The feeling of complete isolation is not achieved only at a large federal wilderness area or a similarly large place. It can be achieved by screening the camp from the outside world's activity with vegetation or topographic features.

Also, intruders are unwelcome in organization camps where activity programs are being carried on; therefore, the isolation technique of external security plays a large part. That is, people will be less likely to intrude into an area if it is not readily accessible or is not visible from regularly traveled roads. Privacy is difficult to insure in sites that are divided by public roads or are crossed by easements; therefore, one contiguous tract of land located off a forest or township road offers the ideal situation for privacy. By constructing only one access road into the organization campsite, the developer will make the job of excluding trespassers easier than if he opens several entrance points.

Size

The requirement for size is related to the general environment and ownership of the surrounding lands. When the adjacent lands are in private ownership or are public lands that are not managed with recreation as a major factor, a large area of ownership is needed to provide protection from the impacts of activities that would have adverse effects on the organization camp. Organization camps that are surrounded by or located in state parks or on national forests do not require as much acreage because the quality of the general environment is protected. Also, those areas will always be open for use by the participants.

Land is needed within the campsite area to provide room between each of the individual camp units, to permit separation of the camping areas and the administrative buildings, and to allow for some roaming and activities within the boundaries of the camp. One rule of thumb for the amount of land required for a privately owned organization camp calls for one acre of usable land for each camper space available.[6] This rule of thumb will give a rough approximation for determining the required size based on capacity. Space must be available for play, nature study, crafts, and group activities as well as for the existence needs of sleeping, eating, and sanitation.

Accessibility

The accessibility requirements for organized camps will vary somewhat according to the type of camp. Camps that serve one select group such as the Boy Scouts must be located so as to be near the troops using it. The closer the camp is to the municipality or council that is sponsoring it, the more it will be used. It may be necessary to encourage short-term use throughout most of the year in order to justify the high cost of establishing the camp. Long-term summer camp planners can be more independent of distance while selecting a site; however, they should keep the round trip short enough to be completed during daylight hours.

Location within an area served by good highways is a must, even though the camp itself should be away from the main roads. Long or difficult access will cut down on use, raise the cost of construction, and make operation costly and inconvenient. Good roads and nearby communities enable camp personnel to obtain the necessary supplies for camp operation without great inconvenience or cost.

Accessibility also has a bearing on the type of caretaker staff that will stay in the camp over the winter. Directors and owners of isolated camps state that they have difficulty in hiring competent caretakers to live at their facilities through the winter.[4]

Topography

The topography or configuration of the land should be as varied as possible in the vicinity of the organization campsite. Variations in the landscape increase the value of the setting and offers more opportunities for different activities.[3] Nearly level spots are necessary for living, play, and administrative areas, while streams, ponds, or lakes add considerable value to the area. Water for recreational purposes is very important for the success of organizational camps; therefore, every effort should be made to include some usable body of water nearby the camp. For user safety, site protection, and administrative control, a buffer area should be left between the camp and the water's edge. Organization camps can be located on relatively rough terrain because they do not require the large flat athletic field play areas that are needed in cities. Organization camps located within the forests should be designed to encourage participation in activities that are not available in towns and playgrounds. Hiking, nature study, and water-based activities should be some of the major forms of recreation activities included when planning such camps.

Swamps, marshes, and other low spots can be both disadvantages and advantages. They breed mosquitoes and restrict passage without special modifications. On the other hand, swamps and marshes provide the habitat for much unusual and interesting flora and fauna. These wetlands make outstanding nature study areas when developed for the purpose.

Natural features in the topography make the best boundary lines. Ridgelines and bodies of water give dimensions to property that painted boundary lines can never impart. Besides being easily located, they provide natural barriers against intruders and they convey a feeling of ownership.

The roughness of the topography will have a marked effect upon campground layout. Gently rolling terrain permits the camp to be developed with the minimum consideration for topographic advantages and limitations. The structures, trails, and service facilities can be dispersed or concentrated where they are most suitable to the users and the administrators. Rugged topography, however, inflicts severe limitations on the layout. Because of the lack of large areas with gentle slopes, the facilities must be spread out over a large area to take advantage of the existing sites, or else the facilities must be concentrated into a few of the available spots. The ideal situation lies somewhere between the two extremes. The terrain should be irregular enough to provide variations in scenery and in activities, but not rugged enough to prevent the proper dispersal of facilities.

LAYOUT

The organization camps of today are generally based upon the dispersed-unit theory or "dice-throw" arrangement where small subcamps are scattered around a common administrative site. [2,7] Besides the subcamps that meet the needs of living, sanitation, and limited activities, an organized camp must include dining facilities, infirmary, administration buildings, and both extensive and intensive forest recreation opportunities.

Subcamps

The subcamps are scattered around the developed area in such a way as to break the overall camp population into several smaller units. As shown in Figure

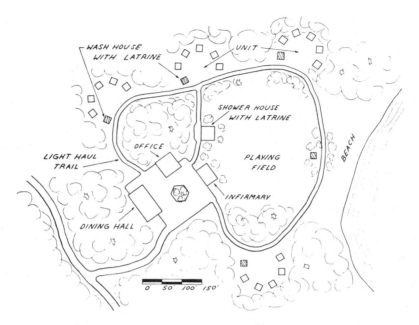

Fig. 11.1.

11.1, each of these smaller units occupies its own area where its users live and partake in limited group activities. The subcamp theory fits in well with unorganized groups because it organizes the campers into small groups with which the individual camper can identify himself as a part. This immediately gives him common ground with his fellow unit members and sets the stage for the establishment of an esprit de corps as the season progresses. Each subcamp should accommodate between 16 and 32 people. The smaller number is best for the camper, but the higher number will reduce overall camp development costs. Twenty-four persons to each subcamp provides a good compromise figure.

Participating groups that are already organized into units such as the Boy Scout–type organizations fit right into the subcamp layout. Each troop can have its own subcamp to operate without friction from other troops. Generally, these groups have between 16 and 32 members so that they can fill one unit. Also, the troops are broken down into patrols that can each fill one housing unit.

The subcamp provides for all of the living requirements of the camper except for eating. This means that besides the group play area and housing facilities, the subcamp must contain a washhouse and latrine. The trails that connect the subcamps with each other and with the administrative site should be eight feet wide and suitable for light-haul maintenance and operation vehicles.

Housing

Usually, living quarters should be large enough to accommodate eight persons in each structure.[7] Organized groups that do not rely upon paid counselors prefer to use cabins accommodating four or six persons.[6] Local ordinances often govern the size of cabins, but a good minimum to follow is to reserve 30 to 40 square feet of floor space for each occupant of the cabins.[8] The U.S. Forest Service states that 500 cubic feet of space within the building is sufficient when there is adequate ventilation.[7] Wide eaves overhanging the building walls permit the windows and doors to be left open during rainstorms and when the occupants are temporarily away when rain threatens.

The three basic forms for housing that are used in organization camps are the cabin, the tent, and a combination of the two called a tentalow or tent-cabin. The choice of shelters will depend upon available funds, desires of the user groups, and permanence of the individual units. Some camps are developing unique housing units to portray a theme. Figure 11.2 shows a covered wagon design living unit.

Fig. 11.2. Unique subcamp housing employing an interesting theme, good sunlighting, and adequate ventilation.

The housing units should be placed approximately 50 feet apart when some supervision of the campers is required.[4] When supervision is not required as in family organization camps, the distance can be much greater between units. In part, the distance between subcamps will have some bearing on the distance between the cabins within the one subcamp. The organization camp with enough land to permit a wide dispersal of the subcamps can have greater spacing within the scattered units without losing each subcamp's identity. Conversely, camps that do not have enough space to disperse the subcamps should not have such a wide spacing of the housing. Wide spacing between housing units under the latter conditions could mean a loss of the individual subcamp's integrity because of diffusion with adjacent subcamps.

Each cabin or tent should be situated so that it receives sunlight during the morning hours and shade during late afternoon. Morning sunlight will warm the cabin and dry off the predawn moisture that will accumulate within the cabin. Sunlight will also make the morning seem more pleasant to those arising. The afternoon shade will permit the cabin to cool off before bedtime.

Sanitary Facilities

Each subcamp should have its own washhouse and its own toilet facilities. Because of the dispersed location of the subcamps, flush toilets will be impractical in all but the most highly financed camps. The light use of the subcamp toilets will also help to justify the use of a nonwater carriage sewage disposal system. Not only is the number of campers in each subcamp small, but also much of the time those occupants will be off to other parts of the camp where there are central sanitary facilities. Since most states are developing camp sanitation codes, the local board of health should be consulted during the early planning states.[4]

The pump-out vault privy is probably the most suitable type of toilet facility under these conditions. It has more permanence than simple pit toilets; therefore, more elaborate efforts can be put into making it a satisfactory sewage disposal set-up. The problems associated with pumping out of the accumulated excreta should not prove to be a problem in most rural areas since commercial operators are present to service septic tanks and similar systems. Details on sewage disposal systems are presented in Chapter 14.

The unit washhouse should be a separate structure from the toilet facilities with an underground sump located nearby to catch the waste water and leach it into the soil. A porchlike shelter with a concrete floor, a central row of sinks, and self-closing faucets is a simple and commonly used design for a washhouse. Hot water is a luxury that might prove to be uneconomical at subcamp washhouses. For this reason, one or more central washhouses that are supplied with hot water and equipped with showers should be constructed at strategic locations so as to serve campers in many subcamps. These central washhouses should also contain flush-type toilets to handle the concentration of use.

Dining Facilities

One large dining hall is usually employed to feed all the campers and staff of an organization camp. This enables the camp to furnish the proper meals that are prepared in an adequate kitchen area. The large dining hall area can also be used as a meeting place for camp activities.

The kitchen must be enclosed, and it must be adequately screened to exclude insects and rodents. At least 12 square feet of floor space are required for each diner.[8] Also, it is desirable to have the kitchen connected to a screened dining area.[7] Massive log construction is now out of favor for dining halls because of its expense and its dark and dreary atmosphere. Open, airy, and light structures offer more pleasant and more practical buildings for dining halls.

Although dining halls should occupy good sites within the camp, they should not dominate the scene by being placed on the spot with the best view or along the water's edge. These locations satisfy adult values, but do not make the best sites for dining halls. The dining hall should be located so that it is easily accessible from all of the subunits, where the soil and terrain conditions are suitable, and where the access road construction costs will be kept at a minimum.

Administration areas are favorite places for dining halls. This is a satisfactory location only when the administration area is centrally located. If the dining hall is part of the administration area, it must be kept separate from the other administration buildings. It should not be attached to any other structures and it should not be modified for use as anything but a dining hall and a meeting place for the campers and staff.[6]

Campfire Circles

The campfire circle, or council ring, is a very popular part of most organization camps. As are many other facets of the organization camp, the campfire ring is oriented to Indian lore in that it represents the council fires of by-gone tribal gatherings. Singing, games, and other social activities dominate today's council ring fires. These campfire circles should be centrally located within the camp so as to provide the easiest access from all parts of the camp. Since much use will be made of the council ring after dark, the trails leading to it should be well marked and well maintained.

The campfire fireplace should be circular and ringed by a low wall of stones to retain the fire and ashes. Circles or semicircles of rough benches around the fire will add to the convenience of the user, and make the group placement more orderly. If the fireplace is located on a flat spot next to a gently sloping hill, the benches can be placed on the slope so that they are higher than the fireplace and the stage area surrounding it. When a sloping area is not available, the fireplace should be raised above the ground level so that the fire will be visible to those persons in the rear of the audience. The fireplace should be raised above the ground level by a stone platform that is approximately 24 inches high. The stage area between the fireplace and the benches should be raised approximately 12 inches.

Administration Area

The administration area contains all of the structures and facilities that are needed to administer and manage the organized camp along with certain other facilities that will improve the general quality of the camp. This area contains the administrative offices, infirmary, equipment storage sheds, service personnel living accommodations, and camp store. A central washhouse is generally included in this area.

The best location for the administration area is at the end of the public access road. This is the logical point to supply information and to greet incoming campers. Since the road terminus is the major concern in locating an administration area, the area might not be centrally located within the camp. This is probably a good situation since it would be undesirable to have public access all of the way to the camp's interior.

It is the administration area that the visitors and campers will see first upon arrival at the camp and last when departing. That area should therefore present a good picture of the camp. The public road should pass in front of the buildings where there are adequate parking facilities and avoid such necessary eyesores as the garbage can racks behind the dining hall. [2]

Water-oriented Sports

Although organization camp structures should not be built right along the water's edge, the camp should be oriented so that the campers have easy access to the water. Swimming and boating play a large role in organizational camping and should be considered in the camp's layout. As far as possible, the subcamps should be located in such a way that all have equal access to the water frontage. Also, the layout should provide trails to guide the movement of campers from their subunits to the water-sports area without taking them through other subcamps.

The beach improvements and requirements for swimming and boating are discussed in Chapter 15. A qualified life guard is usually required at organization camps and nonswimmer areas must be marked off.

Extensive Recreation Activities

Extensive recreation activities take place over large areas and require the minimum of facilities. Hiking, nature study, fishing, and horseback riding are some of the extensive recreation activities enjoyed by organization campers. A system of hiking trails should be developed to provide the camp with access to points of interest within the area. Those camps located on or adjacent to state or national forests have the advantage of being able to use the state or federally maintained trails for riding or hiking. The trails should be accessible from all the subcamps, but they should not pass through them.

Certain stream improvement projects could be undertaken to increase the recreation potential of any suitable streams flowing through the camp's property. Fishing is the second most popular activity at privately owned recreation areas and should not be overlooked when developing an organization camp.[5]

REFERENCES

1. Meszoly, Robin D. 1973. The Careful Consideration of Camps. In *The Washington Post*, June 3, 1973.
2. National Park Service, 1938. *Park and Recreation Structures.* U.S. Department of the Interior. Government Printing Office, Washington, D.C.
3. Neff, P. 1965. Applied Silviculture in Managing Outdoor Recreation Sites. In *Proceedings of the Society of American Foresters*, Detroit, Mich.
4. Ohio Department of Health. 1964. *Camp Sanitation-Laws, Regulations and Recommendations.* Columbus, Ohio.
5. Outdoor Recreation Resources Review Commission. 1962. *Private Outdoor Recreation Facilities.* Study Report 11. Government Printing Office, Washington, D.C. 154 pages.
6. Salomon, J.H. 1959. *Campsite Development.* Council Administrative Series, No. 5B. Girl Scouts of the United States of America, New York, N.Y.
7. U.S. Forest Service. 1963. *Recreation Management.* Handbook Title 2300. U.S. Department of Agriculture, Washington, D.C.
8. Young Men's Christian Association. 1960. *Developing Camp Sites and Facilities.* Associated Press, New York, N.Y.

12

Trails

INTRODUCTION

Although the dictionary defines a trail as a track worn by passage through the wilderness, the modern concept of a trail is quite different. Trails are meant to provide safe and adequate passageways to an objective. Even though it guides the user to an objective, not every trail goes to some point or destination. Indeed, most hiking trails are designed to provide the opportunity for aesthetic enjoyment by taking the trail user to vistas, unique spots, and diverse environments.[11] Trails, by definition, can be difficult to separate from roads because in certain instances trail-design standards approach road levels. This text considers trails to be those passageways designed for modes of land transportation other than cars, trains, buses, and trucks. The manager or developer must consider trails for snowmobiles, bicycles, horses, ski tours, and even pedestrians. Actually, marked boating trails could be considered here; they are not, however, because they are treated as part of the water-oriented recreation covered in Chapter 15.

This chapter will consider the interior trail, the cross-country trail, and the nature trail. Each of the three types of trail has its own characteristics and requires somewhat different specifications. Common to all trails is the need to consider safety, topography, and alignment. Also, strict zoning and separation of competing user groups appear to be necessary.[1]

Since trails serve as safe and adequate passageways to an objective, they tend to control use of an area by people walking or using some type of vehicle. Probably more than any other cultural feature, trails impact on accessibility of recreation areas by handicapped persons. Planners and managers should be aware of the problems associated with access. The public estate is prohibited by law from excluding anyone by creating a physical barrier to the handicapped.[2] That prohibition is summarized by excerpts from the three pieces of national legislation listed below:

1. *The Outdoor Recreation Act of 1963 (PL 88-29)*: "all American people of present and future generations be assured adequate outdoor recreation resources."

2. *The Architectural Barriers Act of 1968 (PL 90-480)*: "Any building, or facility, constructed in whole or in part by federal funds must be made accessible to and usable by the physically handicapped."
3. *The Rehabilitation Act of 1973 (PL 93-112)*: "no otherwise qualified handicapped individual in the U.S. . . . shall solely, by reason of his handicap, be excluded from participation in, be denied the benefits of, or be subjected to discrimination under any program or activity receiving federal financial assistance.

INTERIOR TRAILS

The trails constructed to guide people around the intensely developed recreation area should be designed for economy of purpose and site protection. Trails are the key to reducing the potential pedestrian impact on the recreation site because they channelize and direct foot traffic over a designated route. In areas of heavy use, the trails should be surfaced with mulch, gravel, or paving according to the situation. Since the primary purpose of the interior trail is to get people around the area, the trails should be as direct as possible and well marked by interior directional signs.

All trails must serve some purpose in order to justify their construction and maintenance costs; the major problem in planning, however, is designing a workable trail system. Thoughtful planning is the best ingredient in trail layout. Unfortunately for the planner, people do not always react as they are expected to react. Because of this, the manager quite often follows the practice of "path paving" within recreation areas. That is, he lets the people wear a path and then he paves it. Path paving has been quite common on large college campuses for decades. After all, the people will find the route of travel that is best for them. This technique has some drawbacks. First, the public might wreck the vegetation of the entire area before they wear out a satisfactory path. Second, the public-worn path may be located in such a way that it is objectionable for administrative or management reasons. For instance, it might cross the road at a place where it could cause a safety hazard. The third drawback to applying the path-paving technique is that not all people know where everything is located. This means that they must follow roundabout existing trails and roads or go stumbling about the forest in search of the washhouse. On the other hand, planned trails might require more cultural treatment than path-paved trails to keep users from wandering off them or from shortcutting.

The foot trail should be at least two feet wide and cleared to eight feet in height. Stairs should be used to reduce the slope of the interior trail on steep grade changes to make pedestrian travel easier and to reduce erosion and paving slippage. Surfacing material tends to work downward below each barrier on steep slopes. If the trail is to be cleared, drained, and graded without structures, then the problem of barriers to handicapped persons will be minimized.

Structures such as stairs, however, could exclude access by handicapped people. Because of the need for barrier-free structures on public sites, ramps can be used to cover or by-pass the steps. Otherwise, low-riser steps should be used so that they can be climbed by wheelchairs. Sections of the trail that are not paved should have sufficient water-removal structures such as water bars to prevent channelization of surface runoff on the trail. Although a zero-grade interior trail is not desirable because of the drainage problem, gently sloping trails are desirable for ease of movement by pedestrians who might not be prepared for strenuous walks to the facilities within the recreation area.

Steps must be properly employed and designed or they will be by-passed. The grade of trails can be lessened by using railroad ties or squared timbers. Two 18-inch-long pieces of half-inch steel-reinforcing rod placed through the wood and driven into the ground will hold the ties or timbers in place.

Shortcutting switchbacks is another unfavorable practice of trail users. They will shortcut to different levels of a trail if it appears convenient. They will trample the vegetation on the steep slope and cause the soil to unravel. Barriers, screenings, or signs will be needed to stop the shortcutting practice.

EXTERIOR TRAILS

Exterior trails are those passageways designed to serve extensive recreation activities such as hiking and horseback riding. The end of the 1960s saw the beginning of a boom in hiking, horseback riding, bicycling, snowmobiling, and ski-touring. Simultaneously, changes in forest management policies and fire protection procedures have reduced the mileage of trails through the forest. For all the interest in trail use, no market situation has been established; therefore, most trail use takes place on public lands where trails were built for nonrecreation purposes or as secondary use of logging roads. Less than one yard of trail exists for each U.S. citizen, and this is being reduced at a steady rate in spite of the National Trails System Act of 1968 (PL 90-543).[11] Even though national inventories list the country's total trail system as being 136,000 miles long, over one-half of all trail mileage in the United States is on national forest land. Of the 88,000 miles of federal recreation trails, 83 percent cross the Forest Service land and 10 percent are in National Park Service areas. The remaining mileage is administered by the Bureau of Land Management, Bureau of Sport Fisheries and Wildlife, Bureau of Reclamation, or the Department of Indian Affairs.[13,14] Trail users are inconspicuous because of the dispersed nature of their activity, and the active campaigning that they have done has been absorbed in the wilderness preservation movement.

This chapter will treat extensive trail design for snowmobiling, bicycling, horseback riding, hiking and ski-touring.

Hiking Trails

Walking over relatively long distances for recreation purposes has continued to gain in popularity in nonwilderness situations as well as within established wildernesses. Aesthetic enjoyment ranks as the highest value among hikers.[11] For this reason, the trails should be laid out to take advantage of vistas and unique beauty spots. Ridgeline and high-elevation trails will present the walker with the most favorable scenic situation. Generally, the aesthetic appeal should take precedent over length of route or destination. Trails presently in existence tend to follow one type of landform such as a mountain range or a shoreline.[14]

Most hiking is done as a day-use activity. Backpacking enthusiasm is spreading rapidly; however, research to this point indicates that long-length stays on hiking trails account for a small percentage of the trail's use. Even hikers going into established wilderness areas return to their home at night. Emphasis on various-length trails is needed to achieve the variety needed to accommodate day hikers as well as the deep penetration of wilderness areas. The Green Mountain Club of Vermont maintains the 400-mile network of the Long Trail across the north-south length of their state in such a way that 19 one-day walks are marked and described in detail on a freely distributed brochure.

The basic purpose of a hiking trail is to provide a safe and aesthetic route for the foot traveler. Easy access is important and vehicle parking areas are needed. Vandalism to parked cars is a serious enough problem to cause concern to most hikers. One method of combating the vandalism menace is to lay out the trails so that they originate or pass near intensive recreation areas or administrative areas that can be used as "trailheads." Hikers can use parking places where some degree of protection is given by the recreation or forest management personnel. Even designated and improved parking areas along the trail will help by concentrating vehicles where law enforcement personnel can check on them.

The trails should run along ridges and high ground as much as possible with side trips to lakes and ponds. A five- to eight-foot right of way should be cleared to a height of eight feet. A two-foot trail width is sufficient in the locations where surfacing is required. Generally, surfacing should not be done except in problem locations. Straightness is of little value in hiking; therefore, trail alignment should not be done at the expense of felling trees. Switchbacks should be avoided on heavy-use trails whenever possible so as to eliminate the temptation to shortcut between intervisible spots. Grades of 8 to 10 percent should be followed with short pitch grades in excess of 10 percent used only when necessary. Steps can be considered when practical; however, they will cause maintenance problems and limit the trail to foot traffic only. Since much trail mileage will be on side slopes, the back slope must be constructed with sufficient care to insure a stable condition and to permit a vegetative cover to be established. Most soils obtain an angle of repose at a ½:1 or ¼:1 ratio between rise and horizontal distance of cut. Surface water must be removed from the trail by slopes, open-top culverts, or water bars when necessary.

Water bars and culverts should be used near the top of each grade to get the water off the trail before it can pick up velocity along the trail. Trail bends are another good location for water bars to be used to get the water from the inside edge of the trail and dump it out into the forest litter. Rises and dips in the trail can also be employed to get water to run off the trail instead of being captured by the trail.

Trails should pass by facilities such as campsites, water supply points, shelters, or toilets without going directly to them. Well-marked and short spur or side trails should lead from the main hiking trail to the facilities. By-passing the facilities, the trail will not lead everyone through every facility. Wear and tear on the sites will be reduced, the integrity of the trail will be maintained, and the facility user will get somewhat more privacy.

Development of vistas should be considered along the hiking trail. People prefer ridgetop trails so that they can enjoy the panoramic scenes. All too often, hiking trails lead on between two walls of trees. Short spur trails can lead off to scenic overlooks that occur near the trail. Vista sites that are visible from the hiking trail will tend to draw users more frequently than those that are off some walking distance down a side trail.

Horseback Riding Trails

Trails designed to accommodate horses are a necessary part of an integrated trails system. Approximately 10 percent of the U.S. population participates in horseback riding.[3] In specific locations, the demand for equestrian trails might be great enough to justify exclusion of other trail users. Heavy use by horses and hikers can create safety and sanitation problems. Most hikers indicate that they prefer not to meet horseback riders on the trail.[11] However, in the West, where horseback riding and back-country use are closely related, the exclusion of horses would be illogical and unenforceable. Horseback riding trails could be designed to serve as snowmobile or ski-touring trails in parts of the country where these winter sports are popular.

The minimum width for equestrian trails is three feet; however, an eight- to ten-foot wide right of way is recommended to permit access by emergency vehicles. The tread width for the horses' hooves must be at least 18 inches wide. A ten-foot vertical clearance should be maintained.[9] The 10 percent maximum grade can be exceeded by short stretches of pitch grades of up to 15 percent. The minimum tread width on switchbacks is eight feet. Overnight campsites can be placed along the longer trails at appropriate locations. All rest areas and campsites should provide a hitching rail of pipe or cable. Water needs to be supplied only at the overnight sites. Parking lots at the termini or trail heads should allow space for cars pulling trailers to turn around and to park. The pull-through lot design can save a lot of tempers and repair costs because it permits cars to enter a long parking space with trailer attached and then exit by pulling on through the parking space.

Bicycle Trails

The bicycle has become established as part of the forest recreation scene. Many state and private campgrounds have some rental arrangement with campers. In most cases, the existing trails are insufficiently surfaced for bicycling; therefore, most of the riding is done on the road network. In recent years, the pressure for exclusive bicycle trails has been mounting at all levels of government.

Bicycle trails should be separate from motor vehicle traffic. However, the public's participation in jogging, running, and walking requires a sharing of the improved surface trail. The cost of trail construction is too high to justify a single use when the demand is so high for other activities. In cities where managers have attempted to give bicyclist priority, more conflicts have occurred than when shared use has been publicized. Bike-to-bike collisions seem to be more of a problem than biker-pedestrian conflicts.

Bicycle trails should have nearly level grades whenever possible with pitch grades of approximately 6 percent. Long grades should be avoided or broken by nearly level or reverse grades for resting, restarting, or changing gears. Five feet is the minimum trail width with eight feet being recommended for heavy-traffic areas. An eight-foot vertical clearance should be maintained. Because of possible high speeds by bicyclists, extra care should be taken in designing the turns. The radius of turn should be at least ten feet and warning signs posted if necessary.

Bicycles are more sensitive to trail surface than most other trail users. It is the surface condition that impedes progress in turning many abandoned rights of way into bicycling trails. Asphalt makes the ideal bicycle trail surface, but that can become quite expensive on long trail systems. Soil cementing agents used on course soils or compacted gravel are acceptable surfacing materials. [11]

Snowmobile Trails

The snowmobile epitomizes the recent large-scale entry of motorized vehicles into recreation (Fig. 12.1). In order to enhance snowmobilers' enjoyment, decrease environmental impacts, and resolve conflicts, land managers have begun to develop trails for snowmobile use. Snowmobiling was originally confined to the snow belt states that have snow cover for more than 100 days each year. However, states that have far fewer snow days have been sharing in snowmobiling as a result of its popularity. Snowmobiling trails are classified as general-use, rally, or race courses. This book is concerned with only the general-use trail that has a place in the forest setting. A study of snowmobilers in Ontario

Fig. 12.1. The snowmobile epitomizes the recent large scale entry of motorized vehicles into recreation.

showed that 45 percent of them preferred wooded sites with no development other than trails.[6]

Snowmobile use should be confined to designated and marked trails. This can only be enforced if adequate trails exist.[5] Many linear openings already exist in the forest that can be used without creating an entire new system. Roads that are not needed for winter travel, abandoned rights of way, firebreaks, power-line rights of way, and existing equestrian or hiking trails can form the framework for the snowmobile. Connector trails can be used to complete the snowmobile system and provide variety and circular traffic flow (see Fig. 12.2).

In most general-use situations, the trails should be 15 to 30 miles long and utilize a variety of landscapes.[5] The recommended maximum length of a trail is 40 to 50 miles and the minimum length trail is 5 to 10 miles. One-way loops that return to the starting point are necessary. Two-directional trails may be required in certain situations, but they should be short and very well signed. Trail width should be between 6 and 15 feet and the two-way trails should be 15 feet wide. Trail turning radius must exceed 25 feet. All vertical clearing should be done to ten feet above normal snow depths and the brush should be cut back

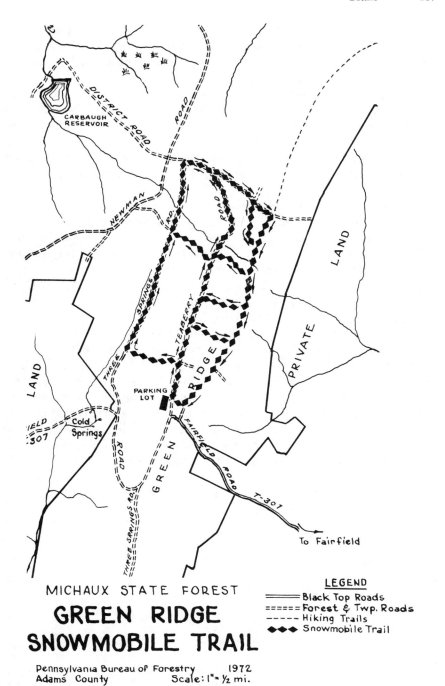

MICHAUX STATE FOREST

GREEN RIDGE
SNOWMOBILE TRAIL

Pennsylvania Bureau of Forestry   1972
Adams County   Scale: 1"= ½ mi.

Fig. 12.2. A layout of a designed snowmobile trail using connector trails to tie existing roads into a system of one-way loops.

two feet from the edge of the trail to minimize danger to the snowmobiler. General trail grades of 6 to 8 percent are recommended with short pitch grades up to 25 percent permitted. Snowmobiles need a straight in-run route at least as long as the pitch grade to make the climb.

Openings along the route permit the snowmobilers to rest or to move without the confines of the trail. Snowmobiles do not perform well on sideslopes and will require a cut and fill trail there. It is better to take the trail across the contour at right angles whenever possible. Since drowning has become the leading cause of snowmobile-related fatalities, trails should never be routed across frozen lakes and rivers.[4] Eight-foot-wide bridges will serve to cross the trail over streams.

Signs play an important role in snowmobiling. They inform the snowmobiler of trail direction and hazards, reassure the user that he is still on the trail, and warn highway and foot-trail users of crossings. The Department of the Interior and the snowmobile manufacturers have made an effort to standardize snowmobile trail signs. Trail markers are orange diamonds seven inches high and five inches wide. Caution signs are black on yellow and are offset squares 12 inches to the side, while stop signs are red, 12-inch octagonals with white letters. All signs should be made with reflective surface.

Facilities required to support a snowmobiling trail will include a parking lot, loading area, a warm-up or test area, and trash cans. A warming hut and sanitary facilities are recommended at the trail terminal. Table 12.1 gives the chill-factor relationship between temperature and wind. This should be posted at a trail head sign or in the warming hut to remind snowmobilers of the dangers involved. The parking lot should have pull-through stalls for cars with trailers, regular parking for cars and pick-up trucks, and a parking area for snowmobiles. A loading ramp next to the snowmobile parking area will facilitate loading and reduce the danger to pedestrians within the parking area.

Table 12.1. Chart Showing the Equivalent and Actual Temperatures for Various Wind Velocities.

| | Actual Thermometer Reading ($-$°F) | | | | | | |
	30	20	10	0	-10	-20	-30
Wind Speed in MPH	Equivalent Temperature (°F)						
calm	30	20	10	0	-10	-20	-30
5	27	16	6	-5	-15	-26	-36
10	16	4	-9	-21	-33	-46	-58
15	9	-5	-18	-36	-45	-58	-72
20	4	-10	-25	-39	-53	-67	-87
25	0	-15	-29	-44	-59	-74	-88
30	-2	-18	-33	-48	-63	-79	-94
35	-4	-20	-35	-49	-67	-82	-98
40	-6	-21	-37	-53	-69	-85	-100

Ski-touring Trail

Ski-touring, or cross-country skiing, is the original form of skiing. [7] It is the Scandinavian version of snowshoeing and it is rapidly becoming a leading winter sport where there is snow cover. Ski-touring trails are built up of one-way loops of one- to three-mile length that bring the skier back to the starting point. Old logging roads and fire trails can be tied together with connector trails to form various patterns of loops. Ideally, the trail should run along a nearly level grade with occasional up and down slopes.

A 12 percent grade should be the maximum slope for general-purpose trails and a run-out area should be at the bottom to permit slowing down before turning. A seven-foot trail width to permit snow plowing descents or herring bone climbs should be allowed whenever an 8 percent or greater downhill slope is used. A single-lane, one-way trail needs a minimum width of four feet. Two-way trails, on the rare occasions when they are rarely required, need a six-foot right of way. Vertical clearance should be done to a height of eight feet above the expected snow depth. Cross-sections of the trail need to be fairly level with a slight outward grade to assist drainage.

Signs are necessary to provide route direction, reassurance, level of difficulty, distances, and warnings. Generally, a trailhead sign is used to provide the basic information as to routes, distances, sanitation facilities, and rest stops. Trail marker signs should occur in sufficient numbers to reassure the skier that he is not lost.

The number of sanitary facilities required along the trail will vary with the number of users. A three- to four-mile spacing will match the approximate speed of the average party. [9]

Nature Trails

The nature trail, or interpretive trail, is a route designed to lead users to places where points of geologic, biologic, historic, or cultural interest can be explained to them by guides, signs, pamphlets, or electronic devices. They are thematic in subject matter. Interpretive trails are designed for use by every form of transportation used in the forest from automobile to cross-country skiers. Some of the best possibilities for interpretive trails exist in and along water areas. Trails for pedestrians are the most common form of nature trail. The general principles of planning and designing pedestrian trails will apply to most other forms of nature trails.

One-way loop trails of less than a half-mile length that begin and end at an explanatory, or trailhead, sign or at interpretive structure are the most common form of nature trail. Short loops can be tied together into figure eights or stacks; they must, however, be kept short to retain interest and reduce fatigue. [1] Nature trails are not meant to provide the average user with a physical challenge.

Bends and curves should be placed in the trail to help provide the feeling of isolation and privacy for each group on the trail. Care must be taken in designing the trail to avoid intervisible points between nearby trails so that the trail layout does not encourage shortcutting at the expense of the environment.

A four- to six-foot width permits the gathering of small groups at each point. Surfacing of the trails or boardwalk construction will protect the ground from trampling and will assist in keeping the users on the trails. Wood chips, shredded bark, and soil-cementing agents will retain the natural environment. Gravel or native stone set in cement provides a compromise, whereas asphalt or cement might be necessary in heavy-use areas. Split or sawn rail fences will add to traffic control without any serious reduction of aesthetic quality.

Nature trails should follow nearly level grades with very short pitch grades of up to 15 percent. Steps should be used to reduce grade whenever practical. Views into points of interest and vista points will need to be used to reduce grade whenever practical. Views into points of interest and vista points will need to be brushed out so as to increase the scene length. Interpretive signs or numbers keyed to self-guiding pamphlets should be placed at the points of interest along the trail. The subject of signs is covered in Chapter 17.

REFERENCES

1. Ashbough, Byron L. 1965. *Trail Planning and Layout.* National Audubon Society Information Education Bulletin No. 4. New York, N.Y.
2. Bunin, N., D. Jasperse, and S. Cooper. 1980. *A Guide to Designing Accessible Outdoor Recreation Facilities.* Heritage Conservation and Recreation Service, U.S. Department of the Interior. Lake Central Regional Office. Ann Arbor, Mich. 58 pages.
3. Bureau of Outdoor Recreation. 1972. *The 1970 Survey of Outdoor Recreation Activities.* Preliminary Report. U.S. Department of the Interior. Washington, D.C. 105 pages.
4. Cordell, Harold K., and James, George A. 1972. *Visitors' Preferences for Certain Physical Characteristics of Developed Campsites.* Southeast Forest Experiment Station. USDA. Forest Service Research Paper SE-100. 21 pages.
5. Fleming, John P. 1969. In *Proceedings of International Snowmobile Conference.* Bureau of Outdoor Recreation. New York State Conservation Commission. Albany, N.Y., pp. 23–36.
6. Hollenbaugh, William C. 1969. Trails and Signs. In *Proceedings of International Snowmobile Conference.* Albany, N.Y., May 20–21. New York State Conservation Commission.
7. Klopie, Peter. 1971. *An Analysis of Snowmobiling in Ontario: Winter 1969–1970.* Report No. 52. Department of Tourism and Information. Province of Ontario, Canada. 92 pages.
8. Knopp, T.B., and Maloney, J.P. 1972. The Ski Touring Trail Planner. Unpublished manuscript. North Star Ski Touring Club of Minnesota. 25 pages.
9. Lane, Fred W. 1971. Equestrian Trails. In *Proceedings of National Symposium on Trails.* Bureau of Outdoor Recreation, Washington, D.C., pp. 38–40.
10. Larson, R.D. 1966. Ski Touring Trails. In *Trends in Parks and Recreation*, vol. 3, no. 2, pp. 20–22.
11. Lucas, Robert C. 1971. Hikers and Other Trail Users. In *Recreation Symposium Proceedings.*

Syracuse, N.Y. October 1971, pp. 113–122. Northeast Forest Experiment Station, Upper Darby, Pa.

12. Pennsylvania Department of Forests and Waters. 1969. *State Park Planning and Guidelines.* Bureau of State Parks, Harrisburg, Pa. 90 pages.

13. U.S. Department of Agriculture. 1977. *The Nation's Renewable Resources: An Assessment, 1975.* Forest Resources Report No. 21. Government Printing Office. 243 pages.

14. Wagar, J. Alan. 1966. Quality in Outdoor Recreation. In *Trends in Parks and Recreation.* vol. 3, no. 3, pp. 9–12.

13

Water Supply

INTRODUCTION

What are the water needs of a picnicker or a camper? What constitutes usable water? What determines water quality? How can it be made safe? Where can it be found and in what quantities? For what will the water be used? How many uses will occupy an area and when will they be there? How should the water be distributed? These are questions that soon come to the mind of people attempting to plan a water supply system. They deal with problems of quality and quantity requirements, sources, treatment, and distribution. The answers to these questions will aid a recreation area planner to develop a water system that is both safe and adequate for the uses intended.

Water is an essential ingredient for most forest recreation activities. It is important from two views in that water is needed for existence requirements and is desirable for the recreation wants of the user. The comfort level of recreationists is highly dependent upon water. Intensive forest recreation areas are in demand near ponds, lakes, streams, rivers, and oceans. Private picnic and campground developers generally include nearby recreational water as a must for success. This view is substantiated by the heavy development of recreation sites along lakes shores and riverbanks. The development of swimming and boating facilities is covered in Chapter 15, and the supply of water required for the existence needs of recreationists is discussed in this chapter.

QUANTITY OF WATER

Demand

The quantity of water required for a recreation area depends upon the number and types of facilities and upon the intensity of use of those facilities. By investigating the probable uses that people will have for water, the planner will have a start in determining how much water he needs to supply. Average figures of water volumes used with various types of recreation facilities have been published by the United States Public Health Service.[12] Recreation area users need water for drinking, cooking, washing, laundering, and sanitation. Table 13.1 gives a planning guide for water use that is based upon the U.S. Public Health Service estimations.

The use of water in recreation areas fluctuates widely throughout the day; therefore, a planner must consider the average daily water use as well as the peak demands that occur at certain times during the day. The peak demands must be anticipated in order to determine the pipe sizes, pressure losses, and storage requirements necessary to provide sufficient water during these periods.[12]

Certain patterns of peak use of water occur with each type of activity. The peak use in a picnic-swimming area will vary directly with the use of the facilities. As the number of users increases at a beach area through the afternoon, the bathhouse use becomes heavy and the water demand rises. Camping areas probably tend to follow the more familiar water demand patterns found in rural and suburban areas where water-use rates are highest during mealtimes, at midmorning, laundry times, and at bedtime.[12]

Using the figures in Table 13.1 as a guide, one can determine that a picnicker or camper uses an average range of 10 to 50 gallons of water per day when there is running water available. The planner must realize that the availability of water is an invitation to its use. Therefore, the more readily available water is, the more it will be used. The very fact that water is under pressure stimulates its use.[14] The problems of heavy water use must be weighed against the benefits of user satisfaction when deciding for or against a pressure water system.

Campgrounds are generally organized around the basic camping unit which is designed to accommodate a family-sized group. When investigating the water requirements within a campground, the planner should think in terms of water demand per unit rather than per person. Cooking, dishwashing, and laundering are group functions that use the water for the entire family. By using the following five-step method, a planner can approximate the quantity of water that will be required for a planned campground.

The five-step method of approximating the quantity of water needed to supply a planned campground is:

Table 13.1. United States Public Health Service Estimates of Water Requirements.*

	Gallons per Day
Campground with flush toilets each camper	25
Trailer with bath unit each camper	50
Picnic areas with flush toilets each picnicker	10
Showers and bathhouse each person	10
Laundry — self-service per customer	50
Horse drinking	12

*U.S. Public Health Service Manual of Individual Water Supply Systems.

Step 1. *Number of units.* The number of units must be decided upon in the early planning stages. The figure arrived at does not need to be the final size of the campground because expansion may take place at a later date; however, a fixed number of units must be decided upon as a basis for initial planning. Factors influencing the number of camping units are discussed in Chapter 2.

Step 2. *Number of people per unit.* The number of people occupying each camping unit will have an overall effect on the total water consumption. Therefore, some estimate should be made to obtain this figure. Campground managers in the nearby areas probably will be willing to pass on their experiences. Some state or federal recreation areas will produce complete records concerning the size of user groups. The research that has been done to determine figures for user groups indicates that the average camping party consists of four or five people. [3,5]

Quite often the recreation area being planned will have unique attractions that make its appeal different from any other development operating nearby. In this case, intuitive reasoning of the planner will be needed to estimate the probable size, age distribution, and wants of the user groups. Deductive reasoning based on experience, attractions, facilities, and expected clientele should give estimates of sufficient precision for use here. Many campground managers limit the size of a party occupying a given camping unit. This practice does aid both the planner and the manager in their duties; however, it may alienate certain users.

Step 3. *Percent occupancy.* Most campgrounds are developed on the premise that a certain percentage of the camping units will be occupied at all times during the season. Actual percent occupancy figures are generally prone to be much lower than the original estimates. Fifty percent is the maximum figure that should be used in estimating seasonal occupancy.

Having estimated the number of units occupied each day, the planner will have an estimate of the continuing minimum water requirements during the season. Next, he must determine the peakload requirements that must be met periodically on such occasions as holidays and weekends. The difference between the minimum occupancy requirements and the peakload demands will be the volume of water that must be stored throughout the weekdays and before holidays.

Step 4. *Special use.* Irrigation of lawns and shrubbery requires additional water above that needed for peakloads. Sprinklers should spread approximately 300 gallons per hour over 100 square feet. This amounts to 5 gallons per minute or ½ inch of water. The water system should be capable of supplying this volume once per week in addition to meeting the regular demands. Adequate fire protection will require a much larger flow rate than most campgrounds need for normal use; however, the larger water system capability will provide users with more conveniences. The U.S. Public Health Service recommends that a capacity of 500 gallons per hour be specified for new water systems. [12] This is probably beyond the requirements of most campgrounds.

Step 5. *Making estimates.* After the planner has taken the first four steps, he can apply simple mathematics to ascertain the campground needs. For example, consider a campground with 100 units that is expected to have a predicted occupancy of 40 percent on weekdays and 100 percent on weekends. This means that 40 units will be drawing water on a daily basis during the five weekdays; however, 100 units will be used on Friday and Saturday nights. Step 2 indicated that the average group occupying the camping units will probably be composed of five persons and will require approximately 200 gallons per day. A two-acre play area will be irrigated at the rate of ½ inch per week through the summer months.

Requirements	Gallons
Normal occupancy/day 40 × 200 × 5 weekdays	40,000
Irrigation$\frac{43,560}{100}$ × 2 acres × 300 gal/day	261,360
Peakload 100 × 200 × 2	40,000
Weekly requirement	341,360

In this case, the water supply must be capable of providing a minimum of 341,360 gallons per week throughout the season. Large storage areas for retention of water are an alternative to continuous flow; however, costs for such structures are generally prohibitive for recreation area water supply.

Sources of Water

After making the estimate, a planner must consider the water supply available to determine whether or not it is adequate to meet the volume demanded by the proposed project. The obvious step to take here is to compare the anticipated demand with the quantity available at the source. Does the source supply sufficient flow to satisfy the need? The effects of prolonged dry seasons must be considered when evaluating the source. Some water sources may be adequate during the fall, winter, and spring seasons when much of the planning is done; however, they fail during the long dry periods of late summer. Even if the source does not completely fail, it will be at its low point while the recreational load is at its highest.

Aside from personal observation, the planner has many recourses for determining the reliability of the water source. In a few cases, the hydrological records for specific water sources are maintained by the U.S. Geological Survey, the U.S. Army Corps of Engineers, the U.S. Bureau of Sports Fisheries and Wildlife, or some interested state agencies. The use of witness evidence is probably the easiest and often the most reliable way of determining the dependability and fluctuations of a water source in the past. A little investigation will often turn up several "old-timers" who have been familiar with that specific water source for many years back. True, the reliability of the witness's statement could be questioned, but that is a problem for the investigator to weigh. Certainly, the statements of several witnesses would carry more weight than the statement of one witness. One specific reading reference recommended is the U.S. Department of Agriculture's *Climate and Man*.[11] This yearbook of agriculture discusses seasonal variations in rainfall for each state over a long period. The historic rainfall variations should give the planner an idea of what to expect in the future.

If the continued flow of the source is inadequate for direct usage, an alternate solution must be sought. Three choices are available for the planner. One, the size of the recreation area can be reduced until it is in line with what the water source can supply. Two, additional sources can be found to meet the continuous use. Three, a storage system can be developed to store enough water during periods of low demand to satisfy the total need. The use of one or more of these choices might be necessary to bring the water supply into balance with the proposed demands.

Occasionally, a forest recreation area is situated where it can hook onto a municipal water system that has pipelines passing nearby. In many cases, the costs of this connection will be money well spent when balanced against the expense and inconvenience of maintaining a safe and adequate water system. Some parks take water from municipal water systems during the periods of low demand that occur from late evening until early morning. This water is placed in storage for use within the park during the following day.

Unfortunately, municipal water lines seldom run through or near to forest recreation areas. Therefore, the planner must look elsewhere for his source of water. Water is available as it flows over the surface or in the aquifers underground. Surface water is the water on the surface of the earth that makes up the rivers, streams, lakes, and ponds. It is the result of direct runoff or of the surfacing of ground waters. Ground water is the water that has infiltrated into the soil and has percolated downward until reaching an impervious layer. This ground water moves laterally and downward as a result of gravity. In areas of deep soils accumulation, the ground water table establishes a huge underground reservoir.

Certain strata of bedrock, usually sandstones, permit water to move through them. If the next lower bedrock strata are impermeable, they block the downward movement of the water. The sandstone strata then become both an aquifer which serves as a storage area and a pipeline for the trapped water. Hydrostatic pressure buildup as the sandstone strata dip down provides the force for flowing artesian wells. A well tapped into this aquifer will provide water that might have entered the ground many miles away.

When the impermeable rock strata or the impervious soil horizon contacts the earth's surface, the trapped water flows out onto the surface as springs or seeps. Figure 13.1 shows a stylized concept of the perpetual circulation of water

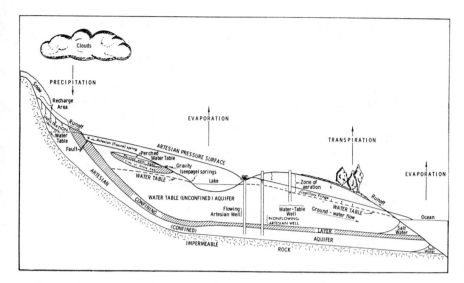

Fig. 13.1. A sketch of the hydrologic cycle showing the various routes of water movement from and toward the ocean. (U.S. Public Health Service.)

from the ocean to the land and back again. This circulation of water is known as the hydrologic cycle.

Surface Water

Some areas of the United States still contain lakes that are pure enough to be used for drinking water. The campground operator who can use such a lake is very fortunate indeed. Some operators use the water directly from adjacent lakes, while others treat it in one or more ways. Maine's Lake Sebago State Park has a water system to supply over 200 camp units. This installation has a chlorination system that handles more than 70,000 gallons of water per day without filtration. Campgrounds on the heavily used Lake Winnipesaukee in New Hampshire pump the water directly from the lake to the user. As the lakes occur further from population centers, they have a better chance of remaining free from contamination.

Wells

Depending upon locality and need, wells may be made by digging, drilling, boring, or driving.[2] Dug and bored wells are usually shallow wells that utilize the ground water table. Drilled and driven wells are usually narrow and deep. Some states require special approval of the health officer for dug wells and other types that are less than 25 feet deep.[7] Pumping of the water from the underground water table lowers the water table around the pump. It is possible to pump a well dry for periods by pumping water out faster than it can be replaced by the water-bearing strata. Aquifers can also be depleted of their water supply by well outlets. However, the results of a depleted aquifer can be more serious than just the occurrence of dry wells. The presence of drinkable water in the aquifer may have been keeping out undesirable salt water. With the water pressure depleted, the aquifer can accept the flow of salt water from the ocean or saline deposits. [12]

Any well should meet the minimum specifications listed below. [2,8,9,12]

1. The well opening should be higher than adjacent ground so as to prevent the flow of surface water into the well.
2. Wells should be placed at a minimum of 100 feet from any possible source of contamination.
3. Upper 10 feet of any well should be cased to prevent seepage of polluted water into the well.
4. Every well must be covered with a waterproof cover or seal.
5. Artesian wells should be cased down to unfissured bedrock so as to prevent loss of pressure.
6. All newly constructed wells should be decontaminated before use to neutralize contamination caused by construction. Usually household bleach will suffice if mixed as two parts water and one part bleach. This mixture should be added to the well at the rate of two quarts for each estimated 100 gallons. This is not necessary for a free-flowing artesian well.

A well must be tested for capacity to determine the amount of water that it can supply. This is done by pumping out water at a given rate per hour and then determining the recovery rate after pumping is stopped. The testing techniques used and the pumps required might differ with the standards of each state health department. In many areas, dug or drilled wells are not possible because of the shallow soil mantle. The deep drilled wells are quite common in the eastern rural areas. However, without the costs of casing included, a drilled well represents an investment of approximately $2 to $3.50 for each foot of depth. In forested areas where a history of successful wells is lacking, investment in a drilled well becomes speculatory. On the other hand, the location of a well near the use area might mean a considerable savings in transmission costs required to move water from an existing surface supply.

Springs

Springs offer an excellent water source for forest recreation areas. Quite often one or more springs providing the proper quality and quantity of water can be found uphill from the recreation area. Gravity feed from these uphill springs will greatly simplify the water storage and distribution system. Springs occur where water-bearing rock strata or impervious soil horizons contact the surface and allow trapped water to flow out of its confinement.

Unfortunately, not all springs produce pure drinking water. The entrapment areas may be so close to the outlet as to permit insufficient filtration. Also, fissured limestone may provide open channels for water to flow through without the benefits of filtration. Glaciated areas have a similar problem to the limestone areas in that contaminated water can seep into underground channels remaining in the glacial drift. As with deep artesian wells, pollution can enter the aquifer at a far distant point and be carried to the spring. Placing an outhouse on the reverse side of the knob from a lower spring will not prevent contamination from entering the spring. Figure 13.2 shows how contamination is believed to have entered a spring by flowing through or along rock strata on the Monongahela National Forest in West Virginia. The spring had been a producer of good water for a long period of years until two privy-type toilets were built on the reverse slope of the hill to accommodate visitors to the fire tower located there.

Any spring should be checked by state health authorities before it is used for drinking purposes. The occurrence of turbidity after a rainstorm is an indication that surface runoff is reaching the spring. The spring should be enclosed to protect the water from contamination from outside sources. Also, the water should not be stored at the spring house but moved to a storage area where any pumping is to take place. Overflow pipes should be at least 6 inches above the ground and should be screened to prevent entrance of rodents and insects.

The minimum precautions for protecting a spring are as follows: [2,12]

1. An open-bottomed, watertight basin should be constructed on bedrock or into

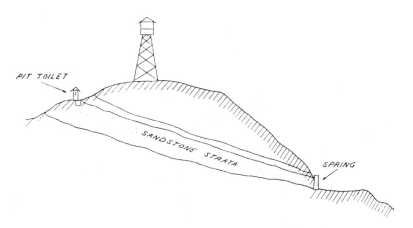

Fig. 13.2. Probable source of contamination of a mountain spring from a reverse slope recreation area.

the impervious layer trapping the water. Allowance must be made for expansion and contraction of the concrete.

2. A tight-fitting, heavy cover should close the top of the spring box. It should overlap the edge of the opening by approximately four inches with downward edges and it should be locked in place.

3. A clean-out drain that is separate from the distribution system should be provided.

4. Provision should be made to permit water to flow into a separate storage facility for eventual distribution.

5. Overflow precautions must be taken. This is generally accomplished by placing an outlet pipe at the maximum desirable water height. This pipe should carry the extra water far enough away from the spring-box to prevent it from undermining the structure.

Measuring Quantity

How can the quantity of flow be measured to determine whether or not a source is adequate? The solution is quite simple if the planner remembers that all he must do is measure the water flowing by a given point each second. This is a three-step problem. Step one is to determine the square feet of area in a vertical cross-section of the stream. The second step is to ascertain how fast the water is flowing through that cross-section. The third step is a simple multiplication of the cross-section area in square feet by the stream velocity in feet per second. Generally, the stream or spring flow serving as a source for drinking water will be small and easily waded. The cross-section should be established on a reach of the stream where the water if flowing smoothly because this technique is not applicable to turbulent flow.

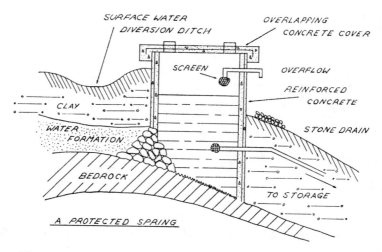

Fig. 13.3. Sketch of a spring house enclosing and protecting a spring.

A simple but effective way to obtain an approximation of flow in a small stream can be made by using a string, a yardstick, and a piece of cork. A point should be placed on each stream bank and a string stretched between them. The points must be placed so that the string is perpendicular to the stream flow. At one-foot intervals along the string, the water depth is measured by placing a yardstick vertically into the stream. These depth measurements and the width measurements are used to find the cross-section area. Directly plotting the cross-section on graph or cross-section paper to scale will provide sufficient precision for finding the area in square feet.

Stream velocity is usually measured slightly below the surface; however, surface measurements are very satisfactory for this technique of stream gauging. Simply place a cork in the water and record the time it takes to float over a premeasured distance. If the cork moves downstream 10 feet in 20 seconds, its velocity can be determined by the following formula.

$$\frac{distance\ (ft)}{time\ (sec)} \times 60\ sec/min = answer\ in\ ft/min$$

Example

$$\frac{10\ ft}{20\ sec} \times 60\ sec = 30\ ft/min$$

The cross-section area in square feet is multiplied by the velocity of the water flow in feet per minute. The answer is given in cubic feet per minute. Since each cubic foot contains 7.48 gallons, a simple conversion gives the answer in gallons per minute.

Example

$$\begin{array}{ccccccc}
\text{stream cross section} & & \text{velocity} & & & & \text{flow} \\
(ft^2) & \times & (ft/min) & \times & 7.48\ gal/ft^3 & = & (gal/min) \\
1.5 & \times & 30 & \times & 7.48 & = & 337\ (approx.)\ gal/min
\end{array}$$

Stream or spring flow may vary greatly during the year; therefore, it should be checked for its potential during the periods that it will be receiving use. In much of the United States, heavy forest recreation use takes place during July and August when the stream flow is characteristically at its lowest.

Elaborate measuring stations are constructed for the purpose of measuring stream flow where the need justifies the expenditure of thousands of dollars. However, recreational planners are basing their needs on educated guesses that are justified by approximations and intuitive reasoning. The expensive and precisely constructed measuring dams, or weirs as they are technically termed, would be unnecessary in all but the largest recreation areas.

If the stream flow is turbulent or if the quantity measurements is critical, a small weir can be constructed and the stream flow computed by mathematics. A 90-degree V-notch weir with a sharp-edge blade will best serve the purpose for this project. Although several designs of weirs have been developed for measuring stream flow under various conditions, the 90-degree V-notch weir provides the greatest sensitivity at low flow and is best suited for small watershed areas of between 5 and 50 acres. They are generally designed to handle a maximum crest of two feet.[10]

A simple V-notch weir can be constructed from a half-inch-thick sheet of exterior or marine plywood. It should be embedded into the bottom and in the banks of the streambed so that it effectively dams up the stream flow. Four-inch baffles should be fastened to the plywood below the soil line with resorcinal glue and screws to prevent seepage.[15] The 90-degree notch should be centered on the top edge of the board. It should be cut to a depth of one or two feet and edged with metal to form a sharp crest. Since the principle of the V-notch weir relies on the water breaking away from the lip of the weir, the crest must be sharp enough to produce this breakaway action. Galvanized metal is used for the blade in the larger and permanent structures; however, any sheet metal will serve the purpose for this operation if it can be cut accurately to form a 90-degree V-notch.

Placement of the weir is important. The bottom of the notch must be at least twice the height of the maximum stream flow.[11] This is to prevent drowning of the notch during high-flow periods. In cases where the stream gradient is so steep that it will interfere with the operation of the weir, a small ponding basin should be scooped out to hold the pool behind the weir. Precautions must be taken in areas having coarse soils to prevent by-pass of the weir by leakage.

The amount of flow can be determined by measuring the head of water be-

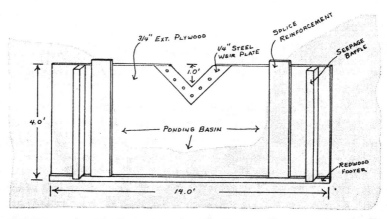

Fig. 13.4. Schematic view from upstream side of an installed plywood cutoff wall as developed by R.Z. Whipkey.

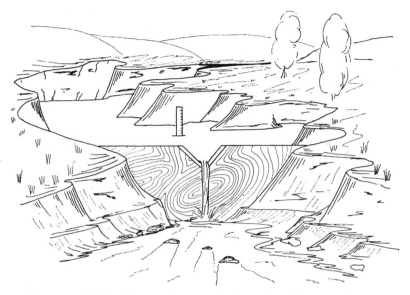

Fig. 13.5. Sketch of low-cost homemade V-notch weir in operation.

hind the notch and using a formula developed by King for this purpose.[6] A measuring stick should be firmly mounted in a vertical position upstream from the weir. The distance between the weir and the measuring stick should be at least twice the depth of the notch. Calibration of the measuring post should be done in tenths of feet with the zero-point level with the bottom of the notch. For convenience and accuracy, the calibration should take place after the stick is implaced. If an engineer's level is not available to locate the zero point, the water level can be used with sufficient precision. At the instant the water level reaches the point of the notch, it will mark the zero point on the post. The calibrations should be measured upward from that point. The flow over the blade cannot be used to determine height of head because of the downward curve of the water. Table 13.2 gives flow values over the weirs described here as they would be determined by King's formula for computing flow over sharp-crested 90-degree V-notch weirs.[6]

STORAGE OF WATER

The storage of water becomes a consideration if the source does not supply a continuous and sufficient quantity to assure uninterrupted usage or if the source is not elevated to provide the proper pressure for usage. The problem of water pressure can be solved as part of the storage for sufficient quantity. Elevated tanks and ground-level cisterns provide the best solution to recreation

Table 13.2 Approximate Flow over 90-Degree V-notch Weirs for Each Tenth Foot of Head.*

Height of Head	Discharge	
	ft³/sec	gal/min
0.1	0.008	0.060
0.2	0.047	0.352
0.3	0.129	0.965
0.4	0.262	1.960
0.5	0.455	3.404
0.6	0.714	5.341
0.7	1.044	7.810
0.8	1.452	10.862
0.9	1.943	14.535
1.0	2.520	18.852
1.1	3.189	23.857
1.2	3.954	29.579
1.3	4.818	36.043
1.4	5.785	43.278
1.5	6.860	51.320
2.0	13.960	104.435

*1. By Formula: $Q = 2.54 H^{2.47}$ (King, 1954).

area water storage problems. The pneumatic pumps and tanks used in home water systems generally lack sufficient volume or require too large an investment and upkeep for use in recreation areas.

Above-ground storage tanks can be made of wood, metal, concrete, or brick; however, redwood or cypress wood is the most commonly used material. Redwood and cypress will probably produce the cheapest tank and will remain watertight while the tank contains water. Generally, a two-day peak supply of water is planned for an elevated storage tank.[12] Water can be moved into the tank by gravity or raised by pumping. Whenever the terrain will permit it, gravity flow frees the recreation area manager from the worry of pump operation and maintenance.

The ground-level cistern or reservoir is the best facility for storing large quantities of water for recreation area use. The ground-level reservoir is a large waterproof container that is set down into the ground and covered to prevent the contamination of its contents. The reservoir should not be placed where high water or surface runoff could enter. The overlapping cover should be raised at least 4 inches above the ground surface and locked into place. The floor should slope toward the drain to permit complete drainage and all openings should be screened to exclude rodents.[12] Overflow systems must be independent of any sewage system.[2]

The concrete and brick reservoirs can be made watertight by an interior coating of rich cement. The U.S. Public Health Service objects to the use of asphalt

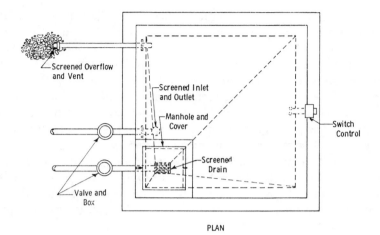

PLAN

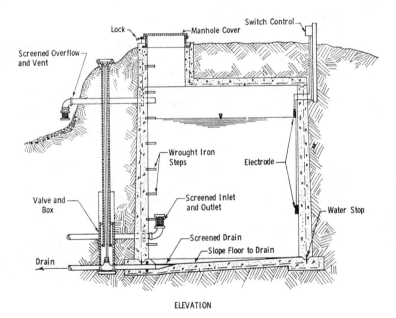

ELEVATION

Fig. 13.6. Typical ground-level reservoir. (U.S. Public Health Service.)

or tar for waterproofing because of the objectionable taste it can give to the water and because it might react chemically with some of the chemicals used for treatment. [12]

As with wells, the reservoir should be disinfected before use and after repairs that could pollute the water supply. The system should be flushed clean of any dirt and particles resulting from construction. Next, a disinfecting solution of calcium hypochlorite should be added and allowed to stand for 24 hours. The

American Water Works Association recommends that the 1.2 pounds of high-test 70 percent calcium hypochlorite be used for each 1,000 gallons of water in the reservoir. If no chlorine is present at the end of the 24-hour period, the process should be repeated.[1] Flush out the disinfecting solution before putting the reservoir into operation.

The size of the storage facility required will depend upon the quantity of water demanded at peak usage and the system's ability to replenish the supply during the dry season. The problem of water quantity requirements was discussed earlier in this chapter. As mentioned earlier, water use generally is confined to the half day beginning at breakfast and ending at evening. Because of this one-sided distribution of use, the water supply or storage must be larger than it would if the use was spread evenly over the recharge period. The peakload expectation is used to determine the minimum storage facility required. This is done as shown in the steps below.

1. Estimate daily water requirement during peak use of campground.
2. Determine hourly recharge rate.
3. Subtract twelve times hourly recharge rate from maximum water requirement.
4. Remainder is the minimum size of storage required. Example of method for determining minimum water storage requirement:
   Estimated daily water use during full capacity = 40,000 gal
   Recharge capacity of spring during lowest flow = 2000 gal/hr

   40,000 − (12 × 2000) = 16,000 gal (approx.) to be stored.

This example is based on the assumption that the water supply is capable of producing enough water over a 24-hour period to supply the peakload requirements. If it cannot do this, additional storage must be built in order to collect water during low-use days, or supplemental sources must be developed. The size limitations caused by costs or space may preclude too large of a storage space. The reservoir needed to hold 16,000 gallons, approximately large enough to fulfill the requirements in the example would have to contain 2,120 cubic feet of space. Such a reservoir would require inside dimensions of 14 × 14 × 11 feet.

DISTRIBUTION SYSTEM

The distribution system must accomplish two objectives. First, it must transport water from the source and storage area to the point of use in the most efficient manner possible. Second, the distribution system must protect the water from contamination during transit. No water-quality reductions should occur as a result of the distribution system. Most state health departments have regulations and guidelines for water supply systems. These are available without charge upon request and should be consulted prior to construction of the system.

Pipelines for small distribution systems are usually made from the standard galvanized pipe and fittings, although pipes of many other materials are suitable. Plastic pipe material is often used for hot or cold water transmission because of its lower cost and convenience of installation; however, plastic pipe requires more protection from crushing than does galvanized pipe. All plastic pipe should be certified by the National Sanitation Foundation or similar testing laboratory as being nontoxic or nontaste producing.[12] The transmission lines should be as straight as possible to reduce cost and maintenance and deep enough to avoid danger from freezing if they are to be used during cold weather. The expense of deep burial of the water lines can be avoided if the lines are drained prior to the danger of freezing. Air vents should be placed at high points to bleed air out of the lines, and valves should be placed in convenient locations for lines drainage or repairs. A standard "T" connection can be used instead of the valves that are to be used for drainage. The open end can be capped during normal-use periods. Besides providing for a savings in the capital investment, the "T" connections can permit future expansion of the system with a minimum of effort.

Although state regulations may vary somewhat, they generally agree that water lines must always pass above any sewage lines and that the two kinds of pipelines must remain ten feet apart when parallel. Also, no connections of any kind can be tolerated between the drinking water system and a contaminated source. Decontamination of a pipeline with a 40- to 60-milliliter solution of chlorine for 24 hours is necessary after its construction or after any repairs that could contaminate it.

Self-closing nonthreaded faucets cost more initially. However, they will save money in the long run by conserving water and reducing the muddy mess that can be associated with a water tap. Occasional threaded faucets should be available for irrigation or fire control.

The question of the pipeline construction need not be difficult to solve. The line should be laid as straight as possible in a trench for efficiency and safety. Although most reliable textbooks and consultants will advise that the pipes be buried in trenches, many recreation areas have surface lines. In certain situations, the surface lines have proved satisfactory. They save digging in the very rocky areas that are often associated with forest or mountain land. Also, leaks are easily detected and repaired. Surface lines have two problems that are not as serious with subsurface lines: (1) they must be drained to prevent freezing, and (2) the pipeline should be inaccessible to the public so as to guard against accidental damage or vandalism.

Determining the proper diameter pipe is a problem facing the developer. The three variables that must be calculated in order to calculate the pipe size are (1) the water pressure, (2) the hydraulic gradient, and (3) the flow per minute.

Water pressure is measured in pounds per square inch (psi). A column of water that is 2.31 feet high will produce one pound per square inch of downward pressure. Therefore, the normal domestic water pressure of 15 to 60 psi will require a head, or column of water, that is 35 to 140 feet high.[12]

Figure 13.7 gives the pipe size that is required to obtain a given quantity of water at a given head loss per foot. The term "head loss" refers to the head or column height in excess of that required to give the required water pressure. In order to obtain the average domestic pressure of 30 psi, a head of 2.3 × 30, or 69 feet, is required. If the reservoir is 200 feet above the outlet, a head loss of 200 − 69, or 131 feet, occurs within the distribution system. The head loss per foot is calculated by dividing the head loss by the length of the pipeline in feet.

$$\text{hydraulic gradient (head loss/foot)} = \frac{\text{head loss}}{\text{length of line in feet}}$$

If the reservoir is 1,000 feet from the point of use, the head loss per foot is equal to the head loss (H) of 131 divided by the length (L) of 1,000.

$$\frac{H}{L} = \frac{131}{1000} = 0.131.$$

Now that the pressure and hydraulic gradient have been determined, the only remaining factor to be resolved is that of quantity of water required at the distribution point. The U.S. Department of Health, Education, and Welfare recommends that any new system be designed to supply at least 8.5 gallons per minute.[12] Although this may be excessive for some recreation areas, it provides fire protection for a slightly higher development cost than for a smaller water system. Also, with the increasing use of outdoor recreation facilities has come the need for more complete sanitation facilities that include flush toilets, showers, and laundries. All of these facilities require large quantities of water. In general, the recreation area that will continue to satisfy its users must be able to provide these facilities and be ready to expand or enlarge them.

After the desired water pressure, the hydraulic gradient, and the flow per minute have been determined, the pipe diameter can be obtained from Fig. 13.7. By entering the calculated values into the table, one determines that the required pipe diameter for galvanized iron pipes in the example is approximately ⅞ inch.

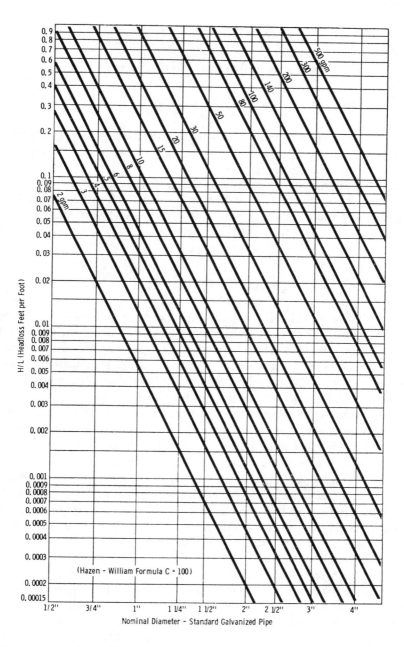

Fig. 13.7. Required pipe diameter is dependent upon head loss and desired flow.

Example

$$H = 200 - 2.3 \times 30 = 131 \text{ (feet)}$$

$$\frac{H}{L} = 0.131 \text{ (head loss in feet/foot of line)}$$

$$\text{Flow} = 8.5 \text{ (gpm)}$$

Therefore, 7/8-inch pipe is required (Fig. 13.7). Because pipe comes in inch and half-inch sizes, the next larger size above the calculated value must be chosen to meet the desired specifications.

The distribution system should be thoroughly flushed out and disinfected prior to use. Also, no outlets should be placed down in bowls, sinks, or other containers that could fill up to the outlet. This is to protect against back-syphoning through a flooded outlet.

QUALITY OF WATER

The U.S. Public Health Service published standards for drinking water in 1962.[13] Many of the states are now following with similar standards that will assist the campground planner in his development plan. A check with the state health service is advisable right at the beginning of the recreation area planning stage and will determine if an unsurmountable stumbling block exists. Some states have drinking water standards, but they do not require any testing for purity. Many recreation area operators have the drinking water tested as a matter of safety to their customers and a safeguard for themselves against lawsuits that might develop as a result of providing contaminated water.

What does the term "water quality" mean? It is the relative bacteriological, physical, radiological, and chemical characteristics of water in relation to its safe and desirable use by humans.[12] The bacteriological or biologic quality is probably the most serious and widespread problem concerning water quality. It is the biologic quality that is considered when the term "purity" is used among laymen. The other facets of water quality are locally limiting, but not universally troublesome.

The bacteriological characteristic is determined by counting the number of coliform bacteria present in a water sample. Although the coliform group of bacteria are nonpathogenic, they are used to measure pollution of water for two reasons. First, they dwell in human intestines and have life cycles that are similar to pathogenic bacteria. Second, they are more numerous and easier to detect than the pathogenic bacteria. Techniques for sampling the water are available from the health departments of each state. The U.S. Public Health Service standards permit only one coliform organism for each 100 milliliters of water.[12,13] This amounts to about two bacteria in each cup of water.

The use of the coliform count gives only an indication of the pathogenic bacteria present in the water. It does not measure the enteric viruses present. Evidence points out, however, that water supplies are not frequently guilty of carrying viral infections. Fortunately virus organisms are far less numerous than are the coliform bacteria; therefore, if the virus count were too high, the coliform count probably would be proportionally higher and thereby drawing attention to the pollution.

The physical characteristics of water are turbidity, taste, and odor. Turbidity refers to the presence of suspended mineral and organic material in the water. When the suspended particles are readily visible in a glass of water, the turbidity level is too high. Even though the water is biologically safe, it is aesthetically undesirable.

The dark color often seen in woodland streams is generally caused by organic acids given off by decaying vegetation. The local terms of "pine water" and "cedar water" aptly describe appearance of organically colored water. This phenomenon is generally associated with water that has collected in a bog area. Coloration of water also can be caused by dissolved inorganic substances and by algae. Coloration caused by organic acids or dissolved minerals is often accompanied by a taste. Tastes in water are very objectional to the consumer and should be avoided if possible. Certain treatment can be done to lessen or eliminate some offending tastes.

Turbidity, color, and taste may cause the user to seek an alternate source of water. In the case of forest recreation, the user might not remain in the recreation area.

The chemical characteristics of water in an area are closely tied to the geology of the area. Limestone valleys generally have hard water springs and streams, while the coal-bearing sediments of the carboniferous era produce very acid water. When water falls as precipitation, it is relatively free from dissolved chemicals. As it flows over, around, and through the rocks and soil, the water dissolves and carries away chemicals inherent in the geology of the area. The usual chemical analysis of water determines the total hardness, alkalinity, acidity, and the presence of sulfates and chlorides. However, there are local problem areas where water contains an excessive amount of toxic chemicals and cannot be used. Tests for these chemicals should be made in areas where they are commonly found.

Water Treatment

Water that is destined for human consumption should be of the highest possible quality. It should be technically safe from bacteriologic pollution, free of suspended particles, colorless, and without odor or taste. Some recreation areas supply water that meets these standards and do not need to treat the water in any way. Others are not so fortunate and must be involved in extensive water treatment. The majority of forest recreation areas probably are in an intermediate position. That is, they have a water supply from wells, springs, streams, or lakes that meets most minimal standards, but are near enough to the danger point for concern. The possibility of pollution is something to be considered by a private operator from a business standpoint. Even a temporary closure because of poor water quality could have a disastrous effect on a private business establishment. Many large developments chlorinate water as a general practice for protection against possible pollution even though the water is biologically safe for drinking.

The treatment that water gets will vary according to the conditions of the water. There are several treatment processes used in preparing water for drinking. Any one or more may be required in any specific instance. These processes and their purposes are given in Table 13.3.

The most important treatment process is that of disinfecting the water. Chlorine-bearing compounds serve this purpose quite well and are easy to administer. The most popular form of chlorine is calcium hypochlorite which is commercially available in tablet and powder form. Sodium hypochlorite solutions are commonly used in small water systems where the household bleaches are available at local stores. The available chlorine in the sodium hypochlorite solutions varies in strength from 3 to 15 percent.

The chlorination of the water should be done by one of the many commercially designed systems on the market. The equipment should be installed and operated so that the water is treated and rapidly mixed with the chlorine continuously. The U.S. Public Health Service states that "at least two parts per million of free residual chlorine should be in contact with the water for not less than twenty minutes before the treated water reaches the first consumer."[14]

State health authorities should be consulted during the early stages of devel-

Table 13.3 Water Treatment Processes and Their Purpose.

Process	Purpose	Technique
Sedimentation	Removal of heavy suspended particles	Gravity settling in quiescent pond or tank
Coagulation	Removal of very fine suspended particles	Flocculation of solids by adding alum in still water
Filtration	Removal of suspended particles	Passage of water through sand or diatomaceous earth. Sometimes used with sedimentation when water is very turbid
Disinfection	Destroy pathogenic organisms	Addition of chemical disinfectant with high germicidal power

opment planning. Their advice early in the planning might help to prevent their wrath later on. Most state health authorities are quite willing to help an operator get off to a good start, but it is their responsibility to protect the citizens that will be using the facility. If the water supply system is going to be disapproved, it is better to have it happen before hundreds of dollars are invested in it.

REFERENCES

1. American Water Works Association. 1954. *Procedure for Disinfecting Water Mains.* Report C601-54. Park Avenue, New York, N.Y.
2. Elhers, V., and Steele, E. 1965. *Municipal and Rural Sanitation*, 6th ed. McGraw-Hill, New York. 643 pages.
3. Fine, I., and Werner, E. 1960. *Camping in State Parks and Forests in Wisconsin*, vol. 1, no. 3. University of Wisconsin. 18 pages.
4. Forbes, R., and Meyer, A.B. 1961. *Forestry Handbook.* Ronald Press, New York.
5. James, G., and Repley, T. 1963. *Instructions for Using Traffic Counters to Establish Recreation Visits and Use.* Southeast Experiment Station Paper SE-3. Asheville, N.C.
6. King, H. 1954. *Handbook of Hydraulics*, 4th ed. McGraw-Hill, New York. 556 pages.
7. Michigan Department of Health. 1965. *Regulations for Certain Water Supplies in Michigan.* Act No. 146, Public Acts of 1919 as amended.
8. Ohio Department of Health. 1964. *Camp Sanitation — Laws, Regulations, and Recommendations.* Columbus, Ohio.
9. Ort, D.R. 1963. Recommended Campground Sanitation Requirements. In *Guidelines for Developing Land for Outdoor Recreational Uses.* Cooperative Extension Service. Purdue University, West Lafayette, Ind.
10. Reinhart, K., and Pierce, R. 1964. *Stream-Gazing Stations for Research on Small Watersheds.* Agriculture Handbook No. 268. U.S. Forest Service NE Experiment Station, Upper Darby, Pa.
11. U.S. Department of Agriculture. 1941. *Climate and Man. Yearbook of Agriculture.* Government Printing Office, Washington, D.C.
12. U.S. Public Health Service. 1962. *Manual of Individual Water Supply Systems.* Publication No. 24. U.S. Department of Health, Education, and Welfare, Washington, D.C.
13. ———. 1962. *Drinking Water Standards.* Publication No. 956. U.S. Department of Health, Education, and Welfare, Washington, D.C.
14. ———. 1965. *Environmental Health Practice in Recreation Areas.* Publication No. 1195. U.S. Department of Health, Education, and Welfare, Washington, D.C.
15. Whipkey, R.Z. 1961. *Plywood Cutoff Walls for Temporary Weirs.* Central States Forest Experiment Station Note 150. U.S. Forest Service, Columbus, Ohio.

14

Sanitation

INTRODUCTION

Sanitation, as it is covered in this chapter, refers to the collection, treatment, or processing of sewage, refuse, and wash water. Sanitation facilities are necessary for the protection of the visiting public, the employees, and the nearby communities from diseases.[13] Although sewage and refuse are menaces to health, they are to a much greater extent creators of aesthetic nuisances. They are offensive to both the senses of smell and sight and cause aesthetic devaluation that is far out of proportion with their danger to human health.[2]

Adequate sanitary facilities at forest recreation areas are of the utmost importance. The user will often judge the recreational quality of the area by the sanitation facilities. In fact, research has shown that the sanitary facilities are more often criticized than any other part of camping.[4] By definition, the U.S. Forest Service considers sanitary facilities a part of any of its developed recreation areas.[9] Of course, user reaction is just one reason, and perhaps not the most important one, for providing sanitary facilities at such areas.

SEWAGE

Sewage is, by definition, human excreta that has been mixed with water; however, in the field of forest recreation where water systems are not always used, sewage has become a synonym for excreta.[3] This change has probably occurred because of the social acceptance of the word sewage and not of excreta. In this book, we shall consider sewage to be any human waste products.

The recreation area manager or planner needs to have an understanding of the basic principles involved in sewage treatment so that he can sensibly investigate the available systems or analyze troubles in existing systems. In other words, knowledge of the capabilities and limitations of the various sewage systems will aid the manager in giving the best service to the public for the money that he has at his disposal.

Characteristics and Biology of Sewage

Solids make up only 800 parts per million of water-borne sewage so that the actual volume of solids is very small for the problems it creates. Furthermore, only half of the solids are organic matter and therefore decomposible. Why should the reader be concerned over such a small amount of solids since the solids themselves are not pathogenic? Why not simply be concerned with killing the disease-bearing organisms? The reason for being so concerned about the organic solids is that it is the decomposing organic matter that produces the offensive odors and dark colors that are associated with sewage. The organic matter must be decomposed before the sewage effluent is put into the soil or run into streams or else serious problems occur. Organic matter will plug up the pores in the soil mantle and prevent the infiltration of the effluent. Also the aquatic structure of the stream will be changed because of the presence of the undecomposed organic matter.

The decomposition of organic matter is a result of bacteriological processes that take place either in the presence or in the absence of free oxygen. Organic matter is decomposed by aerobic bacteria when sufficient free oxygen is present and by anaerobic bacteria when free oxygen is not present.

The aerobic bacteria carry on their life process in the presence of free oxygen that occurs in the air or is dissolved in the water. The aerobic process is odorless and relatively rapid in that it takes a matter of hours. Nitrates and sulfates are produced through the oxidation of nitrites and sulfur compounds occurring in the organic matter. These products are available for use as plant fertilizer.

Anaerobic bacteria act on the organic compounds in the absence of free oxygen. Since the bacteria require oxygen to survive, they take it from oxygen-containing compounds within the sewage. This is a reduction technique that occurs commonly in nature. Swamp gases such as methane are products of anaerobic activity occurring in the wet areas. The gray mottling that is asssociated with poorly drained soils is a result of the reduction of the iron compounds in the mineral soil by anaerobic bacteria.

Decomposition by the anaerobic action is very slow, and the organic matter may require many weeks to stabilize completely into the dark and almost odorless humus.[3] Ammonia and hydrogen sulfide are two very odorous products of this process. In cases where the free oxygen supply is limited, the aerobic action might use up all of the free oxygen supply, and the decomposition process will switch to an anaerobic action.

Decomposition of organic matter dumped into streams will occur if the water temperature is above 40°F. If the quantity of sewage is sufficient, the stream's supply of free oxygen will be depleted, setting the stage for anaerobic processes to begin with its accompanying odors and colors. Fish cannot live in streams that do not contain dissolved free oxygen. With the use of its open streams for sewers, society has created widespread channels of aesthetic degradation through the countryside. Fortunately, all is not lost because nature has the ability to correct some of man-created sewage problems.

The streams can "cleanse" themselves to a certain degree if the pollution is not overwhelming. As the stream water moves along, it absorbs oxygen through the surface and ripple action. Algae growing in the water use carbon dioxide and produce oxygen which greatly adds to the recovery rate of the dissolved oxygen. As the stream recovers and the oxygen approaches saturation, aerobic bacteria again take over the decomposition of organic matter. Although pathogenic organisms die off as time passes, some survive for a very long time. These surviving pathogens make the danger of disease too great to ever consider once polluted water safe for drinking purposes without treatment.

Neither aerobic nor anaerobic bacteria are associated with disease; they are naturally occurring bacteria that function when the conditions are favorable for growth of such organisms. If the conditions of food, temperature, and moisture are favorable, the bacteria will grow. On the other hand, anaerobic and aerobic action do not remove infectious agents from the sewage.[11] They simply decompose the organic solids within the sewage without having any great effect on pathogenic organisms.

Pathogenic organisms contained within sewage are relatively small in number, and they meet a hostile environment immediately upon leaving the human body. Within five days, most of the typhoid and typhus bacteria are dead.[3] A much more common group of bacteria organisms are the coliforms. Although these coliform bacteria are not pathogenic, they do have a life cycle that parallels the pathogens. Therefore, the coliforms are used as indicators of water contamination.[10]

Sewage Disposal

Sewage disposal at forest recreation developments will generally be less elaborate than those in municipal areas; to the user, however, they are every bit as important. Of course, there are the wilderness seekers who do not want to see any signs of sewage disposal systems other than a shovel. This chapter confines its interest to the developed forest recreation areas and leaves the wilderness user to his own digging.

Many different methods of disposing of sewage are being used in developed forest recreation areas. Basically, these systems either store the human waste in some sort of container or they move it in water through a treatment process. Therefore, the fundamental classification of the disposal systems is made on the basis of whether or not the system uses water for carrying the sewage.

The decision to use water carriage or nonwater carriage systems will depend largely upon available capital, expected use, soil conditions, and water quantity. Nonwater carriage systems are considerably cheaper to build than water carriage systems. However, they are the less desirable of the two classes of sewage disposal from maintenance costs and user satisfaction standpoints. The public favors the flush toilet systems at the present time. For this reason, private campground owners who must cater to the will of the customers should make an effort to install a water carriage system. [8]

State sanitary codes in many states are just beginning to be written up for forest recreation developments. In the absence of specific legislation, many states have made trailer park or tourist accommodation regulations apply to campgrounds. Picnic and other day-use areas have been ignored except as they are controlled and guided by local ordinances. Some states are presently attempting to pass laws for state licensing of campgrounds in addition to establishing sanitary codes. [2]

In all cases, the best arrangement for sewage disposal is the tying into a municipal type sewage disposal system. Although the initial costs may be higher than for a separate system, the problems will be fewer. Most of the problems concerning soil and water pollution from disposal of sewage are solved when a municipal system is used. Unfortunately, most forest recreation areas are not situated near a municipal sewer and must be served by some other sewage disposal system.

Nonwater Carriage Sewage Systems

There are five types of nonwater carriage sewage systems that can be used in recreation areas. They are:

1. Pump-out vault privy.
2. Simple pit privy.
3. Composting toilets.
4. Chemical tanks.
5. Incinerator vaults.

Of these five, the simple pit privy and the pump-out vault are the types usually employed in forest recreation areas. They are the cheapest to construct and the easiest to maintain.

Nonwater carriage disposal systems are not as desirable as water carriage systems, but they are adequate under certain situations and used under almost any condition. [13] Light use, insufficient water, or unsuitable soil conditions for water carriage systems are three valid reasons for the use of nonwater carriage disposal of sewage. The cost factor is often used as a reason to avoid flush toilets; however, this argument does not always hold up in heavily used recreation areas. Temporary-use areas that are not designed for continuous use and therefore do not warrant a large investment would be a place where costs could be held down by less elaborate sanitary facilities. Overflow, or peakload, areas for campgrounds are not intended to give the user more than adequate facilities; therefore, privy toilets would satisfy the short-term use and the minimal facility requirements.

Although water carriage systems are best from the sanitation and user satisfaction standpoints, they do not preclude the use of other systems. Many large and heavily used picnic and campgrounds in some states are still using privies with no adverse effect. However, this is because of excellent construction and maintenance techniques such as those used at Point Beach State Park in Wisconsin, where pump-out vault toilets are proving satisfactory. Whether because of poor planning or insufficient maintenance, privy type toilets are generally not satisfactory in heavy-use areas.

Pump-Out Vault Privy

The pump-out vault privy has proved to be the best nonwater carriage system in places where use is moderately heavy. The pit is lined with concrete so that it is waterproof and prevents the escape of any liquids into the soil or water table. Periodically, the contents of the tank are pumped out by a contractor with the appropriate equipment. In order to facilitate the emptying of the pit, a tightly sealed exterior pump-out opening should be built. The state sanitary codes may vary on pump-out vault size requirements and should be checked in advance of building. Figure 14.1 shows a pump-out vault toilet built in accordance with U.S. Forest Service designs. The land should slope away from the structure in order to carry away surface runoff. The U.S. Forest Service recommends a 12:1 slope away from the building to accomplish satisfactory runoff.

Simple Pit Privy

The oldest and still very common type of sewage disposal system is the simple pit toilet. This is little more than a small building placed over a hole in the ground. For safety, the sides are often shored with lumber or stone, and the floor is made from a precast reinforced concrete slab.[9] A 50-foot safety zone is needed between a privy and water sources; however, some states require as much as 100 feet between the privy and the water source.[3]

As with pump-out pits, it is desirable to keep out surface runoff water. This can be done by maintaining at least a 12:1 slope away from the privy.[9] The pit privy functions better if the contents are dry; therefore, if the area is situated where there is a danger of high water, some other system should be considered. Also, the rising water table would increase the danger of subsurface water pollution and make the pit privy undesirable. Any water that has collected in the pit will be a breeding place for mosquitoes unless treated. A cup of kerosine added to the contents each week will control their breeding.

Any biologic action taking place in the pit will be impeded by disinfectants;

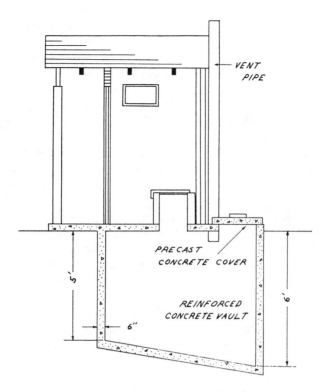

Fig. 14.1. Diagram of pump-out vault toilet.

care should therefore be taken to prevent their introduction. Also, screening and a self-closing toilet seat will help to exclude rodents and insects from the pit.

Odors and pit toilets have appeared to be inseparable over the years. Some odors can be reduced by the application of burnt lime; but this has proved to be of limited value. In recent years, the U.S. Forest Service has come up with a satisfactory technique for controlling these bad odors. Wagar has developed a convection stack device to move air currents down through the seat opening and out through a ventilating stack.[14]

Simple ventilation stacks have proved to be satisfactory only when the pit contents were warm enough to permit the air to rise through the stack. The convection stack developed by Wagar uses a gas or kerosine burner in the stack to create convection currents. Besides causing the desired movement of air, the flame in the stack burns and modifies some of the offensive gases as they move upward through the stack.

A flash barrier is needed with this convection system to prevent ignition of volatile fuels that might be dumped into the pit. These flash barriers can be fabricated from wire mesh scouring pads that have been unrolled and repacked until they are packed so densely as to block all but pinpoint spots of light, the theory here being that any flash originating at the flame would be cooled below ignition when passing through the copper strand barrier.

Completely prepared convection stack units can now be purchased from the commercial forest supply companies. If this system of odor control is to be installed, the developer should obtain Wagar's research note from the USFS Northeastern Forest Experiment Station.

Unfortunately, the effectiveness and simplicity of this system of odor control do have a drawback. It has encouraged the use of pit toilets in some eastern state parks where the use is much too heavy to warrant such a method of sewage disposal.

Toilet buildings need all the help that they can get to be appealing to most users. Large central washhouses with tile floors and electric lights require an enormous investment and do not fit in small recreation areas. Two very important steps have been taken in recent years to improve the lot of privy users. First, the homemade toilet risers are being replaced by the commercially sold stainless steel risers with plastic seats.[9] The size and shape of these risers make cleaning up easier and reduce horrifying thoughts in the minds of parents of young children. Second, public agencies are abandoning the strict policy of constructing dark and dreary buildings just to avoid using "unnatural" building materials. The use of

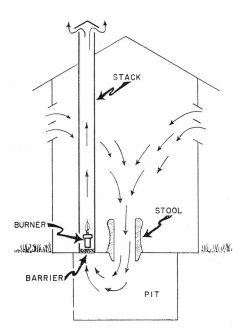

Fig. 14.2. Diagram of pit toilet showing air circulation caused by convection stack. (Forest Service.)

corrugated translucent fiberglass roofing has done a lot to brighten up the privy and make its interior more attractive. The translucent fiberglass roofing should be used whenever possible.

Some attempts have been made to use prefabricated light-gauge corrugated metal buildings for privies. The author's observations indicate that these are unsuitable for forest recreation areas. The metal does not withstand the beating that it receives, and the entire structure is very susceptable to severe damage by vandalism.

Composting Toilets

The composting toilet employs the aerobic bacteria for digesting organic wastes. The human waste is combined with cellulose material such as grass clippings, paper products, or woodchips in a sloping fiberglass tank where the aerobic microorganisms digest the mixture. Gases are vented through tall roof stacks. The roof stacks should be taller than any adjacent structure on the building and they should be topped with a wind propelled, rotary ventillator. Also, a small electric fan can be placed in the stack to insure an adequate flow of air.[1]

The composting process creates heat that serves to kill harmful bacteria. Temperature is an important condition for the composting process that operates most efficiently near 104°F. When the internal temperature rises to above 131°F, it begins to inactivate the composting microorganisms even though the internal temperatures often reach as high as 160°F.[7] Solar collectors are used in some cases to keep the composting temperature high enough during cooler weather. Electric heating cables can be used to supply heat in colder climates having limited sunshine.

No water is needed and the cost for a park-quality restroom facility is half the cost of a normal flush-type facility.

Water Carriage Sewage Systems

There are three types of individual water carriage sewage systems that are satisfactory for use in a recreation area. The underground distribution system employing a septic tank and a leaching field is very commonly used in areas that are not serviced by municipal sewage systems. An aerobic tank digestion method with a leeching field is a second system. The surface distribution into a stabilization pond is a less common system that is ideally suited for many forest recreation areas. Many regulations governing use and many prejudices based upon misuse of these systems exist at all levels of government. Local sanitation codes should be consulted prior to construction. On-the-ground investigation and rigid engineering standards are necessary to assure that these systems will perform satisfactorily.

The investment is too large and the dangers are too numerous to leave the sewage disposal system at the mercy of a contractor. The developer should either plan the system himself or have it done by a qualified person for his approval. Most important, the developer should oversee every step of the construction to assure proper installation.

Septic-tank systems

The septic-tank system is probably the most economical and practical method of sewage disposal where the quantities of sewage are small and the soils are suitable for dispersing the effluent.[13] Proper planning and installation are critical for the satisfactory functioning of a septic-tank system. Improper construction or indiscriminate use of septic-tank systems has created many serious economic and health problems.

A septic-tank system is made up of a buried waterproof tank, a distribution box, and a tile drainfield all connected together by continuous iron or terracotta pipes. The purpose of this system is to get the sewage effluent dispersed into the soil mantle. This purpose is accomplished by passing the sewage through the septic tank where it is conditioned by anaerobic bacteria. When the conditioned effluent passes from the tank, it moves through the distribution box and into the porous leaching lines where it infiltrates into the soil.

The success of a septic tank depends upon the soil's ability to absorb the effluent rapidly enough to prevent the fluid from breaking out onto the ground surface or backing up into the plumbing fixtures. Some soils are loose enough to handle large quantities of liquid, while others are not suited for effluent disposal. A percolation test should be run to rate the soil for effluent disposal.

The percolation test measures the rate at which water will infiltrate and percolate into moist soil. At least six test holes must be drilled or dug on the proposed absorption site. The holes can be from four to twelve inches in diameter and should reach as deeply as the proposed absorption trenches. The sides of the holes should be roughened slightly and all loose material removed. A two-inch layer of pebbles or gravel on the bottom of each hole is needed to protect the soil from "puddling" when the water is poured into the hole. The test holes should be kept filled with water for at least 4 hours. Overnight soaking of the holes is often recommended to be certain that the soil will be as wet as it will be during the wettest part of the year. Do not overdo this part by waiting for the soil to soak more than 24 hours.[6,11]

To measure the percolation rate, adjust the water level to six inches above the gravel layer. Measure the drop in water level for a 30-minute period. This drop determines the suitability of the soil for septic-tank absorption or leaching fields. If the water requires more than 60 minutes to drop one inch, the soil is unsuited for a septic-tank system.

In order to determine the size of the absorption field required, the developer must correlate the soil's percolation rate with the amount of effluent produced by the facility. An estimate of the amounts of sewage flow that can be expected from park facilities during use is listed in Table 14.1. By multiplying the quantity of sewage from each type of fixture by the number of fixtures, the total flow of effluent can be estimated.

Using the information in Table 14.1, a developer can obtain an estimate of what volumes of sewage he will need to dispose of. The example following Table 14.2 will show how to use this information in determining the size of the absorption field. Table 14.2 gives the maximum rate of sewage that can be applied per square foot of trench bottom. Always plan on a minimum of 225 square feet of area or 114 linear feet of 24-inch-wide trench.[6] This is the minimum that is to be used in lieu of local ordinances that require more minimum area.

Example 1

Determine length of line required for a washhouse containing four flush toilets, two showers, and four faucets in area that has a percolation rate of 5 minutes. The campground is expected to operate at peak capacity on holidays.

Step 1. Number of each facility × estimated flow gallons
         4 toilets × 36 each   = 144 gallons
         2 showers × 150 each = 300 gallons
         2 faucets × 15 each   =   30 gallons
         _____
                    Total   474 gallons per hour
Step 2. Assume 12 hours of use for each facility 474 × 12 = 5688 gallons per day.
Step 3. Determine number of square feet of trench required to absorb a day's total sewage. 5688 gal/day ÷ 2.2 gal/ft² = 2585 ft² of absorption area required.
Step 4. Compute the length of required two-foot = wide trench. 2585 ÷ 2 ft² linear foot = 1293 linear feet

Nearly 1,300 feet of absorption trench might appear to be excessive for one washhouse. The percolation rate of the soil cannot be changed by different calculations, but perhaps the sewage flow as estimated from Table 14.1 appears too high. Another approach to the estimate of sewage can be made by basing

Table 14.1. Estimate of Sewage Flow at Public Parks During Park Use Hours.

Type of Fixture	Gallons per Hour	Type of Fixture	Gallons per Hour
Flush toilets	36	Showers	150
Urinals	10	Faucets	15

U.S. Public Health Service.

Table 14.2. Allowable Rate of Sewage Application to a Soil Absorption System.

Percolation Rate (minutes for one-inch drop in water level)	Maximum Sewage Application Rate (gallons per square foot each day)
2	3.5
3	2.9
4	2.5
5	2.2
10	1.6
15	1.3
30	0.9
45	0.6

U.S. Public Health Service.

the estimate on the expected use of the area as described in the following paragraphs.

The ideal situation is to have one toilet for each sex for every 10 camping units. This is not widely followed, and some states use a recommended minimum of one toilet for each sex for every 30 camping units. [5] It would be safe to assume that the example used above would apply to a 30-unit campground.

The average camping group consists of four or five persons who will each produce approximately 35 gallons of sewage daily. [4,11] Example 2 computes length of trench required using the figures for water requirements per camper for the same area that was used in Example 1.

Example 2

Step 1. Determine daily volume of sewage produced at the washhouse when campground is at capacity and all 30 units are using the washhouse facilities.

35 gal/person/day × 5 persons/unit = 175 gal/unit/day

30 units × 175 gal/day = 5250 gal/day of sewage

Step 2. Determine length of 2-foot-wide trench needed to absorb a day's sewage from 30 campgrounds when the soil percolation rate is 5 minutes per inch.

5250 gal/day ÷ 2.2 gal/ft²/day = 2386 ft² of absorption area required

2386 ÷ 2 ft² linear foot = 1193 linear feet of 2-foot-wide absorption trench required

Most tables that list recommended absorption trench areas are designed for the private residential dwelling and not for a recreation area. Table 14.1 listing the sewage flow at public parks can be used to compute the absorption area. These figures will work well for most day-use areas. [11] Table 14.3 presents the length of absorption trench required for each campground as determined by

Table 14.3. Linear Footage of Absorption Trench Required for Each Camping Unit as Related to Percolation Rate.

Percolation Rate (minutes per 1-inch drop)	Recommended Linear Feet of Absorption Trench[a] per Camping Unit[b] (approx.)[c]
2	25
4	35
5	40
10	55
15	70
30	100

[a]24-inch-wide absorption trench.
[b]Based on average of five persons per unit.
[c]Rounded up to nearest 5 feet.

the percolation rate. The computations for Table 14.3 are based upon U.S. Public Health Service data concerning percolation rates.

Septic tank. The purpose of a septic tank is to condition the sewage so that it will infiltrate into the ground more readily than the unfiltered sewage would do.[13] The effluent from the septic tank is nearly as polluted with bacteria as that which flowed into the tank. Also, while in the tank, the organic solids are attacked by anaerobic bacteria, causing the effluent to be "septic" and therefore bad smelling. In accomplishing its purpose of conditioning the sewage, the septic tank removes the solids, permits anaerobic bacterial action on the organic solids, and stores the sludge and scum accumulations.

As illustrated in Figure 14.3 the solid matter settles to the bottom of the tank, where it remains quietly while the anaerobic bacteria work upon it. This bacterial action changes some of the solids into liquids or gases.[2] The anaerobic action is very important in the treatment of the sewage and in decreasing the amount of sludge and scum that must be disposed of. No additives are necessary to make the septic tank function properly. Actually, the many additives sold on the open market to improve septic-tank operation will not improve its functioning.[13,3]

Most normal household wastes will have no adverse effects upon the septic system. Common types of detergents and cleaning fluids in normal amounts will not interfere with proper functioning; however, the introduction of large quantities of disinfectants will kill the bacteria and interfere with the anaerobic action. Surface drainage water should not be piped into the septic tank because a large flow of water will flush sludge from the tank and into the dispersal field. Sludge passing through the drain tiles will clog up the soil pores and cause the sytem to malfunction.

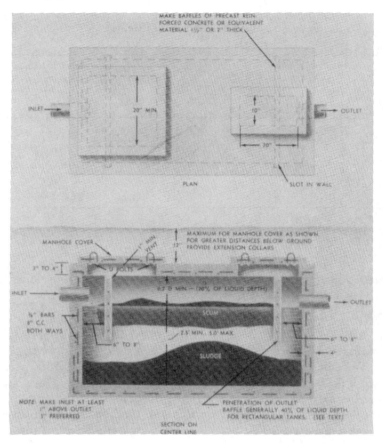

Fig. 14.3. Longitudinal section of septic tank (U.S. Public Health Service.)

The accumulated sludge and scum must be cleaned from the tank to prevent its being moved out into the drainfield when too much collects within the tank. Definite intervals for cleaning are difficult to recommend; however, yearly inspections are probably wise in order to protect the large capital investment and to avoid the inconvenience of having trouble with the sewage system right in the middle of the recreation season. Once the field becomes blocked, it might never function properly again and will probably need replacement. Generally, only 1 tank out of 20 will reach the danger point within three years.[11]

A white towel wrapped around a stick will serve to measure the sludge accumulation if it is placed down through a break in the surface scum and forced to the bottom of the sludge (Fig. 14.4.) The scum that floats upon the surface between the baffles will block the field if it is carried out through the outlet device. If the scum is three inches or less from the bottom of the outlet device, the tank should be pumped out.

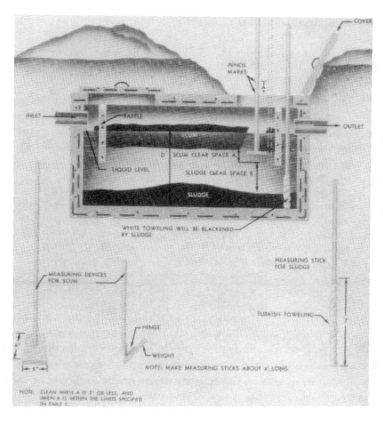

Fig. 14.4. Diagram of devices for measuring sludge and scum within a septic tank. (U.S. Public Health Service.)

No part of the septic-tank system should be closer than 50 feet to a water source in order to assure against pollution. Some state codes require that the minimum distance be 100 feet. Also, the U.S. Public Health Service recommends that the septic tank be at least five feet from any building, while some states require an eight-foot spacing.[6] The pipes that are used to carry the sewage to the tank and then from the tank to the distribution box should be of durable material with the joints tightly sealed. Cast iron pipe is often recommended for this purpose; however, vitrified clay, concrete, bituminized fibers, plastic, and asbestos cement can also be used. Local ordinances will probably require the use of cast iron pipe within five feet of a building, 50 feet of a water system, or underneath a road.

Septic tanks can be constructed in place with noncorrosive waterproof materials or purchased as a prefabricated unit. The latter method probably eliminates the problems of sealing and of health authority approval; however, it is limited to the smaller tanks. Many tanks are built in place from reinforced concrete. It is recommended that a sloping bottom be built into a septic tank to aid in cleaning.[3]

It is difficult and probably unnecessary to determine the exact septic-tank size required; however, the trend is toward larger septic tanks that require less cleaning. Also, the difference in price between a 750-gallon capacity tank and a 1,000-gallon tank is relatively small, and many local ordinances require a minimum capacity of 750 gallons. For an effective septic system, the tank volume should have a one day's retention capacity. That is, the tank should have a large enough usable volume to store one day's sewage output. When sewage flows are expected to be greater than 1,500 gallons each day, the tank capacity should equal 1125 gallons plus 75 percent of the daily expected flow.

Example

anticipated sewage $= 5250$ gal/day

Formula for determining required tank volume:

$$V = 1125 + 0.75 \text{ quantity/day}$$
$$V = 1125 + 3937$$
$$V = 5062 \text{ gal}$$

Two-compartment tanks are more effective than single ones and are recommended for large flow establishments. The relative absence of solids in the second compartment serves as an indication of how successfully the first tank is functioning. Two tanks in series will serve as a two-compartment tank which may be difficult to purchase. The capacity of the first tank should be twice that of the second or outlet tank.

Distribution boxes. The distribution box is necessary to ensure equal distribution of the effluent into all parts of the absorption trenches. It prevents the overloading of one line while the rest remain underused. There is nothing complicated about distribution boxes in that they are just concrete boxes tht receive the effluent from the septic tank and let it flow out through outlets that lead to the absorption trenches (Fig. 14.5.) To ensure equal flow through all absorption trenches, the outlets from the distribution box must be at the exact same level and at least four inches from the bottom of the box. The flow into the distribution box should be baffled to prevent a direct flow-through situation.

Absorption field. The purpose of the absorption field or leaching field is to distribute the septic-tank effluent into the soil mantle. The effluent moves through four-inch diameter cement tiles that are placed loosely end to end so that approximately one-quarter-inch spacings occur between tiles. As the effluent moves along down a grade of two to four inches per hundred linear feet, it leaks out of the tile pipe and into the absorption trench where it infiltrates into the soil. The lines should follow the contours if necessary to keep

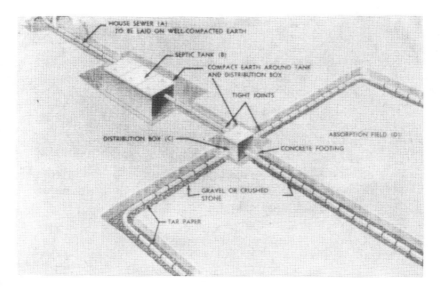

Fig. 14.5. Diagrammatic sketch of septic-tank disposal system. (U.S. Public Health Service.)

the proper grade since the top of the tile should be one to two feet below the ground surface.[6] Each open joint between tiles should be covered with a piece of roofing paper to exclude water from above. Sharp turns in the line are exceptions to this arrangement of the tiles in that all joints on the turns should be sealed.

The tile should be set down within an aggregate-filled trench that is between 18 and 36 inches deep and between 12 and 36 inches wide. At least six inches of one-half- to one and one-half-inch size aggregate stone material should lie below the tile pipe and at least two inches of aggregate depth should cover the pipe. The absorption trench should then be covered over with roofing paper and then approximately one foot of soil.

Drainage lines should not exceed 500 feet in length and should not be placed within six feet of the septic tank. Parallel lines should be at least seven feet apart to provide sufficient space for lateral movement of the effluent in the soil. Whenever the total line length is greater than 750 feet, a dosing tank should be used in conjunction with the septic tank.[6] A single dosing tank setup will permit the operation of two 500-foot lines for a 1,000-foot-long field.

The dosing tank is a concrete box that has a capacity equal to one-third that of the septic tank (Fig. 14.6). The septic-tank effluent empties into the dosing tank, where it is stored until enough effluent has accumulated to fill 75 percent of the drainfield's capacity. An automatic siphon functions every two or three hours to discharge the dosing tank contents through the distribution box and into the lines. This system has three advantages over one without a dosing tank.

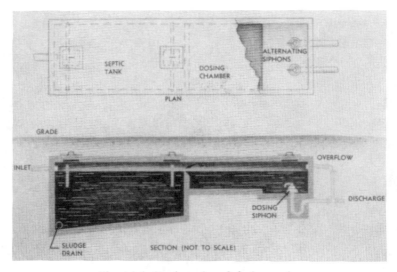

Fig. 14.6. Septic tank and dosing tank.

First, it gives the field periodic rests so that it gets an opportunity to dry out between uses. Second, proper distribution of the effluent throughout the absorption trenches is achieved by the use of the dosing tank. Third, alternating halves of the absorption field can be used by incorporating two siphons and two distribution boxes to handle lines requiring more than 1,000 feet of total line.

Automatic dosing siphons do not contain any moving parts; therefore, they give satisfactory service over long periods of time. Prefabricated dosing boxes with automatic siphons are available on the open market from plumbing supply houses or builder supplier corporations.

Aerobic tank system

An aerobic tank system relies on the presence of oxygen to permit aerobic bacteria to digest the organic matter. These units have some form of air pump to bubble or force air through the tank contents. Solids are broken up by rotating blades. A settlement chamber is needed to keep the solids from floating into the drain pipes where they would clog the disposal field.

An aerobic system costs more to install and to operate than a septic tank system. However, one-third less drain field is required if an aerobic tank system is used.[7] If the equipment is not properly maintained, the system will loose sufficient free oxygen and switch over to the anaerobic process for which it was not designed.

Stabilization pond

The stabilization pond is a shallow pool of sewage that is being worked on by aerobic bacteria which use the dissolved oxygen in the water. The biochemical oxygen will be satisfied in the pond; therefore, the pond is sometimes called an oxidation pond.[3] The dissolved oxygen is replenished from the atmosphere and from the algae growing in the water. The pond should have a regular perimeter and be approximately three feet deep. This depth is shallow enough to permit the penetration of sunlight to all parts of the liquid and thereby encourage algae growth; however, it is deep enough to discourage some rooted aquatic plants. Usually two to five feet is the range of depth acceptable in a stabilization pond.

The pond should be formed from constructed dikes in order to eliminate the collection of surface runoff. The pond site should be located at a practical distance away from the recreation developments to prevent its becoming a nuisance. The oxidation process in itself does not cause unfavorable odors; however, large concentrations of sewage in parts of the pond can cause anaerobic activity with its odors. The Michigan State Park System is using stabilization ponds with success at such large parks as Harrisonville State Park. Two hundred yards appears to be a satisfactory distance from the developed recreation sites for a properly functioning pond. More than one inlet to the pond will help to solve the problem of large concentration of unstable sewage in the pond. If only one inlet pipe is provided, it is usually placed near the pond's center.

The stabilization pond does not require daily maintenance and is relatively free from operation problems other than the switching of input pipes to prevent sewage concentrations. The grass and weeds must be mowed, the mosquitoes eradicated, and unauthorized people excluded. The exclusion of trespassers will require a high fence and warning signs. Weeds and willows can be controlled by soil sterilants and by mowing. Also, the dikes must be protected from erosion and from tunneling by burrowing rodents.

Additional sewage can be oxidized in a small pond by using a method of increasing the free oxygen. Figure 14.7 shows an electrically powered floating pump used to aerate the small stabilization pond on the Chippewa National Forest in Minnesota. The stabilization pond shown in Figure 14.7 is less than a half-acre in size; however, it satisfactorily oxidizes the sewage from a large campground with flush toilets and hot showers.

The local health authorities should be contacted in order to ascertain what design criteria exist within their jurisdiction. For a rough estimation, one can plan on one surface acre of pond for every 1,000 users.

REFUSE

Refuse collection and disposal are becoming a monstrous problem in forest recreation areas. The average camper produces approximately four-tenths of a cubic foot of refuse every day.[13] After the picnicker, hiker, water skier, and fisherman has piled on his refuse, there is quite a heap. Things are getting

Fig. 14.7. A stabilization pond with an aeration spray pump in use on the Chippewa National Forest.

worse from the standpoint of litter. Even the beer bottles are disposable nowadays, and aluminum soft drink cans never rust away. Although the picnicker produces less than a tenth of a cubic foot per day, numbers make up for the small contributions.

Refuse, as used here, means both garbage and rubbish. The recreation area manager must face three major problems connected with refuse. He must decide how to keep it stored on site, how to get it collected, and how to dispose of it after collection.

Storage and Collection of Refuse

The on-site refuse container should be watertight and made of 26 to 30 gauge galvanized metal. Thirty-gallon capacity cans are the maximum that workmen should be expected to handle when collecting refuse. The 55-gallon oil drums that are used in some recreation areas might be less expensive than a properly designed refuse can; however, they are also unsatisfactory in the long run and should not be used. Each can should have a tight-fitting lid to keep out insects and rats. A pair of handles to facilitate lifting should be attached to each can.

Refuse cans must be kept clean or else they will become a nuisance as well as a health hazard. The refuse containers can be collected and washed periodically to prevent odors and breeding of flies. Approximately six days are required for the complete development of the fly adult; however, cleaning will be necessary much more often than every six days. Some progressive recreation areas combine a daily pickup with a double set of cans so that one set of containers can be in use while the other set is being washed and dried. The use of plastic bag liners for refuse cans has become common practice in recent years. They will more than pay for themselves in convenience, in work saved, and in can protection. Refuse can be collected simply by picking up the plastic bag and setting it in a truck.

The proper containers for storage of refuse at the point of origin will minimize health hazards and odor nuisances as well as speed up the collection process.[12] The containers should be located so that they are convenient to the user as well as being readily accessible to the collector. Special storage containers may be required in most forest recreation areas in order to thwart scavenging bears, dogs, and racoons. In addition to being durable, these containers should have some way of being firmly anchored in order to minimize the scattering of refuse by the scavengers. Buried cans with foot-petal lids, special flap-top locked lids, or anchoring pipes can be used to help overcome spillage of refuse by animals.

The scheduling of refuse collection in intensive recreation areas is a simple matter. It should be collected daily in most areas. In situations of very light use, the collection interval can be stretched to two- or three-day intervals. However, this longer period is probably not much of a money saver in any but the more isolated areas since the manager of work crews will be traveling through the area each day anyway. Frequently, heavy-use picnic areas need more than one pickup on busy days.

A contractual arrangement between the campground manager and a reputable collection firm is the most advantageous arrangement when large quantities of refuse are involved. A contract stating definite collection means, times, equipment, and routes of travel should be signed by both parties involved. Unfortunately, not all forest recreation areas are conveniently located in an area serviced by a commercial refuse collector, and therefore the managers must find other means of collecting refuse.

Any truck can be used to haul refuse that remains in the cans or plastic liners; however, trucks with waterproof beds should be used if the refuse is to be dumped into the truck bed. The dumping of refuse into open bed trucks is generally the less desirable collection method. This method permits spillage, causes odors, and makes the truck dirty. If the quantity is too great to pick up the individual bags or cans, an enclosed packer truck should be considered. Refuse-packing trucks reduce the cost per trip by carrying refuse compacted into two-thirds of its original volume. They permit low loading levels that make dumping easier on the man lifting the can and lessen the spillage that accompanies high lifting of the refuse cans. Also, refuse packers reduce odors and spillage along the road because all refuse is enclosed within the truck body.

Disposal

Once the mountain of refuse has been collected, it must be put somewhere or treated so that it will not become a health problem or a public nuisance. Open dumping, sanitary landfill, and incineration along with modifications of each are methods that are suited for recreation area refuse disposal. Separate collection of rubbish and garbage along with hog feeding is often mentioned in publications, but it is not practical for use in disposing of recreation refuse.

Open dumping

Open dumping of refuse in some out-of-the-way place is a very common, perhaps the most common, of the refuse disposal methods. Publications on sanitation generally avoid admitting that open dumping does occur and concentrate their efforts on more desirable refuse disposal techniques. Fortunately, many local governments have ordinances prohibiting open dumping. Odors, fire danger, windblown debris, rats and mosquitoes are some of the problems that accompany open dumping. [3] Some managers have stayed with this undesirable practice because at first inspection it is the cheapest and most convenient method of disposing of refuse. In some areas open dumps even provide a form of offbeat recreation. Rat hunting and depraved bear watching attract visitors to many dumps. However, in consideration for public health and general aesthetics, the enlightened manager will avoid the open-dumping method of refuse disposal.

Sanitary landfill

If the recreation area manager cannot work out a satisfactory contract for the collection and the removal of the refuse from his area, he should then investigate the next best method of refuse disposal which is the sanitary landfill method. The sanitary landfill method is just an elaborate way of burying the refuse. The refuse is placed into a predug trench, compacted by a crawler tractor, and buried under a six-inch layer of soil each day. This is a very good method of refuse disposal that lends itself to use at forest recreation areas. Sanitary landfill provides an economical way of refuse disposal where the proper sites can be selected. A sufficient unforested land area must be available at the proper distance from the recreation site. The disposal site should be close enough to make hauling economical but far enough away so as not to be a public nuisance. Very deep, well-drained loams and sandy loams make the most desirable soil for sanitary landfill sites. Soils with impeded drainage can hinder the operation in wet weather and can cause the fill to become a health hazard through seepage. Also, the landfill areas should be located more than 50 feet from any surface water and should be in areas that are not subjected to high water tables or to flooding.

Approximately one-half acre of six-foot-deep landfill would be needed for an all-year operation servicing 5,000 people.[12] Very few forest recreation areas serve that large number of users so that the required area would be proportionally smaller.

The steps in operating a sanitary landfill are relatively simple. First, an eight-foot-deep trench that is one and a half times wider than the dozer blade is dug out of a flat or gently sloping area. A 30-degree slope is graded at one end of the trench to serve as a base for the first layer of refuse. The refuse should be spread over the base slope to a vertical height of six feet from the trench bottom and compacted by the crawler tractor. After the compacted layer of refuse becomes two feet thick, it should be covered with at least six inches of packed earth. The top two vertical feet should be used to form a soil plug over each layer.

Small developments must make some modifications to fit their economic situation. Most forest recreation areas cannot afford to keep a crawler tractor standing by the refuse dump. Therefore, it is most advantageous for them to have the required capacity trench dug all at one time and the soil stockpiled for use during the season. Mechanical equipment can be brought in twice a week to cover the refuse. Some small recreation areas have been adequately served by a daily burning of mixed refuse in a prepared trench followed every couple of

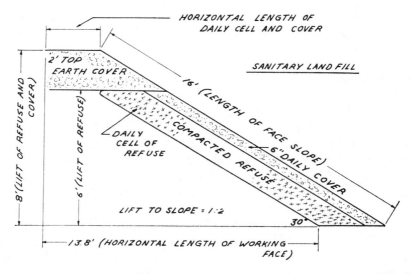

Fig. 14.8. Diagram of sanitary landfill operation. (Texas State Department of Health.)

weeks by burial.[12] This system has been stretched by many campground operators who bury the refuse only at the end of the season. This practice favors the breeding of rats, flies, and mosquitoes and is not to be recommended.

Hand-dug trenches can serve some very small forest recreation areas where mechanical equipment is not available. A one-foot-deep layer of refuse is spread in a two-foot-deep trench and burned. After the burning is completed, the trench should be filled with soil.

Incineration

The complete burning of all refuse to ashes eliminates breeding of rats, flies, and mosquitoes. It removes the material that attracts bears, dogs, racoons, and other animals to refuse dumps. This process of burning refuse at high temperatures in specially designed enclosures is called incineration.[12] Incinerators have been used for many years to aid in the disposal of municipal refuse; however, they have been used only to a limited extent in forest recreation areas. Incinerators are expensive to build and to operate and can compete with sanitary landfill only where use is extremely heavy and landfill sites are scarce. Neither of these situations really exists in forest recreation sites in spite of the crowded conditions of some areas. Some U.S. Forest Service personnel in the Northern Rocky Mountain Area now are considering the increased use of incinerators because of the piles of debris that will need disposing of when the projected figure of 86 million visits a year is reached on those national forests alone.[4]

For most situations, the initial cost of approximately $5,000 per ton of rated 24-hour capacity is too high.[3] The smallest incinerators, capable of burning 50 pounds of refuse per hour, have a rated 24-hour capacity of 12,000 pounds and will cost approximately $3,000 to build. The need for skilled operators and maintenance people to operate incinerators, the operation cost of $3 to more than $7 per ton burned, and the high initial costs of the incinerator make the incineration method unsuited for most forest recreation areas. Publications on the subject of incinerators are available from the U.S. Public Health Service for those persons wishing to investigate the subject further.

REFERENCES

1. Anonymous, 1980. Composting Toilets Save Recreation and Parks Money. In *Parks and Recreation.*, December, p. 6.
2. Babbit, H.E. 1947. *Sewage and Sewage Treatment.* John Wiley, New York, 691 pages.
3. Elhers, V., and Steel, E. 1965. *Municipal and Rural Sanitation.* 6th ed. McGraw-Hill, New York. 643 pages.
4. Fine, I., and Werner, E. 1960. *Camping in State Parks and Forests in Wisconsin*, vol. 1, no. 3. University of Wisconsin, Madison, Wisc.
5. Ort, D.R. 1963. Recommended Campground Sanitation Requirements. In *Guidelines for Developing Land for Outdoor Recreational Uses.* Cooperative Extensive Service, Purdue University, West Lafayette, Ind.
6. Shephard, W. et al. 1958. *Questions and Answers about Home Sewage Disposal.* Joint Public Circular E-9. Cooperative Extensive Service, Michigan State University.
7. Stoner, Carol H. 1977. *Goodbye to the Flush Toilet.* Rodale Press, Emmaus, Pa. 285 pages.
8. U.S. Forest Service. 1962. Forest Recreation for Profit. *Agr. Information Bull.*, No. 265. Washington, D.C.
9. ———. 1963. *Recreation Management — Manual and Handbook.* Title 2300. U.S. Department of Agriculture, Washington, D.C.
10. U.S. Public Health Service. 1962. *Drinking Water Standards.* Publication No. 956. U.S. Department of Health, Education, and Welfare, Washington, D.C.
11. ———. 1963. *Manual of Septic-Tank Practice.* Publication No. 526. U.S. Department of Health, Education, and Welfare, Washington, D.C.
12. ———. 1963. *Suggested Design Criteria for Refuse Storage, Collection, and Disposal.* Pacific Southwest Inter-Agency Committee and Columbia Basin Inter-Agency Committee, U.S. Department of Health, Education, and Welfare, Washington, D.C.
13. ———. 1965. *Environmental Health Practice in Recreational Areas.* Publication No. 1195. U.S. Department of Health, Education, and Welfare, Washington, D.C.
14. Wagar, J.A. 1962. *The Convection Stack — A Device for Ridding Pit Toilets of Bad Odor.* NE 133, U.S. Forest Service Northeast Experiment Station, Upper Darby, Pa.

15

Water-oriented Recreation Development

INTRODUCTION

Water plays a major role in forest recreation by providing either the primary purpose for the visit or by supplementing some other activity. Many people come to the forest solely to participate in water-based activities. To them, any other recreation activity is secondary. Almost half of the national population prefers water-based activities to any other type of outdoor recreation.[15] Even land-based activities are enhanced by nearby water that provides a secondary activity or improves the setting.

Most participants engage in more than one activity on each forest recreation visit; the primary purpose of the visit therefore generates use of supplementary facilities. People who travel into the forest to swim often combine that activity with picnicking for one or two meals. Campers prefer to have swimming, fishing, or boating opportunities available to them in order to supplement their primary activity. Here again, the forest manager must not be too concerned about exact descriptions. Too much can be made of whether the activity is primary or supplementary because more of the user's total time might be spent in supplementary activities than in the primary activity.

As with forest recreation in general, water-oriented recreation is developed and managed according to the type of use. Activities that require developed facilities to handle a concentration of use on a limited area are intensive-use activities. Swimming epitomizes the intensive-use type of water-oriented recreation. Conversely, an extensive-use recreation activity takes place over a relatively large area and requires a minimum of developed facilities. Fishing and downstream canoeing characterize extensive-use recreation activities.

INTENSIVE WATER-ORIENTED RECREATION

Swimming

Picnicking and swimming are supplemental activities that rely upon each other for mutual success.[31] Swimming, wading, and sunbathing are very important supplementary activities for camping as is borne out by the emphasis placed on available swimming areas in camping advertising. In most cases, swimming becomes an intensive-use forest recreation activity when it is supplemental with another type of forest activity.

Swimming sites

Swimming sites can be located on either natural bodies of water or at swimming pools. Much literature is available concerning the design and operation of a swimming pool; however, the swimming pool is not favored by the forest recreation user. Good, natural waterfront areas are superior to manmade structures.[21] Even the Forest Service Handbook on recreation discourages the use of manmade pools.[29] In this text, the term "natural water bodies" is meant to include ponds, lakes, streams, rivers, and oceans. Reservoirs are included as lakes in this chapter because they have most of the shoreline characteristics and limnological characteristics of lakes.

Safety

The safety of the user is the prime obligation of any recreation manager. Therefore, he must supply the user with a swimming area that is bacteriologically safe and physically free from unreasonable hazards. Water pollution or physical hazards can be limiting factors when selecting a swimming site on a natural body of water. That is, the pollution or the physical hazard eliminates the site from consideration.

Quality. The bacteriological quality of the water must be sufficiently high so as to be considered safe for swimming by the local health code. The safe range for the bacteriological quality of swimming water is generally listed as that water having less than 1,000 coliform organisms per 100 milliliters of water.[20] This is approximately 1,000 times more coliform organisms than are permissible in public drinking water.[30] The permissible rate of pollution varies widely among states. There is so much disagreement on this point that some states permit nine times the number of coliforms in swimming water than do other states. These accepted figures range from 250 to 2,400 coliforms per 100 milliliters of water.[26,31]

The volume of water present will have some bearing on water quality. Some pollution of the water will occur as a result of human bathing; therefore, a sufficient quantity of water should be available to keep the pollution diluted to less than the permissible coliform count. Streams, creeks, and rivers should have a flow-through rate of more than 500 gallons for each user-day.[35] This turnover rate of water must occur during every day that the area is in use to prevent pollution. The rate of flow can easily be estimated by following the simple stream gauging procedures described in Chapter 13.

Bodies of standing water are more susceptible to contamination from bacteria introduced into the water by bathers. Small ponds with little or no flow through will soon become polluted with heavy use; therefore, they will satisfy the demand generated at small campgrounds or similar light-use developments. Each user requires 50 square feet of water surface in small ponds and lakes. In the larger bodies of water where surface area is obviously sufficient, the area for standing in the water can be as small as ten square feet per person.[21]

Disinfection of natural water bodies has not been satisfactory except under research conditions and does not hold any immediate solution to the pollution problem. The elimination of the pollution cause is the best control over natural pollution.[21]

Physical hazards

Physical hazards are the second limiting factor associated with user safety. They occur as submerged, water-edge, and in-water hazards. All hazards should be removed from improved swimming areas when possible. Warning signs and barriers should be erected to protect the public from hazards that cannot be removed.

The submerged hazards are the most common and probably the most dangerous forms of hazards. Beaches should have a gentle, even underwater slope that extends to a depth of approximately 6 feet.[29] Drop-offs, escarpments, and underwater rocks must be considered as submerged hazards. Snags, logs, metal, and glass are common hazards that must be removed from under the water in the improved swimming sites.

The depth of the water itself constitutes a form of hazard and must be considered in designing and managing the site. It is advisable to erect markers in the water to denote depth. The Forest Service has done an effective job of depth marking on unprotected bathing beaches such as the improved beach on Lac Vux Desert where they have placed two rows of vertical posts out from the shore. Each post has calibrations marked on it to indicate the actual depth of water at that point. In natural water bodies, this method is better than simply giving the depth on a sign because it automatically indicates fluctuating water depth.

The water-edge hazards are easier to eliminate or to compensate for than are

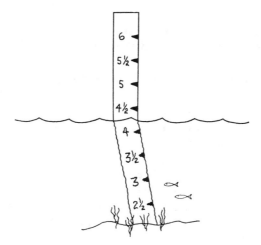

Fig. 15.1 Sketch of self-reading depth rods that are recommended for use in areas with fluctuating water depth.

the submerged hazards. Cliffs, overhanging banks, snags, rocks, metal, and glass are common water-edge hazards. Overhanging banks can be bulldozed down, and rocky ground can be covered with sand or soil. Cliffs usually are desirable for scenery, but dangerous as climbing or diving spots. Fencing or signs might be necessary to keep swimmers from climbing around on the cliff. General cleanup techniques will eliminate many other water-edge hazards.

Poison ivy, wasps, and spiders are water-edge nuisances found around stream banks and muddy spots. Poison ivy eradication needs more management attention than it gets in most recreation areas. An intensive noxious plant eradication program is very important to user safety although the sad effects of these plants are not as spectacular as that of a broken bottle or similar hazards. Wasps and other stinging insects can be controlled by a direct assault on their nests with insecticide and by the elimination of the muddy conditions that attract them. Spiders present more fright value than danger; however, the spider population should be kept under control by the judicious use of insecticides.

The depth and velocity of mountain streams can vary widely throughout the swimming season. This fluctuation must be considered when the site is being selected and when the swimming area is being designed. Low flow can prevent swimming completely or cause a pollution hazard, while very high flows will combine with higher water velocities to flood over the banks, tear out improvements, and alter the stream bottom. Some of the depth fluctuations can be compensated for by the use of the self-reading depth rods that are mentioned earlier in this chapter. These rods will keep the user-public informed of the actual depths. Flood waters will necessitate closure of the swimming area.

Stream water should be flowing less than two miles per hour when passing through the swimming area. High velocities in the stream create a hazard to those who could be pulled downstream by the flowing water and to small nonswimming youngsters. Low dams can be used to pool stream water and thereby reduce its velocity as it moves through the swimming area. Some water movement is desirable to prevent pollution and to give the swimmer a chance to swim without going too far from shore by swimming upstream.

Low-water dams can be made by lining large boulders across the stream. Concrete low-water dams are rather expensive and not necessary in most cases. A rather recent development in stream improvement work has been the introduction into this country of the gabions. Gabions are one cubic meter or larger wire baskets that are set up in place and filled with local stone material. A detailed description of gabions is given later in this chapter under extensive water-oriented recreation developments. Since gabions are porous, they permit water to flow through them and thereby do not cause stagnant pools during periods of low flow.

The placement of low dams both downstream and upstream may be necessary to create a permanent and safe pool in the stream. The downstream dam will form the pool and reduce the velocity of flow through the swimming area. The low dam on the upstream side will protect the bottom of the swimming area by reducing the velocity of the inflowing water before it damages any improvements. The energy of the downward flowing water is dissipated in the drop over the first dam and not in tearing through the swimming area. This is much as if the water were being let down a ladder rather than flowing down a chute. Sedimentation takes place in the upper pond and does not fill up the main swimming zone. The scenic value of the water falling over the low-water dams is an added bonus for the area.

Safety equipment. Some states require lifeguards to be stationed at any paid swimming area. Even where the law does not require their presence, lifeguards should be employed to protect swimmers in heavy-use areas. Often, forest recreation areas do not have enough use to warrant the cost of a lifeguard, so other methods of bather protection must be utilized. Lifesaving equipment such as floating rings, ropes, and long poles should be readily accessible at the beach. Concise and clear descriptions of water-rescue techniques employing the available equipment should be posted on a conspicuous display board next to the equipment Ropes and floats are often used to mark certain depths. The floating ropes restrict the bather and provide a safe place for him to reach for if he gets into difficulty in the water. A nonswimmer area is usually roped off at a depth of three and a half feet. An outside rope at the seven-foot depth will mark off the swimmers' area and tend to set the outside limit even when restrictions are not posted.

Beach development

The bottom of the swimming area should have uniform and gentle slope into a water depth of six feet. In order to be safe for children, this slope should have a one-foot drop for every 12 or 15 feet of horizontal distance.[10] When sand or gravel bottoms exist, as they do in New England lakes and ponds, they are both firm and comfortable to walk on. A minimum of grading and underwater work usually will be required to make a good beach.

Coarse sand or fine gravel makes the best bottom for swimming areas. It is too heavy to remain suspended in the water and fine enough to walk on with unprotected feet. Firm bottoms can be covered directly with 12 inches of coarse sand to achieve the desired results; however, muddy or soft bottom soil will not remain beneath the sand. Muck, clay, and silt loam mud will work its way up through the sand as a result of trampling by the bathers. Soft bottom areas will have to be stabilized with a crushed rock base that is overlaid with coarse gravel and then 6 to 12 inches of sand. One problem besides cost that arises with the use of crushed stone is that of exposed stones. It is advisable to keep the base material well below the water's edge so that the rocks do not get uncovered and become safety hazards or missiles.

Stream flow will remove sand from the bottom and wash it downstream. This downstream movement of sand will be speeded up by the churning action of the user's feet. The particle size that a stream will move increases exponentially with the increase in stream velocity. The actual effect of velocity on the movement of sand particles will vary with channel and flow characteristic; however, empirical data indicate that a one-half-mile per hour flow will carry one millimeter size sand. A flow of one mile per hour or 1.46 feet per second will transport bean-sized gravel.[28]

In order to prevent the erosion of the beach bottom, the developer should use a coarse gravel and reduce the velocity of the water where necessary on fast-moving streams. The problem of bottom erosion should be considered during the site selection process. Since the size of particle movement is dependent upon water velocity, it makes sense to choose spots where the stream gradient is low or where low-water dams can be employed. Erosion is most damaging in stream sections where steep gradients occur since the stream velocity will double with every 4 percent increase in gradient.[28]

A beach-play area should be constructed at the swimming area when one does not exist naturally. The size of the beach depends upon the use that it is expected to receive. The Department of the Interior plans on 75 square feet of beach for each activity-day of use.[4]* The beach should have at least a 12-inch layer of sand or pea-sized gravel on it to serve both as a play area for children

---

*An activity-day of use means a full day's use by one individual.

Table 15.1. Velocity of Flowing Water Required to Move Particles
of Various Size Classes.[a]

Particle Size Class	Water Velocity Required to Start Movement (ft/sec)
Clay	0.27–0.35
Angular sand	0.70–1.10
Pea-sized gravel	0.62–0.70
Bean-sized gravel	1.10–1.55[b]
Half-inch gravel	2.30–3.20
One-and-a-half-inch angular gravel	3.20–4.0

[a]U.S.D.A. Forest Service.
[b]One mile per hour equals 1.46 feet per second.

and as sunbathing spot for adults.[10] For protection of bare feet, the beach area should be kept clean of rocks, glass, and pieces of metal. In areas where grass will grow well, it can be used to improve the quality of the waterfront area. A grass-covered strip with scattered shade trees will provide a place for relaxation near the water without being on the sand or in the sun. Some limited research indicates that grass-covered beaches are preferred to sand beaches by sunbathers.[22] A portion of this grass area could be designated as a play area that would serve to keep ball games off the beach.

Except for mass bathing areas in high-use locations, the beaches should provide some privacy from nonusers. A little space and some screening should separate the beach area from the picnic grounds and from the parking lot. Camping areas are generally situated more than 200 or 300 yards from the beach so that day-use visitors do not intrude in the campgrounds.

Required supporting facilities

The development of a swimming area involves more than just the improvement of the waterfront area. It also includes the building, the maintenance, and the operation of sanitation, drinking, dressing, and parking facilities. Here again, these supporting facilities accomplish a dual objective. First, they provide conveniences to the user and thereby make his visit more pleasant. Second, they keep the user's activities controlled to specific spots and thereby protect the site from damage.

The sanitation facilities should be constructed near the beach to permit ready access to the swimmers. Every effort should be made to construct the best possible toilet facilities in a convenient location so as to encourage their use. At least one toilet per sex is needed at all swimming areas. The U.S. Public Health Service recommends that one toilet be constructed for every 50 man-days of use

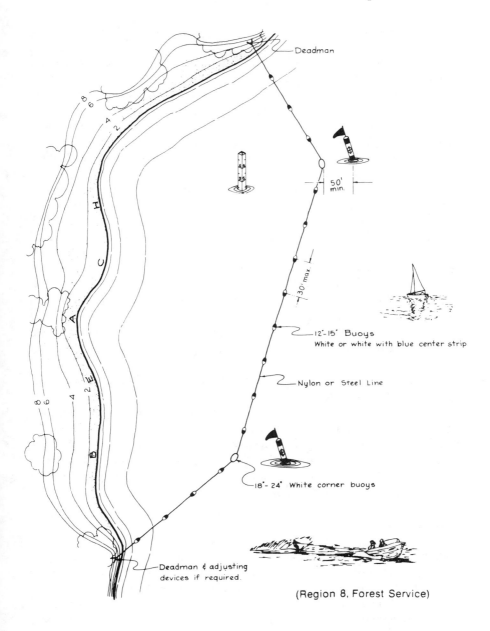

Fig. 15.2. Sketch of swimming beach showing contours, self-reading depth rods, boat warning buoys, and safety cable.

that the swimming area is designed to handle.[31] A more realistic figure is one toilet fixture for each 160-person capacity.[19]

One drinking fountain should be located next to the beach area where it is accessible to the swimmers. The drinking fountain is not to be placed in the toilet rooms. If the fountain is not located on very porous soil such as sand or gravel, it should be placed on a paved pad that has a water-collecting drain and sump. This will help to prevent the muddy spots that are associated with so many drinking fountains in poorly designed recreation areas. When people are walking around the beach without shoes on, they are not inclined to walk in the mud or upon mud-gathering wasps in order to get a drink of water.

Refuse containers should be placed at the entrances to the beach and at convenient locations on the beach. These containers should meet the standards for refuse cans that are given in Chapter 14. Even though picnicking on the beach area should be discouraged, people will still produce some litter from snacks, newspapers, and enough other sources to require a trash collection and a regularly scheduled cleanup of the beach area.

Bathhouses will be necessary for the changing of clothes. There should be at least one bathhouse, or dressing room, for each sex except when the swimming area is used exclusively by campers from a nearby campground. In this case, the additional cost of dressing rooms can be avoided. Bathhouses should be placed near the beach but on the route from the parking lot so as to make their use convenient.

A central parking lot designed to serve the swimming area should be located approximately 50 to 100 yards from the beach. Surfaced trails should connect the two areas so as to provide good access and to channel the use along the designated route of travel. The parking lot can serve as a control on the amount of use the beach receives by limiting access to the area. Each parking spot will require 300 square feet of area and will probably account for four people when occupied.[34] A central parking lot with a usable area of 30,000 square feet will hold 100 cars which will probably mean 400 visitors.

Supplemental facilities

Swimming often attracts day users to the area. These day users will combine other activities with swimming so that additional facilities will be required to satisfy the demand and to protect the site from misuse. Facilities for play, picnicking, and food purchase are the common supplemental facilities associated with forest recreation swimming areas. These facilities should be located away from the beach area so that their use is a separate activity from swimming and sunbathing.[29]

Play fields that are improved for use with swimming and picnic areas should be level, cleared areas that are suitable for impromptu games of tag, volley ball, softball, and other "pickup" games. No improvements are necessary other than what is required for clearing and leveling the area to make it safe and suitable for play. Occasionally, local demand will justify the construction of playground equipment for the children's use. Private operators often include playground equipment in the development to encourage the use of the facility by family groups.

Picnic grounds should be near the beach area, but separate from it. This type of picnic area should be of the general-use design that is described in Chapter 10. Some planners believe that a separate parking lot should be constructed to serve the picnic areas in order to handle those persons who are going to picnic but not to swim. Another advantage of the second central parking lot is that it does spread the users out. At least it gives them a choice of which lot they want to use. Since picnickers generally do not want to walk very far from the cars, they will be closer to the tables if a special parking lot is placed at the picnic area.

Hot dogs, hamburgers, soda, ice cream, and other such foods traditionally have been part of a day at the beach. The sale of prepared foods is both a convenience to the user and a method of making a profit for the operator. In recreation areas, the place of business where food and sundry items are sold is commonly called the "concession stand" although the business might or might not be operated under a true concession agreement as is described in Chapter 5. Private operators claim that the concession stands supply much of their profit.[18]

The concession stand should be placed off the beach, but convenient to both the beach and the picnic area. A couple of bars, stand-up counters, or tables should be clustered around the concession stand to encourage the bathers to eat the food there and not to take it back to the beach. Several trash containers should be placed around the concession stand and along the trails leading to the picnic and beach areas in order to help keep the trash from being discarded along the way or carried into the beach or picnic areas.

Boating

Boating for pleasure has more than kept pace with the outdoor recreation boom. It is probably responsible for the tremendous upsurge in visits to the Corps of Engineers Reservoirs where recreation visits have soared from 16 million in 1950 to 300 million in 1980.

There is a wide variation in the types of boats used by the American public. The user's choice or financial limitations include everything from large sonar-equipped cabin cruisers down to fold boats that are tucked into the automobile trunk. Forest recreation is normally concerned with the smaller types of craft that are associated with users of forest recreation facilities. Small power craft and outboard motorboats that can be moved by the family car, sailboats, rowboats, and canoes are the major concern of the forest recreation developer or manager.

Water quality

Water to be used for boating should meet certain quality limitations. Bacteriological pollution in itself is not a limiting factor to prevent boating. However, many of the symptoms associated with bacteriological pollution do downgrade the water's usefulness for pleasure boating.

Odor. Offensive odor probably is the biggest detracting factor in boating-water quality. Since a person is obliged to smell the odors in the air that he breathes, he will be affected by odors before any other degrading factor of the water. Most people can make the association between certain odors and organic pollution of water; therefore, those people lose a certain sense of enjoyment with the first smell. Anaerobic bacteria action causes both bad odors and dark colors which is a second degrading factor.

Color. Much of the dark color in water is caused by the decomposition of organic matter in the absence of dissolved oxygen. Decomposing organic matter uses up free oxygen by the aerobic process and then switches to the anaerobic process which does not require free oxygen. Anaerobic action is a slow process that produces a foul odor and forms dark-colored products. As long as there is enough dissolved oxygen in the water to maintain the aerobic process, organic solids will not cause dark-colored water or offensive odors. Chemical pollutants are a different matter and must be controlled at their source. Coloration caused by suspended clay and silt particles is not too great a degrading factor for boating water if people do not object to their craft having a dirty hull.

Reaction. The acidity and alkalinity measurements are often listed as being important criteria for boating water; however, there are indications that it is overplayed. A suggested limit for the pH values are from pH of 6.0 on the acid side of neutral to a pH of 8.5 on the alkaline side.[16] Water that is any more acid or alkaline than these suggested limits could cause some corrosion of the craft's surfaces. Usually, the local problems are known to the users who can take precautionary measures to protect the surfaces of their boats whenever such conditions exist.

Supporting facilities

Points of access are needed to permit the public to put its boats into the water. If unlimited access to the water exists, the danger of indiscriminate boat launching also exists. Indiscriminate launching destroys the vegetative cover, breaks down banks, and causes widespread litter and sanitation problems. Unloading of boats along highways creates a serious safety problem to the boat owners as well as to the general motoring public. Since the cars and trailers have to be left somewhere, they are just pulled off the road wherever it is convenient to the driver. This parking causes increased damage to the waterfront zone. Management and cleanup of such an area can become an impossible task when more than the lightest use takes place.

Boat landings should be built along bodies of water that have recreational boating value to meet the public demand, as a site protection technique, and as a management aid. In very heavy-use areas of California, one boat-launching site is recommended for every 160 surface acres of boating water.[6] Under normal conditions fewer launching points will be adequate. This does not mean that launching sites should be built only on lakes and reservoirs. Relatively small streams can provide some very enjoyable, and sometimes exciting, experiences for canoeists. The Tennessee State Planning Commission recommends that "float streams" be established as part of the state's total recreation plan.[25]

A formal boat-landing area usually consists of a loading ramp, a turnabout area, a parking lot, and adequate sanitary facilities. Certain supplemental facilities such as picnic grounds and campgrounds are often developed adjacent to the boat-launching facilities. Since most people participate in more than one activity on each recreational visit, they enjoy the flexibility that supplemental facilities provide. Swimming beaches are often accompanied by a boat-launching ramp as shown in Figure 15.3. Quite often, these supplemental facilities are necessary just to improve the comfort and safety of those people who are going to participate in the activity anyway. Therefore, the construction of the supplemental facilities at boat-landing sites is justified by the same reasons used to justify the landings themselves. That is, they are justified on the basis of public demand, site protection, and area management requirements.

Launching ramp. A launching ramp is used to back the boat trailer down into the water so that the boat can be floated off or onto it. Concrete is the recommended material for the ramp construction. A minimum ramp width of ten feet is required in order to allow some maneuverability for the backing automobiles.[31] The Department of the Interior specifications call for 12-foot-wide ramps to give an added measure of safety.[3] Twenty-foot-wide ramps are recommended by the U.S. Public Health Service; however, the costs for such structures probably would be prohibitive for any establishment except the federal and some state governments. The launching ramp must cross the soft shore line or beach and protrude into the water far enough to permit its use at any expected water level. Also, the ramp should be built with a maximum grade of 10 percent.

Fig. 15.3. A typical back-in boat-launching ramp next to a bathing beach.

Approach road. A two-way road ending in a paved or gravel circle at the shore end of the loading ramp will provide normal head-on driving for the maximum distance toward the water. The circle should have a sufficiently large diameter to permit the car to maneuver into position for backing the trailer down the ramp. The two-lane approach road should pass next to the parking lot that is located within a short walking distance of the ramp.

Parking. Since many of the cars will be towing trailers, they will need approximately twice as much room for parking and maneuvering as do cars without trailers. One solution to the problem of moving and parking trailer-pulling cars is to provide special drive-through parking stalls instead of the double rows of head-in stalls commonly used in central parking lots. The drive-through stalls will enable the driver to head into the stall when parking and to drive straight ahead to get out of the stall. By driving forward, the driver avoids the hazardous practice of backing up with a trailer attached to the car. Cars without trailers can be parked in a separate section of the lot where the normal head-in stalls are provided.

Boat storage. The concept of on-site, dry-rack storage has been given wide application in recent years. Dry-rack storage permits boats to be stored in large buildings on racks when not placed on the water surface. A forklift is used to launch and to retrieve the boat. By leaving the boat at the recreation site, a boater avoids the need to trailer the boat back and forth between home and the point of use. That means that the boater can use a gas-efficient, small car instead of the van or pickup truck when going boating. This form of energy savings and convenience is gaining wide acceptance in most parts of the country.

Water and sanitation. Some form of outlet should be constructed to provide drinking water. A well and pump with a built-in fountain is very satisfactory where the use is relatively low or no central water supply system can be developed. The sanitation facilities are also dependent upon amount of use and the water system. An out-of-the-way and lightly used area can be adequately serviced by water pumps and pump-out pit toilets if flooding is not a problem. Pit toilets are not recommended in areas that lie on low terraces, flood plains, or other such areas that are susceptible to periodic flooding. As in any other recreation development, flush toilets and drinking water under pressure should be provided when the use becomes heavy.

EXTENSIVE WATER-ORIENTED RECREATION

Water provides recreation opportunities far in excess of those occurring at developed facilities. Millions of recreationists range over the country's streams, rivers, lakes, and ponds in search of pleasure in one form or another without requiring many developed facilities. Inland fresh water, exclusive of the Great Lakes, covers more than 25 million acres within the contiguous 48 states.[17] About 20 percent of that surface is made up of natural lakes and ponds, and the remaining 30 percent was produced by manmade reservoirs. Extensive use of fresh water includes the activities of fishing, hunting, and boating.

Fishing

In large areas such as national forests and national wildlife refuges where fishing is available, it is the leading recreation activity.[17] Almost half of the adults in the United States engage in fishing; their impact on recreation, however, is difficult to measure.[24] A comparison of the four National Outdoor Recreation Surveys shows that participation in fishing rose from 29 percent of the respondents in 1960 to 50 percent by 1977.[27] This is largely because of the extensive nature of fishing. Fishermen spread out along the streams and on the lakes to engage in their selected sport without much concern about developed facilities. Regulation of fishing practices and stocking of fish in streams and in large lakes are usually not the concern of land managers except where local restrictions on trespass or conflict are needed.

Land managers should be concerned with increasing the man-hours of fishing use to meet the carrying capacity of the water for fish. Wildlife biologists state that fish and game are a renewable resource that must be harvested or wasted. Each stream has a limit to the number of fish that it can support; therefore, any number of fish above the capacity of the stream to support them will die if they are not harvested.

Developed facilities

Some of the most significant actions that land managers can take in encouraging fishing visits deal with the fisherman's access to the streams. Parking clearings should be provided at ends of trails leading to the streams. The combination of well-identified trails and parking spaces provide the fisherman with a positive access point, spreads use away from congested and overfished roadside points, and keeps the automobiles within defined locations so as to protect the roadside vegetation.

Footbridges provide the fisherman access to both banks where streams are too deep for wading. Bridges can be made from trees growing along the stream. All that is required is to fell the tree across the stream, limb off all the branches and top, and anchor both ends to the banks. The banks must be high enough to suspend the log well above the high-water level so that it does not block floating debris and dam up the stream. Also, the log must be placed so that it reaches far enough back onto the shore so as not to cause the banks to crumble. An ad can be used to flatten the top of the log for safe walking and a handrail will greatly decrease any danger in using the bridge. The U.S. Forest Service has earned much user goodwill by the installation of footbridges.

Forest-type campgrounds should be provided at the places where fishermen already have been staying for overnight fishing trips or at locations where the fishing pressure could be increased. These camps provide camping units, water, and sanitation facilities for the fisherman and make outdoor life somewhat easier on the family if it goes along on the fishing trip. Here, as in most recreation developments, the campground will concentrate the wear into one place and protect the surrounding vegetation. True, the developed campground might encourage more visitors who will cause more wear. For that matter, some fishermen probably do not want their families to go with them and will not be able to use the primitive conditions as an excuse to go fishing with the "Boys."

Sanitary facilities, refuse cans, and even picnic tables have their place at locations of relatively heavy use. If road access is convenient for the general public, these fisherman-oriented developments also can serve as general-purpose picnicking grounds for day-use visitors. Such areas are ideally suited for families with young children who want to combine some fishing with a day's outing.

Fig. 15.4. A small footbridge over a deep fishing stream.

Increasing the carrying capacities of streams and ponds

Most hunters want to do more than hunt wild game; they want to find some once in a while. The same is true for fishermen. Much has been made concerning the recreation values of fishing. The fact is that fishermen want to catch fish, not just fish for them. As a result of this obvious fact, efforts are being made by trained biologists and others to find ways of providing better fishing by manipulating the habitat. Some of these efforts have paid off in better fish yields, while others remain of doubtful use. Rehabilitation or stocking of ponds and the modification of stream flow are the two major methods of producing more catchable fish that were investigated by the researchers.

Pond stocking and rehabilitation. Trout pond rehabilitation programs have been a success in that they actually have produced more fish for the angler to catch.[14] Ponds have proved to be highly successful in the production of trout and bass and can provide fishermen with a great number of recreation hours although they have not proved to be a good financial investment. Fee fishing lakes tend to be money losers when all depreciation and labor costs are considered. The construction and management of fishing ponds are well outlined in a publication by Wingard and Heiney at The Pennsylvania State University.[34] Warmer water ponds are more suited to bass, while the cool water ponds will support trout. The species are generally not mixed even in waters where they both can survive because trout cannot compete with other fish for available food.

Ponds that are less than six-feet deep should be stocked with fish only when there is a constant inflow or water from a stream or a spring. Approximately 600 trout or 100 bass can survive for each surface acre of water. However, since natural mortality is high, the originally stocked fish will die off in two or three years if they are not caught. Trout do not reproduce well in pond waters, but bass do; therefore, many people who want the pond for light fishing use prefer to raise bass.

A larger population of trout than the natural carrying capacity can be raised in a small pond by supplement feeding. Bass lakes can be fertilized with an inorganic 10-10-10 fertilizer to produce more plankton for the food chain; however, trout lakes should not be fertilized. There is no point in fertilizing ponds that have a high flow-through rate because the effort is wasted by downstream dilution.

Stream management and improvement. Every effort should be made to avoid heavy stream siltation as a result of improperly constructed roads, poor logging practices, or overgrazing. Excess runoff should be controlled in an effort to stabilize the stream flow and thereby lessen the extremes in flow between flooding and no-flow periods. In the North where rainfall is relatively adequate, the riparian vegetation should be encouraged so that it will stabilize the bank and shade the water. In the Southwest, riparian vegetation draws off enough water to cause a significant lowering of stream flow.

The building of structures to improve the carrying capacity of streams might turn out to have been an enormous waste of money throughout the United States if their only purpose was to raise catchable fish. Although the construction of such structures as groins, low dams, and V-deflectors appear as structures recommended in handbooks on stream improvement, there is no research that indicates that the structures produce additional fish.[14] The arguments favoring the use of the so-called stream improvement structures are based on intuitive reasoning that has a very strong emotional appeal, but no scientific backing.

There are some limited situations in which local application of structures will speed up the recovery of a reach of stream that has been damaged by construction. However, even where creel limits supposedly have increased, the issue is cloudy. The findings of one study indicated that the increase in trout catch over five years cost $16.68 per pound as a result of construction cost.[14] At this rate, even successful stream improvement projects are losers since stocked fish cost $2.00 per pound of catch.

Fish biology researchers cannot see much value in using structures to increase the number of catchable fish. The structures are strongly favored by sportman's club's, magazine article authors, politicians, and manufacturers of the materials used in constructing the structures.[11] State fish commissions are often pressured into giving their auspices to structure projects out of the necessity to do something to make the fishermen and therefore the politicians happy.[14]

Since fishermen like to fish the streams where structures are located, the structures do serve the purpose of increasing use. The increased use raises the harvest while providing more hours of recreational enjoyment.

Stream structures are very important for hydrologic purposes. They are needed to retard flows, to stop unraveling of stream beds, to keep the stream in the desired channel, and to stop bank erosion. These are measures that improve the streams, but do not in themselves increase the carrying capacity of the stream.

Stream Floating

The preservation or the development of float streams has been given very little coverage in today's clamor for recreation activities. This is, in part, because of the nature of the stream floater. He is usually very enthusiastic about his water-oriented activity and is eager to have friends join him; he does not, however, want his favorite float area overrun or commercialized. So while he hopes the stream will remain protected from destructive change, the stream floater does not want to advertise his favored recreation pursuit. Although it presently is a matter of opinion, the reason for the lack of stream-floating publicity probably is not only because the number of enthusiasts is small, but also because they are reticent about the activity.

One segment of stream floating that has risen rapidly in popularity and commercialization has been the sport of white-water rafting. While the season lasts, many American rivers are filled with pneumatic rafts loaded with thrill seekers. While some rafting rivers such as Pine Creek and the Youghiogheny are in the Eastern states, the ultimate rafting ride is down the Colorado River canyons. In 1955, 55 persons made that white-water float. In 1972, 16,000 persons paid outfitters between $195 and $455 a person to make the thrilling ride.[1] By 1973, a quota or limit was established to limit the numbers.

President Carter's rain-soaked float down Idaho's Salmon River in 1978 splashed white-water rafting into national headlines. The 20 commercial float-trip operators that split an annual gross of more than five million dollars are continually battling to keep their share of the trip allocations. Since 1973, the National Park Service has been regulating river rafting on the Colorado River. Commercial tours had been alloted 92 percent of the share until 1978 when individuals and organizations brought legal suit to change the allocations to a 70–30 split between commercial and individual rafters.[23] An attempt to phase out the outboard motor in the canyon is causing greater controversy than the commercial allotment argument. Eighty percent of the canyon users go through in motorized rafts.[2]

By 1978, recreational use limits existed on at least 45 river segments within the United States.[12] Managers of rivers use allocation policies that differentiate between the commercial outfitters who provide river-riding experiences for market value and the private users relying on their own equipment and skills. The rationing of trips is made within each allotment. Generally, the commercial outfitters ration trips through the market value of pricing. The private users' allotment is generally rationed through some nonmarket process such as first come, first served or lottery.[32]

Seven allotment techniques and six rationing techniques were described and tested for public and commercial acceptance by Utter, Gleason, and McCool. The "Even-Pool" allotment technique appears to be the most prefered technique of alloting trips to each of the two sectors. The "Even-Pool" technique is a variation of a 50–50 split whereas any unclaimed float opportunities could be shifted to meet the demand upon the other sector.[32]

The rationing of the float opportunities within each allotment apparently is being done by using techniques favored by the river users. The USDA Forest Service employs a lottery system to select those private users of the river. Commercial outfitters use the advance reservation and piecing system of rationing. Research done at the University of Montana indicates that the users prefer the application of those two rationing techniques.[32]

Another form of river floating that is catching on in a big way is "tubing" or free floating in an innertube of some convenient size (see Fig. 15.5). Although tubing is done on streams all over the land, Apple River, Wisconsin, considers itself to be the "Tubing Capital of the World."

White-water canoeists seek and get a great deal of publicity; many of the other stream floaters, however, have personal interests to protect and are therefore satisfied with general anonymity. Much of the appeal of stream floating lies in solitude. The therapeutic effects that are often discussed in connection with fishing are certainly to be considered again when evaluating the enjoyment of stream floating. In some cases, the float is made as an end in itself for the enjoyment of floating down the stream; however, floating is often combined with other extensive recreation activities such as fishing and hunting.

Float fishing is very popular in much of the United States and some of the state planning commissions have included it in their recreation planning.[25]

Fig. 15.5. "Tubing" on the Apple River, Wisconsin.

Hunting along the small tree-lined streams has a relatively small number of very devoted adherents who regularly hunt waterfowl and squirrel from the bow of a canoe or on the stream banks.

Stream development and management

The streams selected for floating should have adequate water flow through all but the driest periods of the year. Within the limits of practicability, there is very little that a land manager can do to control the quantity of water flow down the streams. Therefore, he must choose the reaches of stream to be developed on the basis of existing flow. A minimum depth of 12 inches is desirable; however, canoe floats can have eight-inch minimum depth over very short distances.

Some states are now becoming active in developing streams into canoe trails systems that will justify more attention being given to the stream from the boater's viewpoint. [5] Here, as in most recreation decisions, the land manager must be aware of the conflicts within recreation. The increase in stream use for boating has been causing conflicts with fishermen who have been using the streams for many years.

Structures. Some stream improvements can be made by channeling the water through shallow spots by the use of water deflectors. Many streams are not floatable because shallow "riffles" block the boat passage at points along the stream reach. Some of these riffle areas can be made passable by the construction of a double-deflector structure on the shallow spot. Each water deflector in the pair is anchored to the bank and to the stream bottom and angles down current at a 30-degree angle as shown in Figure 15.6. Structures can be used also to close off meander channels or to stop bank undercutting where it will be detrimental to stream floating as illustrated in Figure 15.7.

The gabion is the recommended building block for making stream improvement structures. The gabion is a rectangularly shaped basket made out of heavy-gauge galvanized wire. The gabions are set up on a prepared spot and filled with small rocks that are present at the site. The number of baskets needed to complete one part of the structure is assembled and wired together. As each gabion is filled, it is closed and wired shut. By wiring each gabion to an apron gabion on the stream bottom and then to every other gabion touching it, the builder forms a strong but flexible structure. Gabion structures have proved themselves superior to concrete or log structures because they do not crack or rot. Also, they are not left suspended in space if the stream bottom changes shape because they are flexible enough to conform to the shape of the stream bottom.

The manufacturer of gabions claims that litter, flotsam, and soil will gradually fill in the spaces that occur above the water level and permit the establishment of vegetation. [11] Maybe this will happen in certain localized spots after

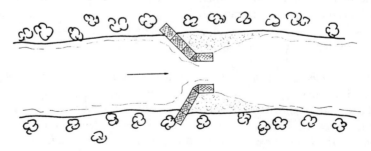

Fig. 15.6. V-deflector made from two gabion groins used to concentrate stream flow and cut a deep channel.

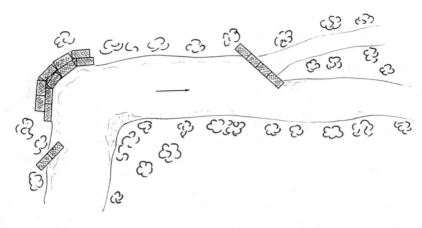

Fig. 15.7. Gabion wall used to block off stream meander channel and to concentrate low flows in one channel.

many years; however, on the basis of observations made on six-year-old gabion structures, it is just a claim and not a fact. This is really of very little importance anyway since the gabions usually are filled with stones from the creek bottom and blend into the scenery very well without a vegetative cover.

There is only one manufacturer of river gabions that produces a product acceptable to the U.S. Forest Service. It is the Maccaferri Gabions of America, Inc., which is an Italian corporation with offices in New York. Complete handbooks on the uses and the methods of installation of gabions are available through the manufacturer.

Riparian vegetation. In areas where sufficient rainfall occurs to permit the growth of vegetation along stream banks without an appreciable decrease in water flow, the vegetation is a definite asset to the quality of the stream for floating. Trees, shrubs, and herbaceous vegetation provide food and cover for birds and animals, form a screen to provide privacy, stabilize the banks, and shade the water. In the East, woodduck hunting is confined largely to streams flowing through wooded bottomlands containing a lot of pin oak trees and streamside cover. Squirrels thrive among the hickory and black walnut trees found on the low terraces next to the stream. In the Southwest, streamside or riparian vegetation is an enemy of stream floaters because it extracts large quantities of water from the stream. As a result, western forest land managers will be in step with other people concerned with water resource when they discourage the growth of riparian vegetation.

Safety. Periodic stream cleanups will be necessary to remove blockages and hazards caused by deposited debris. Any unusual hazards should be marked so that they are easily avoided. Warning signs and markers should be placed well upstream from such serious hazards as treacherous water or waterfalls. When access points are constructed, the serious dangers should be clearly indicated to the floating party prior to launching by signs describing the float area.

Access points. The people must be able to get to the stream by automobile in order to float down it by boat. This means that all weather roads should reach to the stream bank at convenient points along the stream. In areas where roads cross or parallel the stream, boat landings can be established to permit the boater to "put in" or "take out" of the stream. Usually, downstream floats require road connections between landing points; however, as any duck hunter will know, the connecting roads should not be anywhere near the stream.

In certain situations, river-area managers have found that they could obtain their management objectives more easily by requiring users to pack all equipment to the river.[8] Recreation use is subordinate to natural feature protection in the Wild and Scenic Rivers System. To that end, managers have found that less litter is left behind if the bottles and other future debris must be carried into the river. Such a philosophy can work on those rivers used for canoes, kayaks, and rafts where the entire river corridor is controlled. Caution should be exercised, however, in cases where casual access could be more convenient to the user than the official access points.

Stream floats usually are made in small, car-top boats or canoes; an elaborate ramp and trailer space are therefore unnecessary. All that is needed at a stream landing is a parking area and gently sloping spot cut out of the bank. Sanitation facilities might become necessary at points of heavy use; however, the use they would receive generally would not justify their cost. The Minnesota Department of Conservation has taken a different stand on this issue in that it has developed the Crow Wing River into a canoeing waterway and has developed boat access campsites along the river at specific intervals. Similar arrangements occur on many of the heavily used rivers in the United States. If the overnight use of streams continues to rise, then open camping will probably have to be stopped in favor of developed sites.

Designated campsites should be used when camping becomes heavy enough to cause significant damage to the natural features. The linear layout for backcountry camping explained in Chapter 9 (Fig. 9.3) is recommended for use in primitive river corridor camping. A sign can be placed on the river bank to identify the camping site that is more than 100 feet from the river's edge. Studies in Minnesota suggest that group limits per camping units are needed to protect screening vegetation from destruction.[8]

LIMNOLOGICAL ASPECTS OF RECREATIONAL WATER

Limnology, or the study of fresh water, is a science that is important to the field of forest recreation. As water-oriented recreation becomes more popular—as it surely will—it will necessitate a better understanding of the aquatic environment that is so often ignored by those who should have learned their lessons from land-based studies of ecology. A freshwater lake is more than a slippery surface to ski on or a mysterious medium for growing sport fish. It is a dynamic and complex balance of many interacting physical, chemical, and biological forces.

Environment

The physical forces of temperature and light are very important factors in controlling the environment within a body of water. Thermal stratification takes place within the water of lakes and ponds as a result of heating. The character of the stratifications will vary according to the water depth, the climatic conditions, and the area of surface; however, the basic influence of the stratifications on the lake's internal environment remains the same. Thermal stratifications restrict circulation of oxygen and nutrient-bearing water so that only the top layer is replenished by the wind-mixed water.

During the early spring weeks, in the northern part of the country, the stratification breaks down so that there is the necessary circulation to raise the level of dissolved oxygen throughout the deep lakes. The amount of dissolved oxygen contained in fresh water is critical because freshwater fish require more than five parts of oxygen per million parts of water to survive.[16] If good fishing is to take place at varying depths as the fish retreat down to cooler water in the summer, the fish must have an adequate supply of oxygen at the deeper levels.

Oxygen is placed into the water directly from the air or as a result of aquatic plant functions. However, aquatic plants grow only as deep as light will penetrate through the water. The penetration zone of light, or the tropogenic zone, will vary from 5 feet to 90 feet in depth according to the amount of suspended materials and stains present in the water. Most plants live within the upper ten feet of water so that they do not add oxygen directly to the lower strata of water.[7]

Plant Pests Affecting Recreational Water Use

Plants have a dual role in their effect on the recreational quality of water. They are friends of the duck hunter, the bass fisherman, and even the sightseer; however, plants are enemies to the swimmer, the boater, and some fishermen. Excessive numbers of plants actually interfere with fish propagation.[7] Since plants migrate into water areas and become troublesome to the recreationists, this text will consider the plant pests that are commonly encountered. These plants are classified as algae, submergent weeds, or emergent weeds.

Algae

Algae are the simplest form of oxygen-producing plants.[33] Although algae grow in both fresh and salt water, this discussion will be confined to the blue-green and green algae that are found in fresh water. The blue-green algae, which are the most primitive form of plant life on earth, form a characteristic dark green scum on polluted or overfertilized water. Although the green algae occasionally form blooms upon the water surface, they are usually floating free or else attached to any solid object within the water.

The algae provide the basic building block in the food chain within and dependent upon the lake waters. All forms of suspended algae are part of a large collection of microscopic plants and animals known as plankton. A great number of algae blooms make the water undesirable for swimming or drinking because of the discoloration or slimy scum formed by the blooms. The odor of the decomposing algae is another degrading factor that arises when the algae population gets too high.

Temperature, sunlight, water quality, and shape of the water basin are important factors affecting algae growth. Warm temperatures and direct sunlight encourage rapid growth of algae. Algae, as plants, need food in order to grow. Large concentrations of phosphates and nitrates in the water enable large masses of algae to develop. Nutrients are either washed into the water from the surrounding watershed or they are introduced by sewage disposal systems. Even well-treated sewage contains nitrates and phosphates. [7] Algae do not flourish far out to sea or in a large lake because the introduced nutrients cannot get out that far. [33] This is why the shape and the size of the water basin are important factors in algae growth. Wind mixing of the water is most effective on lakes or ponds that are oriented so that the wind can regularly blow along the long axis. The orientation is especially important in areas of rough terrain where the water surface could be shielded from the wind.

Certain algae have toxic effects on birds, fish, and animals when present in concentrated quantity; however, no toxic effect on man has ever been proved. There are some cases where algae were the suspected cause of intestinal disorders, but they could never be isolated as the causal agent. [13] Poor aesthetic quality and obnoxious odors are the primary problems caused by algae.

Algae control. Algae can be controlled in lakes and ponds by treatment with either copper sulfate or diquat. Diquat is a relatively new aquatic herbicide that is effective in killing algae when used properly. However, water treated with diquat cannot be used for domestic drinking water. Since diquat-treated water can be used for recreation purposes ten days after treatment, that herbicide can be used in recreational water that will not be used for drinking. It should be applied to the water surface at a rate of one-fourth to one and a half parts of active ingredient per million parts of water. Tables 15.2 and 15.3 give the quantities of chemical required to achieve certain treatment concentrations.

Copper sulfate has been the favored method of controlling algae since it was first used for this purpose in 1904. [13] Besides the fact that it can be conve-

Table 15.2. Gallons of Liquid Chemical Needed (Based on the Pounds of Active Ingredient per Gallon) to Treat One-Acre Foot of Water with 1 to 10 Parts per Million Concentration.*

Pounds of Active Ingredient per Gallon	Parts per Million									
	1	2	3	4	5	6	7	8	9	10
1	2.719	5.438	8.157	10.876	13.595	16.314	19.033	21.752	24.471	27.190
2	1.359	2.718	4.077	5.436	6.795	8.154	9.513	10.872	12.231	12.590
3	0.906	1.812	2.718	3.624	4.530	5.436	6.342	7.248	8.154	9.060
4	0.680	1.360	2.040	2.720	3.400	4.080	4.760	5.440	6.120	6.800
5	0.544	1.088	1.632	2.176	2.720	3.264	3.808	4.352	4.896	5.440
6	0.453	0.906	1.359	1.812	2.265	2.718	3.171	3.624	4.077	4.530
7	0.388	0.776	1.164	1.552	1.940	2.328	2.716	3.104	3.492	3.880
8	0.340	0.680	1.029	1.360	1.700	2.040	2.380	2.720	3.060	3.400
9	0.302	0.604	0.906	1.208	1.510	1.812	2.114	2.416	2.718	3.020
10	0.272	0.544	0.816	1.088	1.360	1.632	1.904	2.176	2.448	2.720

*Agriculture Extension Service, The Pennsylvania State University.

Table 15.3. Pounds of Chemical Needed (Based on the Percent of Active Ingredient) to Treat One-Acre Foot of Water with 1 to 10 Parts per Million Concentration.*

Percent Active Ingredient	Parts per Million									
	1	2	3	4	5	6	7	8	9	10
1	270.0	540.0	810.0	1080.0	1350.0	1620.0	1890.0	2160.0	2430.0	2700.0
2	135.0	270.0	405.0	540.0	675.0	810.0	945.0	1080.0	1215.0	1350.0
3	90.0	180.0	270.0	360.0	450.0	540.0	630.0	720.0	810.0	900.0
4	67.5	135.0	202.5	270.0	337.5	405.0	472.5	540.0	607.5	675.0
5	54.0	108.0	162.0	216.0	270.0	324.0	378.0	432.0	486.0	540.0
6	45.0	90.0	135.0	180.0	225.0	270.0	315.0	360.0	405.0	450.0
7	38.6	77.2	115.8	154.4	193.0	231.6	270.0	308.8	347.4	386.0
8	33.8	67.6	101.4	135.2	169.0	202.8	236.6	270.4	304.2	338.0
9	30.0	60.0	90.0	120.0	150.0	180.0	210.0	240.0	270.0	300.0
10	27.0	54.0	81.0	108.0	135.0	162.0	189.0	216.0	243.0	270.0
11	24.5	49.0	73.5	98.0	122.5	147.0	171.5	196.0	220.5	245.0
12	22.5	45.0	67.5	90.0	112.5	135.0	157.5	180.0	202.5	225.0
13	20.8	41.6	62.4	83.2	104.0	124.8	145.6	166.4	187.2	208.0
14	19.3	38.6	57.9	77.2	96.5	115.8	135.1	154.4	173.7	193.0
15	18.0	36.0	54.0	72.0	90.0	108.0	126.0	144.0	162.0	180.0
16	16.9	33.8	50.7	67.6	84.5	101.4	118.3	135.2	152.1	169.0
17	15.9	31.8	47.7	63.6	79.5	95.4	111.3	127.2	143.1	159.0
18	15.0	30.0	45.0	60.0	75.0	90.0	105.0	120.0	135.0	150.0
19	14.2	28.4	42.6	56.8	71.0	85.2	99.4	113.6	127.8	142.0
20	13.5	27.0	40.5	54.0	67.5	81.0	94.5	108.0	121.5	135.0
21	12.9	25.8	38.7	51.6	64.5	77.4	90.3	103.2	116.1	129.0
22	12.3	24.6	36.9	49.2	61.5	73.8	86.1	98.4	110.7	123.0
23	11.7	23.4	35.1	46.8	58.5	70.2	81.9	93.6	105.3	117.0
24	11.3	22.6	33.9	45.2	56.5	67.8	79.1	90.4	101.7	113.0
25	10.8	21.6	32.4	43.2	54.0	64.8	75.6	86.4	97.2	108.0
50	5.4	10.2	16.2	21.6	27.0	32.4	37.8	43.2	48.6	54.0
100	2.7	5.4	8.1	10.8	13.5	16.2	18.9	21.6	24.3	27.0

*Agriculture Extension Service, The Pennsylvania State University.

niently purchased at agriculture supply stores, it is a relatively safe and effective chemical to use under most circumstances even though it does have some disadvantages. Copper sulfate will kill trout when applied in sufficient quantity to control the algae. Any application in excess of the amount prescribed to kill the algae will have an adverse effect on all species of fish. Therefore, if fishing is an activity, the results of the continued use of copper sulfate must be watched carefully. Also, copper-sulfate solutions will corrode metal, and the copper-sulfate dust is very irritating to human eyes and nostrils.

A concentration of one half part of copper sulfate per million parts of water should be a satisfactory application for most water; however, the concentration will have to be increased for hard water. If the kill is unsatisfactory after one week, a 50 percent stronger application should be made.[7]

The control of algae should begin before dense populations of algae form. The killing of a dense population will cause a severe strain on the dissolved oxygen supply within the water. If a dense population has built up, it should be divided and treated by sections so as not to make an overwhelming demand upon the oxygen needed in aerobic decomposition.

Copper sulfate can be spread by boat or airplane and applied as a solid or a liquid. Small ponds can be treated by dragging a bag of crystals off the stern of a rowboat until they have dissolved.

Submergent plants

Submergent plants are higher forms of plant life that live in deep water. They are either attached to the bottom or they float freely. Nutrients are absorbed directly from the water and only anchorage is supplied by the roots. These weeds provide some cover for fish when not too plentiful, but they cause fish population problems when they are too dense. Submergent plants make swimming hazardous and fishing unpleasant; therefore, they must be controlled.

Submergent plant control. Mechanical methods of removal should not be used to control submergents. Many submergent water weeds will reproduce by vegetative propagation. Raking, dragging, or chopping will leave pieces behind to develop into full plants in a very short time. Mechanical attempts to remove submergents will only succeed in multiplying the plant's numbers and extending its area coverage.

Milford, some of the pondweeds, and other submergents can be controlled by modifying the environment. A lowering of the water level during early winter will permit some of the bottom areas to freeze and kill the submergents. Unfortunately, the oxygen supply is proportionally smaller and might have an adverse effect on the concentrated fish population.[33]

Ponds with a slow rate of water turnover can be fertilized to increase the plankton growth and thereby cutting down on sunlight penetration. The photosynthesis of the submergents is slowed down and their growth is inhibited. Fertilization with a 10-10-10 fertilizer should be done until visibility is limited to 15 to 20 inches of water depth by algae growth. Fertilization should not continue beyond September in locations where the pond will freeze in the winter because of the problem of oxygen depletion. This technique of submergent weed control is not recommended in ponds that will be used for swimming.

The chemical control of submergents used to be done with arsenic compounds; however, they are dangerous and have been replaced by herbicides.[13] Some of the herbicides used in the control of submergents today are 2,4-D, 2,4,5-T, simazine, silvex, diquat, and endothall. The note of caution that must be sounded here is that these materials have not been tested long enough to ascertain their long-range effects. As a result of the uncertainties involved in applying these chemicals to water, some states require approval from the fish commission or health authorities prior to application. Table 15.4 lists some of the methods used to control various aquatic plants.

Floater plants

Floaters are shallow water plants that have their foliage at or slightly above the water-surface level. They generally obtain nutrients from the muddy bottom except for the unattached duckweeds of the North and the water hyacinth of the South.[33] These two floaters obtain their nutrients directly from the water and are not as dependent upon depth as are the other floaters.

The infamous water hyacinth was introduced into this country from Venezuela during the 1889 New Orleans Cotton Exposition. This showy water floater now clogs streams, ponds, and canals throughout Louisiana and Florida.[9] Spadderdock and the water lily are characteristic of the rooted floaters. The dense shade caused by the floater plants eliminates the submerged vegetative growth.

Emergent plants

The aquatic plants that send their stems, leaves, and flowers well above the water surface are known as emergent plants. Cattails, bullrushes, and rice are good examples of emergents. Emergents are favored by shallow water, gently sloping shorelines, stable bottoms, cold water, and nutrient-poor water.[11] The emergents reproduce by seed, runners, and fragmentation.

Control of floaters and emergents. Mechanical, environmental, biological, and chemical controls can be used effectively against floaters and emergents. Mechanical control of floaters and emergents is a common practice in both large and small bodies of water. Care must be taken, however, to remove the cut-up pieces of plants from the water so that each piece does not develop into a mature plant. If mechanic control is not done with care, the weed problem is intensified and not alleviated by the effort.

By manipulation of the factors that affect the shallow water environment, control of emergent plants can be established. If the shoreline can be altered so that it dips steeply to a depth of ten feet, the emergent will be permanently eliminated. The placement of black plastic sheets on the bottom will block the light and thereby stop plant growth. The plastic sheets are available in most agriculture supply stores where they are usually sold for mulching gardens.

Biologic controls have been tried on many land plants with success; however, no practical biologic control is available to the private landowner in his battle with aquatic plants. Waterfowl and muskrats eat some plants; however, they probably contribute more to the plant's growth and spread than to their eradication. Manatees were introduced in an attempt to control the water hyacinth, but so far they have not been able to do much. In the Congo River Basin of Africa where herbicides are not widely used, the manatee has proved to be a more effective biologic control than it has in this country.

Chemical controls offer the best solution to aquatic plant control. The common herbicides used to control submergents will also kill floaters and emergents. [11] Tens of thousands of acres of water surface have been freed of the strangling water hyacinths.

Herbicides can be spread in either liquid or granular form and can be applied from boats, airplane, or the shoreline. Even distribution of the chemical is the key to successful herbicide application. The quantity of chemical required and its application rate can be determined by using Tables 15.2, 15.3, and 15.4.

Animal Pests Affecting Recreational Water Use

Within the environment created by the fresh water and the factors affecting it, there is a natural balance of life. Small things eat smaller things so that they can be eaten in turn by larger things. Competition for light, oxygen, or nutrients keeps every species of living things battling the other species for survival. Some of the animals that are part of this deadly fight for survival are also pests to humans and therefore undesirable creatures. However, to eradicate all the pests and their hosts completely will sometimes destroy the ecological balance within the entire body of water. Before a person sets out to destroy his enemies, he had better understand how much his friends need those enemies. He must realize that by killing off the populations of undesirable creatures, he might also eradicate the indigenous fish population or kill waterfowl at the same time. The common animal pests associated with the freshwater environment are mosquitoes, leeches, and swimmer's itch.

Table 15.4. Summary Table of Aquatic Plants and Control Measures Recommended[a]

Plant Species	Mechanical Methods	Environmental Methods	Chemical and Dosage[b]
ALGAE			All dosages are in terms of active ingredient
Green, blue-green, filamentous forms and other types	In very small ponds, rake or drag. This is only effective with the mat-forming filamentous types.	Reduce nutrients in water (ex. sewage effluent animal wastes, fertilizer runoff, fertilization, etc.)	Copper sulfate ½–1 ppm Diquat ½–1½ ppm Copper sulfate ½–1 ppm Diquat ½–1½ ppm
Stonewort algae (Charophyceae)	None	None	
SUBMERGENTS			
Coontails (*Ceratophyllum* sp.)	Mechanical harvesting machines of some use. Many species reproduce vegetatively from plant fragments and cutting may only make problems worse. This is true for most submergent plants.	Increased water depth, steeper sides	2,4-D granules 20 lb/acre Endothall ½–3 ppm
Pondweeds (*Potamogeton* sp.)	"	"	Endothall ½–3 ppm Diquat ½ ppm
Fanwort (*Cabomba* sp.)	"	"	Silvex 2 ppm
Bladderwort (*Utricularia* sp.)	"	"	Diquat ¼–½ ppm Silvex 2 ppm
Bushy pondweeds (*Najas* sp.)	"	"	Diquat ¼–½ ppm
Milfoil (*Myriophyllum* sp.)	Mechanical harvesting machines of some use. Many species reproduce vegetatively from plant fragments and cutting may only make problems worse. This is true for most submergent plants.	Increased water depth, steeper sides	Diquat ¼–½ ppm Endothal 2–3 ppm 2,4-D granules 20 lb/acre
Waterweed (*Anarcharis* sp.)	"	"	Diquat ¼–½ ppm Silvex 2 ppm

268

FLOATERS—ATTACHED Water lily (*Nymphaea* sp.)	For small ponds or limited areas, repeated cutting and pulling can be successful.	Increased water depth and steeper sides will reduce the problem.	2,4-D granules 20 lb/acre Silvex 6–8 lb/acre as a foliage spray
Spatterdock (*Nuphar* sp.)	"	"	Silvex 6–8 lb/acre as a foliage spray
FLOATERS—FREE Duckweed (*Lemma* sp.) Watermeal (*Wolffia* sp.) Giant duckweed (*Spirodela* sp.) Giant duckweed (*Spirodeal* sp.)	None	None	Diquat ¼–½ ppm
EMERGENTS Cattail (*Typha* sp.)	For small areas, repeated cutting and pulling can be successful.	Increased water depth and steeper sides will reduce the problem.	2,4-D granules 20 lb/acre
Arrowarum (*Peltandra* sp.) Arrowhead (*Sagittaria* sp.) Bulrush (*Scirpus* sp.) Burreed (*Sparganium* sp.) Pickerel weed (*Pontederia* sp.) Rushes (*Juncus* sp.)			2,4-D; 2,4,5-T liquid Silver liquid 2,4-D; Silvex liquid

[a] Agricultural Extension Service, The Pennsylvania State University.
[b] Diquat may not be used in domestic water supplies.

Mosquitoes

The most important pest associated with fresh water is the mosquito. Besides being a vicious biting insect, it is the vector, or carrier, for encephalitis and malaria. [33] Mosquitoes breed best in shallow, still water where there is an abundance of cover and organic matter on the bottom of the water body. The amount of mosquitoes that an area produces is directly related to the amount of intersection of the water's surface by vegetation. The mosquito population increases when the amount of intersecting vegetation increases. An exception to this occurs when the vegetation becomes so dense that the vegetation is nearly packed solid. This situation actually cuts down on the intersection line formed by the vegetation protruding through the water's surface. [11]

Mosquito control. Good preparation of the shoreline and nearby land will greatly reduce the mosquito population. All of the vegetation should be removed from the water's edge. This strip should be kept clear to eliminate the intersection of the water surface by plants. All wet spots should be filled with soil or drained.

Chemical spraying is effective in killing the land-based adults; however, this only results in a temporary reduction of the population. Saturated hydrocarbons such as DDT have been used successfully in the past. Since its use has created some controversy and the mosquitoes are breeding a resistance to it, DDT is being replaced by an organophosphorous pesticide named Malathion. Malathion applications have been very effective when used as a fog application of slightly less than .10 pound per acre. [33]

Leeches

Leeches are flat, dark-colored parasites that range in length from one to five inches. They prefer warm, shallow water where the water is usually calm. Stones, plants, and debris on the bottom provide shelter for the leeches during the daytime when they are the least active. As a result of this shelter requirement, leeches do not flourish where the bottom is made up of clay. During the winter, leeches burrow into the bottom and become dormant. [11]

Although leeches do not feed very often, they are a serious pest when present. Their presence can completely destroy the swimming value of a body of water. Even the sight of leeches that do not attack humans ruins the swimming experience for many people. When they do feed, leeches attach to their victims by an oral suction device and painlessly penetrate the skin. As with other blood-sucking pests, the leeches inject a salivary anticoagulant into the wound in order to encourage a free flow of blood. It is the anticoagulant that causes the itching associated with leech bites.

Leech control. Leech control is possible by making environmental changes or by the application of chemicals; control, however, is difficult and seldom becomes 100 percent effective. The control of leeches is difficult for two reasons. The first reason is the leech's ability to swim over long distances in a short period of time. This means that local eradication of the leech population is only a temporary solution and must be repeated periodically. Second, the chemical applications needed to kill the leeches will also kill the fish. A large fish kill is undesirable in many places where fishing is a major attraction.

A technique of killing leeches by changing their environment has been employed successfully in northern lakes or ponds that can be drawn down. When the cold weather arrives and the leeches bury into the muddy bottoms, they are protected from freezing by the shallow water above them. If the water is removed rapidly during freezing weather, the leeches will be killed. If the water level is lowered four feet and held there for two months during subfreezing weather, the leeches in the frozen mud flats will be killed. Temperatures below 20°F are fatal to leeches.

Chemical applications are usually considered to be temporary because of rapid reinfestation by the leeches. However, complete elimination can be accomplished in small lakes if danger of reinfestation is not great, if the fish population is expendable, and if the treated water is not released to flow downstream. A concentration of five parts of copper sulfate per million parts of water will kill the leeches, the fish, and a few other forms of aquatic life.

Temporary control around swimming beaches is a compromise measure that can be employed. One method of temporary control calls for a daily application of 100 pounds of powdered lime per acre each day. This is an expensive technique to get temporary control. Weekly treatments with ten pounds of copper sulfate and five pounds of hydrated lime per acre have proved to be effective.

Swimmer's itch

The swimmer's itch is caused by a small free-swimming worm larva (*Schistosome cercariae*) that burrows into human skin where it dies. These larvae are not parasites of man; they attack man by accident after leaving certain snails that act as alternate hosts to these bird and mammal parasites. The larvae are just visible to the naked eye when there is proper illumination. [11]

When the larvae burrow into human skin, they die and their remains cause inflammation and itching. Each red spot is discrete, does not spread, and disappears after a couple of days. The swimmer's itch is most common in the north central lake region of the United States where it has become a serious threat to lake swimming; it has, however, been reported in nearly all regions of the country.

Control of swimmer's itch. The application of five parts per million of copper sulfate will kill the snails that act as alternate hosts for the swimmer's-itch-causing larvae. Since this concentration of copper sulfate will be toxic to fish and other aquatic life, it should be applied only at the beach areas. The application is more successful when mixed with copper carbonate or hydrated lime. These chemicals should be applied at the rate of two pounds of snow-grade copper sulfate and two pounds of copper carbonate for every thousand square feet of bottom surface to be treated.[11]

REFERENCES

1. Anonymous. 1973. Troubled Waters. In *Newsweek* Magazine, June 18, p. 62.
2. Anonymous. 1978. Cleaning Up the Canyon. "Life/Style," In *Newsweek* Magazine, April 17, 1978, p. 74.
3. Bureau of Outdoor Recreation. 1966. *Wabash River Basin Comprehensive Study—Louisville Reservoir, Helm Reservoir.* BOR Lake Central Region. U.S. Department of the Interior, Ann Arbor, Mich.
4. ————. 1966. *Water Oriented Outdoor Recreation, Lake Erie Basin.* BOR Lake Central Region. U.S. Department of the Interior, Ann Arbor, Mich.
5. ————. 1972. *Outdoor Recreation Action.* Report 24. U.S. Department of the Interior, Washington, D.C. 32 pages.
6. California Public Outdoor Recreation Plan Committee. 1960. *California Public Outdoor Recreation Plan, Part II.* Sacramento, Calif.
7. Cole, Wingard, Butler, and Bradford. 1966. *Aquatic Plants, Management and Control in Pennsylvania.* Natural Resource Series. Special Circular 79. The Pennsylvania State University Agriculture Extension Service, University Park, Pa.
8. Craig, William S. 1977. Reducing Impacts from Recreation Users. In *Proceedings: River Recreation Management and Research Symposium.* USDA, Forest Service General Technical Report NC-28, p. 155–162.
9. Farb, P. 1963. *Ecology.* Life Nature Library. Time, Inc., New York, N.Y. 193 pages.
10. Humphery, C. 1963. Recreation Ponds and Beaches. In *Guidelines for Developing Land for Outdoor Recreational Uses.* Cooperative Extension Service, Purdue University, West Lafayette, Ind.
11. Maccaferi Gabions of America, Inc. 1966. *Stream Improvement Handbook.* Steller Press, New York, N.Y. 16 pages.
12. McCool, S.F. 1978. Recreation Use Limits: Issues for the Tourism Industry. In *Journal of Travel Research*, vol. 17, no. 2, pp. 2–7.
13. Mackenthun, Ingram, and Porges. 1964. *Limnological Aspects of Recreational Lakes.* U.S. Public Health Service Publication No. 1167. U.S. Department of Health, Education, and Welfare, Washington, D.C.
14. Mullen, J.W. 1961. *Stream Improvement Prospectus for the Streams of the George Washington National Forest.* U.S. Forest Service, Washington, D.C.
15. Outdoor Recreation Resources Review Commission. 1962. *Outdoor Recreation for America.* Superintendent of Documents, Government Printing Office, Washington, D.C. 246 pages.
16. ————. 1962. *Water for Recreation—Values and Opportunities.* Study Report No. 10. Washington, D.C. 130 pages.
17. ————. 1962. *Sport Fishing—Today and Tomorrow.* Study Report No. 7. Washington, D.C. 130 pages.

18. Owens, G.P. 1964. *Income Potential from Outdoor Recreation Enterprises in Rural Areas in Ohio*. Research Bull. No. 964. Ohio Agricultural Experiment Station, Wooster, Ohio.

19. Pennsylvania Department of Forests and Waters. 1969. *State Park Planning and Guidelines*. Bureau of State Parks, Harrisburg, Pa. 90 pages.

20. Pennsylvania Department of Health. 1957. *Regulations for Bathing Places*. Chapter IV, Article 442, Rules and Regulations, Harrisburg, Pa.

21. Salomon, J.H. 1959. *Campsite Development*. Council Administrative Series No. 5B. Girl Scouts of the United States of America, New York, N.Y. 160 pages.

22. Shafer, E.L., Jr. 1967. Management Suggestions for Water-Oriented Outdoor Recreation. Unpublished manuscript. NE Forest Experiment Station, U.S. Forest Service, Upper Darby, Pa.

23. Stevens, Mark. 1978. Custodianship of Wild Rivers Challenged. In *The Christian Science Monitor*, August 21, 1978, p. 7.

24. Stroud, R. 1966. Key Values in Outdoor Recreation Planning. *Proceedings of the Northeast Fish and Wildlife Conference*. Boston, Mass.

25. Tennessee Planning Commission. 1962. *Public Outdoor Recreation Resources in Tennessee. Inventory and Plan for Development 1962*. Publication No. 323. Nashville, Tenn.

26. Tennessee Department of Public Health. 1965. *Suggested Regulations Governing Organized Camps*. Chapter 65 of Public Acts 1965. Nashville, Tenn.

27. U.S. Department of the Interior. 1979. *The Third Nationwide Outdoor Recreation Plan: The Assessment*. Washington, D.C. 264 pages.

28. U.S. Forest Service. 1961. *Handbook on Soils*. Category 2. Handbook Series 2512.2. Division of Administrative Management. USFS Department of Agriculture, Washington, D.C.

29. ————. 1963. *Recreation Management*. Manual and Handbook, Title 2300. U.S. Department of Agriculture, Washington, D.C.

30. ————. 1962. *Manual of Individual Water Supply Systems*. Public Health Service Publication No. 24. U.S. Department of Health, Education, and Welfare, Washington, D.C.

31. ————. 1965. *Environmental Health Practice in Recreational Areas*. PHS Publication No. 1195. U.S. Department of Health, Education, and Welfare, Washington, D.C.

32. Utter, J.W. Gleason, and S. McCool. 1981. User Preceptions of River Recreation Allocation Techniques. In *Proceedings of the Second Conference on Scientific Research in the National Parks*. USDA, Forest Service General Technical Report NC-63.

33. Went, F.W. 1963. *The Plants*. Life Nature Library. Time, Inc., New York, N.Y. 193 pages.

34. Wingard, R., and Heiney, C. 1966. *Pond Construction and Management in Pennsylvania*. Special Circular No. 78. Natural Resources Series, Agriculture Extension Service, The Pennsylvania State University, University Park, Pa. 24 pages.

35. Young Men's Christian Association. 1960. *Developing Campsites and Facilities*. National Committee on YMCA Camp Layouts. Building and Facilities Association Press, New York. 63 pages.

16

Management of
Forest Recreation Areas

INTRODUCTION

Management is defined by Webster as the "judicious use of means to accomplish an end: skillful treatment." This implies that learned skills are applied to situations in such a way as to bring about an intended condition. In the management of a recreation area, the end product is user enjoyment. The skillful treatment used to obtain this end in a recreation area consists of techniques in planning, maintenance, and protection coupled with proper administration. The judicious use of each of these techniques must be dependent upon the desired end product. In that user enjoyment is the end product, the user's interests in the managed area must be analyzed. True, many areas have specific attractions and thereby can attract only those users interested in what the area has to offer.

Resources of any kind are managed for one, or a combination, of reasons. Those reasons are:

1. the production of goods;
2. production of services;
3. protection of the resource; or
4. protection of the user.

The management objectives are generally set by policy goals of the company or the agency administering the forest land. In every case, more than one management reason is applicable even though one might be dominant. Park land is managed primarily to provide services to the visitor, protect the resource, and to protect the user. Industrial forest land is dedicated to the production of timber, but it must be managed to protect the resources and to provide protection for the visitor. Additionally, industrial forest land can be managed so as to provide services. Federal forest lands generally are managed under the multiple-use concept thereby equally covered by all four management reasons.

Today, the forest resources are used for recreation by everyone who comes in contact with them. One of the major pitfalls of the land manager, most notably the professional forester, has been his failure to recognize that almost everyone within the forested area is a recreationist of one kind or another. As a result, the public has become very vocal in its dissatisfaction with the forester's techniques of managing the nation's timbered lands. The land manager must recognize that the public should have more than campgrounds and picnic areas for recreation.

Forest recreation is loosely lumped into either intensive- or extensive-use activities. Intensive forest recreation activities are concentrated in a relatively centralized area that has been developed for use. Camping, swimming, boating, picnicking, and certain types of hiking are generally considered as intensive, or developed, forest recreation activities. The fisherman, hunter, and overland hiker move about over large areas where the minimum of developments is required. These forest users are engaging in extensive forest recreation activities. One of the most important users of extensive forest recreation facilities is the sightseer who wants to be surrounded by as much natural beauty as the area can offer. Almost everyone who drives through forested areas is a user of extensive forest recreation facilities.

Many recreation users are involved in a combination of recreation activities. A camper is often a sightseer before, after, and during his camping. Although his primary use of the forest is in an intensive recreation area, he engages in extensive use of the forest. The intensive-extensive recreation area user, such as the camper, probably gets more attention from land managers than does his opposite number. In opposition to the intensive-extensive user is the person who comes to the forest to use its extensive facilities, but also gets involved with intensive-use areas such as roadside rests. Many sportsmen prefer to camp in the forest while fishing or hunting, but they came for the fishing or the hunting and not for the fun of camping.

The land manager would soon need psychiatric help if he tried to characterize every visitor to his area. He would do better to deal only in generalities and to compare those generalities to what his area can continuously produce. Often, the recreation area manager has nothing to say about planning of the layout, its implementation, its governing policy, or even its insect control program. Even when the manager has been placed squarely in the position of the technician, he must still be able to show ingenuity within the existing limitations. Many state park supervisors have done remarkable jobs of managing their parks in such a way as to make them better than other parks that have much better natural advantages. Even though he may not be permitted much freedom in planning the development of his area, the recreation area manager still has the other methods of treatment at his disposal. He can skillfully apply techniques of management, operation, and protection to provide an area that will continuously provide a given level of user enjoyment.

MANAGEMENT OF INTENSIVE-USE AREAS

Intensive-use areas provide facilities and services that are required for specific types of forest recreation. The range of intensive-use recreation areas extends from ski lifts and lodges to a developed swimming hole. Public agencies tend to give camping and picnic areas the highest priority and the most attention.[22] Whether private or public, these areas need a high priority. More than half of the ski resorts in the country are on Forest Service land. Such high-investment ventures as ski lifts and lodges are operated by experienced operators and generally are not the direct problem of the forest land manager beyond concern over site impact and general service to the public. The intensive-use development tends to concentrate use into the managed area, thereby requiring more facilities and services. As the intensity of use increases, the need for increased management climbs. People control, site protection, maintenance, user safety and comfort, fire protection, and general aesthetics are the major management concerns of a recreation area supervisor. These six items do not include the administrative problems of public relations, operation, personnel management, and policy.

The people who visit a forest area tend to destroy what they have come to admire. Their very presence in the forest has an impact upon the environment.[5,9] Research has shown that even lightly used areas lose 50 to 99 percent of their original ground cover simply by trampling. This concentration of traffic wears out the vegetation, compacts the soil, accelerates erosion, kills the shade trees, and reduces the amount of barrier vegetation. Bare soil causes dust or mud problems, and personal cleanliness becomes a full-time job for a family with small children. The summation of these effects is a deterioration of the site and a sharp decrease in user enjoyment. Also, the presence of people does lessen the appeal of solitude that a forest can offer. However, the impact of crowding on satisfaction is not well understood by research personnel even though several theories have been advanced and studied.

Originally, wise planning can lessen some of these problems; however, to some extent, the problems will always remain for the manager to handle. Research does show that overstory density in tenting areas tends to remain uniform or increase in spite of the wear on each unit of a well-maintained campground.[4] Even though the research showed an increase in canopy closure, it also showed a loss of lateral screening between sites and in the number of smaller trees. The coarse granitic sands of southern Maine do not rise up as dust or turn into mudholes; therefore, they support good recreation sites with the minimum of paving. The limestone soils of West Virginia grow magnificent vegetation, but they have the poorest possible trafficability characteristics. Roads and even trails on such soils need surfacing to be serviceable in wet weather. Also, these limestone areas should be crossed in as short a route as possible.

Not all recreation areas can be located on the ideal soil. They must be developed where the need and the attractions are. As a result of putting the developments where the demand occurs, the recreation planners will have to put facilities in locations that do not have the best site characteristics. This means that recreation managers are going to inherit problems when they take charge of these new areas.

Site Protection

In order to maintain a given level of satisfactory use within an area, the manager can follow two courses. He can estimate the carrying capacity of the recreation area and provide administrative restrictions to limit use to that capacity. To a certain extent, the available facilities will limit the number of users; however, this is not satisfactory in all cases because people might not seek substitution areas or activities until the overuse of the area has done its damage. The second course of action is to apply land management techniques to the area. The supervisor can use various management techniques in order to maintain the attractiveness of the area.

Three interdependent tasks are required to lessen the long-term destructive impact of use. Those tasks are:

1. To concentrate the use to specific locales and channels whenever possible.
2. To modify or treat the ground surface at the concentrated use points to prevent wear.
3. To apply silvicultural techniques required to replace, repair, and care for vegetation and soil on the recreation site.

Concentration of use

Since physical carrying capacities are largely unknown for most sites, they can be used only in general terms or in arbitrary decrees. As more research is completed in this field, more weight can be applied to the carry-capacity theory. Although gross excesses in user loads are readily observable, the delicate balance between site quality and amount of use is difficult to achieve. It means that some limit of use must be established to prevent a reduction in site quality. It is very rare that a private operator will turn away income during peak-use periods. It is probable that he would rather invest some time and money into repairing the damage from overuse.

The concentration of use to specific locales and channels is of the utmost importance. This can be done by judicious location of roads, trails, screening, barriers, and other developments. In campgrounds, this concentration-of-use technique should be applied to the camping unit interior as well as to the entire campground. The unit interior should be set up to facilitate direct movement among the car, table, and fireplace as well as direct routes out of the unit to the water supply and to the toilet facility. Some people object to a formal unit where the table is tied down, the vehicle is restricted, and the tent must be placed in a certain spot. In attempting to concentrate use, these steps might become necessary. If the tent pad is placed in the best location within the unit, if it is level, if it is high enough for good external drainage, and if it is made of coarse material for good internal drainage, most people will use it. The use of the constructed tent pad also will help to eliminate the destructive practice of "tent ditching" during rainy weather.

Concentration of use by itself will be self-defeating. It must be teamed with attractions and site modifications. People will go where the attractions are or where movement is most convenient. Forcing them to do otherwise would be a violation of the purpose of the managed recreation area and would invite disregard, ill feeling, and substitution. This does not imply that all people should be permitted to roam freely around the area; it simply underlines the need for judiciously placed facilities, trails, barriers, and roads.

Trails. Trails are the key to site protection in an intensive-use area. When judiciously tied into the road system, trails facilitate movement of users to points of concentration. If properly located, the trails will channel traffic into designated routes of travel. Even though people will not always walk where the manager wants them to, they will generally follow the easiest route to their objective. That is, if they know where their objective is located. Trails alone will not be effective. They must be identified by signs or sight. A trail without signs that leads to the pump is of limited value if all the potential users do not know where the pump is located. Also, people will leave a worn dirt trail to avoid mud, steep grades, or unnecessary length. A two-inch thick surface of gravel or black top stops wear and mud and makes the trail more attractive. Chapter 12 treats the subject of trails in greater detail.

Barriers. The word barrier is employed in a limited sense in recreation management. It does not mean an overwhelming wall that completely stops everything. Rather, a barrier in a recreation area should be subtle and suggestive. It should blend with the theme of the forested area so that it does not offend the recreationists. True, a high fence or similar barrier will be needed in some instances; however, they should be avoided when possible. Besides being used for controlling the movement of people, barriers can be used to screen unpleasant sights or to provide privacy. Generally, barriers are constructed from building materials or developed with vegetation.

Constructed barriers can be either permanently implaced or movable. Fences, rows of short posts, and sleepers and rails are the common permanent barriers made from logs and lumber. Figure 16.1 shows a split-rail fence being used to channel foot traffic into the flow pattern desired by the park manager. Rocks

Fig. 16.1. Use of split-rail fence and trail to channel pedestrian traffic through a high-density picnic area.

and seeded soil piles can make use of native materials in very subtle ways for vehicle control. The judicious felling of trees and the piling of brush can form casual, but effective, barriers in locations where more elaborate efforts are not needed or not economically feasible. The stringing of barbed wire has no place in the field of outdoor recreation.

Occasionally, the need arises to close a location to use temporarily. Movable barriers should be used for this purpose rather than constructing a temporary in-place barrier. Movable barriers can be tastefully constructed from durable materials and stored when not in use. Because of their flexibility and continued reusability, movable barriers can justify larger cost per unit than can temporary barriers. Temporary barriers are usually thrift measures and end up looking "junky." Some state parks use as movable barrier that is simply made by fastening a poured concrete block to each end of a six-foot-long log.

Shrubbery and tree plantings make the aesthetically ideal barrier. Vegetative plantings control movement of people, provide screening, and increase the scenic value of the setting. The loop roads that are so popular with recreation

Fig. 16.2. The careful adaptation of native materials and screening vegetation maintains the beauty of the setting at this picnic unit. (Forest Service.)

planners create a minor but irritating problem. Headlights of cars on the loop roads shine into half of the camping units as the vehicle moves along. Campground managers should consider the use of some shrubbery to shield campers from the headlight glare.

Generally, barrier plantings will take a beating from the users and will need replacement occasionally; however, not all areas have had the problem of replacement. Maine's Sebago Lake State Park finds itself in the happy position of too effective barrier plantings. Five years after white pine seedlings had been planted in great numbers throughout the expanding campground area, it became apparent that nearly all the trees were going to continue to grow in spite of very heavy use. The management is now undertaking a thinning and pruning operation to open up the overgrown areas of the campground. Unfortunately, not all barrier plantings are so durable and put the manager into such an enviable position.

The choice of species and the form of barrier planting offer a broad challenge to the manager. Will native vegetation withstand the abuse? Should new spe-

cies be introduced to replace native plants? Quite often, nonindigenous vegetation is more durable than native plants. Will a hedge be superior to a row of
trees? Low hedges will channel traffic without blocking the view. Many recreation area managers have had great success with using low growing native
junipers as barriers along paths. Junipers have been very successful in keeping
bathers on the trails at Point Beach State Park in Wisconsin where extremely
heavy-use areas are strung along the strand. Beaked filbert (*Corylus Carnuta*,
Marsh) is not only a very good barrier planting within its range, but it provides
two other functions. It is a tall, bushy shrub that screens the view, and it produces a nutlike fruit that will attract wildlife. Although beaked filbert is not
suited to every area, it is a good example of the species that managers should be
considering for their areas. Rhododendron and azaleas generally prove to be a
durable shrub species in recreation areas.[17]

Screening has already been mentioned in regards to camping areas where it is
planted to provide privacy within the units or to block the view of an unfavorable sight. Maintenance buildings, sewage plants, and parking lots should be
screened from view by vegetation barriers. Not all campers desire to be completely screened in. Also, not all campers desire to be widely separated from
one another, and screening for privacy within campgrounds is not too important to them.[8] These people are usually content in a central campground
where they have plenty of nearby neighbors. If the present trend continues, excessive vegetation will not trouble these people. Many, if not most, forest recreation areas have been so worn out that regular management programs will be of
limited value. In these cases, rehabilitation projects must be undertaken to raise
the level of quality to the desired point.

Surface modification

The thing to consider when concentrating use onto small areas is the increased
need for better surfaces. Unprotected soil will quickly compact and wear away.
Vegetation will be destroyed by trampling. A water faucet is a spot where use is
definitely concentrated. Anyone who has waded around the muddy water
faucets and fought the hornets there gathering mud will testify to the poor idea
of user concentration. A paved apron with a water carry-off drain is usually
needed to improve such a nuisance spot.

The trampling around a table quickly forms a circle of bare soil which becomes dirt on the children and dust on the food. Periodic movement of the
table will spread the wear over a large area. This course of action might be satisfactory under certain conditions. However, in this period of heavy recreation
demand, few managers can afford to donate enough land to one table to provide room for nature's healing hand. It may be better to tie the table down in
one spot and treat the worn circle, thus permitting the larger area to remain
vegetated. One satisfactory technique that has been employed in very heavily

used picnic areas such as roadside rests has been the construction of a concrete pad that is sufficiently large to hold the picnic table and to provide room for movement around the table. Near the center of the pad, a large eyebolt is imbedded to hold a chain that fastens to the table.

The thought of paving within a picnic or camping site is repugnant to many land managers and recreationists upon first thought. This may go back to the roots of professional training or back to that urge to be Nathanial Bumpo or Daniel Boone. Interestingly, most of the indignant remarks over surfaced places within a campground of picnic area come from those who talk about or plan outdoor recreation, but not from those who regularly use the overcrowded intensive-use areas.

Proper use of material can make surfacing less offensive to those who might object to it. Initial costs of concrete and black-top material are high. Although they might save on maintenance in the long run, hard surfacing materials may be too much of a burden for many an operator's budget. Some natural mulching materials might be used to provide a more satisfactory surface. Entire camping units can be given a light coat of pine needles, wood chips, or sawdust at a very low investment. Parents of the family who have tried sitting around a fireplace on the dusty, worn-out ground would not complain about the reduction of dirt caused by a layer of wood chips. Besides producing the immediate benefit of less dust for the user, mulched surfaces provide an insulating cushion over the soil. The mulch cushion protects the soil from wear and compaction, protects the tree and shrubbery roots from exposure and trampling, and prevents moisture loss through evaporation. A California study on site modification showed that plants mulched with bark were 12 to 114 percent taller than unmulched plants. [12] One added benefit of mulch is that it will decompose over the years to build up the organic contents of the underlying soil. [14] The aging of mulching materials before they are applied will have two benefits. First, the material will lose its new and artificial look and will be less offensive in appearance. Second, it will have a chance to decompose slightly and not be such a great drain on the available nitrogen that it would be if it were used while fresh. The high demand for nitrogen by fresh mulching material can be countered by the addition of high-nitrogen fertilizer when fresh mulching material is used.

Silvicultural techniques

Not all vegetation needs to be considered as screening. In fact, complete screening of the recreationist from scenery is undesirable. People like to see things. They like views and variety; therefore, the forest might need some thinning to increase the viewing distance into it. [18]

The planting of trees and shrubs can provide other improvements to a recreation area. Trees and shrubs provide shade, enhance the area's beauty, and attract wildlife. Shade is an essential ingredient of the forest recreation area. It provides coolness for the user and contrast to the scenery. Shade alternated with sunshine provides part of the picture that forest visitors desire to see.[18] Well-chosen tree and shrub species should be favored by the manager to add color to the forest picture. Redbud, flowering dogwood, wild cherries, and hawthorn are just examples of trees that provide pretty floral displays. Serious consideration should be given to using shrubbery that encourages the visits of birdlife. Species of trees, shrubs, vines, and grasses that the Forest Service recommends planting for area beautification, wildlife, and screening are given in the appendix.[24]

Site damage does not increase in direct proportion to increasing use. Light use of an area destroys more than 80 percent of the ground cover, and increased use over the following years will not cause additional damage equal to the extra use.[3] In fact, research has indicated that the vegetation will adapt to heavy use as the years pass by a replacement of broad-leafed species with fine-leafed grasses. Grasses provide the most durable living ground cover. Areas that were heavily worn during the first year showed some recovery during the second and third season of heavy use.[13,11] It is this natural recovery that should be encouraged whenever possible. Some researchers recommend a policy that they call "reverse silviculture." Reverse silviculture encourages ground cover at the expense of the overstory. This is accomplished simply by the removal of some codominate trees from the canopy. The openings will permit more sunlight to reach the herbaceous and shrub layer, thereby stimulating their growth.[6]

The removal of overstory trees to permit sunlight to reach the understory vegetation is not unacceptable to campers. A study by James and Cordell indicated that campers preferred that they had approximately 60 percent shade.[10] Conifer canopies tend to inhibit herbaceous cover even when seeding, watering, and fertilizing is done. Ground-cover growth improves as the overstory density is decreased.[1]

The planting, irrigation, and fertilizing of grass are becoming a necessity for managers wishing to maintain a beautiful and clean site. Some recreation area managers seed durable grass on worn areas in the early fall as soon as the areas can be taken out of use. By keeping the seeded areas out of use until late spring or early summer, the manager can provide the area with the maximum percent of ground cover and the public with the minimum amount of dust.

Water is probably the most important ingredient in maintaining a durable recreation area. Most researchers agree that irrigation will do more to protect a site than any other cultural treatment.[9,25] Wagar points out that watering helps to maintain the site quality in three ways:[25]

1. Watering permits establishment of durable species of grass where they would not otherwise exist.
2. Watering usually increases the total growth of vegetation.

3. Watering aids in the recovery of vegetation that has been bruised or trampled. Moist vegetation is more likely to recover after crushing than if it were subject to drying.

Herrington and Beardsley found that there were markedly significant results from fertilizing, irrigation, and seeding.[7] Seeding alone did very little to increase grass cover in that study. Irrigation is the most expensive of the three treatments. Therefore, the favorable results of seeding and fertilizing any area irrigated are worth the slight extra costs. Fertilizing without irrigation or seeding does not appear to be worthwhile.[1]

Certain problems occur when an area is irrigated. The soil is more subject to compaction when it is wet, and turgid vegetation is susceptible to damage by trampling. The caution here is to carry on irrigation projects after regular periods of heavy use rather than just before them. A heavy soaking on Monday will aid the trampled vegetation on its way to recovery. Also, the soil will be dry enough to better resist the trampling crowds that will arrive with the following weekend. Admittedly, some areas are recipient of continuous heavy use. These areas will need special schedules of watering, area closures, and more improved walkways for the users.

Occasionally, soils will need to be limed in order to get the soil reaction into the proper range of pH 6.3 to 6.9 that is best for grasses.[22] Several easy-to-use and inexpensive soil-reaction test kits are available through the generally used supply houses. An investment of approximately $5 will purchase an adequate soil reaction kit. By following simple directions and comparing colored reagents with a color chart, the manager can determine the soil reaction to the nearest half pH reading. This is precise enough to determine the proper year to lime. Liming is usually done in the fall with crushed limestone or in the spring with hydrated lime. County agents or local feed and grain cooperatives will gladly furnish assistance needed in determining the quantity of lime and fertilizers needed. The caution on liming of a recreation area is again a warning on timing. Lime should not be spread on the grass shortly prior to periods of public use. From this standpoint, late fall liming is advantageous in recreation areas. Spring liming should be done early enough in the year so that the lime will be washed into the soil before the users begin to arrive. It is unnecessary to lime during the summer when it will interfere with the visitors. If fall liming is impractical, it is best to wait until the following year to lime. The loss of one year in liming is far less serious than the ill feeling created among lime-coated picnickers.

Fertilizer has its place in forest recreation just as it has in agriculture and landscaping. Most home owners would not expect to maintain a lawn without the use of fertilizers. Why should recreation area managers attempt to do so? Many recreation sites receive more than enough use to wear out a well-established surburban lawn. "Complete" fertilizers contain nitrogen, phosphorous, potassium, and several trace elements that might be needed. Wagar points out that the fertilizer that is scattered around on the ground will be used by the understory and not benefit the larger trees. [25] In most cases, it is the understory and grass layers that need the most assistance in resisting wear.

The rapid release of nitrogen from most fertilizers can "burn" the vegetation during dry periods. Urea formaldehyde fertilizers that are known as "slow-release" fertilizers have come on to the market in recent years. These slow-release fertilizers permit one application instead of many light ones and lessen the danger of "burning" the vegetation. Since urea formaldehyde fertilizers cost nearly twice as much as standard balanced fertilizers, their use is not likely to be rapidly accepted by cost conscious operators. However, their convenience and built-in safety for vegetation might prove to be a long-run savings to the manager who does not want to spend the time to spread several light applications of standard commercial fertilizer.

One problem with growing grass is that the grass must be mowed. Mowing gives the area a more pleasant appearance and permits more comfortable use of the grass-covered areas. Most recreation managers mow much of their grass-covered areas regularly without questioning the practice.

In some cases, too much mowing takes place. The mowing and maintenance of large areas and roadsides is expensive and may be unnecessary. High operating costs and tight budgets have forced many recreation systems to cut back on mowing operations. Such reductions in mowing schedules have created more diverse vegetation stands that increase wildlife variety and create visual changes. The public acceptance of the "benign neglect" of formerly mowed and manicured areas has been good.

Research done in the Rocky Mountains areas indicates that watering will do more to help the vigor and growth of the overstory trees while fertilizing will do more to stimulate the growth of the ground cover. [25] This research is not complete; however, it does provide information that lends itself to the logical conclusion that trees are better able to utilize the added water while the more shallow rooted ground cover intercepts and utilizes the broadcast spread fertilizer.

In some cases, grass planting has proved to be an impractical way of rehabilitating recreation sites in that the young grass is unable to withstand trampling and often is wiped out in the first growing season. [3] Certain other management or administrative steps must be taken to supplement the seeding efforts in upgrading the site quality. Site modification or a rest-and-rotation cycle must be established, or the planting effort just becomes a waste of money. Irrigation can be an expensive undertaking especially in the arid West. Costs could be reduced in the East where a temporary or hose system could be used for the less frequent waterings required. The camping units under irrigation on one study had 49 percent grass cover and those not irrigated had 17 percent cover.

Which treatments will be necessary to maintain the level of recreation site quality will depend upon several factors. The cultural improvements required will vary with the type and intensity of use, the soil series, the topography, the vegetation, and other such factors. The most important ingredients in a well-managed recreation area are the manager's initiative and interest in providing the users with a high-quality site.

User Safety

The protection of the user's health and safety is of primary importance. To accomplish that end, the manager must provide the following: [23]

1. Satisfactory sanitary facilities.
2. Safe drinking water supply.
3. Minimization of hazards.
4. Fire protection.

Sanitary facilities and drinking water are each discussed in their individual chapters within this book. Hazard elimination and fire protection are problems that constantly vex the manager. It is the operator's obligation to protect the user within the bounds of common sense. Certainly, there are levels of hazard reduction that depend upon the management goals of the forest area. Hazard reduction appears to be more necessary in a developed campground than in a wilderness area. That actually is not the case. Rather, the method of hazard reduction changes, not the level, when various management goals are involved.

Wilderness users do expect and accept some more or different risks than do users of a central campground. Some wilderness users take an extreme view that even search and rescue operations are not part of the wilderness system. That is not, however, a practical view that forest managers can use. What we see in wilderness hazard elimination is a reduction of tragedies based upon education, training, and administration rather than hazard removal.

Existing hazards must be removed or nullified by means such as signs or barriers. Periodic inspections of the area should be made to check on specific hazards such as dying or damaged trees, snags, areas that threaten collapse, poison ivy, and yellow jackets. These periodic checks should be started just prior to the season's opening and carried on throughout its length. Monthly formal safety inspections will help to maintain the proper level of freedom from hazards. The administrative policy of making records of these formal inspections could prove to be helpful in the case of accidents in the area. Formal inspections and their follow-up are only part of the problem of hazard elimination. Limb hazard control in oaks and bole hazard control in conifers provide the most effective hazard reduction. Paine found that one injury or fatality occurred with every 21 tree failures in a recreation area. [16] Conifers, predominantly pines, appear to be the most dangerous hazard trees in that they fail, or break, at the bole. Oaks tend to lose heavy branches and limbs. Since land managers are operating under limited budgets, they should allocate resources in such a way as to achieve the maximum cost-to-benefit ratio. Areas with high use or unusual hazards should be given priority in hazard elimination. Paine's study revealed that the most favorable cost-benefit ratios resulted in the reduction of bole hazards in conifers and limb hazards in oaks.[16]

Constant observation of the area and a sympathetic ear to complaints of the users will probably uncover more dangerous conditions than the formal inspections; however, the formal inspections accomplish four objectives. First, they turn up hazards. Second, they force a complete check of the entire area, not just where the inspector might happen to wander. Third, they emphasize the need for hazard reduction and set a standard of area safety. Fourth, formal inspections provide records that can help protect the manager in case of lawsuits.

Swimming areas are very touchy places when hazards are discussed. Policies governing use of swimming areas and the employment of lifeguards are administrative matters that must be weighed carefully. Elimination of physical hazards, on the other hand, is a subject that can be dealt with easily by the manager. Cans, bottles, and other hazards should be removed from the water whenever necessary. The bottom of river and stream swimming areas should be checked in the spring after the high runoff passes to determine if any submerged rocks form hazards. A lifesaving ring with attached rope should be located on a display board at the swimming area. A glass-covered display case is an added expense; however, it will discourage the practice of using the lifesaving ring for water sports. Directions on how to get assistance from the recreation area personnel, ambulance, and other emergency services should be prominently displayed throughout the recreation area.

As recreation areas become more common and more closely tied to population centers, they will attract more problems. Unwelcome visitors might be a problem in locations that are easily accessible. Theft has already become a major problem in parks. The manager must take steps to exclude intruders from the recreation area by administrative means as well as by management practices. Problems concerned with the exclusion of intruders will vary according to location, population, and size of the area.

The insulation of the recreation area by space or by barrier plantings and screening will lessen the interest of passersby and make the separation of the users from the general public more distinct. Uncontrolled and unscreened access into a recreation area tends to invite trouble. Persons who are not interested in the type of recreation offered by the area can drift in and out as they desire and with little or no controls. The control of intruders is primarily an administration problem; however, this problem can be greatly eased by cultural improvements to the area. A single entrance with an attendant will serve to control access of unwanted visitors. Visible, internal security and the obvious presence of uniformed workers helps to discourage antisocial behavior within the area.

Fire Protection

Most recreation areas have administrative policies concerning the building of fires. Some areas even exclude the use of fire within the intensive-use area. However, the campfire is inherently part of the great outdoor scene. Campers, picnickers, ice skaters, hunters, and others often feel that their outing would be enhanced by an evening campfire. The campfire is seldom used for cooking; however, it adds the flavor that the outdoor recreationist is seeking. The manager should try to favor the user's view on the matter of campfires and provide a safe place for the fire. The concrete rings that were originally used for charcoal disposal (see Chapter 9) serve as ideal campfire enclosures.

It is cheaper to provide firewood for the fires than it is to permit the users to gather their own. Scrap wood or slabbing is always turning up during the maintenance work on the forest. This wood can be distributed to certain central points to be picked up by the camper. Some of the costs of this service can be recovered by selling measured racks of wood for a small sum. The practice of selling precut wood for 25 cents an arm load or so is well established in many large areas of intensive use. Where the price is more for a control on excessive use than it is for profit, the user is asked to deposit a quarter in a container for each arm load that he takes from the pile. More formal arrangements can be developed by using a measuring rack which the buyer fills with the wood that he wants to buy. The choice between the honor system and regularly scheduled sales hours is an administrative decision that must be made as a result of conditions prevailing at each area. Contracts can be arranged with private operators to sell wood within campgrounds. The shift to "privatization" within public areas is gaining popularity as the tax-supported budgets shrink.

Organic litter accumulation generally is not a problem in intensive-use areas; rather, the reverse is usually the case. The manager, however, must guard against allowing dry leaves and other litter to accumulate under, against, or around structures where they would develop a hot spot and spread a ground fire to the structure. Also, some faucets within the area should be threaded so as to take hose for fire fighting.

The manager should organize into fire crews and train whatever manpower he has available. In line with fire training, the manager should have enough specialized forest fire fighting tools on hand to supply his trained personnel. Even one man with the proper tools can do a great deal to contain most forest fires when they are small. The investment of time and money for forest fire protection is quite small when compared with the investment that would be destroyed by a wildfire. Most state forestry agencies will assist any interested land manager in protecting his land against fire. Also, the State and Private

Division of the Forest Service can give some advice to landowners in the preparation of fire suppression programs.

Site Rehabilitation

Forest recreation areas will deteriorate with use. That is, the original character of the area will change as a result of man's presence. As visits become more numerous, more management is required to maintain a high-quality level of recreation. Now, as often in the past, management techniques occasionally are insufficient or inadequately applied to prevent the destruction of the site. Worn-out recreation areas, eroded lake shores, and gullying of bridle paths and foot trails are all too common of a picture throughout the forests of the United States. Some cases of deterioration could have been prevented by good recreation management practices and administrative policies, while others were inevitable because of failings in planning that did not account for problems inherent in the site or the location. A site located on a soil that is highly erosive and not suited to traffic will wear out in spite of most attempts to protect it. Some recreation areas that were designed for the casual use of 25 years ago are trampled under by today's heavy use. In many cases, ordinary management techniques will not raise the recreation quality to an acceptable level. A completely new program of rebuilding of the site's recreation quality must be undertaken. This rebuilding effort is aimed at rehabilitating the site for high-quality use. Site rehabilitation is an expensive undertaking because it runs head on into the basic problems that caused the site to deteriorate in the first place. The efforts required to repair the site and then to solve the problems involved might prove to be more costly than the original development costs.

Is the area worth saving? Will the improvements hold up under use? Would it be better to abandon the area and to establish another? The fact that use has worn out an area might indicate that the area was heavily used by the public; therefore, it is needed. Closure of an area without substitution could lead to serious consequences. Sometimes the construction of an alternate area simply increases the developed facilities because it becomes impossible to close the original facilities. The establishment of areas on more favorable sites followed by the closure and obliteration of the worn-out areas may be the best route to take. Besides being an expensive undertaking, the obliteration of old areas is difficult to explain to users jammed into an overflow area. These are the problems that must be faced by the land managers who must make the governing decisions.

If the recreation area is worth saving and if it is located on an area where it can be saved, the problems of its original degradation must be analyzed. Certain sites might require closing and replacement in a more advantageous location. In campgrounds and picnic areas, a variety of spacings should be used to satisfy many different tastes. Some researchers believe that relocation decisions should be based heavily upon the opportunity to produce a pleasant and varied experience rather than upon the configuration of the land or type of vegetation.[18] That is, areas should be relocated in such a way as to serve the need of the users and to provide them with the most pleasure because management steps can be taken to protect or to alter the land and the vegetation. This reasoning is most sound with the more expensive developments where the demand justifies ignoring the carrying capacity of the land and the altering of its configuration. A lodge and marina might be located by its need for a large level area that is near the water and accessible by road. The fact that it will be located on an unstable terrace soil does not constitute a limiting factor. It is a problem that must be overcome by some cultural improvements. Costly jetties and stone breakwaters do a questionable job of protecting multimillion-dollar investments along the offshore bar resorts of the Atlantic Ocean. However, small forest recreation areas often are pressed just to support their administration and do not justify the expenditures of funds for more than normal maintenance. Because of this, the relocation or layout of many facilities is rather rigidly tied to the existing land configuration.

The next problem to face after layout is that of erosion. Most activities of man have the same effect on the movement of water. They accelerate the surface runoff and impede infiltration of water into the soil. Control of runoff is necessary to prevent damaging erosion and annoyance to users, especially campers. A storm drain system might be necessary to collect and remove the surface water. Check dams should be built in any existing erosion gullies. A grass cover should be established to stabilize the gully sides. Grasses are more effective soil stabilizers than are tree seedlings which take several years to establish themselves.

Trails located on highly erosive soils should be replaced by trails on more stable soils. If the relocation is not possible, the unstable area should be crossed in the shortest possible distance. This practice means that the steepest acceptable grade should be used if it will shorten the crossing distance. The steep grade of the trail must be accompanied by proportionally more drainage structures to prevent erosion. Culverts and water bars will be needed at closer intervals to remove the water from the road or trail as quickly as possible. The reasoning here is to use the steep slope and drainage structures to remove the water from the highly erosive soil as quickly as possible while exposing the smallest area of that soil to erosion by using a short trail or road across it.

The closure of trails becomes a problem in rehabilitation. How does a manager prevent the use of closed trails? A partial answer is to block the closed path with a barrier or sign. Also, the trail can be obliterated by planting it with shrubbery or trees. These are good steps in closure: however, they will prove to be half measures if an alternate or more desirable trail is not provided for the user.

If an area is to be rehabilitated in order to provide high-quality recreation, it must be modified in such a way as to overcome the degrading effects that wore out the original site. Mechanical work such as grading with earth moving equipment might be necessary to provide the landscape configuration needed to resist erosion. Unwanted wet areas should be drained. Top soil must be hauled in to replace that worn or eroded away. Trees, grass, and shrubs must be planted to complete the site. Serious consideration should be given to the installation of a permanent irrigation system at this time.

MANAGEMENT OF EXTENSIVE RECREATION AREAS

Three out of five recreation visits to the national forests are for uses that do not require developed sites.[2] Hiking, horseback riding, fishing, hunting, and sightseeing use the forest as a setting, but their participants do not need the developed sites that camping or picknicking participants require. Extensive forest recreation use is not limited to the person who travels to the forest exclusively for that purpose. As the land managers are belatedly learning, everyone who passes through the forest feels that he has the right to enjoy the forest setting. More people are traveling more miles each year as a result of rapidly increasing mobility, leisure time, and increased income. This traveling public is very much aware of what natural beauty should be and it expects to see the epitome of natural beauty in the forested areas. As the stress on natural beauty continues, public opinion will have more and more influence on how the forest lands are managed. The forester must begin to apply silvicultural practices in such a way as to increase the public enjoyment and its understanding of the uses of the forests. The engineer must consider the need for unspoiled stream fishing and the counterpressure for water-based sports when he plans an impoundment dam. Soil conservation personnel are being watched by the duck hunter whenever they plan to drain some wetlands. The "bureaucratic ping-pong" game of draining marshland in one spot while blasting potholes for ducks somewhere nearby is a waste of taxpayers' money.

The land manager must begin to think of his entire domain as a potential recreation area. He should search for ways to accommodate the public desires for recreation through management programs that reconcile timber production and watershed protection with recreation.

Silvicultural Techniques for Roadsides

Silviculture is the practice of applying knowledge of tree behavior to the production of timber. Certain timber-cutting methods are premised on the expected reaction of nature. Stand quality and volumes can be improved by the proper silvicultural treatment. Just as the forester can raise the timber value of his land, he can raise the recreation value. Simple understanding of the factors that enhance extensive recreation will aid the forester to make the silvicultural decisions that will benefit the timber economy as well as enrich the recreation quality of the area.

No-cutting zones

"No-cutting" zones along highways and streams were one of the first attempts of foresters to reconcile timber production with recreation pressures. About 100- to 200-foot-wide strips where no cutting is permitted are established along roads. This is, in a sense, a screening technique employed to hide the undesirable vista of a logged area. The establishment of this facade of trees simply underlines the arguments against even-aged cutting practices that leave large areas of the land denuded of trees and covered with slash. As even-age management techniques become more accepted in the Northeast, they run into conflict with the conservation-oriented urbanist of that heavily populated area of the country. The problem of reeducating the layman in the proper use and utilization of forests is a problem that foresters must face if they are not to lose all their powers to make professional decisions; however, the solution of that problem is out of the realm of this book.

The no-cutting strip is a good first step in that it does protect the motorist from the view of a clear-cut area; however, it does not do much to integrate recreation with timber management. It is simply a wise concession to the public's wishes. The leaving of a solid wall of timber along the highway does not necessarily provide the things that mean the most to the recreationist who wants variety, vistas, and combinations of landscapes and water.[18] Also, the nocutting strip withdraws many acres from the production of timber. In spite of its many disadvantages, the technique of establishing no-cutting zones is recommended for a first step. As more positive silvicultural techniques can be incorporated into the timber management programs, they can replace or supplement the no-cutting zones.

Clear-cutting design

Clear-cutting will be tolerated by the general public only if it does not dominate the landscape or occur too close to the road or to their recreation area.[15] The amount of cleanup done after and during cutting should be greater on areas that are readily accessible to the public. Smaller clear-cut areas should be selected when near roads and recreation areas. Foresters and loggers tend to ignore the pressures for the more aesthetically acceptable small cutting area and push for the very large blocks that provide more economy of size. A higher degree of debris clearance will be needed to improve the appearance. Planting might be needed to increase the rate of regeneration and heal the scars more quickly. Small clear-cut areas could give the landscape a multilayer effect that will enhance the beauty of the landscape after the regeneration heals the scars caused by the logging operations.

Sequential small clear-cuts can be laid out so that the standing timber or advanced reproduction of one area screens the slash of another area. This can be accomplished by orienting the cutting areas in strips that have their long axis perpendicular to the line of sight from the recreation area, vista, or road. The closest strip to the recreation area should be screened by an area not designated for cutting. After the first strip is cut, operations should jump to a strip further back or move to another location in the forest. By cutting every third or fourth strip in each cutting cycle, the forester permits the regeneration to become large enough eventually to screen the strip behind it. This technique permits the forester to harvest the allowable cut by using the best-known silvicultural practice while protecting the aesthetic value of the landscape.

Irregular openings formed by natural causes are considered to be desirable in providing variety to the landscape scene.[24] The term "block selection" or "clear-cutting in blocks" denotes the forester's organized thinking. Uniform blocks are easy to fit into cutting cycles and they produce the minimum amount of edge effect, or degrade, on the neighboring hardwood trees. Irregular shaping of the clear-cut areas may help to make their appearance less objectionable.[15] They could take on shapes of burns, meadows, or slides rather than man-created blocks. This technique may be more readily adaptable in coniferous or low-quality oak stands where degrading of the edge trees is not a serious problem.

Vistas

To increase the enjoyment of the sightseer, the forester can plan vista cuttings at the places where a view is rewarding. Panoramic views, bodies of water, and agricultural patterns are favorites of the sightseers. Vista cuttings open up the world of the traveler so that he can see something besides tree trunks just outside of the window. Besides providing places for the traveler to stop and admire the scenery, the forester has harvested the timber from another clear-cut area. More cleanup of debris will be needed here than in the backwoods; however, this is a small price to pay for increasing the recreation quality of a site at the same time as the timber is harvested along the road edge.

Roadside treatment

Long expanses of forest-lined roads present monotonous corridors to the traveler. Instead of preserving the roadside vegetation, the silviculturist should employ techniques to utilize it and to improve the recreation scenery. Small areas can be cut at uneven intervals along the edge of the road. These open areas provide variety and contrast for the motorist. Also, they break up the straight edges of the right-of-way and give it an irregular appearance which fits into the landscape better. The reproduction on these road-edge cutting spots forms a needed transition zone between the road edge and the forest. The objective of this technique is to harvest the timber over a several-year period while establishing an irregular-edge effect along the road edge.

Road-edge transition. An abrupt change from open road to tall forests is considered less desirable than a gradual change in vegetation size and composition.[15] To obtain this transition zone, the forester should leave groups of trees, clumps of shrubbery, and ground cover to obtain the transition zone. The objective of the transition zone is to lead the viewer's sight from the road edge to the complete scene. Transition zones can be used to lead up to a view of a roadside lake, marsh, or vista. The transition zone is the ideal place to work at that extra touch of beauty by encouraging understory trees and shrubs that have showy flowers, attractive fruit, or bright fall colors. Efforts can be made to protect such species as service berry (*Amelanchier arborea*) or flowering dogwood (*Cornus florida*) when the logging is taking place.

Quite often, the trees that are of little value to the timberman are of the greatest value to the sightseer. Acres upon acres of thrifty Douglas fir represent many important things to the trained forester; however, they are just another mountainside full of trees just like many other trees to the tourist. On the other hand, that silviculturist's nightmare of a misshapen, broken-topped, and scarred sugar pine next to the road might well be the epitome of the forest sentinels to the vacationer. Therefore, trees with unusual character should be left along roads and in recreation areas if they are sound and do not interfere with normal operations.

Open woods. Thick stands of merchantable timber often become a barrier to recreation. They are difficult to move around in and even more difficult to see into. People want to look into the forest and not at the edge of it. Around recreation areas and along roads, the forest can be opened up by thinning from below or by a careful selection of dominate or codominate trees. This appears to be a cross between even-age management's use of intermediate cuts and uneven-age management's use of the selective cutting system. Be that as it may, the dense stands of merchantable timber would be more appealing to the recreationist if they were thinned.

Silvicultural Techniques Favoring Fishing, Hunting, and General Recreation

This book does not excuse all timber cutting as good for recreation or even good for the local economy. The reader must realize that timber cutting has and is being carried on in conjunction with forest recreation activities. The people want selected recreation experiences at the same time as the nation desperately needs lumber. All land cannot and should not be tied up for single recreation purposes any more than large tracts of land should be set aside for timber at the exclusion of recreation activities. Polarization of positions between no cutting and clear-cutting is having a damaging effect on the concept of total use of the forest land.

The time has come when foresters can no longer claim that good timber management is good recreation management. It simply is not true in light of the legislation impacting forest lands. Each time a silvicultural decision is made, it impacts the recreational component of forest use. The decision concerns the deer, elk, grouse, turkey, and any wildlife inhabiting the area. Private land managers must struggle with their own goals or with industrial goals. Public forest land managers, however, have been given a clear set of guidelines over the last three decades. Public forest land is to be managed for a variety of purposes and products. Table 16.1 lists some of the laws that lead to the national policy for forestland which dictates consideration for other than timber production.

Timber-producing lands are a major part of the recreation scene. That recreation and logging can be compatible as well as competitive is most evident with the extensive recreation activities of hunting and fishing. Improvement of forest game habitat by silvicultural techniques is possible if logging operations can be modified and cutting cycles are altered. Modifications of forest management practices offer the best way to improve game habitat throughout the forest. [20]

Streams that provide fishing for sport should be protected in every way possible by the forester. In the East, no clear-cutting should be permitted within 100 feet of a trout stream. This is to protect the stream from exposure to the heat of sun as well as to keep logging debris and erosion from damaging the stream. The uneven-age selection system should be employed along streams wherever possible. If the area in question does not lend itself to being logged by the selective logging system, it might be better left alone rather than to risk the destruction of trout fishing waters.

Riparian zones provide recreational and wildlife management opportunities far in excess of their area. Besides containing a large variety of vegetation

Table 16.1. Some Federal Laws Influencing Recreation on Managed Federal Forest Land.

Fish and Wildlife Coordination Act of 1934
Multiple Use and Sustained Yield Act of 1960
Endangered Species Act of 1969
National Environmental Policy Act, 1969
Forest and Rangeland Renewable Resources Planning Act of 1974
National Forest Management Act of 1976
Federal Land Policy and Management Act of 1976

species, the riparian corridors serve as routes for migratory birds and animals. Wide-ranging animals such as the elk depend upon stream side zones for movement between summer and winter ranges.[6] Management activity within the riparian zone requires considerable thought to avoid unnecessary conflicts.

Research has shown that large expanses of merchantable timber are not compatible with the production of wildlife.[21] Game animals require open areas or the edge of open areas to reproduce and rear their young or to obtain browse. The mature forest does not provide the browse required by the white-tailed deer nor the opening needed for ruffed-grouse nesting. If wildlife is to be a product of the forest, the land manager must take steps to assure that the proper environment exists for the game animals to carry out their life cycle. Turkey or squirrel will be content in the more open mature timber, and black bear prefer some marshy areas for food in the spring. The land manager would do well to seek advice from a wildlife biologist prior to embarking on an extensive cutting program. A little advice from a competent wildlife expert who is familiar with local problems might greatly enhance the chances for a satisfactory wildlife population. Table 16.2 gives a summary of the harmful and beneficial harvesting procedures.

Many foresters are working on the modifications of silvicultural techniques needed to enhance the overall recreational values of the forest. Table 16.3 gives a selected sample of the silvical treatments considered or used in some forests of the Northeast to enhance recreation potential of the stand. While the table is not complete for all forest types, it does give some guidelines. Generally, larger trees are desirable; conifers and attractive species are favored; and natural plant succession is not always desirable for recreation quality. These generalities do not appear to be inconsistent with good forest management. Regionally, foresters certainly can add to the recreational silvicultural techniques most favorable to their forest types.

The logging operations create forest roads that can serve as access for hunters and fishermen. When timber value will permit, the roads should be built to a

Table 16.2. Timber-Harvesting Procedures Affecting Wildlife.

Harmful
 underharvest of timber
 raking for site preparation
 planting all openings
 herbicide treatment of food plants

Beneficial
 winter logging
 scattered small timber sales
 short-term cutting cycles
 sequential sales
 combined even-age and selective timber management

*Minnesota Department of Conservation.

Table 16.3. Suggested Silvical Treatment of Selected Northeast Forest Types to Enhance Recreational Values.*

Northern hardwoods	All-age management with selective cutting of all poor trees and overmature trees on an 8- to 15-year cycle; retain 70 square feet of basal area per acre; some small patch selection to encourage intolerant trees, preserve den and most trees; leave more overmature trees near developed recreation areas.
Red pine — white pine	Plan plantations to have interspersion of other forest types; grow stands at lower densities to encourage larger diameters (40 to 80 square feet of basal area per acre); give attention to associate species; longer cutting cycles (200 years instead of present 150 years); manage for two-age stand rather than even-aged.
Aspen-paper birch	Prevent natural succession to balsam fir; heavy intermediate cuttings to favor paper birch; consider holding thrifty trees past normal 50-year rotation cycle; be alert for high hazard trees.
Jack pine	Even-age management; favor conversion to red pine or spruce-fir types where possible; start thinning at 20 years; hold large trees past normal 60-year cycle.
Upland oaks	Both even- and all-age management; protection of den trees; encourage pine and other associates; confine clear-cuts to 25-acre or smaller blocks; use selective cutting systems on the higher-quality sites with small patch cuttings to encourage more intolerant species. Leave at least 15 oaks, 14-inch diameter or more, per acre.

*Region 9 USFS and Minnesota Department of Conservation.

high enough standard to permit their being maintained as permanent roads. The construction costs of a permanent road are higher than they are for a temporary one; however, a permanent road will open an area up for returning timber operations. The roads can serve to disperse the hunters and the fishermen and thereby assist in obtaining a larger and more uniform harvest of game.

Temporary roads should be closed to vehicular traffic and protected against erosion when the logging operation is completed. Water bars should be used to drain off surface water onto the forest floor where it can infiltrate into the soil. The roadbeds can be planted with grasses or legumes that will serve as game food while they are protecting the soil from erosion. These seeded roads can be incorporated with boundary-line clearings and firebreaks to form a hiking trail network. This trail network would be available for access in case of forest fires.

The land manager or forester can take some positive steps to obtain a suitable environment for wildlife. The even-age philosophy of timber management calls for clear-cutting of areas. This is compatible with wildlife populations for three reasons. First, clear-cut areas provide browse for food and brush for cover. Sec-

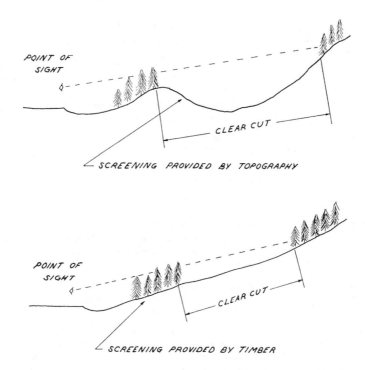

Fig. 16.3. Possible screening methods for use in blocking the view of clear-cut areas.

ond, the clear-cut area can provide the open areas that appear to be necessary for some wildlife species. Third, the valuable "edge effect" is created around the perimeter of the clear-cut block. The edge effect is described as the change in size and type of vegetation that takes place along the dividing line between open and timbered areas. Much of the wildlife can be found in this edge-effect zone.

The size of the clear-cut area is the factor that limits the compatibility of even-age management with wildlife management. Since wildlife prefers the edge effect, animals can make only limited use of huge clear-cuts. In most of the country, the topography and the seed source favor cutting in smaller blocks. Extensive areas of cut-over land remind the general public of an unsightly era that it hopes is past. Many small areas of four or five acres can be cut over a period of many years in order to provide more benefit to the wildlife while lessening the impact upon aesthetics. The irregular borders that were suggested previously would aid in producing more edge effects per clear-cut acre. Most silviculturists have been educated to think in terms of timber production. Therefore, four- or five-acre block sizes probably are an unrealistic hope of hunters, wildlife managers, and the general public. Forest land managers

Fig. 16.4. The seeding and grasses and legumes on abandoned logging roads stabilizes soil and provides food for wildlife.

should strive, however, to keep the clear cuts as small as possible, maximize the edge effect by using irregular cutting boundaries, and minimize the visual impacts by proper orientation of the cutting area shape.

Efforts can be made to get the utility companies to improve the already beneficial edge effect along their rights-of-way. This can be done by selective herbicide application instead of broadcast spraying. A U-shaped cross-section with a central low point planted in a strip of legumes or grasses will give the greatest possible benefit to wildlife. Selective use of herbicides and seeding will cost the utility companies more than the standard broadcast treatment; therefore, cooperative agreements between landowners or government wildlife agencies and the utility companies will be needed to develop the high potential rights-of-way for their maximum benefit to wildlife.

Variety in cover types is needed to produce the best crop of game animals. Open areas are necessary for game animals to build nests, rear young, browse, graze, or just recreate in a different environment. For whatever reasons, the small clearing has proved its value in game management. Some governmental agencies have begun programs of game management that include the construction and maintenance of clusters of small agricultural plots within the forest. Small areas are scraped clean of vegetation which is roughly piled at the clearing edge. The plot soil is then physically and chemically prepared for agricultural crops. Generally, legumes are planted in the area for food, and pines are planted around the edge to provide cover. These plots are very expensive to construct and to maintain; however, they are apparently successful in aiding wildlife production in areas of merchantable timber. Some of the costs to private landowners can be recouped or even avoided by leasing hunting privileges to sportsmen's clubs. Organizations interested in hunting or fishing account for approximately three-fourths of the recreational land under lease.[19,26]

In some cases, the clubs will carry out habitat improvement projects as part of a club project to improve its own hunting. Persons leasing forest land for hunting tend to become acutely aware of the dangers that threaten their hunting rights. Therefore, the clubs might undertake protective measures to safeguard their privileges. These protective and improvement efforts, if properly channeled and supervised, can provide an added bonus to the landowner.

The deer population can become so high that it becomes a threat to continued forest management by destroying tree reproduction. In this situation, the manager must take steps to protect the forest from an excessively large deer herd. He should take the steps necessary to encourage deer hunters to use his land and harvest the deer crop. This can be done by making the public aware of the open hunting area, by constructing and maintaining trails that permit hunter access to large blocks of timber, and by providing some services to aid the hunter.

REFERENCES

1. Beardsley, W.G. and J.A. Wagar. 1971. Vegetation Management on a Forested Recreation Site. In *Journal of Forestry*, vol. 69, no. 10, pp. 728–730.
2. Cliff, E.P. 1965. The Role of the Forest Service in Outdoor Recreation. In *Proceedings of the Society of American Foresters*, Annual Meeting. Detroit, Mich.
3. Cordell, H.K., and Talhelm, D.R. 1969. *Planting Grass Appears Impractical for Improving Deteriorated Recreation Sites*. Forest Service Research Note SE-105. Southeastern Experiment Station, Asheville, N.C.
4. Echelberger, Herbert E. 1971. *Vegetative Changes at Adirondack Campgrounds 1964 to 1969*. USDA Forest Service Research Note NE-142. Northeast Forest Experiment Station, Upper Darby, Pa. 8 pages.
5. Frissell, S., and Duncan, D. 1965. Campsite Preference and Deterioration in the Quetico—Superior Canoe Country. In *Journal of Forestry*, vol. 63, no. 4, pp. 256–260.
6. Forest Service. 1979. *Wildlife Habitats in Managed Forests: the Blue Mountains of Oregon and Washington*. U.S. Department of Agriculture. Agricultural Handbook No. 553. Secretary of Documents. 512 pages.
7. Herrington, R.B., and Beardsley, W.G. 1970. *Improvements and Maintenance of Campground Vegetation in Central Idaho*. USDA Forest Service Research Paper INT-87. Intermountain Forest and Range Experiment Station, Ogden, Utah. 9 pages.

8. Hopkins, W.S. 1965. Outdoor Recreation on Small Woodlands. *Proceedings of 62nd Annual Meeting of the Association of Southern Agricultural Workers.* Dallas, Texas.

9. Hutchison, S.B. 1962. *Recreation Opportunities and Problems in the National Forests of the Intermountain Region.* Intermountain Forest and Range Experiment Station Research Paper No. 66. Ogden, Utah.

10. James, G.A. and H.K. Cordell. 1970. *Importance of Shading to Visitors Selecting a Campsite at Indian Boundary Campground in Tennessee.* Southeast Forest Experiment Station, Research Note SE-130. 5 pages.

11. La Page, Wilbur F. 1967. *Some Observations on Campground Trampling and Ground Cover Response.* Forest Service Research Paper NE-68. Northeast Forest Experiment Station, Upper Darby, Pa. 11 pages.

12. Magill, A.W., and Leiser, A.T. 1972. *Growing Plants on View Landscapes and Recreation Areas. Guidelines,* vol. 2, no. 5, pp. 57–61. Government Printing Office, Washington, D.C.

13. Marquis, R.W. 1965. *Report of Northeastern Forest Experiment Station, 1965.* U.S. Forest Service Department of Agriculture, Upper Darby, Pa.

14. McIntyre, A.C. 1959. *Wood Chips for the Land.* Soil Conservation Service Leaflet No. 323. U.S. Department of Agriculture, Washington, D.C.

15. Neff, P.E. 1965. Applied Silviculture in Managing Outdoor Recreation Sites. *Proceedings of the Society of American Foresters,* Annual Meeting. Detroit, Mich.

16. Paine, Lee A. 1967. *Effective Tree Hazard Control on Forested Recreation Sites.* Research Note PSW-157. Pacific Southwest Forest and Range Experiment Station, Berkeley, Calif. 8 pages.

17. Ripley, T.H. 1962. *Tree and Shrub Response to Recreation Use.* Research Note 171. Southeastern Forest Experiment Station. U.S. Forest Service, Asheville, N.C.

18. ———. 1965. Rehabilitation of Forest Recreation Sites. In *Proceedings of the Society of American Foresters.* Annual Meeting. Detroit, Mich.

19. Rudolf, Paul O. 1967. Silviculture for Recreation Area Management. In *Journal of Forestry,* vol. 1, no. 6, pp. 385–390.

20. Rutske, Le Roy H. 1969. *A Minnesota Guide to Forest Game Habitat Improvement.* Technical Bulletin No. 10. Division of Fish and Game. Minnesota Department of Conservation, St. Paul, Minn. 68 pages.

21. Sharp, W.M. 1957. *Management of a Poletimber Forest for Wildlife Food and Cover.* Agricultural Experimental Station, The Pennsylvania State University, University Park, Pa.

22. U.S. Forest Service. 1961. *Handbook on Soils.* Title 2512.5. Category 2, Handbook, U.S. Department of Agriculture, Washington, D.C.

23. ———. 1963. *Recreation Management,* Handbook Title 2300. U.S. Department of Agriculture, Washington, D.C.

24. ———. 1965. *The American Outdoors. Management for Beauty and Use.* U.S. Forest Service Miscellaneous Publication No. 1000. U.S. Department of Agriculture, Washington, D.C.

25. Wagar, J.A. 1965. Cultural Treatment of Vegetation on Recreation Sites. *Proceedings of the Society of American Foresters,* Annual Meeting. Detroit, Mich.

26. Whittaker, J.C., and Echelberger, H.E. 1971. *Land for Recreation: a Look at Leasing in New York.* Forest Service Research Paper NE-182. Northeast Forest Experiment Station, Upper Darby, Pa. 8 pages.

17

Operation of Developed Recreation Areas

INTRODUCTION

Operation consists of the actions and techniques employed to run the recreation area on a day-to-day basis. The actual operation of a recreation area is the heart of administration. Fee collections, user counts, signs, insurance, publicity, maintenance, and public relations are the most important parts of operation. Internal administration and business operations are not included in this book because they are governed by general principles covered in the field of business administration.

Success of private recreation areas as a business venture generally is measured in terms of profits made. Excluding those people who have other than the profit motive, most entrepreneurs use the dollar as a measuring device. La Page points out that success of private campgrounds involved the capturing of new customers and the stimulation of longer and more frequent stays by active customers. [11] Although many of the reasons for satisfaction stated by users pertain to design and layout of the facilities, other reasons were related to the operational aspects of running the facility.

FEE COLLECTIONS

The general public is willing to pay for the use of developed recreation facilities as is witnessed by the proliferation of private enterprise establishments in this field. Private recreation areas must have efficient methods of fee collection in order to survive as a business. Public recreation areas have been open to the public without admission fees because they have been tax supported; however, this has changed in recent years. As the public demanded more elaborate facilities and as recreation management became more positive in its approach, costs rose sharply. These changes brought about a change in thinking. Now there is a widespread belief that the cost of running tax-supported recreation areas should be supplemented by those users who want the more elaborate facilities. That is, those who derive the most direct benefit from the facilities should pay the larger share. Some sound arguments against fee charging at public areas can be made; however, they are out of step with public opinion. Users have accepted the premise that they should pay a fee for the use of public facilities.

President Reagan's victory in 1980 rode a wave of popular opposition to federal power in local matters. Along with that popular wave went some of the programs funding expanded recreational opportunities through taxation. A subtle shift in recreation concept took place along with, or because of, the shift to lesser federal powers. The people in national, state, and local situations are participating in more activities but supporting public recreation funding less. The trend appears to be well established as of the early 1980s. People will pay much more for their own recreation but do not want to be taxed to support public recreation at any higher level.

All federal land management agencies have seen a consistent reduction of vandalism and an increase in care of facilities where fees are charged.[6] Fees ranging from $2.00 to $12.00 per family are normally charged at such developments as campgrounds, picnic areas, swimming beaches, and boating ramps. Collection usually is made manually by an attendant or mechanically by a self-service device. The manual method of collection is the most popular, although not necessarily the best.

Manual Collection

The manual method has been used successfully for many years. In large areas, an attendant is usually stationed at the entrance point where he collects fees and disburses the receipts. The gate attendant works well where only limited access occurs. If there are many access points, administrative control will be difficult and too expensive. The attendant's time would be wasted at a small recreation area if he just stood around awaiting paying customers; therefore, small picnic and camping areas often require a less formal technique of fee collection. The attendant can make regularly scheduled rounds in between other duties in order to collect fees.

A "roving ranger" system uses a uniformed park ranger to circulate through the campground and collect fees. The "roving ranger" provides security or the feeling of security to the campers. Some objection is raised as to the image of uniformed police collecting money; the "roving ranger" system, however, is commonly used at the state and county level.

Approximately half of the attendant's fee collection time is spent in giving information to the users.[19] At large public campgrounds, the gate attendant is probably as important for the public relations value as for the fee collection receipts. Also, his presence at the gate helps to exclude intruders.

Mechanical Collection

Mechanical methods of fee collection are necessary to reduce fee collection costs. These devices must be economical to operate, reliable, and simple to operate. The two common machines used are the coin-operated gate and the automatic ticket-vending machine.

Coin-operated gates

In a research study, the Forest Service found that coin-operated gates were satisfactory in certain types of areas.[19] These gates are electrically powered barriers that are similar to railroad crossing barriers. They raise up and allow a two-axle vehicle to pass when a certain combination of coins is deposited in the receiving slot. Some problems of equipment maintenance arise; however, the gates generally are successful when properly installed at suitable areas.

The gates are adaptable to areas of day-use sites such as beaches and picnic grounds, but are not satisfactory in areas where the user wants to leave and return to the site. The collection costs are low and refunds are unnecessary; however, the initial costs are high in that each machine that is installed represents a substantial investment.[19] The major drawbacks to the use of coin-operated gates are the high purchase and installation costs and the need for electrical power.

Ticket-vending machines

Machines that dispense tickets when a certain amount of money is deposited provide a good mechanical method of collecting fees at recreation areas where developed sites are used. The common forms of outdoor recreation involving developed sites where ticket-vending machines are used are camping, boating, and picnicking. Two types of ticket-vending machines are available. The rotary-type machine uses a continuous roll to supply tickets in much the same way as would a movie theater box office or "merry-go-round" ticket window. The rotary ticket vending machine's cost runs approximately $300 for each installed unit. The nonrotary dispensers pay out tickets from a stack. This type of dispenser is more likely to make an error than the rotary type because it can discharge more than one ticket with one coin operation.

Since many people will arrive at a campground without the proper change to operate the vending machine, procedures must be established to permit users to proceed to the site and pay later. Usually, the attendant calls on the sites not displaying paid up tickets at some prearranged time. Some campgrounds use a card system where the user signs his name on a printed card requesting the attendant to stop at the unit for payment.

The ticket-vending machines offer the least expensive way to collect user fees and they can be used at isolated or small campgrounds where the use does not warrant an attendant. One of the three major disadvantages stems from the need to provide change. This is especially true during periods of coin shortage when half-dollar coins become scarce. Another disadvantage is a result of the inconvenience caused to the user by not being able to pay in advance. Since the tickets dispensed are dated, they can be valid only for the day showing on the ticket. Therefore, a camper must be present each day to deposit his coins and receive a valid ticket for the coming evening. Also, the checker must make the circuit to check for payment so that much of the savings gained by vending machines is lost in checking and follow-up action.

Ticket Display Post

Regardless of whether the fee was collected by manual or mechanical means, a receipt of payment should be displayed at the camping or picnicking unit to indicate that the fee has been paid. This is especially true in campgrounds where people can stay beyond the prepaid period. Also, the paid-up ticket certifies that the site is occupied even though equipment is not present. With the use of recreation vehicles and the concern over theft and vandalism, many people take everything with them when they go for a day away from the campsite. Boating and other day-use areas can require that the tickets be displayed on a window of the car; however, this method does not work in campgrounds because users often drive the vehicle away for off-site trips. The receipts should have large numbers representing the date, or else as felt-tipped marker should be used to make the numbers visible from 10 or 15 feet away. This display system at each unit consists of a three-foot-tall post with some device on it to hold the ticket. Slotted metal holders, snap paper clips, or glass front display boxes are generally fastened to the post in such a way as to hold and display the ticket. The display post should be at the road edge of the camping or picnicking unit but in the back of a protective barrier. The ticket should be plainly visible to a person riding along the road. This enables an attendant to make an easy check of all sites without getting out of the vehicle.

USER COUNTS

The recreation area manager needs to know how many people are using the developed facilities. The primary interest is in obtaining figures on hours of use, visitor numbers, and peakload use to aid in making administrative and management decisions.[8] Hours of use indicate the amount of wear the site is receiving. From this information the supervisor can predict depreciation rates of the facilities, establish maintenance schedules, and program the trash collection and the cleanup operations. The visitor numbers give an indication of the total number of people who have been to the area. This reflects the number of impressions gained of the recreation development and indicates the need and the required scheduling of visitor information services.[5] Peakload data provide the basis for identifying use trends and for planning overflow areas.

The use can be estimated easily in areas where fees are charged for a specific activity and adequate records are maintained. However, attendance at free admission or multiopportunity recreation developments must be estimated by some technique other than actual count. The attendants at recreation areas usually have other things to do besides count users if they are in the area at all. Therefore, accurate and daily counts would require the cost of hiring additional people to stand around and count the users of various activities.

Obviously, a continuous count is uneconomical and some method of estimating the use must be employed. Three basic methods of estimating the use at recreation areas are (1) the ranger estimate, (2) the periodic attendant count, and (3) the traffic count.

Remote-sensing techniques such as aerial photography or infrared scanner systems offer only limited benefits for user counts. While aerial photography is a widely used tool in forest resource management, it does have limitations when considered for user activity. The cost, weather uncertainties, forest foliage, system resolution limits, and scheduling conveniences are some of the factors limiting the use of aerial photography for forest recreation user inventory. Some success has been achieved by using hand-held cameras in light aircraft to get user counts in open areas and in boats.[10] While color infrared photography has proved to be of great value in forest land resource planning and operation, it does not provide any more information—it may even provide less—than true color film.[5] Aerial photo interpretation can provide a great wealth of information about the physical site and its vegetative cover. By mapping changes in wear pattern and vegetative vigor, the forest recreation manager can assess the impact of visitor numbers directly without actually counting them.

Infrared scanner systems cannot reliably record data that can be directly related to user numbers or activities. There has been much talk about using the emitted infrared portion of the electromagnetic spectrum for detection of recreation users. In view of the inherent limitations of infrared scanning systems available for nonsecret use, the use of airborne infrared scanners for forest recreation activity is not feasible even in future years. Contrary to television thrill show gimmicks, infrared radiation does not pass through the forest canopy without interference. People under a forest in leaf cannot be detected with accuracy by airborne infrared sensors. At the present, there is no serious pursuit of developing infrared scanner methodology for user counts.[16]

Ranger Estimate

The "ranger estimate" technique of estimating use is probably the most used and the least accurate of the three choices. It consists of guesses by the recre-

ation supervisors as to the number of users by type of activity. The ranger estimate method does have some value in that it does give a relative expression of
use when compared to previous days. However, this is a weak assumption even
when the estimates have been made by the same person for the same area.

Why, then, is such an inaccurate method as the ranger estimate still relied
upon so often? The answer to this question probably has three parts. First, it is
easy. Second, it is uncomplicated by statistics. Third, because of reasons one
and two, it is inexpensive to produce. Any other technique of estimating user
numbers will require planning, records, and funds. In some cases, the ranger
estimate has been satisfactory simply because nothing more has been needed.
Other times, other available techniques do not lend themselves to the situation.
On a few occasions, the ranger estimate provides some quick figures to fit into
the monthly report before that report is hustled off to the next higher administrative level.

Periodic Attendant Counts

Periodic counts of users by attendants are sometimes used to get the estimates
of use. An attendant visits the area every day at a given time to count the participants in each activity. Research has shown that the periodic attendant counts
are most accurate when they are made at twelve o'clock noon for most types of
areas.[13] Although this technique is more reliable than the ranger estimate, it
is significantly less accurate than the traffic counter technique.

Traffic Counter Estimate

Intensive-use areas

The most reliable technique for estimating visitor numbers, hours of use, and
peakloads is by counting the entering vehicles and equating that figure with
use. Obviously, this means more than just counting the cars. Unfortunately,
simple car counting is often done under the guise of traffic counter estimates;
however, the only reliable information obtained that way is the number of axles
that passed over the counter. Some technique of correlating entering vehicles to
amounts and type of use must be worked out before traffic counting has any
real value.

Ripley and Jones devised a technique for estimating recreation visits and use
by combining traffic counters and basic statistics. This technique uses a double
sampling method that correlates the use of the recreation area on sample days
to the traffic count for the same day. A ratio is developed between the actual
use of the facilities and the traffic count. The ratio that is developed from the
data gathered on the sample days is used along with daily traffic counts to estimate use for the other days. Once the ratio has been established, it will remain
the same as long as the sites remain the same and no large change in fixed vari-

ables takes place. The traffic count is all that will be needed to estimate the use.

Detailed, step-by-step instructions for using the double sampling technique can be found in the Forest Service Research Paper SE-3 entitled *Instructions for Using Traffic Counters to Estimate Recreation Visists and Use.*[8]

Extensive-use areas

Estimation of extensive, or dispersed, use has been difficult and expensive to accomplish. The U.S. Forest Service researchers had success in precisely estimating visitor-use in a wilderness area by using unmanned registration stations at the entry points and following up with randomly selected interviews.[12] The sampling costs for this method have proved to be too high for operational use. The Forest Service is now working with unmanned registration stations checked by an infrared electric-eye counter located just up the trail from the station. The electric-eye counter gives as check on the numbers passing the registration station. Regression analysis of basic data collected from registration stations (x variables) and from personal interviews (y variables) will help to provide user estimates of the extensive-use area so long as no major change takes place in user patterns.

As of this date, no operational sampling procedure for precise use estimates in undeveloped areas has been obtained. It is apparent, however, that some form of double sampling with multiple regression will provide the answer.[23] Development of mechanical counters such as the portable infrared electric eye produced by the Forest Service Equipment Development Center in Missoula, Montana, should reduce the high costs of personal interviews.[9] The use of remote camera stations has caused sufficient controversy to stop their use. Cameras filming people without their knowledge is a form of unobtrusive observation that many people believe the government should not use.

SIGNS

The use of signs in forest recreation is a major form of communication. Signs are used to give directions, state regulations, identify areas, give warnings, and supply interpretative information. The purpose of signs is to inform the user. They are permanently implaced to give a message to the user at any season of the year or time of the day. Generally, signs can be classed as being either administrative, directional, restrictive, or interpretive.

Administrative Signs

Administrative signs identify boundaries, offices, and field headquarters. The signs identifying boundaries should be durable, easily seen, and small enough to be transported on foot. Because of the need for a large number of boundary signs, the small size will help to keep the total costs down. Yellow, blue, or red make good background colors for boundary-line signs as well as for the tree blazes along the boundary line. Office and headquarter signs should be large enough to be seen and read from a suitable distance to identify the buildings to visitors.

Directional Signs

Directional signs guide visitors to their destination whether it is within or outside of the recreation area. People in the outdoor environment are dependent upon signs to find things ranging from large parks to drinking fountains. Generally, internal direction signs are designed to be read by pedestrians while external directions are meant for motorists. There are exceptions to that generalization when the visitors drive around the interior areas or engage in extensive forms of recreation on foot or by other methods of travel.

Internal direction signs

The internal direction signs are the most important type of sign used. They aid the visitor in finding his way around the area. One of the most frustrating experiences for a camper is to arrive at a campground and have to drive all around the one-way loop roads in order to locate the camping unit that best meets his needs and then find out that it was taken while he was driving on through the rest of the area. Strangers may not know where the water supply is located and must ask other visitors when signs are not available, or else wander around looking for it and other utilities.

Utility signs. The utility signs are used to point the way to drinking water, toilets, boat landings, beaches, and other facilities. These signs should be as small as possible and should conform to the motif of the area. One or two words printed in two-inch-high letters accompanied by simple arrowheads will usually suffice for utility signs. They should be placed as low as possible without reducing their effectiveness. Certain situations force a change in this standard. Some trail signs on the Monongahela National Forest had to be raised seven feet high on metal posts because the black bears like to chew on them.

Orientation signs. Orientation signs showing a diagrammatic sketch of the area and pointing out the reader's location are very important in both intensive and extensive recreation. These signs are well received by the public and are often photographed; therefore, they should be shaded from direct sunlight but easy to photograph. Figure 17.1 shows an orientation sign that greets campers as they enter an unattended campground. The orientation sign should be brightly

Fig. 17.1. A vacation-bound family, with house trailer, stop at camper registration board at entrance of public campground. Here, on a diagram of the area, they can see which camp spaces are already occupied and which remain available. They will insert their own registration card which they will remove and drop in a box on their departure. (Forest Service.)

colored and show the campground layout, the swimming beach, the boat landing, and other facilities located in the campground. Figure 17.2 shows an automobile forest tour on the Nicolet National Forest. This sort of tour should be accompanied by a handout that can be taken along on the trip.

External direction signs

External direction signs are needed to guide visitors into the forest recreation areas from the major highways and roads. Destination signs give the motorist an idea of the distance to his destination as he drives to a forest recreation area. Approach signs alert the driver that he is about to arrive at the turnoff to his destination which is marked by an entrance sign.

Approach signs should be easily read from within the moving vehicle. The wording should be brief and in large letters on a neutral background. The distance between the approach sign and the entrance will depend upon the type of highway involved. High-speed roads will require more distance between the approach sign and the entrance sign than rural roads will require. Rougher forest roads will keep the vehicular speed low enough in some cases to eliminate the need for any approach sign. If no turnoff is required, no approach sign is necessary. Entrance signs to scenic areas, public and private forests, or parks can be placed next to highways that enter them. Recreationists, as do most other people, enjoy knowing where they are; therefore, entrance signs serve the dual purposes of directing area users as well as informing passers-by of their location.

Restrictive Signs

Signs are needed to post regulations, to remind people of their responsibilities, and to control visitor movements in certain situations. These signs bear messages that restrict the activities of the user to various degrees. They must be placed in a prominent place and be made so that they are easily read. Most forest recreationists realize the need for certain restrictions on activities within recreation areas just as there are restrictions in the general society. Administrators must be careful that they do not make up restrictive signs just because it seems like a good thing to do. Many restrictions that are posted around parks are just reutterances of public law. Rules that echo common legal statutes just waste space. Regulations concerning immoral conduct or stealing are favorite ones of administrators who like to make up regulations. Visitors pay very little attention to the rest of the lists of rules and regulations when they read such reutterance of the public law.

Restrictive signs must be prominently placed to be effective, but they should not overpower the entering visitor. Their message must be clear and unambiguous; however, the wording should be suggestive and the thought positive. A big sign with a long list of "Nos" might be effective, but it greatly lessens the enjoyment of the visitor. Also, it immediately sets up two warring camps. Negative signs pit the user against the manager. Granted, in some areas, strong negative action is necessary; however, the positive approach should be taken first. Figure 17.3 depicts the situation as the visitor sees it when restrictive signs take the place of proper planning.

Interpretative Signs

Signs that tell a story about the area in view are becoming very popular with the public. These signs interpret the view and highlight the outstanding attractions, or they briefly tell the history of the area. Interpretative signs enrich the visitor's forest experience by adding a natural or historical interest to just where trees and landforms previously existed. Interpretative signs are recommended for such places as vistas, roadside rests, information sites, and certain forest trails.[21]

Interpretative signs should be eye appealing without distracting attention

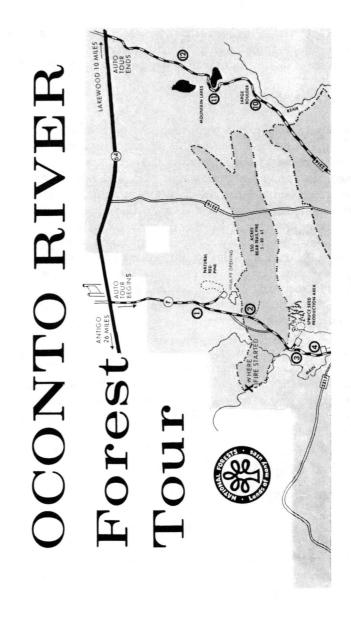

OCONTO RIVER Forest Tour

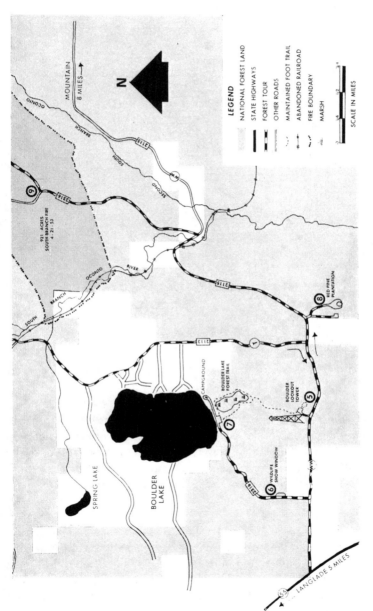

Fig. 17.2. An automobile tour of the Oconto River area of the Nicolet National Forest.

Fig. 17.3. Restrictive signs are sometimes used to cover up planning mistakes or administrative laziness.

from the view. This means that they should not overpower the view with size or overshadow it with extensive use of vivid colors. Some art work and colors will help to gain and to hold interest; however, too much of these will make the sign of greater interest than the scene. Figure 17.4 gives an example of the first-person historical approach by making the reader feel that he was there.

Design of Signs

All signs that are needed for one area should be designed at the same time so as to prevent duplication, conflict, and omissions.[21] The sign should fit into its environment; therefore, its site should be known before the sign is designed. It should never be so large as to be obtrusive in that its size should be determined upon its location and the distance from which it will be read. A sign does not need to be large to serve its purpose; however, small signs must be more carefully placed than large ones to be effective.

Fig. 17.4. "I was there" is a feeling that results from the first-person historical approach in interpretative signs. (Forest Service.)

The sign serves as a frame and background for the text. Its shape should not be novel enough to go out of date or to draw too much attention to the sign at the expense of the view or the text. Wood is the generally used material for sign construction because it is strong, easily worked, and very durable when properly treated. Wood signs also fit into the environment better than do signs of other materials. All signs serving the same function should have the same shape and the same approximate size. That is, the signs along a self-guiding nature trail should be identical except for the text and illustrations. Similar signs make their identification easier.

A well-designed sign has an emotional appeal, a pleasing appearance, dignity, and a purpose.[21] The signs should reflect care and talent in manufacture as well as professional skills in the composition of the text. Cheap or carelessly constructed signs will indicate that the signs are not worth reading or even taking care of. Since people want to gather information from qualified experts, they will expect to find the text presented in a professional manner. To the reader, this means that the signs have been prepared with professional care and that they contain information worth knowing.[20]

Bright colors have a place on signs as part of small illustrations, but not as background for the text. The background should be a neutral shade so as to focus attention on the text. Color contrasts play an important role in making the signs legible. Usually, the letters are routed into the wood and painted white. When the signs serve a purpose at night as do utility signs, the letters should be painted with a white or silver reflective paint. [22]

Text

The text is the reason for the sign's existence. [21] Any other part of the sign or the landscaping should be so designed as to make the text more effective. When composing the text, the author must make it readable, accurate, and brief. The text of interpretative signs should develop only one subject for each sign, and the subjects on a directional sign should not exceed five in number. [12] Table 17.1 presents eight guides for making signs easy to read.

Maintenance of Signs

Signs should be kept in good repair at all times. If the sign has served its purpose and is no longer needed, it should be removed. Damaged signs should be repaired or replaced as soon as possible. If repairs cannot be made in a short period of time and no replacement signs are available, it might be better simply to remove the damaged sign than to leave it up. Common signs can be kept in stock for replacement.

Once signs begin to fall into disrepair, the public loses its respect for them. Many utility signs have ended up in fraternity houses or similar places as souvenirs. Signs are favorite targets for misoriented marksmen. If the dangerous practice of sign shooting becomes epidemic, it makes signs impossible to keep maintained. Quick repair of the damage is probably the best defense against sign shooting in the long run.

LIABILITY INSURANCE

All recreation enterprises should be protected by liability insurance because the private operator assumes some responsibility for the welfare of his customers. He is obligated to pay for any act of negligence that results in an injury or damage. The problem of defining what constitutes negligence is difficult to answer and often must be settled in a court of law. Insurance coverage protects the operator in two ways. First, it puts the insurance company in the position of defending against the claim and saves the operator the costs of legal fees that would occur whether he won or lost the suit. Second and more obvious, the insurance company will pay the claim up to the limits of the policy.

Persons should obtain professional advice from a competent insurance sales-

Table 17.1. Guides for Making Signs Easier to Read.*

1. Do not capitalize the entire text.
2. Do not crowd the text with inadequate margins.
3. Do not set the text in a solid block form.
4. Use upper- and lowercase letters to make sentences and proper names more distinct.
5. Leave extra space between paragraphs.
6. Keep regular spacing between words in a sentence.
7. Spacing of words should be adequate.
8. Leave an extra space at the end of a sentence.

*USFS Publication No. 968.

man and from a lawyer prior to opening a recreation area for profit to help assist him in determining the potential risks and liabilities. Some state laws require a minimum of $5,000 liability insurance for one individual claim.[7] This is a most unrealistic figure since much greater amounts often are alloted in death or disability claims involving liability.[24]

Liability insurance is important enough to be included as part of the operational expense budget. Many insurance companies have not had much experience with recreational enterprises and tend to charge excessive rates in order to be on the safe side.[4] By shopping around from one company to another, the operator will find that the cost of similar coverage varies widely. The Campground Association of Pennsylvania (CAP) cautions its members to be careful about which insurance category their establishment is placed into. Agents often try to place campgrounds into the 301, or general classification, category where premiums are relatively high. CAP recommends that campground operators attempt to have their establishments placed in the mobile home category where premiums are lower.[15]

Many landowners have been afraid to open their land to extensive recreation pursuits such as hunting, fishing, or hiking because of the fear of their liability. Within the last couple of years, many states have enacted liability relief laws which limit the liability of landowners toward recreationists on his land. The liability relief laws have opened up many thousands of privately owned acres of forest and farmland for recreation. A suggested model draft of a liability limitation act was accepted and published by the 1965 Council of State Governments. This draft, "Public Recreation on Private Lands: Limitations on Liability," has been accepted by several states that did not have such legislation in their books.[3]

Limits on liability laws are based on the premise that the landowner who permits, without charge, a person to use his property for recreational purposes does not:

1. Extend any assurance that the premises are safe.

2. Confer the legal status of invitee upon the user.
3. Assume responsibility for any injury or loss of property caused by an act of the users.

Relief laws do not dismiss the landowner from liability for willful or malicious failure to protect the users from a dangerous situation. [25]

PUBLICITY

Private recreation areas are usually in business to make a profit and that profit depends largely upon the number of customers that the area attracts. Good facilities and locations are only part of the solution to getting users. The operator must advertise for customers to keep the area occupancy as high as possible. Some free publicity can be obtained in the local newspaper by news releases concerning happenings at the area.

Many sources of advertising are available. Choosing the best media for investing advertising dollars will be an important decision.

Industry-owned recreation developments are often considered as courtesies to the users and usually are not run at a profit. Publicly administered recreation developments are supplemented by tax funds. As a result, these recreation operators are not interested in gaining users and do not do any direct advertising. They are listed in campground guides when camping is offered and as such receive widespread publicity. The Forest Service makes a conscious effort to avoid advertising. The Forest Service destination signs list geographic points rather than developments to avoid giving direct publicity to concessions on its land.

Private enterprise must advertise to attract customers. Some of the most popular ways to advertise recreation areas are:

1. Local signs.
2. Recreation publication advertisements.
3. Distributing folders through users, mail, conventions, and organizations.
4. Membership in outdoor recreation organizations.
5. Roadside signs and bulletin boards.
6. Good public relations to get repeat customers or to spread the word to other users.
7. Listing in major campground guidebooks.

Folder or brochure distribution was the most common form of advertising after camping-guide listings. Information in the advertisement should include the facilities and the attraction of the development. The exact road directions should be given to guide the interested user to the area. Lists of nearby attractions, stores, restaurants, and entertainment activities are often included. The mailing address and telephone numbers should be given in every advertisement.

RESERVATIONS

Most of the successful private campgrounds have a well-developed reservation system.[1,11] Almost half of the campground's business was arranged by reservation and reservation holders tended to remain for a longer period. Many state park systems are facing the fact that reservations are a necessity. American campers have shown solid acceptance of the reservation system being tried on the national parks.

Computerized systems for reservations are available under leasing arrangements with established reservation firms. The large motel chains and oil companies have their own reservation systems and are in the position of competing successfully for a portion of the resort camping market. In most cases, the private operators accept campground reservations over the counter or through the mail. The advertising brochures usually present the reservation policy followed by the campground owner. A minimum deposit amounting to one day's rate is required when reservations are made in many cases to protect the campground operator from revenue loss caused by "no shows."

MAINTENANCE

The maintenance or upkeep of the area and the facilities is one of the most important parts of recreation area operation. Because forest recreation consists mostly of seasonal activities, the workload of maintenance personnel must be adjusted to fit available time. Generally, a good supervisor will be able to program maintenance into two parts. The daily maintenance required to keep the recreation area operating properly during the use-season will keep the staff busy. All major repairs, construction, or rehabilitation projects should be rescheduled for completion during the off-season.

By scheduling heavy maintenance during the off-season, the supervisor reduces the fluctuation in staff size between the use-season and the off-season. The staff engaged in use-season light maintenance, public relations, and traffic control can be employed at the heavy maintenance projects during the off-season when they are not needed to operate the recreation area. This use of the full-time employees for operation of the park reduces the number of part-time employees required.

Off-season projects do not interfere with the normal operation of the recreation area. Construction, earth moving, pipeline installation, and toilet improvements are examples of the projects that should be completed prior to the use-season. Besides physically interfering with the visitors, heavy maintenance projects create an aesthetic nuisance within an area where users are searching for a picturesque forest environment.

The specific problems associated with light maintenance and the operation of forest recreation facilities are discussed within the appropriate chapters of this book that deal with each type of facility. One rule of maintenance that should not be overlooked is that dirty and run-down facilities will be treated poorly by the visitors. However, the public is inclined to cooperate in taking care of recreation facilities that it finds to be clean, well cared for, and in good repair.[9]

PUBLIC RELATIONS

Public relations are the activities undertaken to establish good rapport with a particular segment of the general population. In this case, public relations are undertaken to establish harmonious relations with the user group. The purpose of a recreation area is to provide user satisfaction. Even private enterprise recognizes that user satisfaction is necessary before the recreation area venture can become profitable.

Good public relations require both active and passive efforts. Active public relations include visitor contacts, information services, activity programs, guided tours, and other similar aggressive actions by recreation personnel. Sufficient signs, proper design of area and facilities, adequate explanation of any necessary restrictions, cleanliness of the area, and appearance of personnel are some of the passive efforts in public relations that weigh heavily on the user's response to the recreation area. Full-time manager, service, and variety have been effective parts of the successful private campground.

Public relations consists of a two-way flow of benefits. The user benefits by having increased satisfaction in the recreation activity. Aside from the profit increases that the private operator is striving for, good public relations techniques provide the manager with information about the user that can be used to improve the recreation area. The visitor's likes and dislikes, suggestions, length of stay, and reasons for visiting the recreation area will help the manager plan improvements and prepare plans to meet the public needs.

Supervisors, or their representatives, who must operate and maintain the recreation area need to ensure the proper use of the facilities and site. To do this, they frequently must enforce regulations concerning the use of the area. The use of tact in enforcing regulations cannot be overemphasized. Enforcement of regulations can cause offense which is out of proportion with the regulation; therefore, every effort should be made to correct the violation without giving undue offense.

Unfortunately, it is in handling minor violations of regulations that many public servants prove inadequately oriented. Many state and local parks have so many regulations that the users are unnerved by the lists of negative expressions that greet their entry into the park. Gruff, unpleasant, or unexplained enforcement of every rule violation leaves the user disgruntled. Many public agencies have recognized the problems associated with proper methods of regulation enforcement and are taking steps to overcome them. Patrolmen should be trained in the proper ways of approaching the user. Also, the new public employees must understand that they are being paid by the taxpayers and should treat them with respect.

An extra layer of law enforcement often faces the public park user. Quite often the trend is for the political leaders or even the rangers themselves to use that extra law enforcement level diligently to pursue the letter of the law on parklands at the expense of common sense. It is because of the harassment attitude that exists in many municipal and state parks that many people are looking to federal and private recreation opportunities.

The operation of recreation areas places personnel in close contact with the general public. Therefore, it is important that all employees be trained to meet the public in an acceptable manner. Any one of the staff will be in the position of influencing the user's opinion of the recreation area. The wearing attire of the employees should be clean, neat, and in keeping with the work being performed.

REFERENCES

1. Brown, T.L., and Wilkins, B.T. 1972. *A Study of Campground Businesses in New York State.* Department of Natural Resources, Cornell University, Ithaca, N.Y.
2. Bureau of Outdoor Recreation. 1972. *Outdoor Recreation Action Report No. 24.* U.S. Department of the Interior, Washington, D.C. 32 pages.
3. Council of State Governments. 1965. Public Recreation on Private Lands: Limitations and Liability. *Suggested State Legislation*, vol. XXVI. 1313 East 60th Street, Chicago, Ill.
4. Crites, R.S. 1965. *Handbook of Outdoor Recreation Enterprises in Rural Areas.* Farmers Home Administration. Government Printing Office, Washington, D.C. 122 pages.
5. Douglass, Robert W. 1973. *Use of High Altitude Photography for Forest Disease Detection and Vegetation Classification within the Sub-Boreal Forest Region.* University Microfilms. University of Michigan, Ann Arbor, Mich. 141 pages.
6. Economics Research Associates. 1976. *Evaluation of Public Willingness to Pay User Charges for Use of Outdoor Recreation Areas and Facilities.* U.S. Department of the Interior, U.S. Government Printing Office. 45 pages.
7. Holcomb, Conklin, and Winch. 1963. *Opportunities for Private Campgrounds as an Alternate Use of Land.* Agriculture Extension Service Circular No. 792. Virginia Polytechnic Institute, Blacksburg, Va.
8. James, G., and Ripley, T. 1963. *Instructions for Using Traffic Counters to Estimate Recreation Visits and Use.* USFS Research Paper SE-3. Southeastern Forest Experiment Station, Asheville, N.C.
9. James, George A., and Schreuder, Hans T. 1971. *Estimating Dispersed Recreation Use Along Trails and in General Undeveloped Areas with Electric-Eye Counters: Some Preliminary Findings.* Forest Note SE-181. Southeastern Forest Experiment Station, Asheville, N.C. 8 pages.

10. James, George A., Wingle, H. Peter, and Griggs, James D. 1971. *Estimating Recreation Use on Large Bodies of Water*. Southeast Forest Experiment Station, USDA Forest Service Research Paper SE-79. 7 pages.
11. La Page, Wilbur F. 1968. *The Role of Customer Satisfaction in Managing Commercial Campgrounds*. Forest Service Research Paper NE-105. Northeast Forest Experiment Station, Upper Darby, Pa. 23 pages.
12. Lucas, Robert C., Schreuder, Hans T., and James, George A. 1971. *Wilderness Use Estimation: a Pilot Test of Sampling Procedures on the Misson Mountains Primitive Area*. Intermountain Forest and Range Experiment Station, USDA Forest Service Research Paper INT-109. 44 pages.
13. Outdoor Recreation Resources Review Commission. 1962. *Sport Fishing — Today and Tomorrow*. Study Report No. 7. Superintendent of Documents, Government Printing Office, Washington, D.C. 130 pages.
14. Poole, D. 1965. States Move on Relief Law. *Outdoor News Bulletin*. Wildlife Management Institute, 709 Wire Building, Washington, D.C.
15. Sandy, R. 1964. *Campground Owners Adopt Standards*. Campground Association of Pennsylvania Newsletter No. 6. Mercer, Pa.
16. Schell, Kerry, F., and Taft, Joe H. 1972. *Application of Remote Sensing Techniques to Measurement of Use of Outdoor Recreation Resources*, Bureau of Outdoor Recreation, U.S. Department of the Interior, Washington, D.C. 110 pages.
17. U.S. Department of the Interior. 1979. *Fees and Charges Handbook: Guidelines for Recreation and Heritage Conservation Agencies*. 77 pages.
18. U.S. Forest Service. 1963. *Recreation Management. Manual and Handbook*, Title 2300. U.S. Department of Agriculture, Washington, D.C.
19. ————. 1963. *Collecting User Fees on National Forest Recreation Sites*. Administrative Study, California Region, San Francisco, Calif.
20. ————. 1964. *Developing the Self-Guiding Trail in the National Forests*. Miscellaneous Publication No. 968. U.S. Department of Agriculture, Washington, D.C.
21. ————. 1965. *The American Outdoors Management for Beauty and Use*. Miscellaneous Publication No. 1000. U.S. Department of Agriculture, Washington, D.C.
22. ————. 1966. *Sign Handbook. Forest Service Handbook*, Title 7161.4. U.S. Department of Agriculture, Washington, D.C.
23. Wagar, J.A. 1964. *Estimating Numbers of Campers on Unsupervised Campgrounds*. Forest Service Research Paper NE-18. Northeast Forest Experiment Station, Upper Darby, Pa. 16 pages.
24. Willsey, D. 1963. Outdoor Recreation Safety. In *Guidelines for Developing Land for Outdoor Recreational Uses*. Cooperative Extension Services, Purdue University, West Lafayette, Ind.
25. Wingard, R., and Heiney, C. 1966. *Pond Construction and Management in Pennsylvania*. Extension Service Special Circular 78, Natural Resource Series. College of Agriculture, The Pennsylvania State University, University Park, Pa. 24 pages.

Index